D0913056

THE MARKETING ENVIRONMENT

THE MARKETING
ENVIRONMENT

JOHN A. DAWSON

ST. MARTIN'S PRESS NEW YORK

Library of Congress Cataloging in Publication Data

Dawson, John A
   The marketing environment.
   Includes index.
   1. Marketing. I. Title.
HF5415.D38   381   78-31580

ISBN 0-312-51530-8

CONTENTS

FIGURES

The figures have been drawn by Mr C. Lewis

TABLES

For Jocelyn

PREFACE

Almost everyone who looks at this book is in direct daily contact with the marketing system whether in buying a ballpoint refill at the student co-operative store, purchasing their daily bread, fighting the vans and trucks on their urban delivery rounds or gazing at the advertisements on the way to work. The many processes which are associated with the movement of goods from producer to consumer constitute the marketing system. The processes, and consequently the system, differ from country to country and from region to region with their varied social, economic, legal and political environments. Many of the processes also have a direct spatial element because production and consumption are spatially separated. The variation in the marketing system and marketing processes through space, provides the first theme of this book. A second theme stems from the evolution of these marketing systems. Conflicts occur among participants in marketing activities and power relationships develop. Evolution occurs as action and reaction in the various parts of systems create and resolve conflicts. An aim of this book is to show how marketing systems change through the development of conflict and its resolution. In considering the conflicts occurring in comparative marketing systems there is a third aim to the book. This, simply, is to provide an introduction to some of the literature relevant to the study of marketing geography.

In the first chapter the marketing system is defined and its importance within the economy is reviewed. This chapter serves to illustrate the spatial variation and the processes inherent in the system. The concept of power and conflict in marketing is introduced in Chapter 2 and conflict within the marketing channels of different societies is illustrated. Chapters 3 through 6 consider the nature of the main institutions in the marketing system and how the marketing processes relate together the main institutions of consumer, retailer, wholesaler and producer. While these chapters consider spatial activity and marketing conflict from the individual's and firm's viewpoint, Chapter 7 provides an alternative perspective and marketing land-use complexes are considered as part of the total system. Society frequently calls on government to mediate when conflict occurs and some reasons for governmental intervention are discussed in Chapter 8. In the final chapter, some broader issues of the social accountability of marketing and the responsibility of partic-

13

ipants in the marketing system are considered.

As in any book which has taken several years to write, the influences on the author are manifold. I acknowledge a debt to many students, colleagues and friends who wittingly and unwittingly have helped formulate the ideas in this book. They are too numerous to mention individually but to them all—thank you. One person has helped more than any other by constant encouragement, advice and companionship. That person is my wife who has visited endless shopping centres in the cause of duty. This book is dedicated to her.

1 THE ECONOMIC ROLE OF MARKETING

The processes involved in the distribution of goods, whether food, consumer goods or capital goods, from their points of production to those of consumption, are managed, manipulated and controlled. This is the case not just with the economies of high mass consumption but it is equally true of the developing and communist worlds. The equation of supply and demand which is the basis of the distribution process is central to both the disciplines of economic geography and marketing and the two subjects have clear points of contact and overlap. Usually supply and demand are spatially separated and the management of the processes which close this spatial gap is relevant to marketing science and geography. Demand structure – the amount and types of good required for consumption – varies through geographical space and this variation again provides central themes in marketing and geography. Government control of marketing activities varies in type both among and within countries, so again geographical variables impinge on marketing decisions.

The Development of Marketing Geography

For many decades economic geography drew strength from classical economics with its concentration on the factors of production. Analyses of land, labour and capital provide the bases for the majority of geographical studies until the late 1950s. The agricultural and industrial sectors were both studied from this productive standpoint. Economic geography followed Adam Smith who argued in the *Wealth of Nations* that

> Consumption is the sole end and purpose of all production; and the interest of the producer ought to be attended to, only so far as it may be necessary for promoting that of the consumer. The maxim is so self-evident, that it would be absurd to prove it. But in the mercantile system, the interest of the consumer is almost constantly sacrificed to that of the producer; and it seems to consider production, and not consumption, as the ultimate end and object of all industry and commerce. (p. 625, Modern Library edition).

Only in the last 20 years has economic geography begun to escape from the stranglehold implied in this philosophy. Hodder and Lee (1974) have outlined the evolution of economic geography from a production based deterministic approach to a wider framed approach using the concepts of economic systems. While markets and the structure of demand were components of economically derived models in economic geography, as Chisholm (1970) points out, they took a subservient place with the market viewed only as a place to absorb production. A classic study is that of Harris (1954) who studied the market as a factor in the concentration of industrial production. The market had no relevance except as a factor of production. With the emergence of systems analytic approaches to the study of economic activity (McDaniel and Eliot-Hurst, 1968), so a more balanced view was taken of the relationship between production and consumption. Manners' (1971) study of the world market for iron ore illustrates this change in emphasis away from production dominated studies to ones involving an evaluation of the market allocation processes. Smith (1973) has taken an even more positive view of the rôle of market forces in his attempts to analyse spatial inequalities in social wellbeing and to relate these to market situations and in turn to industrial production. The market, in such studies, takes on an active rôle in analyses of the economic system. The basis of Hodder and Lee's view of economic geography is a system based economic model in which the driving force is not production but consumption.

With this swing in emphasis in economic geography generally it might be expected that marketing studies would have emerged as a strong, rapidly developing branch of economic geography. Its lack of development is not due to any absence of pleas for its acceptance. Hartshorne (1959) argued that a unitary statement of economic geography could be achieved based on a geography of consumption which he claimed

> of greatest significance for all of geography. To relate such a field to the many essentially separate geographies of production we need to develop far more than we have the geography of exchange, including marketing as well as transportation. (p. 41).

Before this, Applebaum (1954) was suggesting *marketing geography* as a major potential growth area in economic geography. With

> the large section of the working population that is engaged exclusively in marketing functions, the large part of the urban landscape that is devoted to the structures of wholesale and retail trade, and the complex channels of distribution that lead from producing to consuming areas, it becomes even clearer that there is a place and need in economic geography for special attention to marketing geography. (p. 245).

Despite the potential for development, the subject developed slowly with only a few practitioners and a very limited view of what marketing geography entailed. Berry (1967) states that, 'The prime concern of marketing geographers . . . is in *how to measure a trading area*' (p. 127). The scope of marketing geography is much wider than is implied by this statement.

The pleas of Applebaum and also later Green (1967) to develop a cogent branch of economic geography dealing with the economic, social and political processes influencing goods after their production had some effect although development was not rapid. Murphy (1961) points out in an editorial to an issue of *Economic Geography* devoted to retailing that 'In the last decade the practitioners in this adolescent field have grown in numbers and in activity' (p. 1). Whether or not one would agree with Murphy in his view that by 1961 marketing geography had 'come of age', none the less by then certain topics, for example retail trade area measurement, had a considerable literature. Marketing geography, however, had rather more unresearched topics than subjects of which there was partial knowledge. In 1961 while there was a sizable geographical literature on retail trade area measurement and on shop location (Berry and Pred, 1961), at least in its broadest terms, and on fairs and rural markets, one has to turn to the marketing literature to find studies of consumer behaviour, agricultural marketing, wholesaling, channel structure, shopping centres and many other key topics.

Since 1960 some of these subject areas have formed the basis for advances in economic geography. The general change in emphasis in human geography, from a deterministic to a behavioural standpoint, has resulted in consumer behaviour, particularly of shoppers, becoming a significant research frontier. A number of the established subject areas within marketing geography advanced in the 1960s with the evolution of central place theory (Berry, Barnum and Tennant, 1962). Location and trade area studies thus became even more the foci of research of economic geographers concerned with marketing (Kornblau, 1968; Cordey-Hayes, 1968). This development was without doubt at the expense of other equally important topics such as channel structure or the way goods move from producer to consumer. Thus by the 1970s although marketing geography has grown in importance it has neither blossomed nor been accepted widely as a valid field within economic geography. Scott's (1970) important volume reviews the growing body of work on retailing. Other than Eastman's (1930) volume, no book carried in its title the term 'marketing geography' until the publication in 1976 of Davies's text. The review by Beaujeu-Garnier and Delobez

(1977) together with Davies's book suggest, perhaps, that European geographers have taken over from those in North America the marketing geography flame despite the strength of marketing science *per se* in North America.

The slow initial growth of marketing geography and the slight quickening of interest in the 1970s is due, as Berry (1967) points out, to the inward looking nature of geography before the 1960s and the development in the last decade of a greater sensitivity to developments in cognate fields. Even so it is surprising the extent to which economic and urban geographers have failed to appreciate the extent of both theoretical and practical work in marketing. Even Hodder and Lee (1974) who take an essentially consumption orientated view of economic geography do not refer to any recent work by marketing scientists. Despite Berry's view, certainly economic geography has failed to appreciate the advances made in marketing in recent years.

Only recently have research theses in economic geography begun critically to examine some of the marketing literature (Bradford, 1975). Some aspects such as those based on central place theory, drawing relatively slightly on work in marketing, have developed rapidly. Others such as the spatial organisation of distribution or the spatial variation in operating costs and prices have hardly developed at all. It is these branches which require inputs from disciplines other than geography if progress, within a geographical framework, is to be made. Between such extremes lie topics in which there is overlap between various branches of geography itself. Consumer behaviour is a case in point. Research in urban geography and population geography have been drawn on heavily by marketing geographers studying consumer behaviour at a retail level (Clark and Rushton, 1970). Studies of consumer behaviour carried out within marketing and psychology and of consumption within economics have been drawn upon less frequently (Davies, 1973).

The Emergence of Marketing Science

Before considering in detail the specific content of marketing geography, it is worthwhile to look, briefly, at the marketing input into the subject. As with geography the development of the discipline of marketing has been somewhat introverted with frequent discussion on the definition of the subject and vindications for its study (Bartels, 1970). Bartels (1968) argues that marketing has become an increasingly fragmented discipline in the last 30 years. 'Since the end of World War II, marketing thought has developed along a number of different lines, with the result that it has been increasingly difficult to know, teach, or practise the "whole" of marketing' (p. 29). The parallel with geography is very noticeable. Other marketing scientists, notably Revzan (1965) and many of the contributors to Alderson, Cox and Shapiro (1964) view marketing in a more holistic manner, considering the total marketing system as a single entity rather than as separately managed units in a complex process. Revzan (1965) states

> The marketing organization is thought of as the functioning of a system of interrelated structures or organisms; and, its functioning is conditioned by the cultural and political patterns of the geographic unit in which it operates at any given period of time . . . The marketing system, in the above context, cannot be segmented and considered effectively apart from its relationship to the whole economy. At the same time it must be viewed as an entity for study representing one aspect of economic specialization. (p. 38).

The contrast between this holistic view and the fragmented approach which typified marketing philosophy in the 1950s stems largely from the impact of concepts of *system.*

The evolution of the discipline in the United States in the early years of this century has been well documented by Bartels (1968). The emergence of a mass consumption economy in the USA significantly increased the importance of marketing as a concept and marketing science as a discipline (Cox, 1965A). The spread of marketing concepts from North America to Europe and to the remainder of the world has occurred, for the most part, since 1950. The works of Braithwaite and Dobbs (1932), Smith (1937) and Jefferys (1950, 1954) are concerned essentially with economics and the origins of the books lie in academic economics in Britain rather than in the discipline of marketing emerging in the USA.

Attempts to define marketing, in similar fashion to geography, are legion. The consensus of these definitions is that marketing is concerned with the processes governing the transfer of goods and services from points of production to places of consumption. The definition provided by the Marketing Staff of Ohio State University (1965) is perhaps the most comprehensive and most relevant to a geographical interpretation of marketing processes: '*Marketing is the process in a society by which the demand structure for economic goods and services is anticipated or enlarged and satisfied through the conception, promotion, exchange, and physical distribution of such goods and services*' (p. 43). By this definition marketing is concerned with the changes in place, time and ownership through which goods pass in consumption processes. The concern of marketing is thus *consumption* whether consumption is by manufacturer in the production of more materials or by middlemen or by ultimate consumer.

Acceptance of this definition implies a change in attitudes to the study of marketing from the stereotype views of the 1950s and early 1960s. It implies a much wider concept than most previous definitions and necessarily means that workers began to look to other disciplines to understand the processes involved in marketing. Thus the same trends have affected marketing as have affected geography since the mid 1960s. One result of the awareness of useful studies in other disciplines and the broadening of the marketing concept has resulted in the acceptance of a systems approach (Adler, 1967). A number of basic marketing texts, notably Fisk (1967) and Buzzel *et al.* (1972) present systems concepts and proceed to present marketing as a systems related discipline. The acceptance of marketing as a *behavioural* science utilising a *systems* approach encourages an outward looking view to marketing philosophy. Bell (1972) states that the acceptance of behaviour systems

> encourages the introduction of systems concepts borrowed from the behavioural sciences. Ecology is the study of systems discovered among plant and animal organisms and human ecology (which is very close to sociology and cultural anthropology) is concerned with the systematic relations between man and his environment. The concept of the ecological system, with emphasis on survival and adjustment processes, has contributed greatly to an understanding of marketing and marketing management. (p. 42).

Human ecology has been a fertile source area for geographers and marketing scientists alike. Marketing scientists such as Bell (1972), Fisk (1967), Thorelli (1967) and Alderson (1964) have argued forcibly for the relevance of the principles of human ecology to marketing. Robson (1969), however, in a criticism of human ecology on the grounds that it attempts an overtly all-embracing approach and secondly on the dangers of argument by analogy concludes that 'To try to define marketing in ecological terms holds out the seductive promise of dramatic analogies, but in terms of sheer return the analogies offer little and mean less' (p. 169). As a substitute Robson argues for a systems approach based on the application of 'spatial analysis to marketing' which is an approach that also has appeal to some marketing scientists (Hood, 1969).

The more traditional system based approach is typified by Figure 1.1,

Figure 1.1: The Marketing System

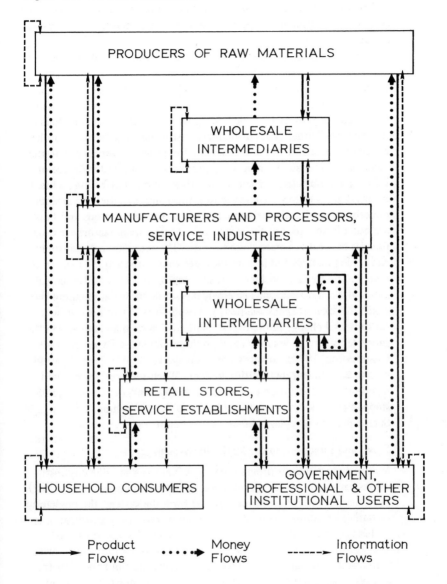

PRODUCERS OF RAW MATERIALS

WHOLESALE INTERMEDIARIES

MANUFACTURERS AND PROCESSORS, SERVICE INDUSTRIES

WHOLESALE INTERMEDIARIES

RETAIL STORES, SERVICE ESTABLISHMENTS

HOUSEHOLD CONSUMERS

GOVERNMENT, PROFESSIONAL & OTHER INSTITUTIONAL USERS

→ Product Flows   •••••▶ Money Flows   ------▶ Information Flows

showing the whole marketing system. The system consists of two types
of element. First is a series of *institutions* which includes those institutions
of production usually central to economic geography. There are, however,
in Figure 1.1 two other sets of institutions – those through which goods
and services pass in the marketing process and those which facilitate the
movement of goods. The first of these is usually composed of various
types of wholesale and retail intermediaries positioned between producer
and final consumer. The efficient functioning of these institutions rests
with facilitating agencies which comprise organisations such as banks,
insurance and other types of financial institution together with brokers,
advertising agencies and other information providing services. The second
element in the system are *flows* of products, money and information
between institutions. Extraneous to this system but affecting its functioning is a set of controls. These controls influence activities but are not
directly engaged in the performance of marketing functions and thus
are not a formal part of the system. Such *influencing* factors are usually
policies of local or national government. They regulate competition
and trade practices and in extreme cases totally control the marketing
system. The role and influence of such factors can change dramatically
over quite a short period. The emergence of distribution planning in
Japan, for example, has resulted, as Yoshino (1971) points out, in a
fundamental change in the overall marketing system and equally in the
subsystems for various individual products (Japanese External Trade
Organisation, 1972). Government has played a major role in the planning of an efficient distribution system: 'When the need for modern-
ization of the distribution sector became apparent, the government
stepped in to assume an active role in this field' (Yoshino, 1971, p. 274).
Such a pattern is typical of many other countries.

Flows and Functions in the Marketing System

Marketing institutions provide specialist functions and like any institutions have a life cycle pattern and location requirements. To illustrate
how the specialist institutions together form the system, the marketing
system of bread may be used. 'The principal raw material, wheat, is grown
by farmers and sold by them, perhaps through a co-operative marketing
association, to millers. The millers process the wheat into flour and sell
it to baking companies. The latter, in turn, use the flour and other raw
and processed materials – such as yeast and packaging materials – to produce bread and other baked goods, which they sell to retail stores. Finally, housewives purchase the bread for their families' consumption.
Because bread is a perishable product, it is not feasible to utilise whole-

sale middlemen in distributing the finished product to retailers. But wholesale intermediaries may participate in the sale of wheat to millers, and in the sale of flour to bakers' (Buzzell *et al.*, 1972, p. 30). Even in the marketing of such a simple everyday product such as bread there are a number of specialist institutions and also a number of institutions which specialise in some other economic function but which also have a subsidiary marketing role. In the first group are the retailers, the agricultural co-operative and the wholesalers, while in the second group are producers (farmers, millers, etc.) and households. In some views of marketing the second set of institutions are all important, for the whole purpose of marketing may be viewed as satisfying demand. The health and wealth of the primary marketing institutions, however, are very important and in the past have sometimes tended to be ignored. The retail and wholesale trades have traditionally been the poor relations in plans for economic growth with a consequence that the institutions involved in marketing have been slow to evolve more efficient techniques. The general lack of effective and comprehensive government policies towards distribution as a whole is very evident from the analyses in Boddewyn and Hollander (1972). The classification of institutions by their function – retailer, wholesaler, assembler, etc. – of marketing institutions is the most commonly used.

Flows of products, information and money interlink the institutions and allow the institutions to operate (Figure 1.1). The flows may be in many different forms. Money may be cash, promissory notes or various forms of credits. Information may be sales promotion, market research or orders. Products may be described in terms of who buys them, how they are bought or how they are consumed. Product flows are usually tangible while money and information are intangible. It is possible to add two further intangible flows to the concept of a marketing system and these are the flow of ownership and the flow of risk. As products pass through the marketing system, title passes from seller to buyer possibly several times; on each occasion goods are transferred from one part of the marketing system to another. There is a flow of ownership. At each transaction and throughout the passage of goods through the system the product is at risk. Risk from physical destruction, from a fall in prices, from availability of a competitor's goods, are all characteristic risks of the marketing system.

The flows within the system serve three purposes – collection, sorting, dispersal. In the initial stages of the system, collection is uppermost, and in the final retail phases, dispersal is most common. Within a simple agricultural marketing system goods are *collected* from the farm and taken to a central wholesale market. The goods are concentrated from numerous small ownership lots to fewer larger ones. From a central market products are *sorted* by a wide variety of agents, brokers and wholesalers and are sent to secondary markets. Finally, the product is *dispersed* to many foods shops and to even more households. Given the most efficient types and pattern of flows, institutions can operate at optimum scale which in turn affects the efficiency and cost of marketing.

The route by which a product passes through the system consists of institutions which handle a product, the flows which link the institutions and the external forces which impinge on the operation of the institutions. In total this route is called the *channel*. Channel planning and control are fundamental to marketing and as institutions have locations and flows move through space, so the channel is basic to a consideration of marketing geography. Marketing channels have been of central concern to marketing and are dealt with fully in the next chapter.

Inherent in the marketing system are exchange functions, physical supply functions and facilitating functions. But there is a rather wider alternative view of the function of the marketing system. Marketing is a major employer accounting for around 25 per cent of employment in most Western countries. Furthermore, marketing decisions impinge directly on everyone's life style. The definition of marketing introduced in earlier pages hints that marketing can create demand and that in so doing it creates a standard of living and consequently a set of social norms. Some marketing scientists would consider that a major function of the marketing system is to change living standards to provide for higher mass consumption (Kelley, 1965; Grether, 1967). Such a view has been questioned and marketing now is becoming vested with a social responsibility. Galbraith (1967) has argued critically of the performance of the marketing system in the matter of social responsibility. Improving the quality of life of consumers is now accepted as a function of marketing where formerly the sole function was increasing the quantity of goods consumed.

The systems view of marketing has resulted in a transformation in the research writing, practice and philosophy of marketing for as Lazer and Kelley (1962) point out in an editorial postscript.

Marketing systems are large, complex and intricate. They are large . . . in dollar amount, volume of goods handled, number of people involved, and quantity of components. They are complex in the number and types of elements and the possible variations within each element. They rely on multiple sources of communications and multiple forecast and feedback loops. There is negligible automatic adjustment in marketing systems. Since they do not adjust automatically marketing management must plan to audit and to adjust the marketing system to better fit the wants, needs, opportunities of a changing market place. Managing marketing systems, therefore, is a difficult and demanding task. (pp. 684-5).

Marketing Geography and Marketing

Given the acceptance of the systems view of marketing it is reasonable to ask how geography has responded to the study of marketing systems. Certainly the traditional view of marketing geography as comprising the measurement of retail trade areas is not sufficient. Even allowing an extension into the analysis of the problems of the location of retail institutions still provides a far from adequate base for marketing geography. Goode (1968), a practising marketing scientist points out that in food marketing the 'geographer spends most of his time providing sales estimates on new locations, working out master plans for large areas, and providing information on specific company problems' (p. 397). The traditional approach thus leaves much to be desired.

Davies (1973) suggests that recent theoretical advances in urban geography have advanced marketing geography: 'A further methodological development in marketing geography, . . . concerns the attempt to use economic rent theory as a framework within which to study especially the internal locational structure of shopping centres' (pp. 138-9). The emphasis is again however on retail institutions, which constitute only part of the marketing system. Retail geography, particularly since Scott's important survey (1970), has become a sub-branch of geography almost as important as marketing geography which encompasses it. A much more comprehensive base for marketing geography is required. A base which includes for example the variety of geographical work on consumer behaviour (Day, 1973; Downs, 1970; Golledge, 1970; Nader, 1969), the increasing number of studies of traditional marketing patterns (Good, 1970; Bromley, 1974; Smith, 1976), studies of agricultural markets (Pyle, 1971; Cassidy, McCarthy, Toft, 1970; Carlyle, 1978; Williams, 1972), wholesaling (Vance, 1970; Kirby, 1974; Jumper, 1974), the transportation of goods (Taafe and Gauthier, 1973; Chisholm and O'Sullivan, 1973; Hay, 1973), as well as the more traditional retail ingredients of marketing geography, both empirical (Clark, 1972; Epstein, 1971; Mikkonen, 1972) and theoretical (Garner, 1970; Dacey, 1972; Jensen-Butler, 1972; Andrews, 1973). A marketing geography to include these studies has been advocated by two authors; strangely neither are geographers, both are marketing scientists. Both Cox (1965B) and Carson (1967) are concerned with the overall structure of domestic marketing systems. In particular they draw together comparative features of domestic marketing systems in what Cox (1965B) calls the 'search for universals' and Carson terms comparative marketing, 'The identification and analysis of common factors and differences in marketing concepts, systems, and techniques among various societies, including nations, may therefore be considered the main thrust of *comparative* marketing' (p. 4). Such a statement is as effective a definition of what marketing geography should be as it is of what comparative marketing is currently. Few marketing scientists or geographers have followed Cox or Carson's lead.

The framework for comparative marketing or marketing geography lies in the concept of the marketing system. The system operates in a socio-economic-political environment in which various cultural, business and governmental factors, particular to the environment, influence the decisions in the marketing system. The system itself, its institutions and flows, again is particular to individual environments but comparisons and contrasts may be made among environments. Furthermore, the functions which institutions are expected to perform differ from place to place. The purchasing of grocery products serves, as an example, to indicate the contrasts which occur. The cultural environment of the household influences, among many things, the items purchased; the economic environment governs the amount on sale and the amount purchased; the political environment may affect prices. Institutions differ — groceries can be purchased in a supermarket or in a village square and flows differ with a shopping trip by car or a walk along a narrow track. In some places the purchaser accepts or declines the price of the goods on offer. In other places haggling is an integral part of purchasing behaviour. These various characteristics of diverse marketing systems are examples of a far wider range of differences. Equally there may be similarities. Supermarkets occur in Accra and London and may appear broadly similar. Perhaps however, contrasts occur in their operation or in buyer attitudes. The aim of marketing geography should be to analyse and hypothesise on the similarities, differences and evolution of domestic marketing systems.

Marketing in the National Economy

With this definition in mind it may be asked 'how important is marketing in the operation of comparative economies?' Marketing is 'the economy's dark continent'; Drucker (1962) has observed 'we know it is there, and we know it is big, and that's about all' (p. 103). Twenty years earlier Clark (1940) threw out his challenge that 'The economics of tertiary industry remains to be written. Many as yet feel uncomfortable about even admitting their existence' (p. 341). Almost 15 years after Drucker's admission and 35 years after Clark we know something more about marketing and services within national economies but when the total of this knowledge is placed alongside comparable information on agriculture or manufacturing industry it is pitiably small.

A major obstacle which faces all attempts to study the contribution of marketing to any economy is the difficulty in measuring the marketing system. Marketing constitutes an activity rather than an industry. For the most part specialist marketing activities lie in the service sector. Retailing, wholesaling, freight transportation, advertising, etc. are all subsumed in service industry. But an agriculturist or industrialist also performs certain marketing functions. A large proportion of clerical type occupations within manufacturing industry could be considered as part of the marketing system. The occupations often are concerned with the sales or purchasing activities of the firm and these activities may justifiably be included in marketing. Fuchs (1965) has attempted to solve this problem for the whole of service activity but even at such a fairly general level a number of assumptions have to be made in the allocation of occupations to either *service* or *goods producing* activities. With marketing the problems are more intransigent and even more assumptions have to be made.

The distinction between occupation and industry group is thus critical in any attempt to define the position of marketing. Most attempts to assess the role of all service activities, including marketing, use an industry based definition of service activity. Ofer (1967) for Israel and Lengelle (1968) for OECD countries exclusively use statistics on an industry classification. The North American studies (Barger, 1955; Stigler, 1956; Fuchs, 1968) also use industry classifications to define service activity although, as mentioned above, Fuchs (1965) does attempt an occupational distribution of the labour force and an occupation based study of the service activity's contribution to GDP. Marketing is only one section of either service occupations or industry and in any attempt to assess the contribution of marketing to the economy certain assumptions have to be made. For the purposes of this chapter, marketing is limited to the commerce (wholesale and retail) and transport sectors which constitute the specialist activities in the marketing system. To divide other services, say banking or insurance, between marketing and non-marketing activities is impossible from published data sources. Equally impossible is the estimation of marketing activity within producing firms. Marketing is assumed as a combination of the commerce and transportation industries of the 1958 International Standard Classification (United Nations, 1958) and the broadly comparable divisions 6, 7 and 8 of the 1968 Classification (United Nations, 1968). Some non-marketing employees and activities are included and some marketing employees and activities are excluded. This definition, for statistical purposes, probably leads to conservative estimates of the position of marketing in an economy but it includes employees and activities of the hard core of marketing institutions—retailers, wholesalers, some facilitating agencies and transporters.

A word of warning is necessary about this definition. Within Western society relatively few elements of productive industries are classifiable as marketing. Usually specialist marketing firms perform the marketing functions. Yoshino (1971) reports a Japanese survey of large manufacturing firms; 'approximately 10 per cent of the total company personnel were engaged in some form of marketing activity' (p. 100). Within the less developed countries of the world, however, the specialist marketing firms are absent and marketing is more often carried out as part of the productive industry. The frequency with which farmers carry their own goods to market and stay to sell them is one example of the lack of the specialist marketing industry sector. The case studies presented by Belshaw (1965) indicate this fundamental difference between the developed and less developed nations. The industry based definition adopted in this chapter thus underestimates general marketing activity in developing economies but partially measures the lack of specialist marketing industries compared with the developed countries.

The proportion of gross domestic product at factor cost accounted for by commerce and transport is one method of assessing the importance of marketing in an economy. The range of values varies considerably from country to country. Even within Western Europe the range is large, from around 13 per cent in Austria to almost 30 per cent in Norway. Generally the values bunch around 20 per cent, higher values being associated with countries having transport sectors contributing more than average to GDP formation. Thus Denmark, Sweden and Norway have a large transport component in the commerce and transport percentage. Typical values are plotted on Figure 1.2.

Figure 1.2: Contribution of Marketing to GDP in Selected Countries—
mid 1970s

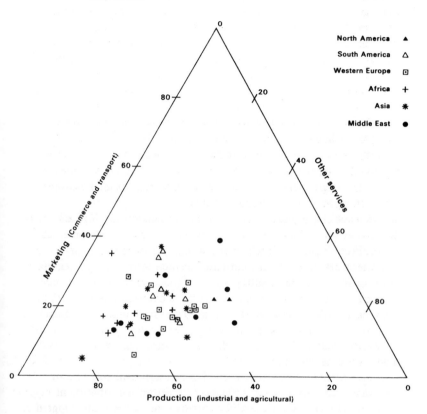

These figures are derived from the *Yearbooks of National Accounts Statistics* (United Nations, 1977) which attempt to provide comparative material over a range of countries. The measurement of service's contribution to GDP is difficult, for with much of the sector there is no easily definable end product which could be termed output (Treadway, 1969) and certainly this is true for marketing. Furthermore, quality is an integral part of marketing services and quality may change (for better or worse) without there being any discernible change in the statistical measurements of output (Cripps and Tarling, 1973). By using a common statistical base however, it is hoped that the errors inherent in the statistics and the difficulties of their interpretation are minimised.

Figure 1.2 also includes a sample of countries outside Western Europe

and the scatter of values is much wider. In Africa the contrast lies
between Lesotho with only 6 per cent of its GDP accounted for by
commerce and transport, and Zaire with 35 per cent. Equally large
ranges occur within Asia, South America and the Middle East. The
countries in these continents with relatively high GDP per head, however, tend to have values in the approximate range 17 to 23 in common
with many Western European countries. Blades, Johnston and Marczewski (1974) have shown however that the contribution of marketing
activity within the service sector of less developed countries is not
statistically related to per capita product. In the poorer countries a
relatively high percentage contribution of commerce can occur not
because marketing institutions are particularly well developed but
because the productive section of the economy is poorly developed and
other services are non-existent. Guatemala is such an example. Over the
last 20 years the contribution of commerce and transportation to GDP
has been consistently over 30 per cent but reflects the low level of
development in agriculture and industry, not an advanced commercial
sector. From Figure 1.2 it would appear that for the majority of
countries marketing activities currently account for probably in excess
of one-fifth of national wealth.

In most countries this level of marketing's contribution to GDP has
been remarkably constant over the last 20 years and in some countries
for even longer. Only in approximately 15 of the 130 or so countries
for which UN statistics are available has the percentage varied by more
than 4 per cent since 1953.

An alternative, but related, method of measuring the role of transport
and commerce is to consider the combined sectors' contribution in
gross capital formation. Generally commerce and transportation together
show a similar rate of capital formation to the total economy. Within
the sector commerce has a very low rate while capital formation in the
transport sector is higher than average. The ratio of commerce's contribution to GDP to its contribution to total capital formation is larger
than the comparable ratio for the economy as a whole. In Sweden the
two ratios were 17.8:1 and 4.4:1 in 1970, and in the UK, in 1973, they
were 9.3:1 and 4.5:1 and the same pattern is present in the less developed
countries (Kuznets, 1966). Since the mid 1960s in most developed
countries the difference between the ratios has been narrowing. So that
while the proportional contribution to capital formation remains low,
capital formation within wholesaling and retailing has been increasing
faster than the economy as a whole. A number of writers have discussed
the *revolution* that took place in distribution in Europe in the late 1950s

and 1960s and in essence this change resulted in considerable investment by retail organisation (Stacey and Wilson, 1965). The effects of this change in retail technique, for example the growth of selfservice methods (Henksmeier, 1960; Channing, 1960) can be seen reflected in the figures of capital formation. A comparable change took place in North America in the 1950s, and a similar lowering of the contribution to GDP/capital formation ratio is shown in the statistics.

While assessment of marketing's contribution to national wealth involves many assumptions about the measurement and interpretation of both national accounts and output from service industries, the proportion of the labour force involved in marketing provides, on the surface, a more easily obtained measure. In reality, however, employment figures are as difficult to interpret as financial statistics, for there are many types of employee with differing working hours and widely varying productivity. In virtually all countries until the end of the 1960s, there was a steady annual increase in the percentage of the total labour force which was employed in marketing industries. In the late 1960s there was an apparent decrease in a few countries, notably the United Kingdom and West Germany. By the early 1970s the percentage was increasing again. How far the decrease was a real one is not certain, for while numbers in transport industries and the distributive trades were falling, large manufacturing firms were increasingly taking on marketing activities such as physical distribution which were formerly carried out by specialist firms. It seems more likely that even in the United Kingdom and West Germany employment in marketing, in its broadest sense, has continued to increase over the last 20 years.

In Western Europe the percentage of the workforce in commerce and transport has risen to be in excess of one-fifth of all employment. Employment in these two sectors has been rising steadily while their contribution to GDP has been steady. The absolute numbers vary somewhat but the trend is the same throughout Europe. Generally employment in commerce and transport is less important in Mediterranean Europe than in Northern Europe. The contrast between North and South and the increase in employment is more apparent in commerce than in transport. The percentage of the economically active population employed in commerce in 1970 varied from barely 10 per cent in Greece and Portugal to over 16 per cent in Norway and Belgium. The corresponding figures for 1950 were 7.2 per cent in Portugal and 11.2 per cent in Norway. Average annual rates of growth are shown in Table 1.1. In the years since the Second World War there has been a major increase in employment in commerce both in relative and absolute measures. The

Table 1.1:   Average Annual Growth Rates in Employment in Trade and Transport in Selected European Countries

Trade	1950-5	1955-60	1960-5	1965-70	1972-3
Austria	6.8[a]	5.4	5.6	1.5	1.1
Belgium	0.1	1.0	2.1	2.2	0.6
Finland			5.6	0.6	6.6
France		1.4	2.7	2.0	2.3
Germany (W.)			1.1[b]	0	0.2
Ireland			1.0	0.4	0.6
Italy		1.0[c]	0.5	0.8	2.8
Netherlands	1.9	2.3	3.1	2.6	−0.4
Norway	2.9	2.0	2.6	2.6	2.3
Spain		3.2[d]	4.2	3.7	5.4
UK	1.8	1.0	1.3	−1.0	
Transport					
Austria	0.7[a]	1.3	0.8	−0.3	1.1
Belgium	−1.0	0.5	0.7	1.4	7.4
Finland			1.0	0.6	0.7
France		1.1	2.4	1.0	1.3
Germany (W.)			1.8[b]	−1.3	1.2
Ireland			1.1	1.0	0
Italy		3.5[c]	3.9	−1.0	1.0
Netherlands	1.4	0.1	0.5	0	−1.3
Norway	1.8	2.0	0.6	−1.1	0.6
Spain		2.8[d]	1.7	1.8	1.0
UK	−0.8	−0.3	−0.2	−0.6	

a. 1953-5.
b. 1962-5.
c. 1957-60.
d. 1950-60.

trend was apparent before the war (David, 1953; Hirsch, 1938) but has become more important in the last 20 years.

Picard (1938) in an attempt to produce comparative statistics of the rôle of wholesaling and retailing in European economies before World War 2, points to the large increases in employment. He suggests these are due to two factors:

First of all, there is the increase in total population, which is greater

than in active population . . . There is also a more or less general
increase in the volume of industrial and agricultural production and
a rise in national income; this has not only made possible, but has
encouraged and even led to the creation of new wholesale and retail
establishments. (p. 11).

For the increase in the numbers employed in postwar years alternative
explanations must be sought, for in many countries population numbers
have remained approximately constant and competition and reorganisation in retailing and wholesaling have resulted in a decrease in the
number of establishments.

Jeffreys and Knee (1962) following Barger (1955) suggest four reasons
for the postwar increase in employment in commerce. First, the decline
in agricultural manpower has made the individual much more dependent
on the marketing system and commerce has grown in response to demand.
Secondly, the increasing division of labour has made the commercial
sector increasingly responsible for connecting producer with consumer.
Thirdly, the very large reduction in working hours and the increasing
use of part-time employees in commerce has in turn increased the relative importance of the sector as an employer. Finally, the volume of
goods distributed per man hour in commerce rose less rapidly than the
corresponding measure in the productive sector. In relation to increases
in employment in other sectors employment rose more rapidly in commerce.

Government attempts to redistribute labour (Reddaway *et al.*, 1970;
1973; Boddewyn and Hollander, 1972) and the continued introduction
of new techniques in retailing and wholesaling aimed at increasing labour
productivity mean that it is likely that the rate of increase in employment
will soon level off. This seemed to be happening in the United Kingdom
in the last few years of the 1960s but since 1971 numbers have again
risen (NEDO, 1974). The earlier decrease and current rates of increase
however are relatively small and the important feature now is the lack
of systematic annual increase seen currently in most countries and until
the late 1960s in the UK. It seems likely that other countries in Europe
will follow the trend set by the United Kingdom. During the early 1970s
Sweden, West Germany, Ireland and Finland all showed an approximately
constant number of workers in commerce.

Outside Europe there is a wide range in the percentage of employees
engaged in marketing industries. Barger's study shows the enormous
gains in employee numbers in distribution in the USA between 1870 and
1950. 'Persons engaged in the commodity-producing industries more than

doubled between 1870 and 1950; those distributing commodities (i.e. in retailing and wholesaling) grew twelvefold' (p. 6). Fuchs (1968) in a later study has shown the increase in employment to have continued through to 1965. Commerce and transportation in 1965 accounted for 27 per cent of non-farm employment in the USA. More recent statistics suggest that employment in distribution continues to rise by about 2 per cent per year while total non-farm employment increases by barely one-tenth of this.

At the other end of the scale are several countries in which marketing activities account for less than 10 per cent of civilian employment. Morocco, Zambia, India and several Central American republics have less than one in ten of civilian employees engaged in commerce and transportation. The distribution of values immediately suggests a relationship with levels of development but the association is far from simple. Fisher (1935) and subsequently Clark (1940) suggested that a characteristic of Western style economic development was a progression from primary through secondary to tertiary activities. Barkin (1966) in preliminary discussion to an assessment of manpower problems in the service industry states:

> Modern Society calls for a wider range of services to maintain the basic productive enterprises whose markets have grown in size and geographical scope. Their relations are moreover more intimate and the responses to developments are quicker. In addition, with the rise in national and personal incomes and the shortening of hours, the human horizons of the good life have been lifted making new demands on the economic system. (p. 11).

The new institutions not only serve the final consumer but also provide services to the productive sector (Greenfield, 1966). Several authors therefore suggest a casual link between levels of development measured by GDP per head and the percentage of manpower engaged in services (Bauer and Yamey, 1951). As marketing constitutes a major element of the service sector, the link also lies with the amount of marketing activity.

Kuznets (1957) has argued for almost a deterministic connection between service sector employment and per capita national product such that either variable can be used to predict the other. This direct relationship is supposedly due to two factors. First, as income increases, the demand for services increases. Secondly, services generally lag behind agriculture and industry in technological development with either a consequent relative decline in real output per unit of input of services or a rise in the relative (and possibly absolute) amount of labour required to produce a given amount of services. Fuchs (1968) goes even further in a search for a direct relationship and fits a curve of the form $x=a+b/y$, where x is the sector share of employment and y is per capita income. Ofer (1973) suggests a range of models but the approach of Fuchs seems to provide the best fit.

Stigler (1956) and Minkes (1954) suggest a much more complex system of connections between service employment and variables in the economy. Stigler lists the processes of urbanisation, technological change, educational achievement, greater equality in income distribution and an ageing population as all affecting the amount of employment in services. Essentially Stigler is arguing for a multivariate measure of development and not the univariate one of per capita income. Ofer (1967), in a study of the Israeli economy, adds a further major variable to Stigler's list. This is the amount to which government meets the demand for public services. In attempts to explain growth in the total service section this factor of government employment is very important but in most countries marketing industries are not public sector services. The general lack of governmental intervention in commerce and transportation perhaps can be seen as a factor in the slow rate of growth of manpower productivity in the two industry groups. Low productivity associated with rises in overall demand has given rise to the expansion of numbers in marketing.

Broadly stated, countries with a high per capita income have a relatively large percentage employed in marketing. The high percentage is not directly attributable to high per capita income but to the increase in demand for services both in final consumption and in the production phases of the economy. Given increasing standards of living the demand for marketing services will increase and manpower will grow in numbers unless productivity increases can be achieved, which will allow an expanding demand to be met by a declining workforce. Evidence from the earlier figures suggested a stabilisation in marketing employment in some European countries in the late 1960s. This coincides with a period of rapid technological change in wholesaling and retailing and a phase of rationalisation in respect of transportation services. Both trends were aimed at increasing productivity and in Britain were associated with positive governmental attempts to encourage higher productivity in service activity generally. The balance between productivity in services and the growth of demand, for which per capita income may be used as a crude proxy variable, is critical in determining the share of the labour force engaged in marketing activities.

Marketing in the Regional Economy

Compared with studies of the national rôle of services generally, and marketing specifically, there is a paucity of work on the position of marketing within regional economies. The regional economists tend to have concentrated on studies of productive activities and have ignored the marketing sector (Nourse, 1968; Hoover, 1971). While regional input-output studies allow the flow of goods through the marketing system to be studied, only very rarely are marketing industries isolated in the input-output matrix. Isard and Langford (1971) introduce marketing margins as an input-output element in their study of the Philadelphia region: 'As goods flow through the marketing system from producer to consumer, they may be subject to three basic margins: The transport, wholesale and retail trade margins' (p. 72). One of the larger sources of inaccuracy in the Isard and Langford study is the difficulty in measuring these marketing margins: 'In practice, the *explicit* determination of these trade margins is extremely difficult' (p. 73). The input-output studies of California (Hansen and Tiebout, 1963) and West Virginia (Miernyk *et al.*, 1970) also had difficulty in accurately representing the interindustry flows involving the marketing industry, but in the West Virginia study the concluding table lists the estimated 1975 impact of $1 million delivered to final demand. Value added to regional wholesale sales emerges as the second highest score over all 48 sectors. Retailing and transportation are both sectors with scores above the median. While these studies indicate interindustry relationships affecting marketing industry, they do not allow conclusions on the rôle of marketing within the regional economy. Perloff *et al.* (1960) states:

> Researchers have, on the whole, failed to recognise the importance of this (i.e. role of marketing and services in the regional economy) area of research. Even Stigler's pioneering study restricts its view of the service industries to the national aggregates . . . Even less has been attempted in the way of an understanding of the functional and regional components of the service industries. (p. 463).

The situation has not improved noticeably in the last 20 years.

Other than the input-output studies, there are a few studies involving analysis of employment patterns. The study of Lengellé (1968) includes a short analysis of employment contribution of services, *in toto*, to the regional labour force. It is more usual, however, for marketing activities to be ignored in regional studies of employment or at least only to be considered in a subsidiary rôle to productive activities. Almost all the regional studies by British regional planning agencies concentrate exclusively on employment in the productive sector. One of the studies of North West England (North West Joint Planning Team, 1973) attempts an assessment of office employment but provides no real insight into employment in marketing. There are, nonetheless, considerable variations among regions in the levels of marketing employment. The amount of such employment is related both to the level of overall development in the region — its economic wealth — and to the level of urbanisation. Urban located marketing institutions have tended to grow faster than rural/ agricultural marketing activities. Just as there are countries where the contribution of marketing to total employment is increasing rapidly while in others the change is less impressive, so within a country there are regional differentials in both the amount and growth of marketing activities.

Regional differentials seem particularly large within the less developed countries where national marketing activities appear to be increasingly concentrated in a few areas or even in a single city. Galbraith and Holton (1955) showed how control of the Puerto Rican marketing system was concentrated in the San Juan region and it might be expected that in consequence employment in marketing would be similarly concentrated. A comparable position has been shown in Columbia (Riley *et al.*, 1970) where both agricultural and consumer marketing activities are concentrated in a few regions centred on the five largest cities. Within the rest of the country market activity is minimal.

In developed countries there are also regional differences both in the amount of employment in marketing and in its proportion of total employment. In the USA the concentration of urban/industrial activity in the North East and in California also corresponds to concentrations of service and marketing employment. Gottmann (1961) indicated the importance of the strength of marketing orientated service industry in the development and functioning of *Megalopolis*. The North Eastern seaboard region has increased its share of marketing activity at the expense of productive activity and Gottmann states:

> while the flow of materials from production to consumption becomes more and more independent of the business districts of the central cities, the management of the swelling flow of materials requires increasing employment and activity in the hubs of commerce. (p. 564).

While the total amount of marketing employment is high in such regions as Megalopolis USA the proportion of the regional labour force engaged in marketing activity may be quite low.

In recent years the operational technique of shift-share analysis has been widely applied to the analysis of regional changes in employment patterns and such analyses provide some evidence for the differential shifts in regional employment in marketing. The basis of the method is to divide regional employment change into three components. First, there is a national component (total employment shift) corresponding to national growth rates. Secondly, there is an industrial component (differential shift) which corresponds to change resulting from national changes in the regional industrial mix. Thirdly, there is a residual component (proportionality shift) which is assumed to measure specific regional performance of industry groups. The basic technique (Dawson, 1974; Stilwell, 1969) has been widely adapted (Esteban-Marquillas, 1972; Parakevopoulos, 1971) and also heavily criticised (Chalmers, 1971; Houston, 1967). The main advantage of the technique lies in its ability to allow overall regional employment change to be disaggregated into broad industry sectors.

Some of the early empirical shift-share analysis paid little attention to service industry. Perloff *et al.* (1960) show that within the mountain states of the USA there is a strong growth in marketing industry, but even so their work is notably weak in analysis of differential shifts for commerce. They do point out however that the total tertiary sector shifts correspond closely to changes in total employment and population. Thus the regions of major population growth also have been the regions of major growth in services. Detailed consideration of their published tables shows that it is not necessarily large shifts in retailing, wholesaling and transport which are associated with population increase. The remainder of the service sector is perhaps more closely linked to population change than is marketing activity. Both Oregon and Nevada of the far West states had proportionally lower differential shifts in marketing industry than did California. In terms of total employment it is the states where population is increasing most rapidly (California, Florida) where marketing industry is most important. Such is only to be expected for much of marketing is concerned directly with supplying final demand.

More recent studies in Ireland (O'Farrell, 1972) and Venezuela (Lasuen, 1971) confirm high absolute differential shifts in market employment in areas of rapid population growth. In Ireland, during the 1960s, the region to show the largest shift was that centred on Dublin while the Galway and Limerick regions which had been the subject of substantial planned employment increase also stood apart from the more traditional regions which were suffering a decrease in employment numbers. The

Venezuelan study, based on change from 1941 to 1961, indicated the very considerable absolute differential shift in the *trade* sector in the Caracas region. There is also evidence that this major increase took place in the latter part of the study period probably following on from increases in productive employment. On the basis of Lasuen's study there would appear to be, at a regional scale, a lag in the appearance of rapid growth in marketing employment after initial population increase and increase in productive employment. There appears to be some contrasts in results in developed and underdeveloped countries whereby the more urbanised regions in underdeveloped countries appear to be increasing their proportional share of marketing employment. The absence of this trend in the developed countries perhaps may be accounted for by the suburbanisation and decentralisation processes operating in urbanised regions.

Marketing in the Urban Economy

The city is the primary agency of distribution and so of marketing activity and industry. The very existence of a concentration of population means a concentration of marketing activity and a focus for certain marketing institutions. Despite the very obvious importance of marketing to the urban economy and while, as Cox (1965A) points out, 'City-forming industries have been much analyzed . . . comparatively little has been done with analyzing the internal trade of cities' (p. 96). An exception to this general statement lies perhaps in studies of retail location. None the less, there have been few attempts to assess the rôle of marketing within the overall operation of urban and metropolitan economies. At an empirical level there are a handful of studies only, while at a theoretical level the details of the rôle of marketing in urban growth processes remains a major gap (Stilwell, 1974).

Greytak (1966) has attempted to test a hypothesis that cities with larger populations have a higher percentage of their employment in tertiary industry generally and in marketing industry in particular. With wholesaling and retailing his results are inconclusive. Among smaller cities in the USA a negative relationship was apparent between population size and increases (1950-61) in employment in wholesaling. Above approximately 50,000 population the reverse appears to be the case. For retailing employment a more consistent positive association appears but if city size bands are analysed the significance of the relationship is extremely variable and Greytak is unable to draw firm conclusions from the analysis.

Greytak's study typifies many of the problems inherent in an attempt

to assess the rôle of marketing to urban growth. A critical problem is
that of measurement. Greytak, in common with several of the classic
studies in urban geography (Nelson, 1955; Harris, 1943; Pownall, 1953)
uses employment as an index of sectoral contribution to the economy.
At least two other measures are frequently available in most Western
developed countries. First is the contribution of marketing industry
and land use to urban finance. For example, in Britain the local property
tax structure allows assessment of the relative financial contribution of
different types of urban establishment. International comparisons of
urban finance are impossible because of different local financial regulation and legislation but intranational studies may well be possible.
During the early 1970s in Britain's larger towns (over 50,000 population)
the contribution of shops to total urban income from property tax
sources varied from less than 5 per cent (Stretford, Port Talbot, Beb-
bington) to over 18 per cent (Crewe, Cheltenham, Shrewsbury, Canter-
bury, Barnsley) and even over 25 per cent in Chester. The determinants
of the relative value of retailing to different cities have never been explored but could be used to provide one indication of the importance of
retailing and probably wholesaling, to urban economies. Many countries
have local business taxes, either on land or turnover, and these could be
as useful as the British statistics.

A second possible but unexplored data source is provided by statistics
on the total floor space accounted for by different industry sectors.
Often such statistics are available by urban and metropolitan areas as in
England and Wales (Department of Environment, 1972, 1974). Changes
in floor space in retailing alone may be quite considerable even over
short periods either as shops close down or as new shopping centres
become operational. In Wales between April 1967 and March 1969 six
towns had a net increase in retail floor space of over 33 per cent while
in the same period in Cwmamman and Tredegar retail floor space decreased by over 20 per cent. Such changes must inevitably have a major
effect on the functioning and organisation of the urban economies of
these towns.

Employment figures remain the only base on which any attempts
have been made to study the relationship between overall urban economic
structure and the marketing component. As yet however there has been
no thorough study even using employment figures. Bergsman, Greenston
and Healy (1973) attempt definitions of groups of industries which
characterise North American cities. In all the cities they studied, the
marketing industries appear as a discrete group fundamental to the pattern of urbanisation in the United States. The ubiquity of marketing

employment in this North American study is argued to be the result of agglomeration processes in urban growth but this appears to be a very simple reason for a complex phenomenon. Glickman (1976) shows a considerable difference between marketing employment growth in central cities and suburbs in Japan and also shows particularly rapid expansion in medium sized cities. In many major world cities the proportion of employment in the marketing industries is constant or even falling. While there may have been an increase in recent years in indirect marketing employment (facilitating agencies for example) there appears to have been a decrease in direct marketing employment in the major cities as attempts have been made to increase productivity in retailing and wholesaling. This decrease also is due to the decentralisation of key marketing industries in most metropolitan areas, with the decentralisation of employment in marketing having been greater than in other industry groups. It must also be remembered that producing firms are increasingly carrying out their own marketing functions and there is a decreasing demand, proportionally but not in absolute terms, for traditional marketing industries. The reason for the decline of marketing in many major cities is not wholly clear but the pattern of change in small towns is even more complicated and the reasons are even less clear.

The Marketing Factors in Economic Growth

Perhaps because social scientists are unsure of the exact rôle of marketing in the economy, marketing industries tend to have been excluded from plans and policies aimed at upgrading levels of national or regional economic wealth. Only in a relatively few cases have marketing industries and institutions been ascribed a specific position in the development process. This has occurred despite both pleas for the realisation of the rôle of marketing industries and also statistical studies on temporal patterns of the growth of GDP and marketing activity outlined earlier and summarised by Moyer (1967) and Preston (1968). The reason for the absence of a specification of marketing's rôle in development policies may well lie in the lack of a theoretical understanding of the position of marketing in the various development processes. Within the realm of the developing countries Anderson (1970) states that marketing

is a relatively neglected aspect of the process of economic development. Whether from the view that it is a passive, self-adjusting mechanism in the economic system which can safely be ignored in a nation's somewhat frantic efforts to raise the level of well-being of its citizens, or from the view that the marketing system is so complex and so intertwined in the private lives of every citizen that it is better left alone, the fact is that development plans and strategies have typically left change in the marketing structure until later. (p. xvii).

Clout's (1975) review of regional development in Western Europe shows that the cynosure of development economists in the so-called developed countries remains with plans and policies for restructuring manufacturing industry and agriculture, although together they often account for barely half national employment.

Drucker (1958) almost 20 years ago provided a powerful argument for development planners to provide marketing with a positive position in growth strategies:

> Marketing occupies a critical role in respect to the development of such 'growth areas'. Indeed marketing is the most important 'multiplier' of such development. It is in itself in every one of these areas the least developed, the most backward part of the economic system. Its development, above all others, makes possible economic integration and the fullest utilization of whatever assets and productive capacity an economy already possesses. It mobilizes latent economic energy. (p. 253).

The need for development policies to take account of marketing became very apparent from a series of studies undertaken by the FAO into development strategies for regions in the Mediterranean and particularly Southern Italy. Both Collins and Holton (1963) and Abbott (1962, 1964) argued that marketing might be the major factor underlying the success or otherwise of expansion of both agriculture and manufacturing industry and furthermore stated that if planned changes in production were to be part of a development policy then there should be concern with planning changes in marketing. Several studies have continued to make this point both in respect of planning agricultural development (German Foundation for Developing Countries, 1968) and manufacturing development—'All too often, marketing is the basic determinant of the destiny of new manufacturing enterprises from the moment they are launched' (p. 29, Sherbini, 1965). Whatever the ultimate aim of the development process and whatever the policy adopted, the basic process is concerned with developing channels in the economy along which goods flow efficiently. Hirschman (1958) suggests how economists isolate two types of linkage in the channel formation procedure. Backward linkage exists when an enterprise requires products or services which are lacking and so creates a demand which is then met. Forward linkage exists when an enterprise produces goods and services which form a launch pad for new activities. In both forms of linkage, and in the whole concept of economic channels, marketing provides the institutions which allow the channels to function.

Why, with the apparent awareness of a significant rôle for marketing, has development planning for marketing been assiduously ignored? Abbott (1967) perhaps provides one answer:

> In part this neglect may reflect a traditional reluctance to enter into the details of marketing on the part of general economists who still carry over the classical view that production is what matters—consumption is mainly a question of income distribution. (p. 393).

The Irish National Industrial Economic Council (1966) in their attempts to develop a policy for the development of distribution point to the major difficulty

> that relatively little theoretical work has been published on the linkages between the distributive sector and the rest of the economy . . . It may explain in part the divergence between the slight attention given to the services sector and the importance of the sector . . . (p. 10).

In several development studies the effect of marketing institutions is minimised and it is even suggested by Solomon (1948) that the inefficiencies of marketing in the less developed countries 'do not seem to have any curtailing effect upon output from existing productive capacity' (pp. 539-40). Consequently there is little need to develop any theory. Holton (1953) suggests a more pragmatic reason why theory has not been developed or policies put into effect, namely that 'inefficient marketing systems afford a dole for the unemployed by means of high margins and prices. Governing authorities are loath to tamper with this convenient method of partially supporting the jobless' (p. 345).

It is however important to distinguish between the *policy* of development planning and the *theory* underlying development planning. A number of recent attempts at development planning have policies relevant to either the encouragement or discouragement of marketing but few of the economic growth models enlarge on the theoretical position of either services or marketing. There is little agreement on the ultimate purpose of marketing in growth strategies. Even within broadly comparable

politicoeconomic units, marketing is used in different ways in development planning. For example, Yugoslavia uses marketing primarily to
develop its international trade, while Romania and Thailand use marketing policies to accelerate the domestic economy. The lack of adequate
theory on economic growth probably accounts for such differences in
policy aims.

Some growth strategies and policies, despite a lack of theory, do have
a significant effect on service and marketing industries. The strategy
for growth in the USSR is based on diverting a very large proportion
of growth resources to heavy industry so letting service industries lag
behind (Bergson, 1964). Consequent on such a strategy there tends to
be a low level of urbanisation, and a small share of GNP allocated to
private consumption—both results tend to hold back the development
of marketing institutions. Ofer (1973) suggests that recent reforms in
the USSR will mean a significant swing to a more positive position for
marketing:

> Every measure of decentralization and increased autonomy of res-
> ponsibility at the firm level is bound to call for more commercial
> intermediaries among firms and production firms and retail outlets.
> This will occur when sales replace production as a major criterion of
> success for managers and when the number of centrally planned items
> is reduced; even the direct contacts between production and retail
> outlets are bound to increase and reduce the number of trade workers
> —in the sales departments of enterprises and the buying departments
> of retail stores.(p. 164).

Ofer sees the situation occurring by the late 1980s. If this occurs then
the Soviet development policy may not look all that dissimilar from
some policies in capitalist countries. The five-year (1960-4) plan of
Morocco attempted to introduce policies of concentration of small shops
and the modernisation of their equipment, storage facilities and services
(Van Nieuwenhuijze, 1963). One possible way of achieving this fairly
widespread aim in developing countries is by a closer integration between
state controlled wholesalers and private retailers.

At a general level however, the promotion of service activity and
increased efficiency in marketing has one particular merit in the development process—growth in marketing involves a proportionally larger
increase in employment than in capital. Marketing and services absorb
a relatively large labour force (Burke, 1975). The Greek economic programme for 1962-71 attempted to promote the service industries gener-

ally, including marketing industries. It provided for a 6.6 per cent annual increase in employment in services compared with a 6.0 per cent increase in national income. The 1968-72 revised plan has similar aims (Ministry of Co-ordination, 1968):

> One of the basic aims of the Plan is the eliminations of the weaknesses and deficiencies of the distribution sector, in order to stimulate competition and reduce the cost of distribution, so that this sector may play a more active role in the development of industry and agriculture. (p. 104).

It was hoped to achieve this end not with a reduction in manpower but with an increase in employment of approximately 2 per cent per year over the period of the plan.

A number of development plans in the developing countries include the planned development of marketing alongside either planned urbanisation or policies to develop agriculture: 'At present the domestic markets for food in tropical Africa are very thin. This is partly due to the still limited degree of urbanization so that opportunities for exchange between country and city tend to be restricted' (de Wilde, 1967, p. 208). Leibenstein (1957) suggested that the most rapidly growing economies and those with rapidly developing marketing sectors are those with a high proportion of population in cities. The processes underlying this relationship are complex. Urbanisation often provides attractive possibilities for industrial growth and capital formation and thus provides a market and capital for the development of marketing institutions. Belshaw (1965) suggests that 'In so far as these relationships hold good, new nations would probably be well advised to encourage the growth of towns as a major impetus for economic growth and agricultural reform' (p. 144). Development poles and development centre planning are clearly a response to such a view. The acceptance of growth pole policies as a means of encouraging marketing industries within the general development process are now widespread in the developing world. The application of growth pole policies in India for example utilises a four-tier system with (a) *growth poles* (major regional centres) into which many of the main marketing institutions are concentrated; (b) *growth centres* (minor regional centres) which concentrate on attracting manufacturing industry; (c) *growth points* (large local centres) which encourage a mix of productive and marketing activities; and (d) *service centres* (small local centres) which provide economic and social services to primarily agricultural areas. Marketing institutions hold a key position in such a policy. Reviews of a number of such policies in other countries are provided by Kuklinski (1972). The urbanisation element within development planning could be considered to be hinged on the provision and planning of marketing institutions and industries.

Of the more commonly argued growth theories only one, usually termed the *stages theory*, relates to marketing industries. The theory argues for growth resulting from internal specialisation and the division of labour within the region. The regional economy, it is assumed, passes through several stages from economic selfsufficiency with little internal specialisation, through phases of increasing internal and external specialisation to a final stage with a high level of internal specialisation and a large proportion of employment in service industries (Perloff *et al.*, 1960). In other theories the growth process usually is assumed to be determined by factors external to the region or city:

> The stages theory . . . places the service sector in a strategic position in the exploration of the growth process of a centre by stressing that:
>   (a) service trades play an expanding rôle particularly for employment growth, as the regional economy develops;
>   (b) since service trades are normally located in the centres, the shift to services means a shift to the centres;
>   (c) the growth of the service sector in the regional economy implies the creation of continuous growth impulses in the centres;
>   (d) the growth of service employment in the centres is a fundamental force in the alteration of settlement patterns. (Allen and Hermansen, 1968, p. 199).

The stages theory has been most commonly applied to the development of urban regions and as a vindication of growth pole policies. The theory also states in general the importance of the whole service sector, not just the marketing elements. Thus while it is relevant to the present discussion it is of a very general nature. This criticism and others are explored by Hilhorst (1967) but alternative approaches often fail to account for the growth of service activities.

During the last 30 years marketing has grown to be a significant discipline within the social sciences, yet geographers generally have failed to appreciate its contribution to the study of economic geography. Marketing geography has developed slowly and in a very patchy fashion. Given some recent changes in emphasis away from production based studies in economic geography it is valuable to reconsider the aims of marketing geography. Its concern with the whole process of distribution within the economy places it in a position to integrate a variety of studies. In the broad international perspective there is both a lack of theoretical basis on which to study the position of marketing within economic units and also a lack of awareness, at least until the 1970s, that marketing processes have a key rôle to play in social and economic change. As domestic marketing systems evolve and respond to changes in their operating environment, so conflicts occur within marketing processes. New techniques replace old methods, the functions of marketing institutions change and the demands made of marketing systems increase. Such changes inevitably result in conflict within marketing processes and in market channels whereby goods move from producer to consumer.

References

ABBOTT, J.C. (1962) 'The Role of Marketing in the Development of Backward Agricultural Economies', *Journal of Farm Economics*, 44, pp. 349-62.
—— (1964) 'Marketing and Area Development Studies', *Proceedings, American Marketing Association Conference, 1963*, pp. 424-38.
—— (1967) 'The Development of Marketing Institutions' in H.M. Southworth and B.F. Johnston (eds) *Agricultural Development and Economic Growth* (Cornell University Press, Ithaca) pp. 364-98.
ADLER, L. (1967) 'Systems Approach to Marketing', *Harvard Business Review*, 45, pp. 105-18.
ALDERSON, W. (1964) 'Marketing Systems in the Ecological Framework', *University of Illinois Bulletin*, 61.
ALDERSON, W., R. COX and S. SHAPIRO (1964) (eds), *Theory in Marketing* (Irwin, Homewood).
ALLEN, K. and T. HERMANSEN (1968) *Regional Policy in EFTA. An Examination of the Growth Centre Idea* (EFTA, Geneva).
ANDERSON, D.A. (1970) *Marketing and Development. The Thailand Experience* (Institute for International Business, Michigan State University, East Lansing).
ANDREWS, H.F. (1973) 'Urban Structure Correlates of Tertiary Activity', *Regional Studies*, 7, pp. 263-70.
APPLEBAUM, W. (1954) 'Marketing Geography', in P.E. James and C.E. Jones (eds) *American Geography – Inventory and Prospect* (Syracuse University Press, Syracuse).
BARGER, H. (1955) *Distribution's Place in the American Economy since 1869* (Princeton University Press, Princeton).
BARKIN, S. (1966) 'Manpower Problems of an Expanding Sector', in *Manpower Problems in the Service Sector* (OECD, Paris).
BARTELS, R. (1968) 'The General Theory of Marketing', *Journal of Marketing*, 32, pp. 29-33.
—— (1970) *Marketing Theory and Metatheory* (Irwin, Homewood).
BAUER, P.T. and B.S. YAMEY (1951) 'Economic Progress and Occupational Distribution', *Economic Journal*, 61, pp. 741-55.
BEAUJEU-GARNIER, J. and A. DELOBEZ (1977) *Géographie du Commerce* (Masson, Paris).

BELL, M. (1972) *Marketing: Concepts and Strategy* (Houghton-Mifflin, Boston).
BELSHAW, C.S. (1965) *Traditional Exchange and Modern Markets* (Prentice-Hall, Englewood Cliffs).
BERGSMAN, J., P. GREENSTON and R. HEALY (1973) 'The Agglomeration Process in Urban Growth' in G.C. Cameron and L. Wingo (eds) *Cities, Regions and Public Policy*, pp. 165-90 (Oliver & Boyd, Edinburgh).
BERGSON, A. (1964) *The Economics of Soviet Planning* (Yale University Press, New Haven).
BERRY, B.J.L. (1967) *Geography of Market Centers and Retail Distribution* (Prentice-Hall, Englewood Cliffs).
BERRY, B.J.L. and A. PRED (1961) *Central Place Theory* (Regional Science Research Institute, Philadelphia).
BERRY, B.J.L., H.G. BARNUM and R.J. TENNANT (1962) 'Retail Location and Consumer Behavior', *Papers and Proceedings of Regional Science Association*, 9, pp. 65-106.
BLADES, D.W., D.D. JOHNSTON and W. MARCZEWSKI (1974) *Service Activities in Developing Countries* (OECD, Paris).
BODDEWYN, J.J. and S.C. HOLLANDER (1972) (eds) *Public Policy towards Retailing* (Lexington Books, Lexington, Mass.).
BRADFORD, M.G. (1975) 'Spatial Aspects of Consumer Behaviour' (Ph.D. thesis, University of Cambridge).
BRAITHWAITE, D. and S.P. DOBBS (1932) *The Distribution of Consumable Goods* (Routledge, London).
BROMLEY, R.J. (1974) 'The Organisation of Quito's Urban Markets', *Transactions of Institute of British Geographers*, 62, pp. 45-70.
BURKE, C.D. (1975) *The Parasites Outnumber the Hosts* (Macmillan, Ottawa).
BUZZELL, R.D. *et al.* (1972) *Marketing: a Contemporary Analysis* (McGraw-Hill, New York).
CARLYLE, W.J. (1978) 'The Distribution of Store Sheep from Markets in Scotland', *Transactions, Institute of British Geographers*, New Series, 3(2), pp. 226-46.
CARSON, D. (1967) *International Marketing: a Comparative Systems Approach* (Wiley, New York).
CASSIDY, P.A., W.O. McCARTHY and H.I. TOFT (1970) 'An Application of Spatial Analysis to Beef Slaughter Plant Location and Size, Queensland', *Australian Journal of Agricultural Economics*, 14, pp. 1-20.
CHALMERS, J.A. (1971) 'Measuring Changes in Regional Industrial Structure: a Comment on Stilwell and Ashby', *Urban Studies*, 8, pp. 289-92.
CHANNING, W.H. (1960) 'Retail Development in Europe', *European Productivity Bulletin*, 36, pp. 16-9.
CHISHOLM, M. (1970) *Geography and Economics* (Bell, London).
CHISHOLM, M. and P. O'SULLIVAN (1973) *Freight Flows and the British Economy* (Cambridge University Press, Cambridge).
CLARK, B.D. (1972) (ed.) *The Retail Structure of Cities*, Occasional Publication 1 (Urban Study Group, Institute of British Geographers).
CLARK, C. (1940) *The Conditions of Economic Progress* (Macmillan, London).
CLARK, W.A.V. and G. RUSHTON (1970) 'Models of Intra-urban Consumer Behaviour and their Implications for Central Place Theory', *Economic Geography*, 46, pp. 486-97.
CLOUT, H.D. (1975) (ed.) *Regional Development in Western Europe* (Wiley, London).
COLLINS, N.R. and R.H. HOLTON (1963) 'Programming Changes in Marketing in Planned Economic Development', *Kyklos*, 16, pp. 127-37.
CORDEY-HAYES, M. (1968) *Retail Location Models*, Working Paper 16 (Centre

for Environmental Studies, London).

COX, R. (1965A) *Distribution in a High-level Economy* (Prentice-Hall, Englewood Cliffs).

—— (1965B) 'The Search for Universals in Comparative Studies of Domestic Marketing Systems', *Proceedings of Fall Conference of American Marketing Association on Marketing and Economic Development*, pp. 143-62.

CRIPPS, T.F. and R.J. TARLING (1973) *Growth in Advanced Capitalist Economies 1950-70* (Cambridge University Press, London).

DACEY, M.F. (1972) 'An Explanation for the Observed Dispersion of Retail Establishments in Urban Areas', *Environment and Planning*, 4, pp. 323-30.

DAVID, M. (1953) *Statistics of Distribution in 15 Countries* (International Chamber of Commerce, Document 17, Paris).

DAVIES, R.L. (1973) 'The Location of Service Activities' in M. Chisholm and B. Rodgers (eds), *Studies in Human Geography* (Heinemann, London).

—— (1976) *Marketing Geography* (RPA, Cambridge).

DAWSON, J.A. (1974) 'Analytical Techniques for Geographers: Shift-share Analysis', *Cambria*, 1, pp. 159-62.

DAY, R.A. (1973) 'Consumer Shopping Behaviour in a Planned Urban Environment', *Tijdschrift voor Economische en Sociale Geografie*, 64, pp. 77-85.

DEPARTMENT OF THE ENVIRONMENT (1972) 'Floorspace in Industrial, Warehouse etc. Shopping and Office Use', *Statistics for Town and Country Planning*, Series 2, No. 2.

—— (1974) 'Floorspace in Industrial, Warehouse etc. Shopping and Office Use', *Statistics for Town and Country Planning*, Series 2, No. 3.

de WILDE, J.C. (1967) *Experiences with Agricultural Development in Tropical Africa* (John Hopkins Press, Baltimore).

DOWNS, R. (1970) 'The Cognitive Structure of an Urban Shopping Centre', *Environmen and Planning*, 2, pp. 13-39.

DRUCKER, P. (1958) 'Marketing and Economic Development', *Journal of Marketing*, 22(3), pp. 252-9.

DRUCKER, P.F. (1962) 'The Economy's Dark Continent', *Fortune*, 65 (4).

EASTMAN, R.O. (1930) *Marketing Geography* (Alex Hamilton Institute, New York).

ESTEBAN-MARQUILLAS, J.M. (1972) 'A Re-interpretation of Shift-share Analysis', *Regional and Urban Economics*, 2 (3), pp. 249-61.

EPSTEIN, B.J. (1971) 'Geography and the Business of Retail Site Selection', *Economic Geography*, 47, pp. 192-9.

FISHER, A.G.B. (1935) *The Clash of Progress and Security* (Macmillan, London).

FISK, G. (1967) *Marketing Systems* (Harper & Row, New York).

FUCHS, V. (1965) 'The Growing Importance of the Service Industries' (National Bureau of Economic Research, Occasional Paper 96).

—— (1968) *The Service Economy* (Columbia University Press, New York).

GALBRAITH, J.K. (1967) *The New Industrial State* (Houghton-Mifflin, Boston).

GALBRAITH, J.K. and R. HOLTON (1955) *Marketing Efficiency in Puerto Rico* (Harvard University Press, Cambridge, Mass.).

GARNER, B.J. (1970) 'Towards a Better Understanding of Shopping Patterns' in R.H. Osborne, F.A. Barnes and J.C. Doornkamp (eds) *Geographical Essays in Honour of K.C. Edwards* (University of Nottingham, Nottingham), pp. 179-86.

GERMAN FOUNDATION FOR DEVELOPING COUNTRIES (1968) *Problems and Approaches in Planning Agricultural Development* (The Institute, Berlin).

GLICKMAN, N.J. (1976) 'On the Japanese Urban System', *Journal of Regional Science*, 16(3), pp. 317-344.

GOLLEDGE, R.G. (1970) 'Some Equilibrium Models of Consumer Behavior',

Economic Geography, 46, pp. 17-24.

GOOD, C.M. (1970) *Rural Markets and Trade in East Africa* (University of Chicago, Department of Geography, Research Paper, 128).

GOODE, N.J. (1968) 'The Professional Geographer's Contribution to the Retail Food Industry', *Professional Geographer*, 20, pp. 396-7.

GOTTMANN, J. (1961) *Megalopolis: the Urbanized Northeastern Seaboard of the United States* (The Twentieth Century Fund, New York).

GREEN, H.L. (1967) 'The Marketing Geographer: His Area of Competence', *Professional Geographer*, 19(5), pp. 261-2.

GREENFIELD, H.J. (1966) *Manpower and the Growth of Producer Services* (Columbia University Press, New York).

GRETHER, E.T. (1968) 'Galbraith versus the Market', a review article, *Journal of Marketing*, 32, pp. 9-13.

GREYTAK, D. (1966) *Urban Growth and Import Substitution in the Service Industries* (Institute for Urban and Regional Studies, Washington University, St Louis, Working Paper CWR 7).

HANSEN, W.L. and C.M. TIEBOUT (1963) 'An Intersectoral Flows Analysis of the Californian Economy', *The Review of Economics and Statistics*, 45, pp. 409-18.

HARRIS, C.D. (1943) 'A Functional Classification of Cities in the United States', *Geographical Review*, 33, pp. 86-99.

—— (1954) 'The Market as a Factor in the Localization of Industries in the United States', *Annals of the Association of American Geographers*, 44, pp. 315-48.

HARTSHORNE, R. (1959) *Perspective on the Nature of Geography* (J. Murray, London).

HAY, A.M. (1973) *Transport for the Space Economy* (Macmillan, London).

HENKSMEIER, K.H. (1960) *The Economic Performance of Self-service in Europe* (OECD, Paris).

HILHORST, J. (1967) *Regional Development Theory – an Attempt to Synthesise* (Mouton, Hague).

HIRSCH, J. (1938) *Standard Figures of Scandinavian Distribution* (Business Research Bureau, Copenhagen).

HIRSCHMAN, A.O. (1958) *The Strategy of Economic Development* (Yale University Press, New Haven).

HODDER, B.W. and R. LEE (1974) *Economic Geography* (Methuen, London).

HOLTON, R.H. (1953) 'Marketing Structure and Economic Development', *Quarterly Journal of Economics*, 67, pp. 344-61.

HOOD, N. (1969) 'Location Analysis in Economic Geography – Implications for Research in Marketing' *British Journal of Marketing*, 3, pp. 170-5.

HOOVER, E.M. (1971) *An Introduction to Regional Economics* (Knopf, New York).

HOUSTON, D.B. (1967) 'The Shift and Share Analysis of Regional Growth: a Critique', *Southern Economic Journal*, 34, pp. 577-81.

ISARD, W. and T.W. LANGFORD (1971) *Regional Input-output Study: Recollections, Reflections and Diverse Notes on the Philadelphia Experience* (MIT Press, Cambridge, Mass.).

JAPANESE EXTERNAL TRADE ORGANISATION (1972) *Planning for Distribution in Japan* (JETO, Tokyo).

JEFFERYS, J.B. (1950) *Distribution of Consumer Goods* (Cambridge University Press, Cambridge).

—— (1954) *Retail Trading in Great Britain, 1850-1950* (Cambridge University Press, Cambridge).

JEFFERYS, J.B. and D. KNEE (1962) *Retailing in Europe – Present Structure and*

Future Trends (Macmillan, London).
JENSEN-BUTLER, C. (1972) 'Gravity Models as Planning Tools: a Review of Theoretical and Operational Problems', *Geografiska Annaler*, 54B, pp. 68-78.
JUMPER, S.R. (1974) 'Wholesale Marketing of Fresh Vegetables', *Annals of Association of American Geographers*, 64, pp. 387-96.
KELLEY, E.J. (1965) *Marketing: Strategy and Functions* (Prentice-Hall, Englewood Cliffs).
KIRBY, D.A. (1974) 'Supply Problems of Small Unit Grocers: a Case Study', *International Journal of Physical Distribution*, 4, pp. 276-85.
KORNBLAU, C. (1968) *Guide to Store Location Research with Emphasis on Supermarkets* (Addison-Wesley, Reading, Mass.).
KUKLINSKI, A. (1972) (ed.) *Growth Poles and Growth Centres in Regional Planning* (Mouton, Paris).
KUZNETS, D. (1966) *Modern Economic Growth Rate Structure and Spread* (Yale University Press, New Haven).
KUZNETS, S. (1957) 'Quantitative Aspects of the Economic Growth of Nations II. Industrial Distribution of National Product and Labourforce', *Economic Development and Culture Change*, 5 (4 supplement).
LASUEN, J.R. (1971) 'Venezuela: an Industrial Shift-share Analysis, 1941-61', *Regional and Urban Economics*, 1(2), pp. 153-200.
LAZER, W. and E.J. KELLEY (1962) (eds) *Managerial Marketing: Perspectives and Viewpoints* (Irwin, Homewood).
LEIBENSTEIN, H. (1957) *Economic Backwardness and Economic Growth* (Wiley, New York).
LENGELLÉ, M.M. (1968) *The Growing Importance of the Service Sector in Member Countries* (OECD, Paris).
McDANIEL, R. and M.E. ELIOT-HURST (1968) *A Systems Analytic Approach to Economic Geography*, Publication No. 8 on College Geography (Association of American Geographers, Washington DC).
MANNERS, G. (1971) *The Changing World Market for Iron Ore* (Johns Hopkins Press, Baltimore).
MARKETING STAFF of Ohio State University (1965) 'A statement of Marketing Philosophy', *Journal of Marketing*, 29, pp. 43-4.
MIERNYK, W.H. *et al.* (1970) *Simulating Regional Economic Development: an Interindustry Analysis of the West Virginia Economy* (Heath-Lexington Books, Lexington, Mass.).
MIKKONEN, K. (1972) 'The Gravitation Field of Forssa', *Fennia*, 115, pp. 1-82.
MINISTRY OF CO-ORDINATION (1968) *Economic Development Plan for Greece, 1968-72* (The Ministry of Economic Development, Athens).
MINKES, A.L. (1954) 'Statistical Evidence and the Concept of Tertiary Industry', *Economic Development and Cultural Change*, 3, pp. 366-73.
MOYER, R. (1967) 'Trade and Economic Progress: an International Comparison', *Journal of Business*, 40(3), pp. 270-279.
MURPHY, R.E. (1961) 'Marketing Geography Comes of Age', *Economic Geography*, 37, p. 1.
NADER, G.A. (1969) 'Socio-economic Status and Consumer Behaviour', *Urban Studies*, 6, pp. 235-45.
NATIONAL INDUSTRIAL ECONOMIC COUNCIL (1966) *Report on Distribution* (Stationery Office, Dublin).
NEDO (1974) *Manpower and Pay in Retail Distribution* (NEDO, London).
NELSON, H.J. (1955) 'A Service Classification of American Cities', *Economic Geography*, 31, pp. 189-210.
NORTH WEST JOINT PLANNING TEAM (1973) *Strategic Plan for the North West* (HMSO, London).

NOURSE, H.O. (1968) *Regional Economics* (McGraw-Hill, New York).
O'FARRELL, P. (1972) 'A Shift and Share Analysis of Regional Employment
    Change in Ireland, 1951-66', *Economic and Social Review*, 4(1), pp. 59-86.
OFER, G. (1967) *The Service Industries in a Developing Economy* (Praeger, New
    York).
—— (1973) *The Service Sector in Soviet Economic Growth* (Harvard University
    Press, Cambridge, Mass.).
PARAKEVOPOULOS, C.C. (1971) 'The Stability of the Regional Share Com-
    ponent: an Empirical Test', *Journal of Regional Science*, 11(1), pp. 107-12.
PERLOFF, H.S., E.S. DUNN, E.E. LAMPARD and R.F. MUTH (1960) *Regions,
    Resources, and Economic Growth* (Johns Hopkins Press, Baltimore).
PICARD, R. (1938) *Distribution in 26 Countries* (International Chamber of Com-
    merce, Brochure 95, Paris).
POWNALL, L.L. (1953) 'The Functions of New Zealand Towns', *Annals of
    Association of American Geographers*, 43, pp. 332-50.
PRESTON, L.E. (1968) 'The Commercial Sector and Economic Development',
    in R. Moyer and S. Hollander (eds) *Markets and Marketing in Developing
    Economies* (Irwin, Homewood).
PYLE, J. (1971) 'Farmers Markets in the United States', *Geographical Review*, 61,
    pp. 167-97.
REDDAWAY, W.B. *et al.* (1970) *Effects of the Selective Employment Tax*
    (HMSO, London).
—— (1973) *The Final Report on Effects of the Selective Employment Tax*
    (HMSO, London).
REVZAN, D.A. (ed.) (1965) *Perspectives for Research in Marketing: Seven Essays*
    (Institute of Business and Economic Research, University of California, Berkeley).
RILEY, H. *et al.* (1970) *Market Coordination in the Development of the Cauca
    Valley Region—Colombia*, Research Reports (Latin American Studies Center,
    Michigan State University).
ROBSON, B.T. (1969) 'Human Ecology, Geography and Marketing', *British Journal
    of Marketing*, 3, pp. 164-9.
SCOTT, P. (1970) *Geography and Retailing* (Hutchinson, London).
SHERBINI, A.A. (1965) 'Marketing in the Industrialization of Underdeveloped
    Countries', *Journal of Marketing*, 29, pp. 28-32.
SMITH, A. (1937) *Wealth of Nations* (Modern Library, New York edition).
SMITH, C.A. (1976) (ed.) *Regional Analysis* (Academic Press, New York).
SMITH, D.M. (1973) *The Geography of Social Well-being in the United States*
    (McGraw-Hill, New York).
SMITH, H. (1937) *Retail Distribution* (Oxford University Press, London).
SOLOMON, M.R. (1948) 'The Structure of the Market in Underdeveloped Econ-
    omies', *Quarterly Journal of Economics*, 62(4), pp. 519-541.
STACEY, N.A.H. and A. WILSON (1965) *The Changing Pattern of Distribution*
    (Pergamon Press, Oxford).
STIGLER, G.J. (1956) *Trends in Employment in the Service Industries* (Princeton
    University Press, Princeton).
STILWELL, F.J.B. (1969) 'Regional Growth and Structural Adaptation' (*Urban
    Studies*, 6, pp. 162-78).
—— (1974) 'Economic Factors and the Growth of Cities' in I.H. Burnley (ed.)
    Urbanization in Australia: the Post War Experience (Cambridge University
    Press, London).
TAAFE, E.J. and H.L. GAUTHIER (1973) *Geography and Transportation* (Prentice-
    Hall, Englewood Cliffs).
THORELLI, H.B. (1967) 'Ecology in Marketing', *Southern Journal of Business*,
    11, pp. 19-25.

TREADWAY, A.B. (1969) 'What is Output? Problems of Concept and Measurement' in V. Fuchs (ed.) *Production and Productivity in the Service Industry* (Columbia University Press), pp. 53-94.

UNITED NATIONS (1958) *International Standard Industrial Classification of all Economic Activities*, Statistical Papers, Series M, No. 4(1).

___ (1968) *International Standard Industrial Classification of all Economic Activities*, Statistical Papers, Series M, No. 4(2).

___ (1977) *Yearbook of National Accounts Statistics, 1975* (New York).

VAN NIEUWENHUIJZE, C.A.O. (1963) *Markets and Marketing as Factors of Development in the Mediterranean Basin* (Mouton, Hague).

VANCE, J.E. (1970) *The Merchants' World: the Geography of Wholesaling* (Prentice-Hall, Englewood Cliffs).

WILLIAMS, O. (1972) 'The Role of the Auctioneer in the Livestock Trade of South Wales', *Geography*, 57, pp. 18-23.

YOSHINO, M.Y. (1971) *The Japanese Marketing System* (MIT Press, Cambridge, Mass.).

CHANNELS AND POWER RELATIONSHIPS IN
MARKETING SYSTEMS

In the outline of the marketing system presented in Chapter 1, the routes
linking the various institutions were termed *marketing channels*. The
marketing channel operates by institutions responding to each other's
behaviour and creating linkages. It is usual to consider the linkages as
one of five types, each type being representative of one feature of
behaviour within the system. The five are ownership, physical possession,
communication, financing and risk. As the market system operates the
pattern of linkage created by any one of these creates a pathway, route
or *channel*. An important survey of the channel concept and a review of
its operation is found in Stern and El-Ansary (1977).

Definition and Function of Marketing Channels

Alderson's (1957) text, *Market Behaviour and Executive Action*, defines
marketing channels as consisting of 'intermediary sellers who intervene
between the original source of supply and the ultimate consumer' (p.
211). By the 1960s a wider definition of the marketing channel was
more in vogue. This included both manufacturer and consumer as
institutions within the channel and may be typified by Clewett's (1961)
view that the channel is

> the pipeline through which a product flows on its way to the con-
> sumer. The manufacturer puts his product into the pipeline, or market-
> ing channel, and various marketing people move it along to the con-
> sumer at the other end of the channel.

By the late 1960s an attempt was being made to define channels in a
more functional manner: 'The two ways in which channels are defined
focus either on the flow of title from producer to consumer or the flow
of physical product. The flow of title is called the *exchange control* . . .
and the flow of product is termed *logistics channel*' (Holloway and Hancock, 1968, p. 384). The logistics channel formed the basis for studies
of physical distribution while the exchange channel represents the more
traditional marketing view. Alternatively, Bucklin (1966) states: 'A
channel of distribution shall be considered to comprise a set of institutions which performs all of the activities (functions) utilized to move

a product and its title from production to consumption' (p. 5). A relatively short step extends the definition to account for other functions of the marketing process—communication, financing and risk (Fisk, 1967; Bell, 1972). By including these non-exchange functions, facilitating agencies become integrated into the channel flows. All the different types of institution within the marketing system then may be linked by channel networks.

The changing definition of channels may be shown in simple diagrams of channel networks. The upper part of Figure 2.1 shows a traditional type of channel diagram. In this case it represents the flow of ownership (exchange channel) of food from farm to consumer in the United States. The lower part shows four types of channel utilised in marketing a table. In this latter example the only major channel left unplotted is the one associated with risk. Risk is both borne by individual institutions and by various specialist facilitating agencies.

Of most direct interest to the geographer, because the spatial factor is vital in their operation, are the exchange channel and the logistics channel and it is with these that most of the remainder of this chapter deals. Clearly there are overtly spatial components to the structure of exchange and logistics channels and these have been recognised for many years. Figure 2.2 is based on the study by Breyer (1934) and illustrates the spatial element in channel structure. The extent to which certain facilitating agencies are used varies with the location of the marketing system but within any one system it is difficult to argue for a meaningful spatial element in finance channels, risk channels or information channels although technological change certainly changes patterns of flow in these channels and can have spatial implications.

Most commonly discussions of marketing channels concentrate on the vertical structure of the channel. There is, however, an important horizontal dimension to all types of channel. At any given channel level there are many different kinds of establishment in terms of method of operation, form of ownership and mix of goods handled. For example, the retail level for the distribution channel of cigarettes extends over a wide range of retail types—independent, co-operative, multiple trader, any of which may sell by self service/counter service in supermarket, corner shop, hypermarket, etc. The horizontal modifications to channels, to be discussed later in this chapter, have become particularly important in the last 20 years, especially since many firms have tended to diversify the range of goods they carry. The horizontal structure, just as much as the vertical structure of marketing channels, both varies from region to region and also influences the spatial relationships in a single market-

Figure 2.1: Traditional and More Modern Views of the Marketing Channel

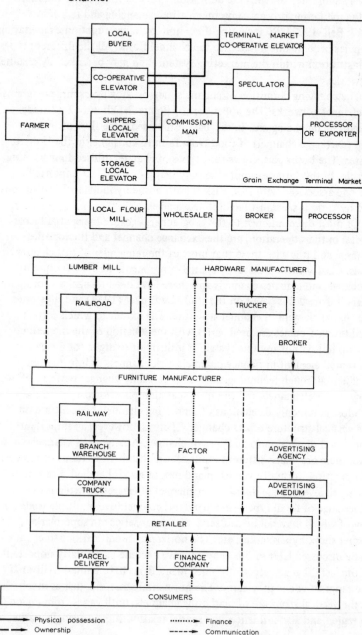

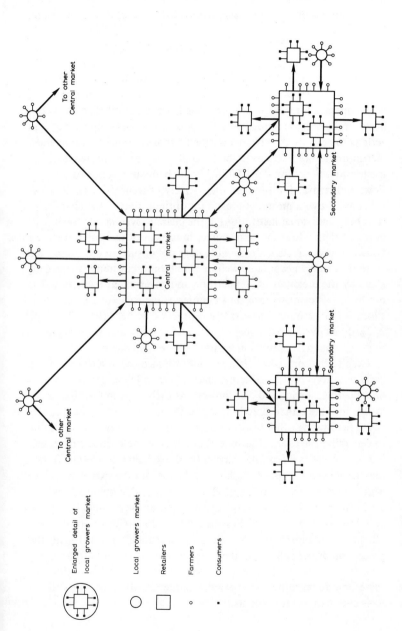

Figure 2.2: A Schematic Example of a Channel Linking Vegetable Producers to Consumers via a Three Tier Market System

ing channel, for the different types of institution at any one level each have different spatial patterns of occurrence. Figure 2.3 shows the horizontal dimension of the physical possession channel shown in Figure 2.1.

The operation of a channel consists of many related sales and purchases of goods and services. Alderson and Martin (1965) have sought to differentiate the concept of an individual flow between two institutions and the entire series of transactions necessary to allow the channel to operate for a single product. The individual unit flow between a buyer and a seller is termed a *transaction*, while the composite of transactions to activate the channel is called a *transvection*. Alderson and Martin use the term transvection in similar way to the more widely used *transaction flow*. This definition of channels in terms of unit flows and transaction flow (or alternatively of transactions and transvections) allows a meaningful basis for optimisation of the channel structure. Individual institutions in the channel system may seek to optimise their allocation of resources in respect of their own transactions. Usually, however, such a procedure does not ensure an optimum transvection. 'From an economic welfare standpoint, consumer sovereignty, aided by the pressures of competition and government regulation, has not been sufficiently powerful a countervailing force to assure optimal allocation of resources in privately operated channels' (Fisk, 1967, p. 222). By analysis of transvections as entities in themselves it is possible to devise channels optimal in terms of predefined goals.

Despite the somewhat different definitions of what a channel is, the basic functions of the marketing channel are widely agreed to be those of collecting, sorting and distribution. At each stage in the channel, institutions are either directly involved in one or more of these functions or are facilitating other institutions in their involvement. It is possible to generalise the channel for petrol in terms of these three functions. Figure 2.4 shows a possible channel (both exchange and logistic) for the distribution of petrol. Within the channel are the extractive oil wells which serve to collect together oil which is stored, sorted and distributed. The refinery is the productive element in the channel system but even this could be conceived as collecting raw materials prior to manufacture of resaleable products. In simpler channels, not involving the processing or the collection, then sorting and distribution functions are even more obvious. The traditional wholesaler and retailer both perform these functions; equally the periodic market in Africa or Asia collects, sorts and distributes products.

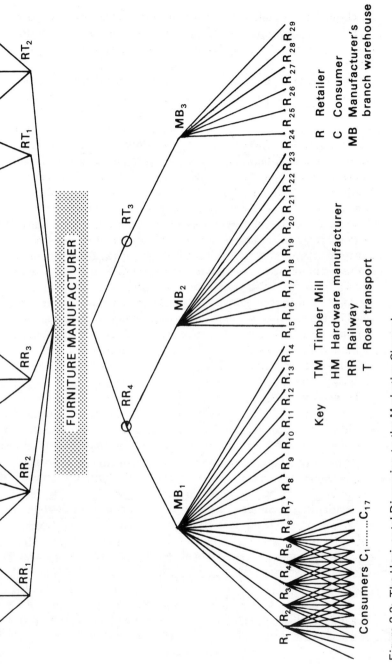

Figure 2.3: The Horizontal Dimension to the Marketing Channel

Key   TM Timber Mill   R Retailer
      HM Hardware manufacturer   C Consumer
      RR Railway   MB Manufacturer's
      T Road transport   branch warehouse

Figure 2.4: The Collection, Sorting and Distribution Functions of a
Typical Marketing Channel

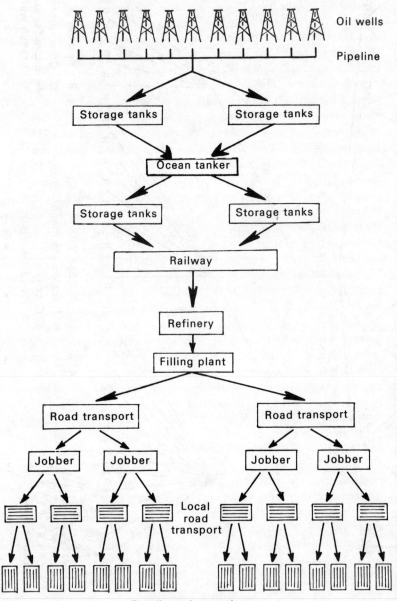

Vertical and Horizontal Evolution of Channels

The length and complexity of the market depends upon the product in the channel and the behaviour of institutions in the channel. The channels in early trade tended to depend heavily on direct exchange occurring between producer and consumer and short, simple channels resulted. Gradually the need for middlemen emerged and Day (1926) has chronicled this change. Zimmern (1924) points out that even in the classical Athenian economy 'though many producers still sell directly to the consumer, a growing number of them require the intermediary of the market, whose function it is to buy and store goods until the consumer is ready to purchase them' (p. 283). The middlemen in such economies had little specialisation and not until the guilds of medieval Europe flourished did marketing channels increase in complexity by any substantial extent. Jones (1954) and Vance (1970) particularly have described the increased complexity of the developing market channels in the USA through the eighteenth and nineteenth centuries. Much of this development has involved the introduction of additional levels in the vertical dimension of the channel. More recent changes have tended to extend the variety of institutions, and hence channel complexity, at each channel level.

The vertical extension of market channels is well shown by the emergence of wholesaling coupled with general economic development. Broadly, the wholesale institutions are strongest in those economies which have advanced beyond the stages of a heavy dependence on agricultural production but have not yet reached a highly industrialised stage. In economies only slightly developed from the subsistence stage, peasant markets allow farmers to supply consumers direct. There is no call for wholesalers or an extensive channel structure. As the economy develops so there develops a need for wholesalers.

A number of examples serve to illustrate this increasing complexity in the wholesale component of the vertical structure of channels. In the peasant, production orientated economy of rural Guatemala (Demyk, 1975; Tax, 1953) and parts of rural Mexico (Beals, 1975) the agricultural producer seeks out a market to sell his produce and either sells direct to the consumer or to a market trader. The farmer and market trader dominate the distribution channel. In Haiti, a slightly more complex system has evolved with the addition of a primitive wholesale function. Peasant producers sell some produce direct in the market place but also sell some to a professional trader termed a *revendeuse* (Mintz, 1957). The *revendeuses* travel from market to market selling in one market unsold stock from another. They may also carry small stocks and run a small warehouse in which sorting takes place. They perform, therefore, a very primitive wholesale function.

In the marketing system of Java five types of trader constitute the wholesale sector (Dewey, 1962).

(1)   First stage carriers buy goods from producers and carry them to the market.

(2)   Middlemen (*bakuls*) operating at the market buy goods from first stage carriers, import agents, etc., bulk these goods, store them, and when appropriate reduce them to small lots for retail sales. The middlemen also sell bulk goods to other traders.

(3)   Second stage carriers buy bulk goods from middlemen, bulk them them even more, ship them to another market and sell to middlemen there.

(4)   Village traders (*makelars*) buy produce in villages, store the produce and subsequently transport it or arrange to transport it to market.

(5)   Transporters hire vehicles to first and second stage traders.

A more complex wholesale function is seen in the North Indian sugar producing regions (Hirsch, 1961). In addition to many of the wholesale channel levels seen in other areas, two specialist levels are introduced. First, commission agents advance to the farmer up to 80 per cent of the expected value of the crop. In this way ready money is provided to the farmer before harvesting. On delivery of the crop the agent sells it on behalf of the farmer and makes over to the farmer the remaining 20 per cent, less the commission, interest, etc. owing to the agent. The agent has many of the functions of an agent-wholesaler. Secondly, within the same area, some cane is sold to sugar factories through co-operative societies sponsored and administered by state governments. The society acts as a wholesaler but sells only to the state sugar factories.

In these few examples it can be seen that the less economically forward regions have a very simple wholesale structure. The complexity of the wholesale channel increases with economic development but only up to a certain stage. More recent trends in wholesaling, particularly in the developed countries, have aimed at reducing the length of the wholesale element in the total marketing channel (see Chapter 5) but the wholesale sector serves as a good example of the vertical extension of market channels.

The more recent horizontal expansion of channels may be illustrated by the increased awareness of segmentation in the consumer level of the total channel. Within the market for any one product there are many groups of individual consumers and each group behaves in a different way and could be conceived as separate institutions within the one level in the channel. This variety has become apparent in the last 20 to 30 years. Within most cities there are well defined ethnic groups who have very different patterns of buying power and behaviour (Feldman and Star, 1968; Bauer and Cunningham, 1970); further discussion is provided in Chapter 3. Similarly segmentation of consumers on the basis of age has become important as the demand structure of a population has become more sophisticated. To talk of the teenage market or senior citizen market has more meaning now than 50 years ago, for both groups have emerged as distinct and discrete consumer institutions. Attempts have also been made to classify consumers in terms of their attitudes to shops, shopping and shopping centres. Johnston's (1974) study of Perth, Western Australia identified four types of consumers:

(1) *Pragmatic shoppers*, who are more concerned with getting what they want rather than being concerned, directly, with their shopping environment. To them shopping is a chore.
(2) *Satisfied shoppers* who are content with whatever, more or less, is provided.
(3) *Shopping trippers* who enjoy shopping and so visit large centres and spend considerable time there.
(4) *Bargain hunters* who are much more involved in shopping as an activity with a goal rather than their shopping environment.

The variety of retail institutions that has emerged has been a response to and has served to fix the different segments within the consumer level of the marketing channel. The variety of types of consumer which now must be catered for serves to show the extent to which horizontal expansion of marketing channels has occurred.

Marketing channels represent an extremely dynamic section of the marketing system. The notion of what they are — their place within the marketing discipline — is under constant review. The functions of channels have altered, in detail, over the last two decades. Most change has occurred in the structure of the channel with both horizontal extension and in some cases vertical extension while in other instances contraction has occurred. Despite these changes the channel remains central to the operation of the marketing system.

Relationship of Channel Form and Type of Goods

The overall design of a marketing channel should be such as to pass goods to their ultimate consumer in the most efficient way. Efficiency in the channel may be defined in terms of minimising time or maximising profit or some acceptable combination of these. Blockages in the channel flow both slow down product movement and increase the costs of distribution. Slater (1968) suggests that the major value of marketing in the development process is to isolate blockages and barriers that exist in marketing channels and to design channels to meet the particular productive and consumption needs of a developing society. Channels need to be designed therefore both for the product passing through them and for the society in which the channel operates.

Revzan (1961) suggests that the form of the marketing channel may be related to characteristics of production and to commodity characteristics and he groups products into the following five categories:

1. Channels of Distribution for Agricultural Products

A. Products to be processed:
    (1)   moving to industrial users;
    (2)   moving to ultimate consumers.
B. Products moving to ultimate consumers without processing:

2. Channels of Distribution for Other Extractive Industry Products

3. Channels of Distribution for Manufactured Industrial Goods

A. Products entering directly into the production of other products.
B. Products facilitating further production.
C. Products for non-manufacturing types of consumers.

4. Channels of Distribution for Manufactured Consumers' Goods

A. Durables.
B. Semidurables.
C. Non-durables (except agricultural).

5. Channels of Distribution for Services

A. Business and government services.
B. Personal services.

The extent to which areas concentrate on the production of these different types of product will influence the comparative mix of marketing institutions among different areas, and in turn gives rise to differences in channel structures among regions. Within each of the five groups of products Revzan argues that middlemen take on a different importance.

With many edible agricultural products, because of the perishable nature of the product, for example, 'The channel structure must provide . . . for rapid physical flows while still permitting such sales by inspection to take place at any transaction centre within the channel'. Under such circumstances pressures exist to shorten the channel as much as possible but the ubiquity of demand coupled with seasonal fluctuations in product supply, mean that direct sales from producer to consumer are not possible unless the consumer has a large demand (for example a hospital or large school, or government— see Chapter 3).

Some broad conclusions may be drawn from Revzan's study as to the effect the product type has as channel form. The main relevant product attributes are: perishability, degree of product standardisation, unit value, product bulk, service requirements and development stage of the product. These will be considered in turn.

Perishability. Because of the dangers involved in repeated handling and delays, perishable products are usually marketed through channels with few intermediaries (i.e. short channels). Long distances may be involved but the goods pass through few institutions. Fresh farm produce passes through a short channel compared with farm products such as grain. Usually individual farmer producers sell to wholesalers or ship direct to a city market where the goods are purchased directly for immediate delivery to retailers. The system is costly, particularly of transport, but no effective alternative has been devised. Although the channel is relatively short it still consists of a complex web of movements (Figure 2.2). A study of channels in North East England (NEDO, 1971) showed that the majority of greengrocery products, both locally grown and imported, pass through only one wholesaler between producer and retailer (Table 2.1). Even when much larger distances are involved, as in the sale of

Table 2.1: Retailers' Sources of Supply for Selected Products in North East England

	Potatoes (%)	Cabbage (%)	Oranges (%)	Tomatoes (%)
Primary producer	17	18	11	8
Market wholesaler	27	28	27	33
Distributive wholesaler	56	52	57	54
Co-operative wholesale society	0	2	5	5
Total	100	100	100	100

Queensland fruit in the city markets in New South Wales (Freeman, 1971) or in the marketing of fruit in continental Europe (OECD, 1956), short channels are normal. Dairy products exhibit equally short, or even shorter channels and the channel diagrams for different European countries presented in OECD reports (1960, 1973, 1974A) show the lack of middlemen in the system. Figure 2.5 reproduces the physical possession channel diagram for milk and milk products in France. The variation from country to country and region to region (National Commission on Food Marketing, 1966) is in the horizontal component of the market — not the vertical.

By contrast, Figure 2.6 shows a generalised channel diagram for a non-perishable consumer product in the Japanese market (Ministry of International Trade and Industry, 1968). While the Japanese market is renowned for its large number of wholesalers the vertical extension of the chain is a response partly to the durable nature of the product being sold.

Degree of Product Standardisation. Non-standard products usually pass through short channels because of the need for direct contact between producer and consumer. Custom built machinery or materials requiring special design are typically sold direct to the consumer. The lack of standardisation in fashion goods also results in short channels and it is not unusual in large cities to see manufacturers delivering clothing direct to retailers in the city while some fashion houses deal direct with the public. Alternatively, standardised products are those most capable of being bulked and they often need distributing to a wide range of retail institutions. Both characteristics allow efficient handling by several middlemen and so relatively long channels result.

Unit Value. In general most manufacturers prefer, all other things being equal, to sell direct to the retailer through a short channel. Inevitably this costs more because more transactions are involved compared with sales through intermediaries. 'The policy of direct sale to retailers is likely to involve the manufacturer in considerably increased transport costs, whether in respect of a transport organisation of his own or of payments to railway companies and other agencies' (Braithwaite and Dobbs, 1932, p. 169). Such a view is equally true today. Costs of packaging and general sales costs will be higher, so resulting in a higher price to the retailer. What is important to the manufacturer is not absolute costs but the percentage of the unit costs accounted for by marketing the product. With a high unit cost the selling costs are likely to be a

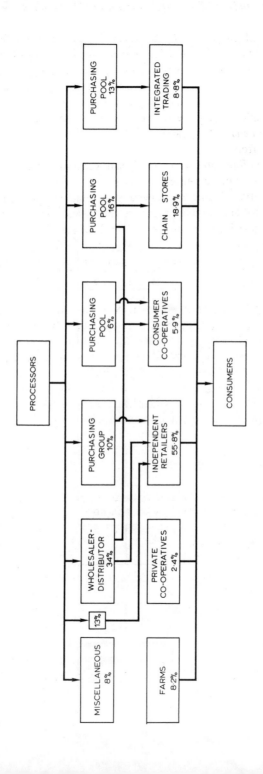

Figure 2.5: The Physical Possession Channel Diagram for Milk in France in 1969

Figure 2.6: A Simplified Channel Diagram for a Consumer Product in Japan

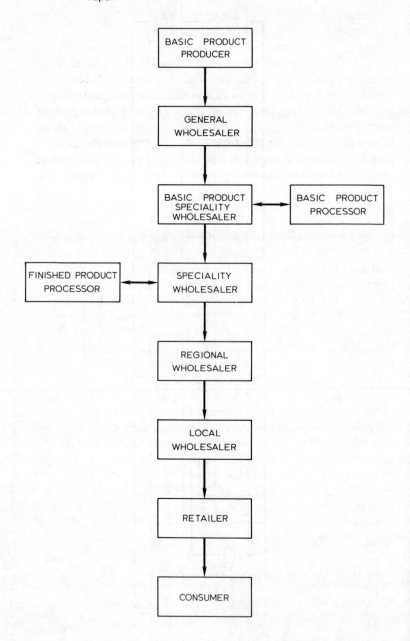

small percentage of total costs, so a short channel results (Lambert, 1966).

The consequence of this is that a manufacturer is likely either to set up a distribution system with regional warehouses (Walters, 1975) or to employ a contract haulier and probably contract warehousing (Hawkins, 1976). One of these methods frequently is used by domestic appliance manufacturers so retailers obtain washing machines etc. direct from the manufacturer, but smaller items such as torches or small batteries (with low unit costs) are obtained through a longer channel involving wholesalers. The relatively high unit costs of many goods in electrical shops often means that goods are distributed direct by the manufacturer (Lewis, 1961) with, from the retailer's point of view, the disadvantage of handling frequent deliveries of goods from several manufacturers. Studies carried out by the Transport and Road Research Laboratory into the patterns of urban freight distribution showed that it was not unusual in British towns for electrical shops to be taking ten or more deliveries per day with consequent High Street congestion (Christie, Bartlett, Cundill and Prudhoe, 1973); while costs are reduced for the manufacturer such short channels may not be the most socially desirable. Thus we begin to see the potential for conflict within marketing channels.

Product Bulk. A fourth characteristic of the product which influences decisions on the marketing channel to be used in its distribution is the size and weight of the product in relation to its value. The bulk of the product affects marketing channels in two ways—one directly and one indirectly. When the bulk is large and physical handling costs are high goods are most economically shipped in truckload or wagonload lots to utilise mechanised handling equipment and to minimise handling. Retailers and industrial buyers seldom buy in these large, economical, shipping quantities and so large bulk products are usually handled through wholesalers. Secondly, the bulk of the product often affects the location of its production. Market orientated locations are chosen for products which increase their bulk in manufacture. The soft-drink bottling industry provides a good example, with local plants in many markets and distribution through truck salesmen to retailers, vending machines, cafes and even direct to the consumer.

Service Requirements. If products require specialised installation or repair services the provision of service facilities may be an important element in the marketing. It sometimes becomes necessary to set up special channels to market the product and provide the back-up services (Ridgeway,

1957). Many franchise (Hall, 1964) and exclusive agency channel systems result from the particular service needs of a product.

Stage of Development of the Product. Lewis (1968) points out:

> The development stage of a product and the growth stage of the company itself have a bearing on the channels used. If a company starts with a rather limited line of unknown products, it probably will depend heavily on full-service, merchant wholesalers and may also sell through agents rather than attempt to develop its own sales organisation. As the line becomes better known and as it broadens in scope, the company will probably experiment with shorter channels. The agent may be displaced, and the company may sell increasingly to retailers. (p. 115).

While the characteristics of the product are a major influence on channel form, there are other variables influencing decisions on how to distribute particular goods. The size of firm (Weigand, 1963) and the type of consumer aimed at are certainly both important variables (Chapter 3 discusses the different types of institutions most favoured by various market segments). The location of the potential market and the shifts in buying patterns going on in that market influence the channel form. Competitive products and broad groups of products tend to be sold through the same channels since consumers expect to buy related items at the same source. Periodically major changes do occur and goods traditionally sold in one way begin to be sold in another way. Supermarkets have extended in recent years the number of lines sold to include many non-food lines. The willingness of retailers to merchandise across traditional product mixes has led many manufacturers to use several channel forms to market the one good. (Preston and Schramm, 1965). In this multichannel market strategy each channel is designed to carry the product to a different market but such dual distribution can lead to considerable conflict between the competing channel institutions (see Chapter 8).

Theories of Channel Use and Channel Structure

While formal theory on the organisation of channels is non-existent there have been a number of general attempts to state the reasons why channels exist in a particular form and to explain the changes which occur in channels.

Aspinwall (1958) states that 'The marketing characteristics of a product determine the most appropriate and economical method for distributing it' (p. 435). The product thus determines the channel form and key characteristics of the product are the variables actually determining channel structure. For this view to be acceptable the characteristics must be applicable to all goods, capable of being measured (either absolutely or relatively) and interrelated. Aspinwall identifies five such characteristics:

Replacement Rate

This is 'the rate at which a good is purchased and consumed by users in order to provide the satisfaction a consumer expects from the producer'. The replacement rate is a consumer, not retailer, orientated idea and shows how often the market must be ready to supply a particular good. Bread, in a Western style society, has a high replacement rate; pianos have a low replacement rate. Aspinwall argues for generality in this measure but because the concept is consumer orientated the rate for a product differs with different segments of the consumer market. It could be argued however that because different consumer groups have different replacement rates for the same good, so it is necessary to have multiple channels for any one good.

Gross Margin

This is defined as 'the money sum which is the difference between the laid in cost and the final realized price'. The characteristic measured here is the summation of all gross margins in the particular marketing channel and is effectively the amount of money required to move a good to ultimate consumer. The gross margin is inversely related to the replacement rate. So when gross margin is high and the replacement rate is low, marketing costs are high.

Adjustments

This is defined as, 'services applied to goods in order to meet the exact needs of the consumer'. Again, this is a consumer orientated characteristic with different groups of consumers requiring special services. Goods with a high replacement rate, Aspinwall states, have low adjustment. The problem then arises as to exactly what is a good? Aspinwall mentions a loaf of bread. But a visit to any baker shows a large range of types of loaves. The good has undergone adjustment to meet specialist demand yet it also has a high replacement rate.

Time of Consumption

This is 'the measured time of consumption during which the good gives up the ability desired'. While relevant to all goods, this characteristic is perhaps most important with non-durable goods in both the industrial and consumer classes. The measure is closely related to replacement rate.

Searching Time

This is 'the measure of average time and distance from the retail store' and so is assumed to measure the effort the consumer will expend to obtain the product.

Aspinwall goes on to cross correlate the characteristics as in Table 2.2, and to colour code goods with particular combinations of characteristics into three classes — red, orange and yellow. Red coded goods Aspinwall argues have long channels of distribution, while yellow goods have

Table 2.2:   Colour Classification in Aspinwall's Characteristics of Goods Theory

	Colour classification		
Characteristic	red	orange	yellow
Replacement rate	high	medium	low
Gross margin	low	medium	high
Adjustment	low	medium	high
Time of consumption	low	medium	high
Searching time	low	medium	high

short channels. The 'theory' allows for channels to change as goods become better known and come to satisfy a wider section of consumer demand. Most goods will thus shift from the yellow towards the red end of the classification.

The *Characteristic of Goods theory* has been discussed in detail because of its impact within marketing science where it has been suggested as a major theoretical contribution. It has also been seen as providing 'a basis for isolating situations in which channel alignments may be uneconomic' (McCammon and Whittle, 1965, p. 359). The real problems of the theory arise when application is attempted and when the characteristics are measured. No overall measure of a marketing channel has been suggested and Aspinwall has to resort to subjective views such as 'long channels' or 'short channels'. Most of the measurements are relative rather than absolute and the definitive base of the theory also poses problems. The characteristics of goods theory is an attempt to generalise on the relationship between product type and channel structure. It does so in a descriptive rather than analytical way but provides a possible foundation on which more rigorous theory could be constructed.

McInnes's *separation theory* is also an attempt to generalise on the structure of marketing channels (McInnes, 1964). Five dimensions resolve the market channel and each dimension is defined as a way in which consumer and producer are separated. The five dimensions are geographical, temporal, perceptual (producers do not know the whereabouts of consumers), ownership and valuation (the consumer and producer may place different values on a product). The 'best' arrangement to close these gaps creates the market channel. McInnes sees the main problem in making his theoretical model operational as one of measurement, for the dimensions have different frameworks of measurement.

Alderson (1954) has attempted to model and theorise channel structure in terms of one variable only—cost. The various gaps and distances in the marketing channel can all be overcome by money. The optional structure of a channel (or transvection) is attained when costs cannot be reduced by changing that structure. Alderson sees the margin, as defined in Aspinwall's theory, as the critical measurement in channel structure.

Underlying all these theories is the argument that the product influences the channel structure to a considerable degree. This is the traditional marketing scientist's approach. Channel structure and channel patterns are generated internally within the marketing system. An alternative, geographer's view might be that channel structure is a response to the social and economic environment which is external to the marketing system. We should not expect marketing channels to be the same in Malaysia as in the USA even for the same product. It would be remarkable if they were. Different social and economic environments have generated, over the years, different types of institution and institutional relationships in marketing channels. To theorise on channel structure within North America and then to use the theories as instruments of management and change in other countries is to impose an arbitrary set of values on a country. Wadinambiaratchi (1965) in advancing points raised by Moyer (1964) and Mehren (1959) argues that the socioeconomic environment relates closely to accepted views of the stage of economic development, so making marketing channel structure and level of economic development closely related.

In a comparison of marketing channels in Japan, Brazil, Venezuela, Puerto Rico, Turkey, Egypt, India and generally in tropical Africa he advances eight hypotheses in support of his theory:

(a) The more developed countries have more levels of distribution, more speciality stores, more department stores and more stores in the rural areas.
(b) The influence of the foreign import agent declines with economic development.
(c) Manufacturer-wholesaler-retailer functions become separated with economic development.
(d) Wholesaler functions approximate those in North America with increasing economic development.
(e) Financing function of wholesalers declines and wholesaler mark-ups increase with increasing development.
(f) The number of small stores decline and the size of the average store increases with increasing development.
(g) The role of the pedlar and itinerant trader, and the importance of the open-garden fair declines with increasing development and
(b) Retail margins improve with increasing economic development. (p. 77).

The surveys on which these arguments are based mostly date from the middle to late 1950s. Wadinambiaratchi concludes: 'given the institutional settings of the underdeveloped countries it should be possible to understand their marketing structure, in terms of their economic development'. Change can then be introduced into the channel either by a response to natural changes in the environment or by inducing changes either in the people or their economy (Anderson, 1970). The very considerable dangers in this latter course are discussed by Bauer and Yamey (1954), who point out that existing patterns are often the result of a long period of evolution and change should only be contemplated if the evolutionary processes are understood fully.

While Wadinambiaratchi does show that channel structure is related to levels of development, the relationship is perhaps not quite as straightforward, direct and simple as he suggests. A number of studies have shown the complexity and variety of channel forms present in the less economically developed countries. Carson (1967) discusses several of these studies, while the studies presented in Bohanan and Dalton (1962) prove the complexity and variety of channel patterns in Africa. Economic development is only one of several variables, composing the socioeconomic environment, which determines channel structure. Attitudes of societies to markets and marketing functions is certainly one such variable and this may well be responsible for the development of channels such as those associated with consumer co-operatives. Political attitudes and their changes may create some of the structures in marketing channels. The attempt by governments in Europe in the 1930s to stem the evolution of large stores and multiple traders certainly had an impact on channel structure. Again in attempts to theorise on channel form and structure only broad, often unmeasurable generalities emerge. While the basic determinants of channel form are now reasonably well known, the precise relationships between factors internal and external to the marketing system have not been specified, nor has any quantitative attempt been made to measure in a scientific way the formal structures in marketing channels.

Channel Relationships, Control and Conflict

'There is very little real understanding of the principles that govern changes in channels of distribution and how they come about' (Cox, 1965, p. 83). Undoubtedly channels do change and while Cox is correct in suggesting that there is no integrated theory of channel change, the last ten years have seen studies which consider the changes which have taken place in channel structure. New products and new institutions inevitably mean that changes will occur.

> The entry of new firms and the departure of old ones; the development of entirely new distribution technologies which make older methods obsolete; and the changing size and composition of markets all demand a constantly changing distribution pattern. Such changes may be drastic . . . More often they are gradual, and the alterations in the channel system are correspondingly slow. (Bell, 1972, pp. 721-2).

What Bell fails to point out is that channel evolution is really a response to changes in the power relationships of institutions in the channel. Each institution attempts to optimise its corporate policy (often profit maximisation) and the most powerful member of the channel will most nearly achieve this objective.

Innovation is fundamental to economic progress no matter what type of political system is operative. Schumpeter (1950) declares that in a capitalist system competition by innovation is as important, or possibly more important than competition by price. Product innovation invariably means a change in marketing channel structure. The impact of product

innovation and its diffusion in time and space is well documented (Fourt
and Woodcock, 1960; Shaw, 1965; Booz, Allen and Hamilton, 1968;
Varble, 1972; Karger, 1960; Levitt, 1962; Robertson, 1969). As new
products emerge, or products are changed, so the channel flows change.
The institutions may or may not stay the same but innovation in institution may well be as great as product innovation in changing marketing
systems (McCammon, 1963; Michman, 1971). The emergence of cash
and carry wholesalers as an innovative institution has had a considerable impact on distributive channels in most western societies (see Chapter 5). Similarly the emergence and subsequent diffusion of the concept
of marketing boards has changed agricultural marketing throughout
the world in the last half-century (see Chapter 6). At a local level the
introduction and diffusion of selfservice retailing in an urban area (Dawson,
1973) changes the channels of distribution in a city. Products change, instit
utions change, causing channels to change.

Over 25 years ago Galbraith (1952) wrote his study of *American
Capitalism* as an essay in the analysis of power and conflict resolution.
'Power on one side of a market creates both the need for, and the prospect
of reward to, the exercise of countervailing power from the other side'
(p. 120). By this argument we may expect that dominance at one end of
a channel will create groupings and reactions in other parts of the
channel. It could be argued that the increase in power of manufacturers
in respect of distributive channels in North America in the post 1950 era
has created the current emergence of consumer groups and indeed the
consumerism movement. In similar fashion Grether (1939) points out
that associations and groupings of small retailers (voluntary chains, buying
groups, etc.) may be seen as attempts by small operators to increase their
power base in response to the increased power of large corporate concerns. The change which occurs in distribution channels is not haphazard
but is a response to the power struggles of conflicting institutions within
marketing.

It is possible to relate together the two approaches of product change
and of institutional conflict as causes of channel changes. Kriesberg
(1955) suggests that within the dominant channel for a particular good
there are five sets of firms. Each set has either different entrepreneurial
values or a different relationship to the total channel. The behaviour of
each set of firms in the channel is regulated largely by the attitudes and
responses of the other sets. When once a channel emerges it becomes self-
regulating with an inbuilt tendency to maintain existing arrangements
but this static nature can be upset by a change in power relationships
among the five groups of firms. The sets of firms are as follows.

Insiders are firms central to the existing channel and have access to preferred sources of supply and a financial commitment to the current channel pattern. As a group they wish to perpetuate the current channel structure and are powerful enough, by reason of economic success, to dictate what will be the relationships in the channel.

Strivers are located outside the channel but want to become part of it. As the striver wishes to become accepted in the channel he adheres to the rules laid down by *insiders.*

Complementors are not an integral part of the dominant channel and do not wish to become such. They are related to the *insiders* in that *complementors* perform functions not normally performed by insiders but which are vital to the continued existence of the current channel structure. Consequently again they respect channel rules and their policy is to perpetuate the existing channel.

Transients again are outside the channel and do not seek membership, often being members of other channels. The transients usually have short-term relationships with the main channel. They are sufficiently far outside the main channel to have little interest in changing it.

Outside innovators lie completely outside the channel but move into the channel and exhibit deviant behaviour in not adhering to the channel rules set out by *insiders.* A number of studies (Corey, 1956; Jack, 1957; Silk and Stern, 1963) suggest that innovators are outsiders to established channels and Hollander (1960) has attempted to formalise that view, at a retail level, into a theoretical proposition. The two concepts of innovation within a changing power structure in a channel may be related to provide a basis for future study of change in marketing channels.

In this scheme one at least of the *insiders* is the channel leader (sometimes termed *captain*). Until ten years ago it was invariably the manufacturer but the emergence of large integrated retail-wholesale organisations has provided many channels with an alternative leader (Little, 1970). Who makes channel decisions depends on the relative bargaining strength of channel members. While large manufacturers have a base of economic power which allows large-scale promotion and the ability to take the initiative in persuading retailers and wholesalers to group into an effective channel, the retailer-wholesaler (multilevel merchandiser) has the benefit of access to the markets into which the manufacturer wants to move. A contrast certainly exists here between the less developed countries and the more developed and also between capitalist and communist. In communist economies channel power and leadership is external to the basic marketing institutions in the channel (Goldman, 1963):

In the early stages of economic development, most manufacturers operate on a small scale and sell directly to users, perhaps producing largely to customers' order . . . In contrast, large-scale specialized production requires marketing on a much wider geographical basis, and economical operation implies marketing in anticipation of demand. As a consequence, the producer . . . must develop some organized system for distributing his products or services to many customers scattered over a regional, national or even international market. (Buzzel, Nourse, Matthews and Levitt, 1972, p. 465).

Clearly in the first instance the manufacturer is channel leader. Little (1970) suggests that in the second case, a developed capitalist society, multilevel merchandising (MLM) 'organisations are in the best position to lead channels because the value to the manufacturer of market access provided by each MLM far exceeds the value of one more product to the MLM merchandising mix' (p. 37). The power balance of leadership is swung away from the manufacturer to a conglomerate middleman. Within the developmental evolution of an economy, therefore, we may expect a period of severe conflict between the two potential channel leaders as the retailer-wholesaler power structure increases and the manufacturer's wanes. In such a period of conflict it is possible that competing channels emerge and the possibilities for innovation increase. The radical changes that occurred in distribution in North America in the 1950s, in Western Europe in the 1960s and which are still occurring in Southern Europe could be related to the change in general channel leadership which is occurring and which was foreseen by Craig and Gabler (1940) over 30 years ago.

Mallen (1963) has considered some of the ways of resolving the conflict between channel leaders and potential leaders but the new strength of multilevel merchandisers has emerged since Mallen's study (Willeman, 1972). Undoubtedly power structures, and *perceived* power relationships, maintained by Granbois and Willett (1964) to be the more important, have changed. Attempts in North America have been made to define power and to measure its interinstitution shifts in marketing channels (El-Ansary, 1973; Beier and Stern, 1969; Bucklin, 1973; El-Ansary and Stern, 1972; Rosenberg and Stern, 1971).

From this consideration of change in marketing channels it can be seen that conflict among members of the channel is inevitable and that it is likely that conflict will be most severe when rapid or major changes are occurring in the channel:

Tensions build to a peak in times of change. Stress is created during the emergence of new forms of distribution or by reshuffling of functions within the channel. Volume is diverted into new channels, leaving less for traditional channels. One agency may take over a sub-task once performed by another, absorbing this portion of the total revenue into its own share. Sometimes the element of conflict is so pronounced that an effective channel can scarcely be said to exist. (Alderson, 1965, pp. 254-5).

Most channels consist of several firms who have joined together to serve customers the better and to receive higher profits. The longer the channel, therefore, the more the likelihood of conflict occurring. To return to the general model outlined above, which suggested length of channel as related to level of economic development, it might be likely that severe channel conflict is expected in countries in the middle levels of development.

Before coming to a conclusion on such a view it is worthwhile to consider briefly the types of conflict which occur. Palamountain (1955), in his now classic study, isolated three types of conflict:

(1) *Horizontal competition* between institutions of the same type, e.g. supermarket with supermarket.
(2) *Intertype competition* between institutions in the same broad level, e.g. supermarket with corner shop.
(3) *Vertical competition* between institutions at different channel levels, e.g. supermarket with merchant wholesaler.

Mallen (1964) goes on to explore in detail the different subtypes within this broad categorisation. It would appear that general developmental models are not a great deal of use as explanations of conflict. More acceptable are explanations in terms of innovative behaviour and such behaviour is not limited to particular developmental levels. A major result of conflict is an attempt by one institution to seek control of a large portion of the channel. These attempts range from the call for legal restrictive trade practices and the formation of cartels through various types of price and non-price competition to attempts at vertical and horizontal integration by a channel member. The various consequences of horizontal and intertype conflict are dealt with in detail in later chapters but one of the most common responses to vertical conflict is vertical integration.

Extensive literature exists on economic integration (Robinson, 1958;

Hirsch, 1950; Penrose, 1968) and additionally there are studies of integration in marketing channels (Haney, 1920; Markin, 1971; Sturdivant, 1967; Cole, 1952; Ridgeway, 1957). The basis of vertical integration is the extension of the control of one firm to other levels in the marketing channel. Manufacturers may establish wholesale and retail outlets and may also integrate backwards towards the source of raw materials. Hirsch (1950) divides vertically integrated channels into two types, each of which has several subdivisions. The two basic types are distinguished in terms of the commodities passing through the channel. The first type consists of an integration of operations in production and/or marketing of *similar* commodities. The second type is concerned with *complementary* products. An alternative view is evident in several contributions in Bucklin (1970), and notably McCammon (1970), in which vertical integration is categorised by its method of operation. A corporate system is when one firm integrates the whole channel. An administered system achieves effective vertical integration by co-operation between a clearly dominant channel leader and other channel members. Thirdly, a contractual system consists of formal agreements between vertically related institutions which still retain independence but relate together in a vertical chain (McCammon, 1965). The various wholesaler sponsored voluntary chains in grocery retailing in Europe and North America produce a vertically integrated system of this last type.

The extent, and to some degree the type of vertical integration will depend on the legal and social sanctions of the society on which the channel operates (Sturdivant, 1967). Some types of collusion among channel members are legally forbidden in many countries. The OECD reports on competition policy (OECD, 1974B) show the extent to which various legal sanctions are applied even within Western Europe, while the difficulties which have occurred in formulating EEC competition policy (Everling, 1964; McLachland and Swann, 1967) testify to the deep nationalistic feelings on this topic. An alternative social variation is in the extent to which consumer co-operatives have been allowed to integrate with producer co-operatives and wholesaler co-operatives. One of the two large co-operative groups in Finland carries out more than a quarter of its own manufacturing. In contrast, in the USA there is only very slight development of a co-operative channel system. Carson (1967) provides many other examples of the influence of the social, economic and legal environment on the extent of the development of vertical integration. Despite the variety of case studies available there have been few attempts to develop general statements on this topic.

Vertical integration in marketing channels usually leads to multilocational firms and a number of studies have considered the locational behaviour of such firms. Pred (1975), Semple (1973), and Williamson (1970) provide extensive reviews of these studies, while case studies are provided by Chapman (1974) and Lorsch and Allen (1973).

Channel Costs

One of the reasons why firms engage in policies of vertical integration is to reduce their distribution costs. Cole (1952) and Douglas (1975) show in detail that under certain circumstances a vertically integrated firm 'will find that it is able to operate at a cost level lower than would be possible were its functions broken up among a number of independent firms' Douglas (1975, p. 325). Before exploring the reasons for this it is worthwhile considering what exactly constitutes costs in a marketing channel.

Total marketing costs embrace the widely discussed distribution costs of wholesaler and retailer as well as the marketing charges for advertising, banking, research, etc. of the manufacturer. Furthermore, the consumers have costs. A visit to a shop to purchase goods costs money and this is part of the total channel costs. A consumer using mail order will have lower personal costs than the apparently more cost conscious shopper who searches many shops before buying a 'bargain'. Consumers' costs in shopping are inadequately understood and few studies have attempted to calculate the real cost of shopping to the consumer or to total up complete marketing costs. Attempts have been made to analyse distribution costs which Bucklin (1972) estimates account for about 75 per cent of total channel costs. The channel costs constitute at least half of the final cost of most products and for some goods considerably more than half. Baumol (1967) suggests

> Since some sort of marketing effort is an inescapable element in economic activity, demand for this service is quite income elastic . . . [marketing will have] cumulatively increasing costs relative to those of other economic activities and the absorbtion of an ever growing proportion of societies resources by this sector is inevitable (p. 420).

Distributive costs are made up of costs related to inputs to the marketing channel, the operations of the channel and the outputs from the channel. The largest cost element of inputs is wages. Although in most Western countries pay in the distributive trades is lower than in manufacturing industry and also increasing more slowly, wage costs still represent a high cost element because productivity is notably low and Schwartzman

(1969) maintains that labour is of low 'quality'. Robinson and Wallace (1976) suggest reasons associated with the composition of the labour force (high percentage of females and large number of part-time workers) as reasons for low wage costs, compared with other sectors in retailing in Britain, but low as they are, they still represent at least 30 per cent of the retail gross margin in most West European countries.

Industrial development is a process of continuing specialisation both of techniques of production and of the products themselves. Marketing, alternatively, is the joining together of the various strands of production. With more strands to link, so the demand for marketing services increases at a faster rate than demand in the total economy. Marketing costs therefore represent an increasing proportion of final product costs. Barger (1955) has chronicled this increase in marketing costs in the USA. In many cases marketing costs are borne increasingly by the productive firm rather than by marketing middlemen. This is only a shift in the responsibility for marketing costs and does not necessarily mean a net reduction in costs.

The costs within a specific channel may vary considerably with the specific mix of goods passing through the channel and with the services provided by the institutions in the channel. The product mix may be changed with a substitution of low margin goods for high margin goods, resulting in a reduction in marketing costs. Unless this change is a response to a real change in consumer demand (in which case a real change in marketing cost results) a switch in product mix usually means a decrease in costs in one channel but an increase elsewhere. Real costs in the output of marketing services can change with a reduction or increase in the service element of transvections in the channel. Quite simply, a reduction in the number of sales staff in a supermarket reduces costs. If sales staff numbers are reduced in all supermarkets then an overall lower level of customer service is provided—queues of customers become longer. Goldman (1963) argues that the low level of service provided by retailers in the USSR is a major factor in the low level of marketing costs in that country compared with many others.

Some channel costs can be related to the inputs, operations and outputs of the channel but some differences in costs among different channels may be related to the length of the channel. Figure 2.7 shows a set of generalised graphs relating marketing cost per unit to number of buyers, and to distance between producer and consumer for direct and indirect channels. In the first graph it is assumed that buyers purchase approximately equal amounts. Indirect channels involve the use of middlemen. Costs of the direct system are approximately constant regardless of

Figure 2.7: Cost Considerations in the Use of Middlemen

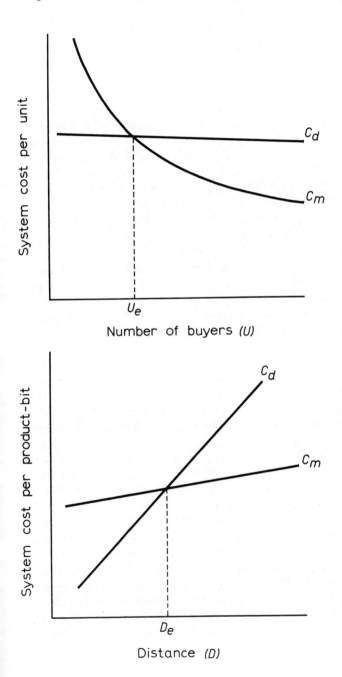

the number of buyers. The slight slope results from some returns owing to large throughput. The use of middlemen results in high costs for a small market but a very considerable decrease for larger markets. The extra handling and transaction costs in the use of middlemen increase total costs per unit when there are few sellers but these costs become offset by the economies of transport costs, by the use of middlemen, when large numbers of buyers are involved. On a cost basis therefore small markets might be expected to be served direct and large markets via a middleman system. The critical number of buyers is U_e.

The second graph shows that because of their high fixed costs but lower transport costs direct channels have lower costs when goods have to be transported a short distance. Middlemen are more likely to be used when longer distances are involved. The size of lot, i.e. number of units per transaction, affects the relative position of the two graphs and the position of *De* which is the point where channel structure is likely to change.

If *Pm* is the unit cost per km of moving the goods by middlemen, F is the fixed cost of inventories etc., D is distance and *Cm* is the costs of using middlemen, then

$$Cm = PmD + F$$

i.e. the line *Cm* on the graph. If Pd is the unit cost per km of moving goods in the lot size purchased by the final user and *Cd* is the cost of direct distribution

$$Cd = PdD$$

The ratio R between these:

$$R = \frac{PmD + F}{PdD}$$

indicates equal costs for the two distribution methods when $R = 1$. Then

$$D = De = \frac{F}{Pd - Pm}$$

Thus the greater the saving from mass transport the further to the left on Figure 2.6 is the equilibrium point between the two competing channels. If the middleman can deal in large lots he becomes viable when distances between producer and consumer are quite small. Therefore the use of middlemen is most viable, economically where users buy small amounts and are located some distance from producers and where savings are available from mass transport.

Distance and number of buyers are not the only variables influencing channel costs and competition. The extent of decentralisation of the market, the assortment of goods and delivery time may all be analysed in some way as above.(Bucklin, 1965, 1972). In summary, middlemen systems may be said to offer greater economies than direct marketing when:

(1) the number of traders (buyers and sellers) increases;
(2) the goods have to be moved farther and the buyer lot size is smaller;
(3) the buyers' time horizons are shorter;
(4) the product assortments built by consumers are large;
(5) the market system is more decentralised.

Given the levels of innovation and product development apparent in most countries together with the level of change occurring in marketing institutions, it is not surprising that the cost differentials between different channel types are frequently in states of flux. This is perhaps one reason why marketing costs, *in toto*, are so difficult to account. Cost differentials together with the pressures of innovation serve to keep marketing channels, in all social and economic environments, in a constant state of evolution and in almost perpetual conflict.

References

ALDERSON, W. (1954) 'Factors Governing the Development of Marketing Channels' in R.M. Clewett (ed.) *Marketing Channels for Manufactured Products* (Irwin, Homewood).
—— (1957) *Market Behaviour and Executive Action* (Irwin, Homewood).
—— (1965) *Dynamic Marketing Behaviour* (Irwin, Homewood).
ALDERSON, W. and M.W. MARTIN (1965) 'Towards a Formal Theory of Transactions and Transvections', *Journal of Marketing Research*, 2, pp. 118-27.
ANDERSON, D.A. (1970) *Marketing and Development. The Thailand Experience* (Michigan State University, East Lansing).
ASPINWALL, L. (1958) 'The Characteristics of Goods and Parallel Systems Theories' in E.J. Kelley and W. Lazer (eds) *Managerial Marketing* (Irwin, Homewood), pp. 434-50.
BARGER, H. (1955) *Distribution's Place in the American Economy since 1869* (Princeton University Press, Princeton).
BAUER, P.T. and B.S. YAMEY (1954) 'The Economics of Marketing Reform', *Journal of Political Economy*, 64(3), pp. 210-35.
BAUER, R.A. and S.M. CUNNINGHAM (1970) *Studies in the Negro Market* (Marketing Science Institute, Cambridge, Mass.).
BAUMOL, W.J. (1967) 'Macro Economics of Unbalanced Growth: The Anatomy of Urban Crisis', *American Economic Review*, 57, pp. 415-26.
BEALS, R.L. (1975) *The Peasant Marketing System of Oaxaca, Mexico* (University of California Press, Berkeley).
BEIER, F.J. and L.W. STERN (1969) 'Power in the Channel of Distribution' in L.W. Stern (ed.) *Distribution Channels: Behavioral Dimensions* (Houghton-Mifflin, Boston), pp. 92-113.

BELL, M.L. (1972) *Marketing: Concepts and Strategy*, 2nd edn (Houghton-Mifflin, Boston).

BOHANNAN, P. and G. DALTON (1962) (eds) *Markets in Africa* (Northwestern University Press, Evanston).

BOOZ, ALLEN and HAMILTON INC. (1968) *Management of New Products* (Booz, Allen & Hamilton, New York).

BRAITHWAITE, D. and S.P. DODDS (1932) *The Distribution of Consumable Goods* (Routledge, London).

BREYER, R.F. (1934) *The Marketing Institution* (McGraw-Hill, New York).

BUCKLIN, L.P. (1965) 'Postponement, Speculation, and the Structure of Distribution Channels', *Journal of Marketing Research*, 2, pp. 26-31.

—— (1966) *A Theory of Distribution Channel Structure* (IBER, University of California, Berkeley).

—— (1970) (ed.) *Vertical Marketing Systems* (Scott-Foresman, Glenview).

—— (1972) *Competition and Evolution in the Distributive Trades* (Prentice-Hall, Englewood Cliffs).

—— (1973) 'A Theory of Channel Control', *Journal of Marketing*, 37, pp. 39-47.

BUZZELL, R.D., R.E.M. NOURSE, J.B. MATTHEWS and T. LEVITT (1972) *Marketing: a Contemporary Analysis* (McGraw-Hill, New York).

CARSON, D. (1967) *International Marketing* (Wiley, New York).

CHAPMAN, K. (1974) 'Corporate Systems in the United Kingdom Petrochemical Industry', *Annals, Association of American Geographers*, 64, pp. 126-37.

CHRISTIE, A.W., R.S. BARTLETT, M.A. CUNDILL and J. PRUDHOE (1973) *Urban Freight Distribution: Studies of Operations in Shopping Streets in Newbury and Camberly* (Traffic and Road Research Laboratory Report 603, Crowthorne).

CLEWETT, R.M. (1961) *Checking Your Marketing Channels* (US Small Business Administration, Washington, DC).

COLE, R. (1952) *Vertical Integration in Marketing* (Bureau of Business and Economic Research, University of Illinois, Urbana).

COREY, R.E. (1956) *The Development of Markets for New Materials* (Graduate School of Business Administration, Harvard University).

COX, R. (1965) *Distribution in a High Level Economy* (Prentice-Hall, Englewood Cliffs).

CRAIG, D.R. and W.K. GABLER (1940) 'The Competitive Struggle for Market Control', *Annals of American Academy of Political and Social Science*, 209, pp. 84-107.

DAWSON, J.A. (1973) 'The Development of Self-service Retailing in Nottingham', *East Midland Geographer*, 5(7), pp. 355-60.

DAY, C. (1926) *A History of Commerce* (Longmans Green, New York).

DEMYK, N. (1975) 'Le systeme des echanges commerciaux au Guatemala', *L'Espace Geographique*, 3, pp. 77-82.

DEWEY, A.G. (1962) *Peasant Marketing in Java* (Free Press of Glencoe, New York).

DOUGLAS, E. (1975) *Economics of Marketing* (Harper-Row, New York).

EL-ANSARY, A.I. (1973) *On the Measurement of Power in Distribution Channels*, Occasional Paper 12 (College of Business Administration, Louisiana State University).

EL-ANSARY, A.I. and L.W. STERN (1972) 'Power Measurement in the Distribution Channel', *Journal of Marketing Research*, 9, pp. 47-52.

EVERLING, U. (1964) *The Right of Establishment in the Common Market* (Commerce Clearing House, New York).

FELDMAN, L.P. and A.D. STAR (1968) 'Racial Factors in Shopping Behaviour' in K. Cox and B. Enis (eds) *A New Measure of Responsibility for Marketing* (American Marketing Association, Chicago).

FISK, G. (1967) *Marketing Systems: An Introductory Analysis* (Harper International, New York).

FOURT, L.A. and J.W. WOODCOCK (1960) 'Early Prediction of Market Success for New Grocery Products', *Journal of Marketing*, 24, pp. 31-3.

FREEMAN, D.B. (1971) *Rail Movement of Fruit in Queensland* (University of Queensland Press, St Lucia).

GALBRAITH, J.K. (1952) *American Capitalism: The Concept of Countervailing Power* (Houghton-Mifflin, Boston).

GOLDMAN, M.I. (1963) *Soviet Marketing: Distribution in a Controlled Economy* (Free Press of Glencoe, New York).

GRANBOIS, D.H. and R.P. WILLETT (1964) 'Patterns of Conflicting Perceptions among Channel Members' in L.G. Smith (ed.) *Reflections on Progress in Marketing* (American Marketing Association, Chicago), pp. 86-100.

GRETHER, E.T. (1939) 'Changing Distribution Channels: the Specific Effects of the Robinson-Patman Act', *American Economic Review*, 29, 1(2), pp. 105-7.

HANEY, L.H. (1920) 'Integration in Marketing', *American Economic Review*, 10, pp. 528-45.

HALL, W.P. (1964) 'Franchising – New Scope for an Old Technique', *Harvard Business Review*, 42, pp. 60-72.

HAWKINS, G. (1976) 'The Case for Contract Warehousing', *Retail and Distribution Management*, 4(1), pp. 45-7.

HIRSCH, L.V. (1961) *Marketing in an Underdeveloped Economy. The North Indian Sugar Industry* (Prentice-Hall, Englewood Cliffs).

HIRSCH, W.Z. (1950) 'Toward a Definition of Integration', *Southern Economic Journal*, 17, pp. 159-65.

HOLLANDER, S.J. (1960) 'The Wheel of Retailing', *Journal of Marketing*, 24, pp. 37-42.

HOLLOWAY, R.J. and R.S. HANCOCK (1968) *Marketing in a Changing Environment* (Wiley, New York).

JACK, A.B. (1957) 'The Channels of Distribution for an Innovation: The Sewing Machine Industry in America, 1860-1865', *Explorations in Entreprenurial History*, 9, pp. 113-41.

JOHNSTON, M.R. AND ASSOCIATES (1974) *Perth Metropolitan Region Retail Shopping Survey 1973* (Metropolitan Region Planning Authority, Perth, W. Australia).

JONES, F.M. (1954) 'The Development of Marketing Channels in the United States to 1920' in R.M. Clewett (ed.) *Marketing Channels* (Irwin, Homewood).

KARGER, D.W. (1960) *The New Product* (The Industrial Press, New York).

KRIESBERG, L. (1955) 'Occupational Controls among Steel Distributors', *American Journal of Sociology*, 61, pp. 203-12.

LAMBERT, E.W. (1966) 'Financial Considerations in Choosing a Marketing Channel', *Business Topics*, 14 Winter, pp. 17-26.

LEVITT, T. (1962) *Innovation in Marketing* (McGraw-Hill, New York).

LEWIS, E.H. (1961) *Marketing Electrical Apparatus and Supplies* (McGraw-Hill, New York).

—— (1968) *Marketing Channels: Structure and Strategy* (McGraw-Hill, New York).

LITTLE, R.W. (1970) 'The Marketing Channel: Who Should Lead this Extracorporate Organization?', *Journal of Marketing*, 34(1), pp. 31-8.

LORSCH, J.W. and S.A. ALLEN (1973) *Managing Diversity and Independence: an Organizational Study of Multidivisional Firms* (Graduate School of Business Administration, Havard University, Boston).

MALLEN, B. (1963) 'A Theory of Retailer-Supplier Conflict, Control and Cooperation', *Journal of Retailing*, 39, pp. 24-32, 51.

—— (1964) 'Conflict and Cooperation in Marketing Channels' in L.G. Smith (ed.)

Reflections on Progress in Marketing (American Marketing Association, Chicago).

MARKIN, R.J. (1971) 'The Retailer in the Vertical Marketing Network', *University of Washington Business Review*, 30, pp. 39-44.

MEHREN, G.L. (1959) 'Market Organisation and Economic Development', *Journal of Farm Economics*, 41(5), pp. 1311-24.

MICHMAN, R.D. (1971) 'Channel Development and Innovation', *Marquette Business Review*, 15, pp. 45-9.

MINISTRY OF INTERNATIONAL TRADE AND INDUSTRY (1968) *A Report on Distribution by Product* (Tokyo).

MINTZ, S.W. (1957) 'The Role of Middleman in the Internal Distribution System of a Caribbean Peasant Economy', *Human Organization*, 15, pp. 18-23.

MOYER, R. (1964) 'The Structure of Markets in Developing Economies', *Business Topics*, 12(4), pp. 43-60.

McCAMMON, B.C. (1963) 'Alternative Explanations of Institutional Change and Channel Evolution' in S.A. Greyser (ed.), *Toward Scientific Marketing* (American Marketing Association, Chicago), pp. 477-90.

—— (1965) 'The Emergence and Growth of Contractually Integrated Channels in the American Economy' in P.F. Drucker (ed.), *Marketing and Economic Development* (American Marketing Association, Chicago), pp. 496-515.

—— (1970) 'Perspectives for Distribution Programming' in L.P. Bucklin (ed.), *Vertical Marketing Systems* (Scott-Foresman, Glenview), pp. 32-51.

McCAMMON, B.C. and R.W. LITTLE (1965) 'Marketing Channels: Analytical Systems and Approaches' in G. Schwartz (ed.), *Science in Marketing* (Wiley, New York), pp. 321-85.

McINNES, W. (1964) 'A Conceptual Approach to Marketing' in R. Cox, W. Alderson and S.J. Shapiro (eds), *Theory in Marketing*, 2nd edn (Irwin, Homewood), pp. 5-67.

McLACHLAND, D.L. and D. SWANN (1967) *Competition Policy in the European Community* (Oxford University Press, London).

NATIONAL COMMISSION ON FOOD MARKETING (1966) *Food from Farmer to Consumer*, vol. 3, *Dairy Industry* (Washington, DC).

NEDO (1971) *Channels and Costs of Distribution in the N.E. Region* (HMSO, London).

OECD (1956) *Marketing Fruit and Vegetables in Europe*, Report of Project 249C (Paris).

—— (1960) *Organisation and Structure of Milk Markets in OECD Member Countries* (Paris).

—— (1973) *Changes in the Distribution of Milk and Milk Products: a Challenge to Farmers*, Vol. 1 (Paris).

—— (1974A) *Changes in the Distribution of Milk and Milk Products: a Challenge to Farmers*, Vol. 2 (Paris).

—— (1974B) *Annual Report on Competition Policy in OECD Member Countries* (Paris).

PALAMOUNTAIN, J.C. (1955) *The Politics of Distribution* (Harvard University Press, Boston).

PENROSE, E.T. (1968) *Growth of the Firm* (Blackwell, Oxford).

PRED, A. (1975) 'On the Spatial Structure of Organizations and the Complexity of Metropolitan Independence', *Papers, Regional Science Association*, 35, pp. 115-42.

PRESTON, R.E. and A.E. SCHRAMM (1965) 'Dual Distribution and its Impact on Marketing Organization', *California Management Review*, Winter, pp. 59-70.

REVZAN, D.A. (1961) *Wholesaling in Market Organization* (Wiley, New York).

RIDGEWAY, V.F. (1957) 'Administration of Manufacturer Dealer Systems', *Administrative Science Quarterly*, 2, pp. 464-83.

ROBERTSON, T.S. (1969) 'The New Product Diffusion Process' in B.A. Morin (ed.), *Marketing in a Changing World* (American Marketing Association, Chicago).

ROBINSON, E.A.G. (1958) *The Structure of Competitive Industry* (University of Chicago Press, Chicago).

ROBINSON, O. and J. WALLACE (1976) *Pay and Employment in Retailing* (Saxon House, Farnborough).

ROSENBERG, L.J. and L.W. STERN (1971) 'Conflict Measurement in the Distribution Channel', *Journal of Marketing Research*, 8, pp. 40-6.

SCHUMPETER, J.A. (1950) *Capitalism, Socialism and Democracy* (Harper Bros, New York).

SCHWARTZMAN, D. (1969) 'The Growth of Sales per Man Hour in Retail Trade, 1929-1963' in V.R. Fuchs, *Production and Productivity in the Service Industries* (Columbia University Press, New York), p. 205.

SEMPLE, R.K. (1973) 'Recent Trends in the Spatial Concentration of Corporate Headquarters', *Economic Geography*, 49, pp. 309-18.

SHAW, S.J. (1965) 'Behavioral Science Offers Fresh Insights on New Product Acceptance', *Journal of Marketing*, 29, pp. 9-13.

SILK, A.J. and L.W. STERN (1963) 'The Changing Nature of Innovation in Marketing: a Study of Selected Business Leaders, 1852-1958', *Business History Review*, 37, pp. 182-99.

SLATER, C.C. (1968) 'Marketing Processes in Developing Latin American Societies', *Journal of Marketing*, 32, pp. 50-5.

STERN, L.W. and A.I. EL-ANSARY (1977) *Marketing Channels* (Prentice-Hall, Englewood Cliffs).

STURDIVANT, F.D. (1967) 'Determinants of Vertical Integration in Channel Systems' in R.M. Hass (ed.), *Science, Technology and Marketing* (American Marketing Association, Chicago).

TAX, S. (1953) *Penny Capitalism: a Guatemalan Indian Economy* (Institute of Social Anthropology, Washington, DC).

VANCE, J.E. (1970) *The Merchants' World: the Geography of Wholesaling* (Prentice-Hall, Englewood Cliffs).

VARBLE, D.L. (1972) 'Social and Environmental Considerations in New Product Development', *Journal of Marketing*, 36, pp. 11-15.

WADINAMBIARATCHI, G. (1965) 'Channels of Distribution in Developing Countries', *The Business Quarterly*, 30, pp. 74-82.

WALTERS, D. (1975) 'Physical Distribution Futures for the U.K. Food Industry', *Retail and Distribution Management*, 3, pp. 21-9.

WEIGAND, R.E. (1963) 'The Marketing Organization, Channels and Firm Size', *The Journal of Business*, 33, pp. 228-36.

WILEMON, L. (1972) 'Power and Negotiation Strategies in Marketing Channels', *Southern Journal of Business*, 7, pp. 71-81.

WILLIAMSON, O.E. (1970) *Corporate Control and Business Behavior* (Prentice-Hall, Englewood Cliffs).

ZIMMERN, A. (1924) *The Greek Commonwealth*, 4th edn (Oxford University Press, London).

3 DEMAND AND THE BEHAVIOUR OF CONSUMERS

Every society develops a system by which goods are produced and distributed. The range of goods available for consumption frequently is large and the processes of distribution and consumption are complex. The two previous chapters have shown how this marketing system is composed of institutions and channels. Consumption is the ultimate goal of this system. During consumption, conflicts arise among types of consumers and between consumers and other marketing institutions. A commonly held axiom is that the customer is always right but, as Katona (1960) points out, usually consumers have exhibited only brief flashes of power. Real marketing power lies with other groups. Consumer attitudes on this however have changed dramatically since the mid 1960s.

Before any consideration of consumer processes can be made it is important to acknowledge the relationships between demand and consumption. It is not the aim to study the variety of demand functions which exist both in theory and practice. These are covered in a number of economics primers (Samuelson, 1970; Thiel, 1971) and specialist texts (Pearce, 1964; Wold and Jureen, 1952; Douglas, 1975; Lancaster, 1971; Houthakker and Taylor, 1970). Demand may be defined simply as *the number of units of a product (or service) that the market will desire to purchase per time period under varying market conditions.* Demand is influenced by many variables. Some are external to the control of the consumer while others are firmly within the consumer's decision making sphere.

Non-household Consumption

The consumer is not a single, or a simple, body. Discussions of demand and consumers and their behaviour usually concentrate on household buying patterns. But there are large and important groups of non-household consumers who each behave quite differently from households and from each other. Three main groups may be seen:

(1)   Institutional buyers that purchase for consumption and use, for example a university or hospital.
(2)   Government buyers that purchase primarily for consumption and use. The goods bought include some items, for example

military equipment, which only governments purchase.
(3)　Industrial, agricultural and general business buyers that purchase for production, resale, and use. A manufacturing firm,
for example, is a consumer of raw materials, semifinished goods
and a range of equipment.

The extent and function of household and non-household expenditure varies considerably between countries. Generally governmental
consumption has increased, in recent years, at a faster rate than household consumption. National account statistics usually indicate the composition of the expenditure of Gross Domestic Product. Private final
consumption (which includes institutional buying) and government
final consumption represent two major expenditure elements. Government expenditure rarely exceeds 25 per cent of GDP. Only in countries
with particularly high defence budgets (Weidenbaum, 1968) is the percentage noticeably over 20 per cent. In 1973 the Israeli Government
accounted for over 40 per cent of expenditure while in Sudan it was
30 per cent and in Syria 22 per cent. Other governments which are large
consumers are those of Denmark and Sweden where spending on government services is high. In the UK, USA, Canada and West Germany the
proportion of GDP spent by government is around 18 to 19 per cent.
In the developing countries percentages fall well below 10 per cent and
are even as low as 5 or 6 per cent for the poorest countries. Private consumption is a proportionately higher fraction of GDP expenditure in
these countries. Although consumption per head is low in these countries,
decisions on the allocation of GDP expenditure is largely in the hands of
individuals. It is in the developing countries that governmental consumption has increased most rapidly in recent years, and has outstripped
the growth in private consumption. In these countries there is the most
leeway to be made up. In general in Africa, for example, governmental
consumption has risen by almost 25 per cent since 1970 while private
consumption has increased by less than 15 per cent. By contrast, as
Table 3.1 shows, in North America, although both markets are considerably larger, the percentage growth rate of government consumption is
relatively low compared with private consumption.

The government as a consumer differs from other types of consumer
in a number of ways. The purchasing behaviour pattern of Western
governments is usually dominated by an extensive network of legal
requirements which are designed to protect the public interest by
ensuring competition on price, quality and performance (Simon, 1970).
Within Eastern Europe and the USSR a very different buyer process is

Table 3.1:   Indices of Final Consumption Expenditure (1970 = 100)

	Government expenditure			Private expenditure		
	1960	1965	1973	1960	1965	1973
Developed market economies	65	80	109	63	80	116
Developing market economies	54	72	123	63	77	117
Africa	48	68	121	69	80	111
North America	64	79	105	66	83	116
Middle East	35	57	147	57	73	123
South East Asia (exc. Japan)	57	77	112	67	78	113
Europe	68	84	113	63	80	115

evident. Here, there is again a very formalised procedure but it is administrative rather than legal. Competition is not as important as purchasing according to a centralised plan.

Within market economies it is probably the ordnance and aircraft industries which are most heavily dependent on government consumption. Over 80 per cent of these industries' outputs in the USA go to government. In government's buying behaviour to these industries, and others which sell a significant amount to government such as electronic components or transport industries, a number of characteristics emerge (Isard and Langford, 1969; Adams, 1968). First, goods tend to be precisely specified as to size, quality, material, etc. prior to purchase. Often standards are imposed by the government consumer and products may even be tested before purchase. The government buyer exerts this power because of the size in either volume or money terms of orders. If any conflict arises the consumer (i.e. government) is in a position of almost total power (Kennedy, 1964). Secondly, decisions by the consumer on where to buy may be influenced by factors totally unrelated to the product or its use. Local government buyers often buy from producers in their own governmental district. Central government may well prefer to buy from manufacturers located in depressed regions. A third feature of governments as consumers is the often lengthy procedure necessary before a purchase is actually made. A report in the *New York Times* suggested that there were 71 steps to be taken by New York City Authorities over the purchase of an item of office furniture. Allegations of executive bureaucracy in town halls are common in all countries. Against such a standard, personal buyer behaviour or industrial buying involve impulse reactions.

The business market encompasses demand by manufacturing industries, agricultural industries and service industries. A glance at input-output tables indicates the size and structure of business markets. The basis of input-output studies is the purchasing pattern of the sectors of the economy (Leontief, 1966; Evans, 1952). The main feature of industrial market demand is that the industrial buyer purchases in a market with a derived demand since his own company's purchases depend on someone else's purchases. The demand for steel, for example, is derived from the demand for cars, refrigerators and equipment, and by other users of steel.

Webster (1969) has summarised the main characteristics of industrial consumer behaviour as follows:

(1)   The purchasing decision is made within an organisation and by a number of individuals including users, decision makers and buyers.

(2)   The industrial buyer is often not the most important factor in the decision process. Often he serves as an executive for others' decisions.

(3)   Decisions can be classed from the simple and routine to complex, expensive and non-routine and the buying process will probably differ according to the type of decision.

(4)   Buyers are motivated by a combination of individual needs and organisational needs.

(5)   There is a tendency to rely upon the familiar.

These characteristics changed little for many years (Duncan, 1940) but now changes are beginning to appear. Industrial buyers often operate within a clearly defined administrative or organisational buying procedure (Klass, 1961). The scope for individual behaviour can be severely limited but a buyer will probably select a supplier – or more usually multiple suppliers (Bucker, 1966) – and be responsible for transportation decisions. In some instances the actions of an industrial buyer are similar to those of a household consumer but he is far more thorough about them and works within a more constrained environment. Henderson (1964) has argued that the behaviour of industrial buyers is changing radically. The purchasing executive will increasingly delegate action and is more likely to be concerned about the overall economic situation of suppliers rather than simply procuring individual orders. Consumer behaviour is then viewed in a systems framework and the purchasing manager will be increasingly an economist, analyst and planner rather than negotiator.

Given the systems approach, perceived interdependencies increase and consequently the scope for conflict is increased both within a purchasing organisation and between consumer and supplier. While the search and evaluation procedures are more thorough in industrial purchasing than in household consumption, increased constraints are thus placed on the actual decision. England (1967) and Holton (1970) stress the importance of collecting and evaluating a very wide range of information in industrial purchasing behaviour. This single feature is the one which most characterises industrial buying: 'Rational buying motives undoubtedly dominate the (industrial) buyer's behaviour' (Holloway and Hancock, 1973, p. 274).

Within the service industries there has been scant research on service business buying behaviour. In tourist regions, for example, very little is known of how hotels and caterers obtain their supplies. A limited study in Jamaica (Lundgren, 1972) suggests that hotels obtain supplies from small scale agriculturalists but 'the hotels showed no consistent behaviour regarding shipment size/unit price . . . thus discounting bulk purchase as a feature in the purchase pattern'. Clearly there is considerable scope for empirical work on buyer behaviour in the service industries.

The third major non-household buyer group is institutions. In this context an institution is an organisation providing, on a non-profit basis, some service to the public or to some sector of the public. Educational and health organisations comprise many such institutions. The public accountability of these institutions and their non-profitmaking basis provide them with particular purchasing behaviour patterns. Public accountability often produces an extensive and complex decision making procedure and cost considerations may override all others in some purchase decisions. The range of goods bought is very wide but often there is little variation in buying procedures. There are 2,400 hospitals in England and Wales and in total in 1971 they spent over £300m on consumable materials. Food, clothing, drugs, equipment and maintenance materials are all purchased regularly. Over the last 20 years consumer behaviour in British hospitals has changed radically. Subsequent to the Messer Report (Ministry of Health, 1957; 1958) on hospital purchasing, many hospitals grouped together to contract for their purchases. Marron (1967), for example, reported an exercise of buying linen for almost all the hospitals in the North of England. A cost saving resulted and a formalised buying process was passed through with decisions made by a committee. More usually the Hospital Supplies Officer takes the bulk of decisions in the buying process and increasingly has put heavy emphasis on large scale contracting.

Household Consumption – the Economic Approach

Government, commercial and institutional markets together represent a larger market than that of the household, yet far more is known about household buying behaviour than is known for these larger bodies. Within Western market economies it has been traditional that household consumption is the catalyst in the economic system and consequently household consumer behaviour has been studied widely. The major difference between household and non-household consumer behaviour is that, in one, buying is an individual process and in the other it is an organisational activity.

Study of household consumption has developed along two parallel lines. One is concerned with demand analysis and the economics of consumption:

> The changing structure of industry over time depends crucially on the evolution of the elements of consumers' expenditure in response to increasing income while knowledge of price responses is an important element in the formation of fiscal policy or any other type of economic control. (Brown and Deaton, 1973, p. 182).

The primary aim is the study of how much of a household's income is spent on different items, whether in terms of allocation of income or of allocation of expenditures. The second approach has as its central concern the process of buying and seeks to determine the influences controlling the buying process. The two approaches are quite different in aim and philosophy. The estimation of demand equations, the study of the *utility* of goods and services and consumers' evaluation (or indifference) to competing goods are well developed and integrated branches of economics. Conversely the reasons behind consumers' visits to a particular shop in a particular place and purchasing particular goods depend upon cultural, social, psychological, economic, political and geographical variables and constants. The buying process lies within a multidisciplinary area and has been studied by a series of interrelated but essentially non-integrated partial models.

The economic theory of consumer behaviour is one of the most refined theories in the social sciences. The evolution of the theory is given by Stigler (1954). Despite its level of development and conceptual elegance it is necessary to refute it as a central theory to marketing geography for it is derived from a too heavy dependence on economics. The development of studies of the buying process has been largely a revolt from the traditional theory.

Assuming the consumer has limited finance then a choice has to be made regarding which goods will be bought. The utility of a good to a consumer is central in classical economic theory. Marshall argued that it was possible to measure utility on a cardinal scale with consumers stating how much one good was preferred to another. Hicks in 1939 provided an alternative treatment of utility which considered that measurement was only possible on an ordinal scale. Thus, he argues, a consumer can appreciate relative merits of goods but not absolute merits. From Hicks's analysis emerged the concept of the indifference curve and the indifference map. The basis of the indifference curve is that consumers purchase combinations of goods and the acceptable combinations indicate relative utility and the consumer's indifference to certain different combinations of goods. The curve joins acceptable combinations of two products. Indifference itself, however, is a relative concept and there are sets of indifference curves with each curve relating to a particular level of indifference. The set of curves is termed an indifference map and Figure 3.1 shows one such map. All points on each indifference curve have equal preference but combinations on graphs to the right on the map are preferred to lower combinations. Lines AA, BB, etc. represent budget constraints and the income consumption curve relates change in income to changes in consumption of the two products. The slope of this curve is affected by the relative prices of the two products. In this form of analysis consumer behaviour is considered to be controlled only by income and price. Furthermore, the consumer is invariably considered as an individual. A fuller treatment of the approach is provided by most standard economic texts, for example Leftwich (1966), Tucker (1967), and Branson (1972). Attempts by David (1962) to reformulate the theory in terms of the household, rather than the individual, foundered because he found that individual preferences were superseded by a family preference which could be quite different from the individual one. Social and psychological variables became relevant and traditional indifference analysis was incapable of digesting these extra considerations.

Lancaster (1966A, 1966B, 1971) has suggested an alternative view of utility and preference. He maintains that it is not the good itself but the properties or characteristics of the goods from which utility is derived. With this as a base it may prove possible to introduce perceived properties and characteristics which might go some way to breaking the income-price control of the utility and indifference concepts. As yet, however, this step has not been taken and is even absent in Lancaster's formulation. Extension of the theory in a different direction has been

Figure 3.1: A Hypothetical Indifference Map

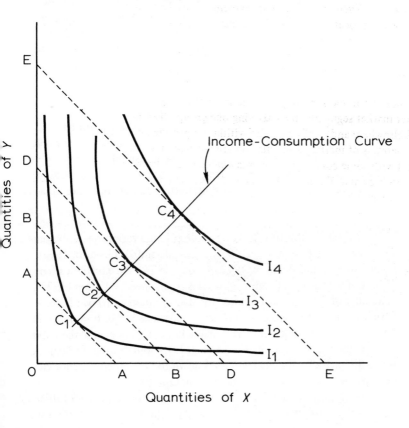

achieved by Devletoglou (1971), who introduces a spatial dimension to consumer indifference and extends the idea of consumer thresholds (Georgescu-Roegen, 1966). In this analysis, triggering mechanisms (income/price) in consumer behaviour are suggested not as specific values but more as bands of values with an upper critical threshold. The size of the band, where in the band the trigger works and the critical threshold, then all become variables outside the traditional formulation of the theory and geographical, social and political variables may be introduced. Devletoglou (1971) concentrates on incorporating the spatial variable and so provides a major step forward in the broadening of consumer economics.

A number of good reasons still exist, however, for the rejection of the traditionally based approach to consumer behaviour in favour of an approach based on buying processes. First, the traditional approach is not operational. It is a normative (and even at times moral) model rather than an empirical one and suggests how consumers ought to behave and not how they do behave. It is also apparent that indifference and the propensity of consumers to consume is not easily measured. Cochrane and Bell (1956) state

> The theory of consumer behaviour as it stands now cannot be used to recommend adjustments in consumption patterns, because where the results of those adjustments cannot be measured, it is impossible to say whether the recommended pattern of consumption yields more or less satisfaction than the previous pattern to the consumer involved. (p. 144).

This statement is still true 20 years on despite the various recent extensions to the approach (Ironmonger, 1972; Agarwala and Drinkwater, 1972; Sommermeyer and Bannink, 1972; Katona, 1974). An excellent review of both theoretical and empirical studies is provided by Ferber (1973). A number of attempts exemplified by MacCrimmon and Toda (1969) have been made to measure indifference functions but in total it is still not possible to make general statements. Price and income, while important, are not the only factors in consumer behaviour. Shubik (1970) suggests: 'Empirically, the question boils down to how much variance can be explained by price and income information' (p. 410).

Secondly, traditional theory remains centred on the product rather than on the consumer despite the study by Lancaster. By definition the economic model is not concerned with behavioural processes but with the result of these processes.

Thirdly, the traditional approach is mechanistic, assuming consumers have perfect information or, at least, all have the same information. It disregards the ways consumers *learn* their behavioural patterns and formulate their attitudes to products. A consumer may be following a behaviour pattern he/she feels to be perfectly rational but in terms of traditional theory it is totally irrational. The economic consumption approach is developed on the basis of norms and averages of behaviour rather than on averages, ranges and extremes of behaviour.

Fourthly, and finally, despite the work of Devletoglou the theory remains essentially non-spatial. It is assumed that consumers have equal real and perceived accessibility to all products. Consumer behaviour involves decisions on where to buy goods as well as what goods to buy. Indifference curves and consumption-income relationships vary over space but the relationships are not inherently geographical. Houthakker (1957), for example, showed that while Engel's laws show a common structure in crosscultural studies there remains spatial variation even in these basic ideas. Engel's laws may be summarised as:

(1) As income rises, the proportion spent on food declines.
(2) As income rises, the proportion spent on housing and house-hold goods remains about the same.
(3) As income rises, the proportion spent on clothing stays the same or rises slightly.
(4) As income rises, the proportion spent on luxuries rises.

Other, more recent, international comparisons (Yneu, 1964) suggest these basic relationships are acceptable but that there may be different indifference curves for different countries and even different times depending on the structure of income distribution at different stages of economic development. The introduction of the structure of income distribution however brings in the complications of different expenditure patterns associated with different income groups and, hence, social groups. Traditional demand theory cannot accommodate this.

Models of Buying Behaviour

The remainder of this chapter will concentrate on consumer buying as a behaviour process with determinants in a range of social sciences. The income variable may be considered as one factor but not, as in the economic consumption model, the only significant one. Kotler (1965) considers economic or *Marshallian Man* as only one model of consumer behaviour. He also isolates

Freudian Man who is motivated by egotistical motives and fantasies.
Pavlovian Man who is influenced by previous buying patterns and the repetition of successful previous patterns.
Hobbesian Man who reconciles his individual desires with social organisational change, and
Veblenian Man who shapes buying patterns in accordance with social group patterns.

To this list could be added

Lewinian Man who is heavily influenced in his buying patterns by external environmental stimuli.

As was suggested earlier, the buying process, because it is both complex and interdisciplinary, has been modelled by means of partial models rather than in a single integrated approach.

As with model building throughout the social sciences it is possible to approach model formulation of consumer behaviour either by inductive or by deductive paths. Figure 3.2 shows the two approaches as idealised by Lazer (1962). The inductive approach begins with the perception of a real situation, for example the arrival at a store of a customer. It is necessary as a next step to determine the relationships among the several perceived variables. The consumer, the store, the environment (including the journey) and the goods purchased are the broad areas of possible variation but each is capable of measurement in a number of ways. Next comes the verification of the relationships with a subsequent generalisation to produce a statement of a model. Application of the model then either leads to further verification or to model adjustment. The alternative, deductive, approach begins with an internally consistent set of propositions about behaviour. This theory is then expressed as abstract, modelled relationships. The abstract relationships are tested against the real world and empirical information gathered. Testing and comparison of abstract and real relationships lead either to acceptance or adjustment of the theory.

Whichever approach is used, the incorporation of models into the study of consumer behaviour has certain advantages. Kotler (1968) itemises five of these in a discussion of mathematical models of consumer and purchasing behaviour:

(1) 'These models will force a more rigorous statement of the variables operating in buying situations and the nature of their relationships.'

(2) 'These models will facilitate the comparison of different theories of buyer behaviour. The similarities will show up more clearly and the differences can be subjected to sharper empirical tests. The models will highlight the degree to which the differences are structural, functional, or only parametric.'

(3) 'These models will help pinpoint more accurately the data needs of marketing decision makers who seek to understand and to some degree influence consumer behaviour.'

(4) 'These models will stimulate inferences not ordinarily obvious

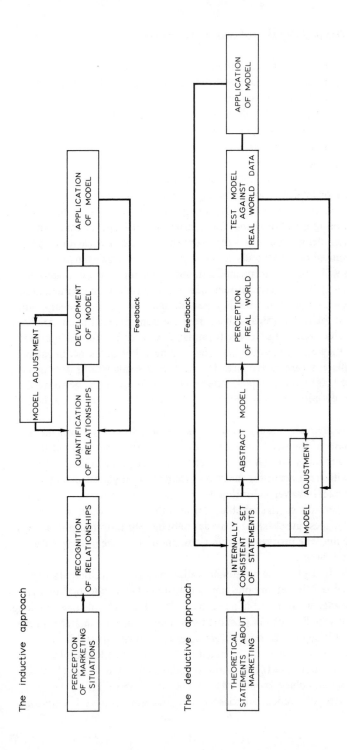

The inductive approach

PERCEPTION OF MARKETING SITUATIONS → RECOGNITION OF RELATIONSHIPS → QUANTIFICATION OF RELATIONSHIPS → DEVELOPMENT OF MODEL → APPLICATION OF MODEL

MODEL ADJUSTMENT

Feedback

The deductive approach

THEORETICAL STATEMENTS ABOUT MARKETING → INTERNALLY CONSISTENT SET OF STATEMENTS → ABSTRACT MODEL → PERCEPTION OF REAL WORLD → TEST MODEL AGAINST REAL WORLD DATA → APPLICATION OF MODEL

MODEL ADJUSTMENT

Feedback

Figure 3.2: Inductive and Deductive Approaches to Model Building

from verbal formulations, much in the way a set of postulates about points and lines stimulates a large number of theorems about spatial relations.'

(5)   'These models will facilitate the construction of microconsumer market simulators. The use of microconsuming units in a simulation permits the study of some important properties overlooked in gross market response models, such as the distribution of preferences, the distribution of delays in response to marketing stimuli, and so forth.'

Modelling consumer behaviour is not without its problems. Sometimes a model oversimplifies the situation. Consumer behaviour, as has been pointed out repeatedly, is a complex process and oversimplified models will only lead to misunderstanding. Furthermore, mathematical models may have an aura of accuracy which is totally unjustified. It is sometimes assumed that the precisely defined idea is, of necessity, fact. A similar difficulty arises with attempts to improve existing models. A logically derived and precisely formulated model has a forbidding appearance for a would-be model mechanic. No model of consumer behaviour is complete, all are partial and often inflexible explanations of reality. As such these models require extension. A series of ideas does not become definitive merely because it is modelled in mathematical language.

There are many models of buyer behaviour. Some attempt general statements of the whole buyer process, others are concerned with single purchasing traits. Not all these latter type are relevant to the present study with its concern for the spatial element in buyer behaviour. It is worthwhile, however, to outline four of the major, general, models and to consider how spatial variables slot into these models. All the general models suggest purchasing behaviour may be split into four phases. It is in modelling the processes within these phases that the models differ from each other.

In the first place the consumer realises he has a need. Bell (1972) has suggested that at any one time a consumer has a collection of wants. These wants are arranged in a relative order which is stable over the long term but which is subject to short-term fluctuations. Ultimately, an event, Howard (1963) terms this a *triggering cue*, of some sort (taking the last packet of tea off the shelf, financial bonuses from work, etc.) forces the consumer to take the decision to make a purchase.

The second phase is one of search and evaluation. This can be a very short phase for a repeat purchase at a regular store of a frequently used item. In other instances it may be long and complicated as alternative styles, brands and prices are evaluated and a search is made of competing suppliers. A survey by Mueller and Katona (1955) indicated that around half of the buyers of consumer goods had a search period of less than two months. Many consumers seeking to minimise the effort involved in a rigorous search procedure substitute information for actual search. Bucklin (1966), Udell (1966) and Dommermuth and Cundiff (1967) all suggest that the environmental aspects of the search procedure constitute a significant aspect of the overall search activity and one where information may prove a surrogate for actual search, notably in unfamiliar environments. Cox and Rich (1964) suggest instances when information on a good, as opposed to the environment, is substituted for actual search processes. Search procedures of consumers tend to be formalised into regular and inflexible shopping habits. A consumer often travels by a particular form of transport to a particular shopping centre to visit particular shops often in a particular order. If the search proves negative an equally formal alternative procedure is set in motion. In some cases the consumer does not need to make a physical search of his shopping environment, it is enough to search his experience or perception of the environment (Downs, 1970; Mackay and Olshavsky, 1975; Mackay, Olshavsky and Sentell, 1975). Whatever the detail of the processes involved (Dommermuth, 1965; Carman, 1969; Shaffer, 1960; Nicosia, 1968) however, all generalise to a search and evaluation exercise.

The actual making of the purchase ultimately takes place although the search and evaluation procedure can be long and hard. The purchase phase may be reached when the search time is considered expired, or when, for the importance of the want, the search effort has been maximised or even when a total search has been made. Perhaps the most critical feature of the purchasing is one of timing—when to make the purchase. Buyers have preferences for days of the week with, in Western Europe, Thursday, Friday and Saturday being the most popular shopping days. Although a search has been made purchase may still be postponed. Usually it is still made even if at a later time.

The final phase is that of consumption and postpurchase feedback. From a producer's point of view this aspect of consumer behaviour is extremely important, for at this stage brand loyalty is forged. Elaborate attempts often are made to assess consumer satisfaction (McNeal, 1969A). From the viewpoint of this book consumer satisfaction, or dissatisfaction, is important in its effect on future purchasing behaviour. If consumers enjoy visiting a particular shop then repeat visits are to be expected. In a survey in 1974 of Exeter (Dawson, 1974) over 40 per cent of shoppers visiting the city centre enjoyed visiting a particular store (Marks & Spencer). The store naturally acted as a magnet in attracting shoppers from the surrounding countryside to the city generally but also influenced patterns of pedestrian flows and behaviour traits such as preferred parking sites. The level of satisfaction achieved may be closely related to the amount of effort expended in the evaluation and purchase phases. Thus, satisfaction may 'depend not only upon the product itself, but also upon the experience surrounding acquisition of the product' (Cardozo, 1965, p. 246). Postpurchase satisfaction with the shopping environment and the article purchased is a key to explaining many aspects of the spatial behaviour of consumers.

In each of the four phases of purchasing behaviour there are variables and processes directly related either to actual or to perceived spatial relationships. The consumer, by operating in a spatially defined area, is influenced by some aspects of environment but also overrides, usually either by decreasing satisfaction or increasing the costs of purchasing, other environmental features. This basic behavioural model is applicable to all Western type societies (Ehrenberg and Goodhardt, 1968) but there is no evidence to suggest crosscultural applicability to either communist society or to the developing world. Intuitively it would seem that the search and evaluation exercise will be severely curtailed if goods are scarce or if information on availability is absent. Slater *et al.* (1969) show that, in the Recife area of North West Brazil, 'Seventy percent of the housewives interviewed purchased from the same group of stores or the same geographic location' (pp. 42-3). This suggests a rather inflexible search procedure. Loyalty, however, is considered as inertial activity rather than the result of cautious evaluation of alternatives. While there are a few studies of the actual purchasing activity of consumers in the developing world (Wood, 1974; Abiodun, 1971) there is a lack of studies of consumer motivation and of the processes involved in buyer behaviour. Undoubtedly processes within the purchase phase are very different in different cultural contexts, but then also there is a wide range of processes operating in Western society. It may be reasonable to assume that the essential four-phase conception of consumer behaviour is generally applicable but the relative strengths of the phases and the processes within each phase vary with society and culture.

Ideally it would be valuable to have a complete model of buying behaviour but knowledge of the subject is still in its infancy. Four major general models have been proposed. These are due to

(1)   Engel, Kollat and Blackwell (1968) with subsequent revision

Figure 3.3: A Model of Consumer Behaviour after Engel, Kollat and Blackwell

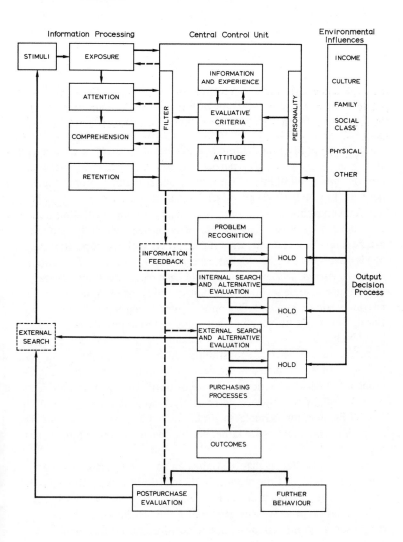

in 1973,
(2)   Andreasen (1965),
(3)   Nicosia (1966),
(4)   Howard and Sheth (1969).

The model of Engel, Kollat and Blackwell is shown diagramatically in Figure 3.3. The greatest detail in the model relates to the first phase which ends with *problem recognition*. Need perception (phase 1) is considered as uninfluenced by the environment outside the consumer. Only psychological processes are considered necessary to explain this phase. This seems a rather narrow interpretation of the need arousal. Both the stimuli and the filter mechanism are influenced by external environment and social influences. This is particularly so if an argument is made for crosscultural applicability of the model. The *stimulus* is often an advertisement (Lipstein, 1965) but advertisements are closely related to the cultural and political constraints on a society. Consequently the stimulus is influenced by outside factors. The *filter* through which 'the stimulus can be screened out or distorted if it conflicts with his dispositions' (p. 55) is essentially a psychological concept but it has sociological underpinnings. Particular social groups could have particular filters. Dietary restrictions of some social groups (Sorre, 1962) for example could provide a common externally imposed filter on a group of consumers. Engel, Kollat and Blackwell do not admit external influences until a problem has been recognised and formalised. The external influences, furthermore, are viewed as constraints which hold up problem solution. 'A *hold* is thus introduced in the decision making process; the recognised problem remains but action is postponed until the constraints are removed' (p. 55). Equally well they could be catalysts to problem solution. A high level of income, for example, might be the opposite to a constraint. The remaining model phases are rather generalised and have been dealt with previously.

The second model is that of Andreasen and it emphasises the consumer's attitudes and the changes in these attitudes owing to feedback throughout the overall process (Figure 3.4). Behaviour is modelled as an information processing cycle in which the behaviour results from the person as a unit making complete decisions rather than behaviour resulting from the sum of many traits. Andreasen raises a number of questions about the model, particularly the extent to which external factors (income, social class, etc.) influence the types of information sought.

Figure 3.5 shows the general form of Nicosia's model. The four-phase

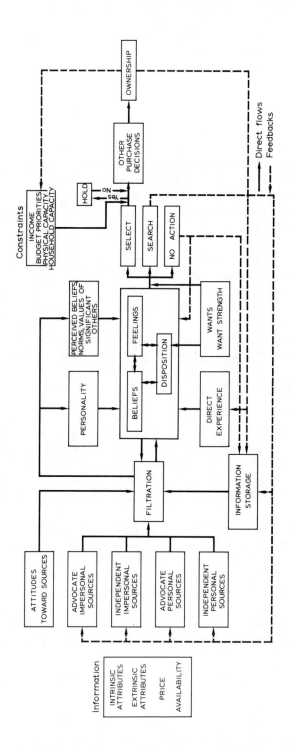

Figure 3.4: A Model of Consumer Behaviour after Andreasen

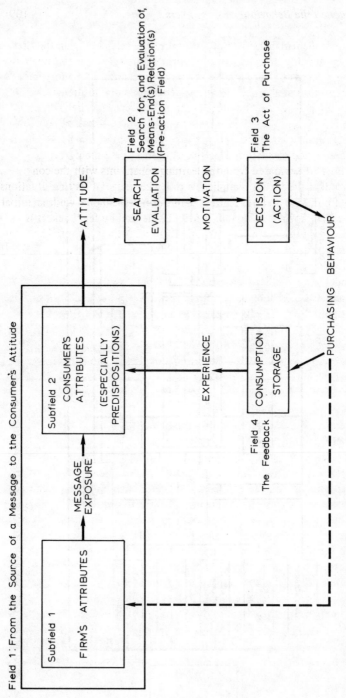

Field 1: From the Source of a Message to the Consumer's Attitude

Field 2
Search for, and Evaluation of,
Means-End(s) Relation(s)
(Pre-action Field)

Field 3
The Act of Purchase

Subfield 2
CONSUMER'S ATTRIBUTES
(ESPECIALLY PREDISPOSITIONS)

Subfield 1
FIRM'S ATTRIBUTES

ATTITUDE

SEARCH
EVALUATION

MOTIVATION

DECISION
(ACTION)

MESSAGE
EXPOSURE

EXPERIENCE

CONSUMPTION
STORAGE

Field 4
The Feedback

PURCHASING   BEHAVIOUR

Figure 3.5: A Model of Consumer Behaviour after Nicosia

structure is identifiable. The noisiest part of the model is again the first phase. By dividing this phase into the firm's action and the consumer's reaction it suggests a very limited source to need arousal. A more important criticism is the absence of external, environmental influences which form an integral part of the overall pattern of purchasing behaviour.

The fourth, and most sophisticated model is that presented by Howard and Sheth and summarised in Figure 3.6. The detail of this model lies in the search and evaluation procedures. In this phase the perceptual constraints are separated from the learning constraints with the consequence that the model is applicable to a wide range of buying situations. A repeat purchase involves a direct path through the model while an initial purchase may involve behaviour heavily influenced by feedback. It is perhaps wrong to see the Howard and Sheth model as sequential between initial inputs and final outputs because within the buying process it is possible to have inputs at a number of stages. The feedback effects in the model allow the inputs to influence the behaviour at a number of stages and in fact more widely than in the previous models. Postpurchase evaluation, for example, is modelled as a particular type of feedback to the inputs rather than a clearly definable separate phase in buying. What remains unclear, however, is the exact relationship between the inputs and their only way into the model through *stimulus ambiguity.* As yet there have been few substantive attempts to test the model empirically so it is far from clear what the general applicability of the approach might be. The most likely area of variation owing to consumers operating in different cultural environments would be in the form of the relationships between inputs and the body of the model. A different range of inputs or different emphases of importance of specific inputs seems likely. The second vague area in the model, and again one subject to cultural influences, is the exit from the *intention* to buy. This seems a simple step in the model but in reality involves the activity of shopping. The Howard-Sheth model is an attempt to model the decision to purchase a particular article and not the purchasing of the article. To achieve the latter it is necessary to include store choice and to model the journey to the store. Given the Howard-Sheth model it is not possible to incorporate the activity of shopping because the model is non-spatial. The process modelled can take place at home (in which case shopping lies between *intention* and *purchase*) or at the store (in which case the shop becomes part of the input mechanism). While the model is a considerable step forward from the economic theories of consumer behaviour, it still lies some way from interpreting real life consumer behavioural processes.

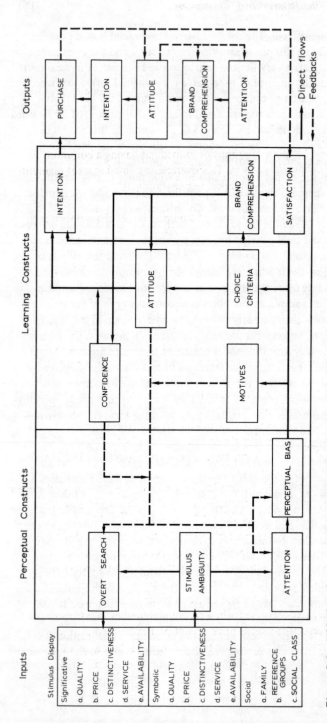

Figure 3.6: A Model of Consumer Behaviour after Howard and Sheth

Consumer Segmentation

In discussion of the main models of consumer behaviour, the influence of environmental variables has been stressed. What exactly are these variables and what is their influence on behaviour? At the one extreme environmental factors could be envisaged as influencing demand such that each individual's demand differs from every other. It is more practical and realistic to ignore the minor differences in demand among individuals and to think of groups of individuals having a common demand and behaviour pattern. This exercise is termed market segmentation. Baker (1971) defines market segmentation as

> identifying a sufficient number of common buyer characteristics to permit subdivision of the total demand for a product into economically viable segments . . . There are no hard-and-fast rules which dictate how a marketer should segment the total demand for a homogeneous product . . . (p. 50).

Consumers may be, and are, segmented along many different axes of measurement. Income, occupation, race, mobility, age, sex, social class, place of residence, language and many other consumer attributes have all been used to segment consumers for particular products (Foxall, 1977). Segmentation procedures may rely on measures along a single variable or may be more elaborate involving multivariate analyses (Arndt, 1974; Engel, Fiorello and Cayley, 1972). Furthermore, consumers are usually individuals or households but the segmentation concept also has been applied to analyses of nations as consumers both in respect of likely demand patterns (Sethi, 1971; Hansz and Goodnow, 1973) and on a behavioural basis (Hall, 1960).

Consumer segmentation pervades the whole of the customer subsystem of marketing and has been discussed in detail by Bieda and Kassarjian (1969), Cravens (1969), Johnson (1971) and Lessig (1972). In the product development, packaging and advertising, the aim is to meet the demands of a particular, often well defined (by market research) market segment. Even in mass merchandising strategies there is frequently an attempt, usually very widely defined, to aim products to one consumer group. The retailer designs the store and carries a range of stock to suit a particular market segment. The seller in a traditional market in Africa or the Caribbean adjusts a product's price to suit particular market segments. The basis of traditional, non-monetary, exchange is based on strict market segmentation. The land-use planner and politician segment the consumer when decisions are made on the provision of particular types of marketing institution in particular places or in the imposition of public policies on marketing enterprises. Even the consumers segment themselves when, for example, they shop at locations which they consider are used by other consumers in the same segment.

In this division of consumers into supposedly homogeneously respons- ive and similarly influenced subgroups lie the seeds of a major area of marketing conflict (Myers and Nicosia, 1968). Products developed, pro- moted and distributed with one subgroup in mind inevitably impinge, adversely, on other market segments. By satisfying one group, dissatis- faction is created elsewhere and conflict can be within the producing firm as different methods of market segmentation are advocated, or at the consumer level with some consumer segments unable to satisfy their demands. The consumerism movement (Herrmann, 1970), to some extent, has its foundations in this dissatisfaction. Equally some consumer segments can come into conflict with government as government defines policies to favour one segment at the expense of another. Legislation to protect small shops, serving the everyday needs of non-mobile consumers, at the expense of large shops in out-of-town locations creates a conflict between the mobile consumer and the large retailer on one hand and the government on the other. The basis of this conflict is the segment- ation of consumers into groups having a common mix of behavioural traits.

For segmentation to be a useful exercise in marketing strategy a number of conditions must be satisfied. Initially the segment must be clearly defined and the characteristics of members of the segment identified and measured. When segmentation is based on socioeconomic characteristics this exercise is not difficult but it becomes more difficult if the segment is defined in terms of behavioural or benefit character- istics. To be of use in market decisions segmentation must yield a sufficient market to make a separate strategy worthwhile. The asses- sment of what is sufficient varies considerably from institution to institution and probably relates to the overall size of the institution. A manufacturer mass producing a good is unlikely to be concerned with market segments of less than several tens of thousands of consumers. Conversely a small, one-person operated shop may have market segments consisting of fewer than 100 consumers. From the point of view of effective marketing strategy a segment must possess effective demand and this demand must be accessible. While it would be possible to seg- ment a market, perhaps on a psychological basis, such that members of a particular segment are widely scattered spatially, shop at different shops and read different magazines, such a segment is of little practical value. Making contact, effectively, with this theoretical segment would be almost impossible and certainly economically not viable.

Geographical and Cultural Segmentation

One of the least sophisticated and first used (Breyer, 1934; Eastman, 1930) methods of segmentation is by geographical area. In most countries there are well documented regional differences in consumption and purchasing patterns. From the marketing strategy viewpoint spatial segmentation is an extremely efficient method but it is essentially a coarse sieve of segmentation. Allen's (1968) study of regional taste in Britain and Piper's (1977) more recent study of ethnic markets exemplify the considerable differences which exist in consumer demand among the British regions. Some of this spatial variation can be explained by other bases of segmentation, for example spatial patterns of cultural or demographic differences, but there remains an element in the regional demand pattern which is unique to the region and cuts across all other segmentation axes. The same is true for any country which has a set of regions identifiable by the mass of the population. Weimar and Stevens (1974) showed wide variation in vegetable consumption among the regions in the USA. In France there are many such regions, for example Brittany, the Auvergne. It is suggested that tastes (Krugman and Hartley, 1960) and culture (Hair and Anderson, 1973) are learnt but most tastes can be manipulated and can be subject to quite rapid change. The existence of intrinsic regional differences would suggest that some characteristics of consumer demand take a long time to learn and change only slowly. Market segmentation on a regional basis serves best in providing for these latter needs. Segmentation of national markets is only an extension of the concept of regional markets and in such an extension the real weakness of regional segmentation is revealed: 'Members of a geographically determined segment tend, therefore, to be far too heterogeneous to qualify as a meaningful target for market action' (Bell, 1972, p. 188). Within-segment variation is as great as between segment variation.

It could be suggested that the underlying reason for geographic differences in consumption is one of culture. It is true that cultural regions will have different demand patterns. Palda (1967) concludes that 'consumption patterns do indeed differ between Quebec and Ontario households of similar size and incomes' (p. 26). But it is possible to segment markets on cultural measures and produce segments bearing little resemblance to those defined on geographical bases. Consumption patterns of broad cultural groups vary enormously. Dewhurst *et al.* (1961) show how food consumption differs in Northern Europe, Central Europe and

Southern Europe while Jureen (1962) increases the number of cultures in his comparative study, of food consumption.

More important than the broadscale differences are the variations shown by subcultural groups. Segmentation of markets along these subcultural dimensions are increasingly common. Alexis (1962) took eight separate studies of Negro/White consumer behaviour in the United States and showed quite different consumption patterns between the two groups although the samples were from the same income stratum. Oladipupo (1970) similarly was able to show that for comparable socio-economic groups Blacks saved more than Whites but spent more on clothing and non-automotive transport. It is not suggested that these differences are a result solely of subcultural differences but certainly some part of the variation is due to this cause. Other studies (Bauer and Cunningham, 1970; Feldman and Star, 1968; Brogowicz, 1977) have shown significantly different Black/White purchasing patterns. There are other studies of the different consumption patterns of different subculture segments. Many have taken place in North American cities with contrasts of different racial (Gibson, 1969), nationality (Jones, 1967) and religious (Bell, 1963) subcultures. The concept is not limited to North America with the European minority and African groups living in Africa (Van Der Reis, 1968; Nel, 1969) and the many different subcultures in the Caribbean (Lowenthal, 1972), for example, each having distinctive consumption patterns. Scott (1970) also points to the urban-rural split of consumers as essentially one of cultural segmentation but which superficially could be considered geographical segmentation. The concentration of subcultural groups into particular parts of cities again yields pseudogeographical segmentation (Herbert, 1972).

Purchasing behaviour differs with subculture. Members of subcultures often use a restricted set of institutions and utilise institutions in different fashion from the majority culture. The shopping patterns of Catholic and Protestant religious groups in Belfast, for example, are different in the shops they each patronise. Murdie (1965) has shown how in South Western Ontario travel-to-shop patterns differ between Mennonites and the majority culture. Travel distance for clothing and shoes, for example, is much shorter for the old order Mennonites than for mainstream Canadians who seek style goods in the larger, more distant, cities. In Eastern Ontario, Ray (1967) has shown that the English and French Canadian subcultures use different shopping facilities. In many developing countries where Western style retail institutions (supermarkets, etc.) operate alongside traditional retail institutions often the Euro-American immigrant subculture groups use the innovative institutions (Boyd *et al.*,

1958; Taylor, 1959).

Within the North American city, Bell (1963) has shown that Jewish consumers are more likely to purchase new products and generally innovate in purchasing behaviour. Dixon and McLaughlin (1971) point out that between Puerto Rican and Negro families in a neighbourhood in North Philadelphia

> There was a pronounced difference in shopping behaviour by cultural groups. Although the Puerto Rican families lived in the same blocks or buildings as the Negro families, only 16% of their expenditures were made in supermarkets, as compared to 39% of Negro family expenditures . . . There was also a difference in the choice among small stores between the cultural groups. The Puerto Rican families shopped mainly in the small Puerto Rican stores, while the Negro families shopped almost exclusively in the white-owned stores. (pp. 96-7).

A major cultural influence on buying behaviour in all countries is again the dichotomy between urban and rural subcultures. The density of population affects purchasing behaviour in fundamental ways (Swedner, 1962). For consumers, the journey to shop is an important component of buying behaviour and the range of alternative shops available influences the journey distance, time, mode and frequency. Much of central place theory has been built on the quite logical assumption that consumers purchase goods at the nearest shop (Berry, 1967). There is considerable evidence to substantiate this behavioural trait in rural areas but in cities it is both a less logical assumption and it has been shown to be a less common trait. Berry's study of consumer movement in South West Iowa, Mayfield's (1963) studies in India, Palomaki (1963) and Kytomaki (1973) in Finland all suggest the consistency of rural consumers in visiting nearest centres. The alternative shopping locations are so unattractive, because of the journey distance, as to be ignored. It must be noted, however, that Thomas, Mitchell and Blome (1962) found a rather more varied pattern of rural behaviour in the non-farm consumer segment. There is ample evidence from studies in metropolitan areas in North America (Brush and Gauthier, 1968; Clark, 1968; Thompson, 1964; Bucklin, 1967), Australia (Johnston and Rimmer, 1967, 1969; Short, 1970) and Britain (Daws and Bruce, 1971; Day, 1973; Davies, 1973) which suggests that urban consumers choose among a relatively wide range of perceived alternative shops and shopping centres. A sizeable proportion of urban consumers even journey to neighbouring cities to visit shops. Dawson and Kirby (1978) showed that in South Wales over 60 per cent of households in Cwmbran New Town are outshoppers for goods they could equally well purchase in their own town centre. Similar results are shown in comparable studies in the USA (Hermann and Beik, 1968; Thompson, 1971). With the greater range of realistic alternative shopping opportunities, the patterns of urban consumer behaviour in all societies are both more varied and more dynamic than those of rural consumers.

Cultural mores, institutions and customs change and so culture's influence on consumer behaviour changes but cultural factors themselves also initiate changes in consumer behaviour. At a broad international level culture is an extremely important influence on behaviour patterns (Hall, 1960). The enormous variations between oriental and occidental consumer behaviour have deep roots in the two areas. On a smaller scale the influence is less obvious but is still present. Changing cultural values about youthfulness in British society (similar to the *Greening of America*) have influenced consumer behaviour and introduced more segmentation, by age, into consumer markets. The changed level of ecological awareness has similarly resulted in different buying patterns. Far more fundamental changes have affected other cultures, for example, Japan in the era after the Second World War. The fact that culture and subculture is learnt and is not present at birth means that changes in cultural values are almost inevitable (Moore and Lewis, 1952) and as such underpin many of the changes which take place in consumer behaviour (Larson, 1970; Tax, 1956). The difficulty in this view lies in the problem of *measuring* the influence of culture on behaviour. Henry (1976), for example, associates cultural variables with social and economic variables (see below) and becomes confused over the difference between social status and stratification and the broader concept of culture. In part this is due to Howard and Sheth (1969) who argue that culture affects buying behaviour not so much directly as through intervening variables. The discussion above suggests that culture can influence consumer behaviour directly. It is usually assumed that culture is composed of attitudes and that a specific attitude yields a particular behaviour pattern (Sargent and Williamson, 1966). Relatively poor correlations have been found, however, even when the measurement difficulties have been overcome. Intuitively it would seem that to expect a one to one correspondence is oversimplifying the situation. While it is accepted that any one of several attitudes produces a particular behaviour trait it would also seem sensible to assume that any one attitude could produce any of several behavioural patterns. This latter assumption is less often accepted but is fundamental to the study of behaviour change, for in that way it would be possible to have behavioural change with or without attitudinal change.

Demographic and Social Segmentation

Many of the behaviour traits shown by consumers are the results of influence by other consumers (McNeal, 1969B). The consumer is a social animal and the social interaction among consumers results in social groupings which may usefully be used as a basis for consumer segmentation. From the social behaviour literature (Homans, 1967; McDavid and Harari, 1968) there are five common group characteristics with relevance to consumer behaviour:

(1)   groups have a common function or purpose and so may create concentrations of a very particular consumption pattern;

(2)   members of the group have specific rôles with the consequence to marketing strategy that there may be key members who influence greatly group behaviour;

(3)   members of the group have differing status;

(4)   within a group there is a class structure with an individual's class position defined in terms of status, rôle and function;

(5)   all members, whatever their class, or position, in the group interact and influence each other.

The argument for using social group consumer segmentation rests with the notion that influence within a group creates a degree of homogeneity in consumption and behaviour patterns (Foundation for Research on Human Behaviour, 1956). While this is true for some types of groups, it is not necessarily true of all types. A consumer can belong to many groups of different types and even to ones with conflicting functions.

Groups may be classified on three criteria. First is the function. Second is the degree of participation. Third is the type of membership. Similarity of function provides groups which might be expected to exhibit some broad common consumption patterns. Membership of a motoring organisation, a football club, or a temperance league will all influence an individual's consumption pattern. The concept of group function may be more nebulous than these three examples of groups with a fairly clear purpose. Even with the groups of less apparent function if the individual identifies with the group – if the group is a *reference* group – then behavioural influences exist. Stafford (1966) suggests:

Reference groups influence behaviour in two major ways. First, they influence the *aspiration levels* and thus play a part in producing satisfaction or frustration. If the other members of a particular reference group (for example, neighbors) are wealthier, more famous, better gardeners, etc., one member may be dissatisfied with his own achievements and may strive to do as well as the others. Second, reference groups influence *kinds* of behaviour. They establish approval patterns of using one's wealth, of wearing one's prestige, of designing one's garden. (p. 69).

Reference groups also relate to the second basis of group classification — degree of participation. Participation can be primary in which face to face communication occurs (Hansen, 1969). Alternatively they may be secondary in which not all members of the group ever meet. For example, political parties provide a typical secondary group while a local branch of Rotary International would be a primary group. In this latter case much of the influence on consumer behaviour would be informal with, for example, one member continually complaining about mechanical deficiencies in a particular make of car. Reference groups are more usually secondary than primary for in many cases the level of participation is very low. The consumer does not have to be a member of a reference group to be influenced by it. A consumer may visit a particular store because she thinks it is patronised by a group to which she would like to belong (Mason and Mayer, 1970). Thus, even spatial behavioural patterns may be affected by group reference beliefs. The influence of group reference on both consumption and purchasing patterns is a notably understudied area of consumer behaviour but the consumer's social perceptions would seem to be a potentially fruitful area for future research.

The third basis for group classification is in terms of type of membership — participatory, automatic, anticipatory and negative. Participating groups usually affect consumer behaviour directly; for example, standards of dress may be established within the group. Membership to automatic groups is governed by such variables as age, sex, race, education, etc. The influence on such groups is what society expects the behavioural position of an individual to be in certain circumstances (Courtney and Lockeretz, 1971). Anticipating groups are groupings of which membership is sought while negative groups are those of which membership is shunned.

These types of group and the isolation of group characteristics have been studied, very largely, within Western society. Certainly all the research on behavioural influences of these groups as consumers is set in a Western capitalist society. Groups and reference groups exist in all societies and probably will exert influence on consumption and purchasing patterns. What the influences are of the caste structure of India or of village groups in Nigeria or of any reference group in the developing world are almost totally unknown.

Age of consumer is a traditional approach to segmenting markets for both broad categories of product and individual items. Consumption, fairly obviously, varies with age (McNeal, 1964; Wallin, 1957; Zwick, 1957) but so do purchasing processes. Spatial variations in age structure are reflected in shopping provision and patterns. The retirement belt of North Wales contrasts with the large number of young adults with young families in British New Towns. Older age groups are less willing to accept innovations in distribution techniques and are more conservative about the goods they choose to buy. While studies such as those of Reinecke (1964), Wallin (1957) and Goldstein (1968) have shown the different consumption attitudes of the older age groups in the USA, Bogue (1959) has shown the spatial concentrations of the different age groups. Contrasts in purchasing behaviour have been studied less frequently. Rich (1963) has suggested that younger shoppers are more likely to become regular patrons of department stores than older shoppers of similar income and social groups, etc. This ties in with some British findings which suggest that older shoppers tend to visit the smaller shops in urban areas (Dawson and Kirby, 1978; Bradley and Fenwick, 1975) and in rural areas (Jospeh, 1977) for a relatively wide range of goods. The range of feasible alternative shopping locations and shops appears to be narrower for the more aged sections of society. This is further evidenced by a study of the acceptance of a new shopping centre in Perth, Western Australia (Dawson and Murray, 1973). In this case it was shown that younger aged households were the earliest to accept the new centre as part of their overall shopping environment while older shoppers, for some weeks, retained their shopping allegiance to small shops which were slightly more distant from their home than the new centre. The greater mobility and higher level of willingness to shop around of the younger age groups is also evident in the figures presented by Daws and Bruce (1971) in their comprehensive survey of shopping in a British city. Most of these findings represent subsidiary elements of surveys for other purposes and there have been few direct attempts to discover the differences in purchasing behaviour between old and young shoppers in either urban or rural areas.

Closely related to age is the concept of family life cycle and this has received more attention, again in North America, in classic studies by

Wells and Gubar (1966), Barton (1955) and Lansing and Kish (1957).
The most common typology segments consumers into nine classes:

(1)   Bachelor stage; young single people not living at home.
(2)   Newly married couples; young, no children.
(3)   Full nest I; young married couples with youngest child under six.
(4)   Full nest II; young married couples with youngest child six or over.
(5)   Full nest III; older married couples with dependent children.
(6)   Empty nest I; older married couples, no children living with them, household head in labour force.
(7)   Empty nest II; older married couples, no children living at home, household head retired.
(8)   Solitary survivor in labour force.
(9)   Solitary survivor, retired.

In addition it is sometimes useful to add to these groups a non-family orientated segment of the older unmarried individual not living at home and a second additional segment comprising married couple without children. In life cycle studies it is useful to distinguish between working and non-working women. The recent increases in female participation rates generally have resulted in working wives becoming a large segment of consumers with both a particular consumption pattern and well defined shopping activities (Strober and Weinberg, 1977; *Shopping Center World*, 1977; McCall, 1977).

The consumption patterns of the different segments are related to differences in disposable income over the groups, for income usually increases with age while the individual is in the labour force. The changes of family status are inescapably associated with age, and result in different consumption patterns for each segment irrespective of the income variation. In the bachelor stage there are few rigid demands and a fashion/recreation orientated lifestyle is more prevalent than in the other segments. Newly married couples have high rates of durable goods purchases while consumption patterns of families with children reflect the demands created by the children. In the later stages consumer durables are replaced and health orientated spending is more in evidence. The combination of age and family rôle create well defined demand patterns. The National Industrial Conference Board (1965) in the United States defined, for the mid 1960s consumption rates, a wide variety of products, related to the life cycle market segments. Again the spatial variation in family composition results in spatial variation in consumption. The differences, even within a metropolitan area, can be considerable with some suburbs favoured by more elderly groups and others by couples with young families, while often the bachelor groups gravitate to city centre locations. Although unstudied, it might be expected that retail provision in a metropolitan area would reflect the spatial pattern of life cycle incidence. Certainly it is not unusual to find specialist baby clothes shops in outer suburban neighbourhood centres while such shops are absent from some inner city shopping centres.

This latter feature also can be explained by the difference in purchasing patterns, as opposed to consumption patterns, of the different life cycle segments. Shoppers with young children tend to visit their local centre instead of travelling to visit stores in a city centre. Groups unencumbered by young children, the married-without-children segment for example, are willing to make longer journeys but probably shop less frequently than similar aged consumers who have families. Impulse buying is more common among the young and store/shopping centre loyalty is less developed. In the retired life cycle segments store loyalty is often very strong and personal service may be more important than competitive prices in determining store choice despite these groups having low disposable incomes. The association of the older consumer with shopping at a corner shop is explained in part by the services these shops provide. A survey of shopping habits in Norwich concluded 'elderly people and mothers with very young children preferred small, local shops' (Consumers Association, 1969). Wilmott and Young (1957) stressed the importance of corner shops as service centres for the elderly in the study of Bethnal Green, London: 'The pubs and shops of Bethnal Green serve so well as "neighbourhood centres" because there are so many of them.'

While it is argued that each segment behaves in a broadly homogeneous fashion, none the less similar segments in different cultural environments behave differently. Goldstein (1966) suggests that the older segments behave differently in urban and rural areas but it is difficult to isolate the individual factors as they relate to consumer behaviour. Behavioural processes have multivariate causation (Alexander, 1975) and even in the two factors of culture and life cycle there is considerable interaction of one on the other.

The decision making process on purchasing often takes place within the family and there is a large body of accumulated evidence on the ways decisions are reached. Most of the ideas relate to the different rôles of family members and there seems no obvious geographical component on spatial variation in these processes. Wolgast (1958) does suggest that joint decision making involving several members of the family is more likely in rural areas than urban areas. It is suggested that the urban house-wife is more likely to make positive buying decisions on her own than is her rural counterpart.

Of more relevance to the study of the spatial element in consumption and purchasing is the variable of social class. It is not proposed to discuss the definition of social class or how individuals become attached with specific class labels. Several sociological texts do this (Lasswell, 1965; Goldthorpe *et al.*, 1969). The aim here is to discuss briefly the value of market segmentation on the basis of social class as an indicator of con-sumption and purchasing patterns.

The different consumption patterns and purchasing behaviour of dif-ferent social classes is a widely used component in the development of marketing strategies (Carman, 1965). Harrods in London sets out to attract a different class of customer than does Fine Fare. The goods on sale are different and the ways they are sold are quite different. It is difficult to isolate social class influences in behaviour from those related to income for generally speaking the higher the social class the higher the income. Wasson (1969) has shown, however, that when social class (defined by occupation) is held constant there is no clear relationship between expenditure allocations and income. Alternatively a study by Myers, Stanton and Haug (1971) in Los Angeles showed that income was a better predictor than social class for low cost package food pur-chases. There is considerable variation in income within a single social class category and within a class, income variation may be greater than variation between social classes. Coleman (1960) and Frank, Massey and Wind (1972) have suggested that this income variation may be the reason for the apparent inadequacy, in some studies, of social class as an explanatory variable of behaviour. Several studies, the earlier ones summarised by Glock and Nicosia (1963) describe, however, how social class affects consumption and shopping patterns.

A study of the lower class and lower income groups in three Manhat-tan housing developments (Caplovitz, 1963) showed that lower income families are consumers of many major durables and often the more expensive brands or models. Martineau (1958) suggests

The Upper-Lower Class man sees his home as his castle, his anchor to the world, and he loads it down with hardware – solid heavy appliances – as his symbols of security. The Lower-Lower Class individual is far less interested in his castle, and is more likely to spend his income on flashy clothes or an automobile. (p. 126).

The middle classes have higher consumption of goods purchased for their symbolic value. Rich and Jain (1968) found the greatest attention to fashion clothes information among the middle social classes.

While consumption studies have tended to be based on North American society, studies of shopping patterns have also been carried out in Britain. In Britain the single most important difference in consumption between high and low status families is the ownership of a car. Car ownership provides mobility, to the higher status family, which becomes apparent in their shopping patterns. Furthermore car-borne shopping is increasing faster than car owners are. In grocery shopping in Britain 34 per cent of expenditure was made by car-borne shoppers in 1975 compared with 24 per cent in 1970. Both Thomas (1974) and Davies (1968) stress this difference. The more mobile groups are able to travel more widely to satisfy their shopping needs. Thomas (1974) suggests 'that a tendency exists for an increasingly mobile population to require a wider choice of convenience goods than is available in neighbourhood centres'. But as Davies (1976) also points out, the lower social class families tend to live at higher densities in the inner city areas where there is a higher density of shops while the higher status families live in low density suburbia where shops are relatively thinly provided:

> The longer trips in more variable directions which are usually exhibited by the higher social classes, therefore, are not necessarily always a direct reflection of class attributes (such as their greater mobility) but are often quite simply an expression of locational constraints. (p. 219).

Even accounting for the difference in provision, however, Davies is able to conclude from his study of Leeds that

> the sample consumers from the lower social class area were found to be much more dependent either on their local facilities or on the main centre of Leeds, whereas those from the higher social class area visited a wide range of centres not only in other parts of the city but also outside. (p. 219).

The use of city central areas by the higher status shopper which is apparent from the British Studies (Nader, 1969; Daws and Bruce, 1971; Schiller, 1972; Holly and Wheeler, 1972) and also in Scandinavia (Hess,

1966; Hadler, 1973; Persson, 1960) contrasts sharply with the North American position. Once again, however, the physical provision of shopping centres is important. Most North American cities are ringed by regional shopping centres which provide goods of a comparable range and quality to central city shops. Such is not the case for many European cities. Consequently in the North American city it is the lower status inner city inhabitants who shop in the CBD. Caplovitz (1963) shows this as does Halper and Debrosian's (1966) study of Fresno CBD. Caplovitz (1963) offers as a partial explanation of the limited range of shops visited by low status consumers the view that their consumption pattern conflicts with their income pattern and consequently credit is required. The low income and status makes the families bad credit risks and often the only credit they can get is from local traders to whom the consumers are known. This consumption pattern creates their shopping pattern. Lower status consumers in the North American city prefer to shop at a few local shops (Ross, 1965) and in face to face situations where they get friendly service and easy credit (Levy, 1964).

Segmentation as a Cause of Conflict

A central theme of this book is the description and explanation of conflicts that arise in the marketing system. Some conflicts in behaviour patterns have been pointed out in earlier sections but several important potential areas for conflict arise out of the social influences on consumer behaviour. Marketing plans almost invariably aim at those social groups with a relatively high disposable income. The majority of marketing effort is aimed at the middle classes. The higher prices and less varied retail provision in lower income/status areas lead to an area of potential conflict. Attempts to apply standard procedures inevitably lead to dissatisfaction from some market segments. Often conflict between social groups in terms of their consumer behaviour pattern is tied in with the interaction of cultural and social influences. Conflicts exist in Britain in cities with large migrant populations where shops have changed from distributing goods for the indigenous population to serving immigrant groups. Shopping journeys of increased length have been substituted for short journeys. At least for some groups, the known, accepted, satisfactory shopping environment has been replaced by an alien one. This situation arises in any neighbourhood which has a change in the mix of distinct market segments—a change in social structure results in conflict.

A second cause of conflict, as has been pointed out in the previous chapter, is the increase in power of one element in the marketing system. Consumers, or more precisely groups of consumers of the same social class, in recent years, have attempted to increase their influence on the traditional marketing system. Earlier attempts in North America to wield consumer power failed (Herrman, 1970) but recent developments although having middle class origins in the USA have now spread to middle class Europe and middle class Australia. There are many definitions of *consumerism* and it is a significant area of conflict in marketing. Aspects of the topic will be returned to in later chapters but 'the most common understanding of consumerism is in reference to the widening range of activities of government, business and independent organisations that are designed to protect individuals from practices that infringe upon their rights as consumers' (Day and Aaker, 1970, p. 12). The importance in the present context is that the movement began as a response to consumer dissatisfaction (conflict) over goods, quality of service and the general environment in which consumers had to operate. The early voices in the movement were middle class consumers and even now this segment remains the most important in determining norms and standards of conduct even to the extent of imposing those standards on other social groups.

Undoubtedly consumerism has had an influence on consumer behaviour and provides one example of how social variables influence and even result in change in established behavioural patterns. The very different purchasing patterns of different social groups is a basic element in controlling the consumer subsystem in any area. The social variable, with its influence on consumption, attitudes and mobility is perhaps the single most important element of the external environment of consumer behaviour.

Psychology and Segmentation

The bases for consumer segmentation discussed so far all relate to the *external* environment of the Engel, Kollat and Blackwell model. The internal influences in the model are due largely to psychological variation among consumers and this variable can be used as a basis for segmentation. Attitude formation, problem recognition, internal search and methods of information processing are all aspects of behaviour which have a large psychological component. Many of these have few if any spatial implications and will not be pursued further here. Markin (1969) provides an excellent study of these processes. Some, however, do affect the spatial behavioural patterns. Three in particular will be discussed here. First is the creation and interpretation of images of alternative shopping environments. Second are psychographic studies which segment shoppers in terms of their *total* shopping behaviour. Third are studies of the diffusion of information through a body of consumers.

Consumers frequently differ in the images they have of stores. Often image is related to social and economic variables. Wyckham (1967) has shown how different social classes have different images of department stores, while again in respect of the same type of stores Heidingsfield (1965) and Lazer and Wyckham (1969) indicate the influence of life cycle on image formation. It is sometimes difficult to distinguish between the image formed by a consumer and the image fostered and created by the store or store development itself (Marcus, 1972). The two are often related but need not be so. Despite a company's attempts to change its image it sometimes finds that the consumer view is extremely strongly held. Attempts by the Woolworth group in Britain to broaden its basic-ally *cheap and cheerful* image met with only moderate success. The images which consumers hold of alternative and competing shopping environments certainly influence their shopping patterns. Walters (1974) argues

> Young married couples, mothers and children, and shoppers in a hurry feel more at home in suburban shopping centres. The reason is that the centres have an image of casual, relaxed informality and they are conveniently located . . . Higher status shoppers look for business-es that appeal on the basis of quality and service. All customers, no matter what income or social class, have an idea of the type of stores that are compatible with their own life styles. (pp. 418-19).

Consumers not only carry and respond to images of the quality and style of stores or types of retail development but they also have images of retail locations and sites. Rich and Portis (1964) concluded that in North America store images are weaker for suburban located stores com-pared with city centre stores. While different department stores were visualised as distinctive in the city centre, their move to the suburbs has resulted in a more standardised image for all department stores. This may be partly a response to the architectural 'sameness' of suburban depart-ment stores contrasting with the individuality of many city centre build-ings.

Specific sites also carry perceptual values to consumers. There are many examples of petrol filling stations opposite one another where one is successful, the other not. North American experience suggests that there are firm images against particular sites in large shopping centre complexes. Consumers living roughly equidistant between two shopping centres tend to visit the one located to their right. Whether this is also the case in Britain where traffic is on the left side of the road has never been tested. Store location is only one further factor in the creation of store image. Design, product assortment, services, and personnel are all individual factors which help in the creation of an image. The ultimate form of this image affects the consumer's decision on whether or not to visit or not to visit the store.

Garner (1970) argues that the perceptual approach to consumer spatial behaviour studies should be advanced on four fronts. He defends a rather narrow view that the only way to advance behavioural studies is through a perceptual framework. The four prongs of attack he lists are:

(1) specification of the nature of images;
(2) the social relationship between consumers and images;
(3) the relationship between the retail provision and images; and
(4) changes that occur in images.

Undoubtedly the image held by the consumer is an important influence in behavioural patterns but it would be wrong, as Garner argues, to consider it the only determinant.

The second area of psychological segmentation lies in attempts to classify consumers according to their overall purchasing behaviour. The classic study is that of Stone (1954) who, on the basis of 150 interviews, was able to broadly categorise shoppers into four groups:

(1) the *economic* shopper who is extremely price/quality conscious and who prefers stores which are obviously efficient;
(2) the *personalising* shopper who is very aware of the service given by store staff and who prefers stores providing high levels of service;
(3) the *ethical* shopper who has a social conscience about the shopping environment patronised and feels, for example, that she should shop at the corner shop to help the small man;
(4) the *apathetic* shopper for whom shopping is a chore and who seeks to shop as quickly as possible. Locational convenience is all important for this shopper.

Stone was able to associate socioeconomic characteristics with the four different types. It does not seem impossible, however, for the four categories to overlap. A shopper who is an *economic* shopper for a major trip, say, each week may well be an *ethical* shopper for smaller purchases. Stephenson and Willett (1969) again in North America attempted a similar exercise and obtained broadly comparable results with a bargain conscious shopper, a shopper with high store loyalty, a recreational shopper and a convenience shopper. Johnston's (1974) study of Perth, Australia, also suggested a four-type classification (see Chapter 2). Again there is some similarity with the earlier studies but in this case there are no clear associations of particular socioeconomic variables with each shopper type. This study, however, extended previous work in considering the types of shopping environment patronised by the different types of shopper. The bargain orientated shopper seldom uses suburban regional centres as these are perceived as expensive. She tends to use unplanned retail streets and discount houses. The recreational shopper, on the other hand, will go to a regional centre for an outing and prefers planned centres to unplanned ones. The apathetic or satisfied shopper uses the most convenient location whatever the type of development. The pragmatic shopper tends to shy away from the very large regional centres in the suburbs but otherwise has no preferred shopping environment. There seems to be evidence for reasonably well defined groups of consumers with common shopping environment patronage patterns. The studies have tended to be of consumers in large metropolitan areas with substantial suburban retail development. Whether these same broad groups are to be found in Britain or in rural areas has never been fully explored.

The third area of psychological studies relevant to the study of spatial behaviour in consumers relates to the acceptance by consumers of changes in their shopping environment. The changes can be either in the product mix available (so affecting consumption patterns) or in retail provision (so affecting shopping patterns). The change can usually be considered as an innovation and the reaction of consumers as the diffusion of the innovation. The process of innovation diffusion is a classic form of conflict resolution. An innovation is injected into a stable or established situation so causing conflict between the *new* and the *old.* The *new* becomes accepted, to some extent, as diffusion occurs; relative power positions of the institutions change, and the conflict is resolved; a changed stable situation is created.

There is a considerable analytical and case history literature on general diffusion processes. The most general statement is by Rogers and Shoemaker (1971) who argue for four structural variables in a diffusion process:

(1) the innovation;
(2) the communication of the innovation;
(3) the social environment in which the process operates; and

(4)   time.

The early studies of the diffusion of behaviour assumed the time variable to be the critical one. Later studies have changed the emphasis to the communication factor as the process control variable. A wide-ranging review of the evolution of diffusion research is presented by King (1966) with Zaltman and Stiff (1973) bringing the review up to date. Two basic types of approach have been utilised.

The more simple approach suggests that the rate of acceptance of an innovation depends directly on the age of the innovation but a ceiling for acceptance is achieved by successively smaller increments of adopters. The number of adopters in week five is fewer than in week four and so on. Fourt and Woodlock (1960) have utilised this approach in indicating acceptance of a new product. Kelly (1967) has suggested that acceptance of a new dairy store may be modelled in that way but the criticism of this approach is its total dependence on the time factor. Differences in consumer attitudes are not included.

The second approach suggests that consumers are of different psychological types depending on their willingness to respond to communication about an innovation.

A few *innovator* types will first adopt the new product [or new environment]because of its novelty and their desire to be different. Then *early adopters* will come along who recognise its intrinsic value or convenience value. To the extent that early adopters enjoy the respect of others as opinion leaders, they are imitated by the *early majority* whose dominant value is deliberateness; these people like to adopt new products before the average member of the social system, although they rarely are leaders. Following them are the *late majority* whose dominant value is scepticism; they adopt the new product only after the weight of majority opinion has legitimatized it. Finally, the last ones to buy the products are *laggards* whose dominant value is tradition. They are suspicious of change, mix with other tradition bound people, and adopt the innovation only because it has by now taken on a measure of tradition itself. (Kotler, 1974, p. 527).

The diffusion process involves communication among these groups. The consumers are scattered over space so that although innovators may pass on the news about an innovation it will not spread evenly through a population. A further complicating factor is that the space and time variable in the basic diffusion process is to some extent interchangeable. Dawson and Murray (1973) have suggested in the case of the acceptance and adoption of a new shopping centre that the time relationship among the types of adopters has a spatial lag effect. Thus, a centre may be visited by early majority adopters who live close to the centre at the same time as innovators living at some distance from the centre.

There have been several attempts to obtain socioeconomic profiles of the different psychological adopter types but often the profiles differ depending on the innovation (Boone, 1970; Robertson, 1971; Arndt, 1968; Andrus, Knutsen and Uhl, 1971; Midgley and Dowling, 1978). In general first adopters are younger and have a higher income and higher social status than later adopters. Innovators are more mobile. They are willing to travel further on shopping visits and they also move home more often. The strategy of aiming marketing information at innovators during the launching of new products is common but making contact can prove difficult. Brown (1968) in one of the few studies of the diffusion of marketed products in a spatial framework suggests mobility as a key proxy-variable in studying psychological groupings. He cites particularly the shopping trip behaviour of potential innovators. While the acceptance and adoption processes in innovation diffusion have been studied in detail by marketing scientists as shown by Robertson (1971) a major gap in most of the studies is the lack of awareness that consumers operate over space.

Other attempts have been made to allocate market segments for market strategy purposes. The extent to which consumers move home (Andreasen, 1966) and brand loyalty (Frank, 1967) have both been used, as has the extent to which consumers buy certain product mixes (Barnett, 1969). In most cases, however, segmentation ultimately falls back on socioeconomic-psychological profile analysis. By considering, descriptively, the major bases of segmentation it is possible to obtain an insight into the environmental influences working on consumer decision processes. Not all the behavioural influences have been considered in the above discussion. Those dealt with have been related in some way to spatial variation in the consumer processes. The spatial element is present either in the different strengths of influence in different areas (concentrations of culture groups) or as an integral part of the decision process (journey to shop and shopping centre choice).

Trade Areas and Shopping Models

The final section of this chapter considers the formal models that have been developed of consumer behavioural processes. The general models discussed in the early section of the chapter provide the broad framework in which consumer behavioural patterns have been discussed. There are, however, a number of well defined statements of particular processes of behaviour. These partial models are important to an overall understanding of behaviour but their development is not yet comprehensive enough to allow aggregation into a formal general model of consumer behaviour. Many of the more sophisticated models have virtually no spatial component and are of marginal relevance to this text. These are the many models of brand choice, for example, which consider the choice of a particular brand as a general stochastic process (after a markov or semi-markov process) and which do not utilise any variable which varies spatially or has a spatial determinant.

There are two related families of model which are directly relevant to consumer processes and which have an inherent spatial component. These are models of trade and market areas and interaction theory models. The second family has grown as a special case of the first but both groups are worth attention.

The area from which a firm, whether retailer, wholesaler or manufacturer, draws its consumers has been a subject for study by economists and geographers for many years. Fetter in 1924 defined a general law of market areas:

> The boundary line between the territories tributary to two geographically competing markets for like goods is a hyperbolic curve. At each point on this line the difference between freight costs from the two markets is just equal to the difference between the market prices, whereas on either side of this line the freight difference and the price difference are unequal. The relation of prices in the two markets determines the location of the boundary line: the lower the relative price the larger the tributary area. (p. 525).

This approach has been generalised to replace the hyperbolic indifference line with a hypercircle (Hyson and Hyson, 1950) and more fundamentally the freight costs have been generalised to transport inputs (Isard, 1956) which may have a behavioural as well as purely economic component (Baumol and Ide, 1956). Other authors, notably Beckman (1968), still concentrate on transport costs as the determinant of market area size and shape. A closely related model is that of Reilly (1931) who states:

> Two cities attract retail trade from any intermediate city or town in the vicinity of the breaking point approximately in direct proportion to the population of the two cities and in inverse proportion to the squares of the distances from these two cities to the intermediate town. (p. 9).

This statement has formed the basis for a very large number of empirical studies as reviewed by Goldstucker (1965). Some of these studies lend credence to the model and some provide conflicting results (Schwartz, 1963). Many of these studies have assumed consumers to be purely mechanistic in motive and the rich variety in attitudes, demands and behavioural patterns of different types of consumers have been ignored. Such an approach is typified by the maps of national systems of trade areas (Strochkarck and Phelps, 1948). A line, on a map, purporting to show a 'trade area' has no meaning. Even when lines are drawn to show the durable goods and convenience goods areas or alternatively the primary, secondary and fringe areas they only provide a very general indication of shopping activity (Bucklin, 1971). Equally the defined 'market areas' for firms are in reality of little value. In a retail trade area it is quite possible that while some shoppers travel 2 or 3 kilometres to visit a particular store others almost next door patronise an alternative store. The reasons for this are many and the earlier sections of this chapter have pointed to the different behaviour processes of different consumer segments. It would be expected, therefore, that there will be a different trade area for each segment. It was argued, however, that segmentation is possible on a number of criteria. The number of possible trade areas thus becomes almost infinite.

An attempt to overcome some of the problems in the trade area model has been made by Huff (1962) who replaces firm trade area boundaries with a probability surface measuring the propensity of consumers to visit a particular centre. The surface is calculated through two probability processes. A broadscale process allocates a certain proportion of consumers in a given area to a particular centre. The probability of visiting a centre decreases as a function of the distance of the home from the centre. A microprocess allows an individual consumer to have assigned a particular probability for visiting a centre. This is necessary, Huff argues, because

the consumer is not able to discriminate among choices perfectly and, as a consequence, is incapable of maximizing in the sense of choosing one alternative exclusively . . . when the perceived differences among alternative choices are small, the consumer finds it difficult to discriminate among them and therefore chooses somewhat randomly . . . if a consumer is confronted with the same choice situation a number of times, he will tend to choose among such alternatives in some constant proportion. (pp. 446-7).

Within this probabilistic framework it becomes relatively easy to incorporate the different behavioural patterns of spatially concentrated market segments. The aim of such a model would then be to forecast the potential consumer attraction (and hence sales attraction) of a particular shop or centre.

From this approach has emerged the second group of models which are best termed interaction models. The family's antecedents are in the gravity type formulations of Reilly and Huff which depend on distance decay functions and the relative attractiveness of different centres as basic inputs for the model of consumer movement. The forms of the attractiveness measure and the rate of distance decay varies considerably from one model to another. The purpose of these interaction models, as with the Huff model, is to forecast the potential sales volume available to a particular store or shopping centre. The concept of lines around a trade area has been abandoned by these models. The family of models are variants on a basic approach suggested, for durable goods shopping in Baltimore, by Lakshmanan and Hansen (1965) who state that a retail centre in a district attracts consumer spending

(a) in direct proportion to the amount spent by consumers;
(b) in direct proportion to its size;
(c) in inverse proportion to the distance to the consumers;
(d) in inverse proportion to competition.

Stated formally

$$S_{ij} = C_i \frac{F_j/d_{ij}{}^a}{\sum\limits_{k=1}^{n} F_k/d_{ij}{}^a}$$

where S_{ij} is consumer retail expenditure of population in zone i spent in zone j, C_i is total consumer retail expenditure of population in zone i,

F_j is size of retail centre in zone j, d_{ij} is distance (driving time) between zone i and zone j, a is exponent applied to the distance variable,

$$\sum_{k=1}^{n} F_k/d_{ij}^{a}$$ is the summation of competition from other centres n.

The equation provides the amount spent by residents of zone i on trips to zone j. If this is summed over the i (residence) zones, it provides the amount spent in zone j by all consumers. If the equation is summed over the j shopping zones, then it provides the total amount spent by residents of zone i.

The variations on this basic model come in three types. First, are different measures of attractiveness or size of centre. Floor space is the most commonly used measure but this can be weighted for different types of shop on the assumption that a department store is more likely to attract trade than a newsagent. Alternative measures which have been used are numbers of stores and their types, or even the position of the centre in some notional hierarchy (Distributive Trades EDC, 1970). The second set of variations is related to the distance impedence. Attempts have been made to disaggregate the influence of distance on the basis of travel mode. Distance decay is then greater with pedestrian shoppers than with car-borne shoppers. Effectively the model is adjusted to take account of market segmentation. Thirdly, again disaggregation has been attempted to take account of different demand patterns of different consumer segments and to model for convenience as well as comparison goods shopping. What has not been accounted for is the willingness or otherwise of consumers to visit certain types of shop or centre. Openshaw (1975) and Scott (1970) provide a comprehensive summary of the main variations on the basic model.

With the increasing disaggregation of the model to account for the different behaviour of consumer segments so the model begins, at first sight, to approach a comprehensive model of consumer trip behaviour. There is an essential failing in this approach to producing a generally applicable model. While the original concept of the direct attraction of size and an inverse function of distance governing trip direction may be applicable at a macro level of consumer behavioural study, the increasing disaggregation of the model means that some consumer segments are no longer governed by the original simple twofold explanation of behaviour. For some segments distance is effectively meaningless and plays no part in their decision making process. Similarly for some segments, size of centre is again irrelevant, yet these segments are forced to fit into the model's strait-jacket. While disaggregation sharpens the model for some segments it introduces errors for other segments.

Despite the extensive recent work on disaggregating interaction models there is still no satisfactory model of consumer shopping behaviour. It must be remembered that the interaction model is a partial model. Two of its advantages lie in the ease with which it is made operational and the relatively small number of variables involved in its formulation. It is therefore an attractive exercise to change, in a controlled fashion, certain variables and to study the results on other variables (Evans, 1973; City of Sheffield, 1973; North West Joint Planning Team, 1974). With such experimentation it is easy to forget the limitations of the model which remains, as Wilson's (1974) description emphasises, a mechanistic derivative of extremely generalised assumptions about mass consumer shopping behaviour.

There are no simple determinants of the process of consumer behaviour. The models of behaviour, both those attempting a general statement about behaviour and those considering detailed parts of the overall process, seek to isolate individual factors which control behaviour. The patterns of consumer behaviour result from an interaction and mix of interdependent factors: 'It is no longer uncommon to find household demand studies that simultaneously take into account the relationships of fifteen or twenty household characteristics to the demand for a particular product' (Frank and Massey, 1971, p. 1). Walmsley (1974) has shown the extent of interdependence among a set of variables relating to shopping behaviour but while this, and other similar studies, are a useful first step, they do not give any indication of the associations of the effects of the variables. This is a much more difficult exercise for it is not merely one of intercorrelating variables but involves associating logical chains of events. No progress has been effected on how such an exercise in 'model addition' could even begin. But this is the sort of exercise which is needed to make headway towards a full model of consumer behaviour. There has to be a radical reorientation of research into consumer behaviour to allow the work of economists and that based in the behavioural sciences to come together. Much of the behavioural science research has not been aimed at any general statement of behaviour but has concentrated on parcelling up behaviour processes to study them in isolation. The influence of social class on car-borne shopping behaviour or the advertisement responses of an ethnic group are examples of typical studies in the behavioural science tradition. Psychology, sociology, even anthropology (Allen, 1971) are called on to describe, and sometimes explain, very particular traits. On the other hand, in economics the general topic of consumer demand has been analysed in respect of a very limited set of measures. Analysis has matured and been formalised into well developed mathematical and logical models. Yet the analyses have moved away from real world processes. Methods to combine the two approaches to consumer behaviour study would seem to be a major area for future research.

A second major area of research, and one in which progress must be made if consumer behavioural processes are to be understood, is the evolution of particular behavioural processes. There are a number of studies on the impact of behaviour of some large event—a space programme, a 20 per cent rise in a consumer's income, the opening of new shopping centre—but there are very few which consider the gradual changes which take place. A study in the early 1960s (Kosobud and Morgan, 1964) attempted this for two years but was concerned only with demand patterns. Bruce (1974) has suggested that shopping patterns are changing rapidly in Britain but the evidence tends to be circumstantial and based on studies of 'big-bang' type changes typified by the studies at the Manchester Business School (Thorpe and Kivell, 1971, 1973). Longitudinal studies and the integration of economic demand analysis with behavioural process study are merely two of many potentially fruitful areas for future research. Hodder and Lee (1974) state after a review of spatial behaviour 'that the geographical understanding of consumer behaviour is poorly developed' (p. 63). The outlook is not total gloom as Hodder and Lee suggest. There is a vast literature, as shown in this chapter, on spatially related consumer processes. What is lacking is a unifying technique to provide the integrated approach to understanding the complexities of the processes of consumer behaviour.

References

ABIODUN, J.O. (1971) 'Service Centres and Consumer Behaviour within the Nigerian Cocoa Belt', *Geografiska Annaler*, 53B, pp. 79-93.
ADAMS, W. (1968) 'The Military-Industrial Complex and the New Industrial State', *American Economic Review*, 58(2), pp. 652-65.
AGARWALA, R. and J. DRINKWATER (1972) 'Consumption Functions with Shifting Parameters Due to Socio-economic Factors', *Review of Economics and Statistics*, 54, pp. 89-96.
ALEXANDER, R.D. (1975) 'The Search for a General Theory of Behaviour', *Behavioral Science*, 20(2), pp. 77-100.
ALEXIS, M. (1962) 'Some Negro-White Differences in Consumption', *American Journal of Economics and Sociology*, 21, pp. 11-28.
ALLEN, D.E. (1968) *British Tastes* (Hutchinson, London).
—— (1971) 'Anthropological Insights into Customer Behaviour', *European Journal of Marketing*, 5(2), pp. 45-66.
ANDREASEN, A.R. (1965) 'Attitudes and Customer Behaviour: a Decision Model' in P.E. Lee (ed.), *New Research in Marketing* (Institute of Business and Economic Research, University of California, Berkeley).
—— (1966) 'Geographic Mobility and Market Segmentation', *Journal of Marketing*

Research, 3, pp. 341-8.
ANDRUS, R.R., J. KNUTSEN and K. UHL (1971) 'The Shopping Behaviour of Innovators', *University of Washington Business Review*, 30, pp. 71-5.
ARNDT, J. (1968) 'Profiling Consumer Innovators' in J. Arndt (ed.), *Insights into Consumer Behaviour* (Allyn & Bacon, Boston), pp. 71-83.
—— (1974) *Market Segmentation: Theoretical and Empirical Dimensions* (Universitetsforlaget, Bergen).
BAKER, M.J. (1971) *Marketing: an Introductory Text* (Macmillan, London).
BARNETT, N.C. (1969) 'Beyond Market Segmentation', *Harvard Business Review*, 47, pp. 152-66.
BARTON, S.G. (1955) 'The Life Cycle and Buying Patterns' in L.H. Clark (ed.), *Consumer Behaviour* (New York University Press, New York).
BAUMOL, W.J. and E.A. IDE (1956) 'Variety in Retailing', *Management Science*, 3, pp. 93-101.
BAUER, R.A. and S.M. CUNNINGHAM (1970) *Studies in the Negro Market* (Marketing Science Institute, Cambridge, Mass.).
BECKMAN, M. (1968) *Location Theory* (Random House, New York).
BELL, E. (1963) 'Consumer Innovators: a Unique Market for Newness' in S.A. Greyser (ed.), *Toward Scientific Marketing* (American Marketing Association, Chicago), pp. 85-107.
BELL, M.L. (1972) *Marketing, Concepts and Strategy* (Houghton-Mifflen, New York).
BERRY, B.J.L. (1967) *Geography of Market Centers and Retail Distribution* (Prentice-Hall, Englewood Cliffs).
BIEDA, J.C. and H.H. KASSARJIAN (1969) 'An Overview of Market Segmentation' in B.A. Morin (ed.), *Marketing in a Changing World* (American Marketing Association, Chicago), pp. 249-53.
BOGUE, D.J. (1959) *The Population of the United States* (Free Press of Glencoe, New York).
BOONE, L.E. (1970) 'The Search for the Consumer Innovator', *Journal of Business*, 43, pp. 135-40.
BOYD, H.W. *et al.* (1958) 'The Marketing Structures of Venezuela', *Journal of Marketing*, 22, pp. 394-9.
BRADLEY, M. and D. FENWICK (1975) *Shopping Habits and Attitudes to Shop Hours in Great Britain* (HMSO, London).
BRANSON, W.H. (1972) *Macro-economic Theory and Policy* (Harper & Row, New York).
BREYER, R.F. (1934) *The Marketing Institution* (McGraw-Hill, New York).
BROGOWICZ, A.A. (1977) 'Race as a Basis for Market Segmentation: an Exploratory Analysis' (Ph.D. Thesis, Michigan State University).
BROWN, A. and A. DEATON (1973) 'Models of Consumer Behaviour' in Royal Economic Society and Social Science Research Council, *Surveys of Applied Economies* (Macmillan, London), pp. 177-268.
BROWN, L. (1968) *Diffusion Dynamics* (Lund Studies in Geography, Lund).
BRUCE, A. (1974) 'Why We Shop where We Do', *Built Environment*, 3(6), pp. 280-4.
BRUSH, J.E. and H.L. GAUTHIER (1968) *Service Centers and Consumer Trips*, (University of Chicago, Department of Geography, Research Paper, 113).
BUCKER, H.P. (1966) *How British Industry Buys* (Hutchinson, London).
BUCKLIN, L.P. (1966) 'Testing Propensities to Shop', *Journal of Marketing*, 30, pp. 22-7.
—— (1967) *Shopping Patterns in an Urban Area* (University of California, Berkeley).
—— (1971) 'Trade Area Boundaries: Some Issues in Theory and Methodology', *Journal of Marketing Research*, 8, pp. 30-7.

CAPLOVITZ, D. (1963) *The Poor Pay More* (The Free Press of Glencoe, New York).
CARDOZO, R.N. (1965) 'An Experimental Study of Customer Effort, Expectation and Satisfaction', *Journal of Marketing Research*, 2, pp. 244-9.
CARMAN, J.M. (1965) *The Application of Social Class in Market Segmentation* (Institute of Business and Economic Research, University of California, Berkeley).
—— (1969) 'Some Insights into Reasonable Grocery Shopping Strategies', *Journal of Marketing*, 33, pp. 70-2.
CITY OF SHEFFIELD (1973) *A Study of Major Shopping Provision in Sheffield* (Department of Planning and Architecture, Sheffield).
CLARK, W.A.V. (1968) 'Consumer Travel Patterns and the Concept of Range', *Annals of Association of American Geographers*, 58, pp. 386-96.
COCHRANE, W.W. and C.S. BELL (1956) *The Economics of Consumption* (McGraw-Hill, New York).
COLEMAN, R.P. (1960) 'The Significance of Social Stratification in Selling' in M.L. Bell (ed.), *Marketing: a Maturing Discipline* (American Marketing Association, Chicago), pp. 171-84.
CONSUMERS' ASSOCIATION (1969) *Which?*, November, pp. 336-41.
COURTNEY, A.E. and S.W. LOCKERETZ (1971) 'A Woman's Place: an Analysis of the Roles Portrayed by Women in Magazine Advertisements', *Journal of Marketing Research*, 8, pp. 92-5.
COX, D.F. and S.U. RICH (1964) 'Perceived Risk and Consumer Decision-making' the Case of Telephone Shopping', *Journal of Marketing Research*, 1, pp. 32-8.
CRAVENS, D.W. (1969) 'The Concept of Market Segmentation', *Tennessee Survey of Business*, 4, pp. 5-14.
DAVID, M.H. (1962) *Family Composition and Consumption* (North-Holland, Amsterdam).
DAVIES, R.L. (1968) 'Effects of Consumer Income Differences on Shopping Movement Behaviour', *Tijdschrift voor Economische en Sociale Geografie*, 60, pp. 111-21.
—— (1973) *Patterns and Profiles of Consumer Behaviour* (University of Newcastle, Department of Geography, Research Series, 10).
—— (1976) *Marketing Geography* (Retail and Planning Associates, Corbridge).
DAWS, L.F. and A.J. BRUCE (1971) *Shopping in Watford* (Building Research Station, Watford).
DAWSON, J.A. (1974) 'Shopping in Exeter' (St David's University College, Department of Geography, Working Paper).
DAWSON, J.A. and D.A. KIRBY (1978) 'Outshopping from a British New Town', *Geo-journal*, 1(4), pp. 57-70.
DAWSON, J.A. and I.D. MURRAY (1973) 'Aspects of the Impact of Karrinyup Shopping Centre', *Geowest*, 1, pp. 1-63.
DAY, G.S. and D.A. AAKER (1970) 'A Guide to Consumerism', *Journal of Marketing*, 34, pp. 12-19.
DAY, R.A. (1973) 'Consumer Shopping Behaviour in a Planned Urban Environment', *Tijdschrift voor Economische en Sociale Geografie*, 64, pp. 77-85.
DEVETOGLOU, N.E. (1971) *Consumer Behaviour. An Experiment in Analytical Economics* (Harper & Row, London).
DEWHURST, J.F. *et al.* (1961) *Europe's Needs and Resources* (Twentieth Century Fund, New York).
DISTRIBUTIVE TRADES EDC (1970) *Urban Models in Shopping Studies* (National Economic Development Office, London).
DIXON, D.F. and D.J. McLAUGHLIN (1971) 'Shopping Behaviour, Expenditure Patterns, and Inner-city Food Prices', *Journal of Marketing Research*, 8, pp. 96-9.
DOMMERMUTH, W.P. (1965) 'Shopping Matrix and Marketing Strategy', *Journal*

of Marketing Research, 1, pp. 128-34.

DOMMERMUTH, W.P. and E.W. CUNDIFF (1967) 'Shopping Goods, Shopping Centers, and Selling Strategy', *Journal of Marketing*, 31, pp. 32-6.

DOUGLAS, E. (1975) *Economics of Marketing* (Harper & Row, New York).

DOWNS, R.M. (1970) 'The Cognitive Structure of an Urban Shopping Centre', *Environment and Behaviour*, 2, pp. 13-39.

DUNCAN, D.F. (1940) 'What Motivates Business Buyers', *Harvard Business Review*, 18, pp. 453-61.

EASTMAN, R.O. (1930) *Marketing Geography* (Alex Hamilton Inc., New York).

EHRENBERG, A.S.C. and G.J. GOODHARDT (1968) 'A Comparison of American and British Repeat Buying Habits', *Journal of Marketing Research*, 5, pp. 17-27.

ENGEL, J.F., H.F. FIORELLO and M.A. CAYLEY (1972) *Market Segmentation: Concepts and Applications* (Holt, Rinehart & Winston, New York).

ENGEL, J.F., D.T. KOLLAT and R.D. BLACKWELL (1968) *Consumer Behaviour* 2nd edn, 1973 (Dryden, Hinsdale).

ENGLAND, W.B. (1967) *The Purchasing Decision* (Irwin, Homewood).

EVANS, S.P. (1973) 'A Relationship Between the Gravity Model for Trip Distribution and the Transportation Problem in Linear Programming', *Transportation Research*, 7, pp. 39-61.

EVANS, W.D. (1952) 'Marketing Uses of Input-output Data', *Journal of Marketing*, 16, pp. 11-21.

FELDMAN, L.P., and A.D. STAR (1968) 'Racial Factors in Shopping Behavior' in K. Cox and B. Enis (eds) *A New Measure of Responsibility for Marketing* (American Marketing Association, Chicago), pp. 216-26.

FERBER, R. (1973) 'Consumer Economics: a Survey', *Journal of Economic Literature*, 11, pp. 1303-42.

FETTER, F.A. (1924) 'The Economic Law of Market Areas', *Quarterly Journal of Economics*, 39, pp. 520-9.

FOUNDATION FOR RESEARCH ON HUMAN BEHAVIOR (1956) *Group Influence in Marketing and Public Relations* (The Foundation, Ann Arbor, Michigan).

FOURT, L.A., and J.W. WOODLOCK (1960) 'Early Prediction of Market Success for New Grocery Products', *Journal of Marketing*, 25, pp. 31-8.

FOXALL, G.R. (1977) *Consumer Behaviour* (Retailing and Planning Associates, Corbridge).

FRANK, R.E. (1967) 'Is Brand Loyalty a Useful Basis for Market Segmentation?', *Journal of Advertising Research*, 7, pp. 27-33.

FRANK, R.E. and W.F. MASSEY (1971) *An Economic Approach to a Marketing Decision Model* (MIT Press, Cambridge, Mass.).

FRANK, R.E., W.F. MASSEY, and Y. WIND (1972) *Market Segmentation* (Prentice-Hall, Englewood Cliffs).

GARNER, R.J. (1970) 'Towards a Better Understanding of Shopping Patterns' in R.H. Osborne, F.A. Barnes and J.C. Doornkamp (eds), *Geographical Essays in Honour of K.C. Edwards* (Department of Geography, University of Nottingham), pp. 179-86.

GEORGESCU-ROEGEN, N. (1966) *Analytical Economics* (MIT Press, Cambridge, Mass.).

GIBSON, D.P. (1969) *The $30 Billion Negro* (Macmillan, New York).

GLOCK, C.Y., and F.M. NICOSIA (1963) 'Sociology and the Study of Consumers', *Journal of Advertising Research*, 3(3), pp. 21-7.

GOLDSTEIN, S. (1966) 'Urban and Rural Differentials in Consumer Patterns of the Aged', *Rural Sociology*, 31, pp. 333-45.

—— (1968) 'The Aged Segment of the Market, 1950-60', *Journal of Marketing*,

32, pp. 62-8.

GOLDSTUCKER, J. (1965) 'Trading Areas' in G. Schwartz (ed.), *Science in Marketing* (Wiley, New York), pp. 281-320.

GOLDTHORPE, J. *et al.* (1968) *The Affluent Worker*, vols. 1-3 (Cambridge University Press, London).

HADLER, A. (1973) *Inn Kjøpsvaner hos befolkningen i Fyllingsdalen* (Bergen Geographical Institute, Bergen).

HAIR, J.F., and R.E. ANDERSON (1973) 'Culture, Acculturation and Consumer Behaviour' in B.W. Becker and H. Becker (eds), *Marketing Education and the Real World* (American Marketing Association, Chicago), pp. 423-8.

HALL, E.T. (1960) 'The Silent Language in Overseas Business', *Harvard Business Review*, 38, pp. 87-96.

HALPER, D.G., and S.G. DEBROSIAN (1966) *Patterns of Retail Shopping with Special Reference to the Fresno C.B.D.* (Fresno State College, Bureau of Business Research, Study 19).

HANSEN, F. (1969) 'Primary Group Influence and Consumer Conformity' in P.R. McDonald (ed.), *Marketing Involvement in Society and the Economy* (American Marketing Association, Chicago), pp. 300-5.

HANSZ, J.E. and J.D. GOODROW (1973) 'A Multivariate Classification of Overseas Country Market Environments' in B.W. and H. Becker (eds), *Marketing Education and the Real World* (American Marketing Association, Chicago), pp. 191-8.

HEIDINGSFIELD, M.S. (1965) 'Building the Image – an Essential Marketing Stratagem' in F.E. Webster (ed.), *New Directions in Marketing* (American Marketing Association, Chicago), p. 138.

HENDERSON, B. (1964) 'The Coming Revolution in Purchasing', *Purchasing*, 20 April, pp. 72-6.

HENRY, W.A. (1976) 'Cultural Values do Correlate with Consumer Behavior', *Journal of Marketing Research*, 13, pp. 121-7.

HERBERT, D. (1972) *Urban Geography: a Social Perspective* (David & Charles, Newton Abbott).

HERRMANN, R.O. (1970) 'Consumerism: Its Goals, Organizations and Future', *Journal of Marketing*, 34, pp. 55-60.

HERRMANN, R.O., and L.L. BEIK (1968) 'Shopper Movements outside Their Local Retail Area', *Journal of Marketing*, 32, pp. 45-51.

HESS, C.F. (1966) 'Geographical Aspects of Consumer Behaviour in the Retail Service Area of Greater Aalborg', *Geographisk Tiddsskrift*, 65, pp. 1-26.

HICKS, J.R. (1939) *Value and Capital* (Oxford University Press, London).

HODDER, B.W., and R. LEE (1974) *Economic Geography* (Methuen, London).

HOLLY, B.P., and J.O. WHEELER (1972) 'Patterns of Retail Location and the Shopping Trips of Low Income Households', *Urban Studies*, 9, pp. 215-20.

HOLLOWAY, R.J., and R.S. HANCOCK (1973) *Marketing in a Changing Environment* (Wiley, New York).

HOLTON, R.H. (1970) 'Consumer Behaviour, Market Imperfections, and Public Policy' in J.W. Markham and G.F. Pananek (eds), *Industrial Organisation and Economic Development* (Houghton-Mifflin, Boston).

HOMANS, G.C. (1967) *Social Behavior; Its Elementary Forms* (Harcourt Brace, New York).

HOUTHAKKER, H.S. (1957) 'An International Comparison of Household Expenditure Patterns, Commemorating the Centenary of the Engel's Law', *Econometrica*, 25, pp. 532-5.

HOUTHAKKER, H.S., and L.D. TAYLOR (1970) *Consumer Demand in the United States* (Harvard University Press, Cambridge, Mass.)

HOWARD, J.A. (1963) *Marketing Management Analysis and Planning* (Irwin, Homewood).

HOWARD, J.A., and J.N. SHETH (1969) *The Theory of Buyer Behavior* (Wiley, New York).

HUFF, D.L. (1962) *Determination of Intra-urban Retail Trade Areas* (Real Estate Research Program, University of California, Los Angeles).

HYSON, C.D., and W.P. HYSON (1950) 'The Economic Law of Market Areas', *Quarterly Journal of Economics*, 64, pp. 319-24.

IRONMONGER, D.S. (1972) *New Commodities and Consumer Behaviour* (Cambridge University Press, London).

ISARD, W. (1956) *Location and Space Economy* (MIT Press, Cambridge).

ISARD, W., and T.W. LANGFORD (1969) 'Impact of Vietnam War Expenditures on the Philadelphia Economy', *Papers and Proceedings Regional Science Association*, 23, pp. 217-65.

JOHNSON, R.M. (1971) 'Market Segmentation: a Strategic Management Tool', *Journal of Marketing Research*, 8, pp. 13-18.

JOHNSTON, M.R., and ASSOCIATES (1974) *Perth Metropolitan Region Retail Shopping Survey 1973* (Johnston & Associates, Perth).

JOHNSTON, R.J., and P.J. RIMMER (1967) 'A Note on Consumer Behavior in an Urban Hierarchy', *Journal of Regional Science*, 7, pp. 161-6.

_____ (1969) *Retailing in Melbourne* (Australian National University, Canberra).

JONES, R.P. (1967) 'The Spanish Ethnic Market Second Largest in U.S.', *Marketing Insights*, 27 November, pp. 10-4.

JUREEN, L. (1962) 'Long Term Trends in Food Consumption: a Multi-country Study' in R.E. Frank, A.A. Kuehn and W.F. Massey (eds), *Quantitative Techniques in Marketing Analysis* (Irwin, Homewood), pp. 281-302.

JOSEPH, M.E. (1977) *The Village Shop in Mid-Wales* (St David's University College, Department of Geography, Lampeter).

KATONA, G. (1960) *The Powerful Consumer* (McGraw-Hill, New York).

_____ (1974) 'Psychology and Consumer Economics', *Journal of Consumer Research*, 1, pp. 1-8.

KELLY, R.F. (1967) 'Estimating Ultimate Performance Levels for New Retail Outlets', *Journal of Marketing Research*, 4, pp. 13-19.

KENNEDY, J.J. (1964) 'A Theory on Principles and Practices in Defense Marketing' in L.G. Smith (ed.), *Reflections on Progress in Marketing* (American Marketing Association, Chicago), pp. 449-53.

KING, C.W. (1966) 'Adoption and Diffusion Research in Marketing: an Overview' in R.M. Haas (ed.), *Science, Technology and Marketing* (American Marketing Association, Chicago), pp. 665-84.

KLASS, B. (1961) 'What Factors Affect Industrial Buying Decisions?', *Industrial Marketing*, 45, pp. 33-5.

KOSOBUD, R.F., and J.N. MORGAN (1964) *Consumer Behavior of Individual Families over Two and Three Years* (Survey Research Center, University of Michigan, Ann Arbor).

KOTLER, P. (1965) 'Behavioral Models for Analyzing Buyers', *Journal of Marketing*, 29, pp. 37-45.

_____ (1968) 'Mathematical Models of Individual Buyer Behavior', *Behavioral Science*, 13(4), pp. 274-87.

_____ (1974) *Marketing Decision Making* (Holt International, London).

KRUGMAN, H.E., and E.L. HARTLEY (1960) 'The Learning of Tastes', *Public Opinion Quarterly*, 24, pp. 621-31.

KYTOMAKI, J. (1973) 'Patterns of Consumer Travel Behavior in Southwestern Finland', *Fennia*, 124, pp. 1-112.

LAKSHMANAN, T.R., and W.G. HANSEN (1965) 'A Retail Market Potential Model', *Journal American Institute of Planners*, 31, pp. 134-43.

LANCASTER, K.J. (1966A) 'A New Approach to Consumer Theory', *Journal of*

Political Economy, 74, pp. 132-41.
—— (1966B) 'Change and Innovation in the Technology of Consumption', *Papers and Proceedings, American Economic Review*, 56, pp. 14-23.
—— (1971) *Consumer Demand: a New Approach* (Columbia University Press, New York).
LANSING, J.B., and L. KISH (1957) 'Family Life Cycle as an Independent Variable', *American Sociological Review*, 22, pp. 512-9.
LARSON, C.M. (1970) 'Changes in the Negro Market', *Atlanta Economic Review*, 20, pp. 22-3.
LASSWELL, T.E. (1965) *Class and Stratum: an Introduction to Concepts and Research* (Houghton-Mifflin, Boston).
LAZER, W. (1962) 'The Role of Models in Marketing', *Journal of Marketing*, 26, pp. 9-14.
LAZER, W., and R.G. WYCKHAM (1969) 'Perceptual Segmentation of Department Store Markets', *Journal of Retailing*, 45, pp. 3-14.
LEFTWICH, R.H. (1966) *The Price System and Resource Allocation* (Holt, Rinehart & Winston, New York).
LEONTIEF, W. (1966) *Input-output Economics* (Oxford University Press, New York).
LESSIG, V.P. (1972) 'Market Segmentation: Theory and Research', *Journal of Business Administration*, 16, pp. 69-76.
LEVY, S. (1964) 'Social Class and Consumer Behavior' in J.W. Newman (ed.), *On Knowing the Consumer* (Wiley, New York), pp. 146-60.
LIPSTEIN, B. (1965) 'Mathematical Model of Consumer Behavior', *Journal of Marketing Research*, 2, pp. 259-65.
LOWENTHAL, D. (1972) *West Indian Societies* (Oxford University Press, London).
LUNDGREN, J.O.J. (1972) 'Hotel Food Supply Systems', paper to IGU Congress, Montreal, abstract P1022.
McCALL, S.H. (1977) 'Meet the Housewife', *Journal of Marketing*, 41(3), pp. 55-65.
MacCRIMMON, K.R., and M. TODA (1969) 'The Experimental Determination of Indifference Curves', *Review of Economic Studies*, 36, pp. 433-51.
McDAVID, J.W., and H. HARARI (1968) *Social Psychology: Individuals, Groups, and Society* (Harper & Row, New York).
MACKAY, D.B., and R.W. OLSHAVSKY (1975) 'Cognitive Maps of Retail Locations: an Investigation of Some Basic Issues', *Journal of Consumer Research*, 2, pp. 197-205.
MACKAY, D.B., R.W. OLSHAVSKY and G. SENTELL (1975) 'Cognitive Maps and Spatial Behavior of Consumers', *Geographical Analysis*, 7, pp. 19-34.
McNEAL, J.U. (1964) *Children as Consumers* (University of Texas, Bureau of Business Research, Austin).
—— (1969A) 'Consumer Satisfaction: the Measure of Marketing Effectiveness', *Michigan State University Business Topics*, Summer, pp. 31-5.
—— (1969B) 'The Influence of Others on Consumer Behavior', *Southern Journal of Business*, 4, pp. 35-43.
MARCUS, B.H. (1972) 'Image Variation and the Multi-unit Retail Establishment', *Journal of Retailing*, 48, pp. 29-43.
MARKIN, R.J. (1969) *The Psychology of Consumer Behavior* (Prentice-Hall, Englewood Cliffs).
MARRON, P. (1967) 'Inter-regional Contracting – an Experiment', *British Hospital Journal and Social Service Review*, 77, pp. 2125-6.
MARTINEAU, P. (1958) 'Social Classes and Spending Behaviour', *Journal of Marketing*, 23, pp. 121-30.
MASON, B., and M.L. MAYER (1970) 'The Problem of the Self-concept in Store Image Studies', *Journal of Marketing*, 34, pp. 67-9.

MAYFIELD, R.C. (1963) 'The Range of a Central Good in the Indian Punjab', *Annals of the Association American Geographers*, 53, pp. 38-49.

MIDGLEY, D.F., and G.R. DOWLING (1978) 'Innovativeness: the Concept and its Measurement', *Journal of Consumer Research*, 4, pp. 229-42.

MINISTRY OF HEALTH (1957) *Interim Report of the Committee on Hospital Supplies* (HMSO, London).

___ (1958) *Final Report of the Committee on Hospital Supplies* (HMSO, London).

MOORE, O.K., and D.J. LEWIS (1952) 'Learning Theory and Culture', *Psychological Review*, 59, pp. 380-8.

MUELLER, E., and G. KATONA (1955) 'A Study of Purchase Decisions' in L.H. CLARK (ed.), *Consumer Behaviour* (New York University Press, New York).

MURDIE, R.A. (1965) 'Cultural Differences in Consumer Travel', *Economic Geography*, 41, pp. 211-33.

MYERS, J.G., and F.M. NICOSIA (1968) 'On the Study of Consumer Typologies', *Journal of Marketing Research*, 5, pp. 41-9.

MYERS, J.H., R.R. STANTON and A.F. HAUG (1971) 'Correlates of Buying Behavior: Social Class vs. Income', *Journal of Marketing*, 35, pp. 8-15.

NADER, G.A. (1969) 'Socio-economic Status and Consumer Behaviour', *Urban Studies*, 6, pp. 235-45.

NATIONAL INDUSTRIAL CONFERENCE BOARD (1965) *Expenditure Patterns of the American Family* (Life, New York).

NEL, P. (1969) *Income and Expenditure Patterns* (University of South Africa, Bureau of Market Research, Research Report 27, vol. 1-19).

NICOSIA, F.M. (1966) *Consumer Decision Processes* (Prentice-Hall, Englewood Cliffs).

___ (1968) 'Consumer Behaviour and Computer Simulation', *Journal of Advertising Research*, 6, pp. 29-37.

NORTH WEST JOINT PLANNING TEAM (1974) *Strategic Plan for the North West — Shopping* (Technical Paper, 17).

OLADIPUPO, R.O. (1970) *How Distinct Is the Negro Market?* (Ogilvy & Mather, New York).

OPENSHAW, S. (1975) 'Some Theoretical and Applied Aspects of Spatial Interaction Shopping Models', *Concepts and Techniques in Modern Geography*, 4, pp. 1-38.

PALDA, K.S. (1967) 'A Comparison of Consumer Expenditures in Quebec and Ontario', *Canadian Journal of Economic and Political Science*, 33(1), pp. 16-26.

PALOMAKI, M. (1963) 'The Fuctional Centers and Area of South Bothnia', *Fennia*, 88.

PEARCE, I.F. (1964) *A Contribution to Demand Analysis* (Oxford University Press, London).

PERSSON, L. (1960) *Kunderai Vallingby* (Economic Research Institute Stockholm).

PIPER, J. (1977) 'Britain's Ethnic Markets', *Marketing*, 46, pp. 18-21.

RAY, D.M. (1967) 'Cultural Differences in Consumer Travel Behaviour in Eastern Ontario', *Canadian Geographer*, 11, pp. 143-56.

REILLY, W.J. (1931) *The Law of Retail Gravitation* (W.J. Reilly, New York).

REINECKE, J.A. (1964) 'The "Older" Market — Fact or Fiction', *Journal of Marketing*, 28, pp. 60-4.

RICH, S.U. (1963) *Shopping Behavior of Department Store Customers* (Harvard University Press, Boston).

RICH, S.U., and S.C. JAIN (1968) 'Social Class and Life Cycle as Predictors of Shopping Behavior', *Journal of Marketing Research*, 5, pp. 41-9.

RICH, S.U., and PORTIS, B.D. (1964) 'The Images of Department Stores', *Journal of Marketing*, 28, pp. 10-15.

ROBERTSON, T.S. (1971) *Innovative Behaviour and Communication* (Holt, Rinehart & Winston, New York).

ROGERS, E.M., and F.F. SHOEMAKER (1971) *Communication of Innovations* (Free Press, New York).

ROSS, M. (1965) 'Uptown and Downtown', *American Sociological Review*, 30, pp. 255-9.

SAMUELSON, P.A. (1970) *Economics: an Introductory Analysis* (McGraw-Hill, New York).

SARGENT, S.S., and R.C. WILLIAMSON (1966) *Social Psychology* 3rd edn (Ronald, New York).

SCHILLER, R.K. (1972) 'The Measurement of the Attractiveness of Shopping Centres to Middle Class Luxury Consumers', *Regional Studies*, 6, pp. 291-7.

SCHWARTZ, G. (1963) *Development of Marketing Theory* (South Western Publishing Co., Cincinnati).

SCOTT, P. (1970) *Geography and Retailing* (Hutchinson, London).

SETHI, S.P. (1971) 'Comparative Cluster Analysis for World Markets', *Journal of Marketing Research*, 8, pp. 348-54.

SHAFFER, J.D. (1960) 'The Influence of "Impulse Buying" or "in-the-Store" Decisions on Consumers' Food Purchases', *Journal of Farm Economics*, 42, pp. 317-24.

SHOPPING CENTER WORLD (1977) 'Big Differences in Shopping Habits of Working and Non-working Women', *Shopping Center World*, 6(9), pp. 12-14.

SHORT, K.C. (1970) *Shopping Patterns in Newcastle, N.S.W.* (Hunter Valley Research Foundation Monograph), p. 33.

SIMON, B.A. (1970) 'Analyzing Government Markets' in V.P. Buell (ed.), *Handbook of Modern Marketing* (McGraw-Hill, New York), pp. 2-54.

SHUBIK, M. (1970) 'A Curmudgeon's Guide to Microeconomics', *Journal of Economic Literature*, 8, pp. 410-31.

SLATER, C. *et al.* (1969) *Market Processes in the Recife Area of Northeast Brazil* (Michigan State University, East Lansing).

SOMERMEYER, W.H., and R. BANNINK (1972) *A Consumption-savings Model and Its Application* (North-Holland, Amsterdam).

SORRE, M. (1962) 'The Geography of Diet' in P.L. Wagner and M.W. Miakesell (eds), *Readings in Cultural Geography* (University of Chicago Press, Chicago).

STAFFORD, J.E. (1966) 'Effects of Group Influences on Consumer Brand Preferences', *Journal of Marketing Research*, 3, pp. 68-75.

STEPHENSON, P.R., and R.P. WILLET (1969) 'Analysis of Consumers' Retail Patronage Strategies' in P.R. McDonald (ed.), *Marketing Involvement in Society and the Economy* (American Marketing Association, Chicago), pp. 316-22.

STERN, N. (1972) 'The Optimal Size of Market Areas', *Journal of Economic Theory*, 4, pp. 154-73.

STIGLER, G.J. (1954) 'The Early History of Empirical Studies of Consumer Behaviour', *Journal of Political Economy*, 62(1), pp. 95-113.

STONE, G.P. (1954) 'City Shoppers and Urban Identification: Observations on the Social Psychology of City Life', *American Journal of Sociology*, 60, pp. 36-45.

STROBER, M.H., and C.B. WEINBERG (1977) 'Working Wives and Major Family Expenditure', *Journal of Consumer Research*, 4(3), pp. 141-7.

STROCHKARCK, F., and K. PHELPS (1948) 'The Mechanics of Constructing a Market Area Map', *Journal of Marketing*, 14, pp. 493-6.

SWEDNER, H. (1962) 'Prediction of Differences in Habits and Attitudes towards Service Establishments in Rural and Urban Settings', *Rural Sociology*, 27, pp. pp. 396-417.

TAX, S. (1956) 'Changing Consumption in Indian Guatemala', *Economic Develop-*

ment and Cultural Change, 5, pp. 147-58.

TAYLOR, D.A. (1959) 'Retailing in Brazil', *Journal of Marketing*, 26, pp. 55-9.

THIEL, H. (1971) *Principles of Econometrics* (North-Holland, Amsterdam).

THOMAS, C.J. (1974) 'The Effects of Social Class and Car Ownership on Intra-urban Shopping Behaviour in Greater Swansea', *Cambria*, 2(1), pp. 98-126.

THOMAS, E.N., R.A. MITCHELL, and D.A. BLOME (1962) 'The Spatial Behavior of a Dispersed Non-farm Population', *Papers of the Regional Science Association*, 9, pp. 107-33.

THOMPSON, D.L. (1964) *Analysis of Retailing Potential in Metropolitan Areas* (University of California, Berkeley).

THOMPSON, J.R. (1971) 'Characteristics and Behavior of Out-shopping Consumers', *Journal of Retailing*, 47, pp. 70-80.

THORPE, D. and P.T. Kivell (1971) *Woolco, Thornaby: a Study of an Out-of-town Shopping Centre* (University of Manchester, Retail Outlets Research Unit, Report 3).

—— (1973) *The Hampshire Centre, Bournemouth: A study of an Out-of-Town Shopping Centre* (University of Manchester, Retail Outlets Research Unit, Report 6).

TUCKER, W.T. (1967) *Foundation for a Theory of Consumer Behaviour* (Holt, Rinehart & Winston, New York).

UDELL, J.G. (1966) 'Pre-purchase Behavior of Buyers of Small Electrical Appliances', *Journal of Marketing*, 33, pp. 50-2.

VAN DER REIS, A.P. (1966) *Motivational Factors in Bantu Buying Behaviour* (Bureau of Market Research, University of South Africa, Research Report 15).

WALLIN, D. (1957) 'A Marketing Profile of the Senior Citizen Group' in R.L. Clewett (ed.), *Marketing's Role in Scientific Management* (American Marketing Association, Chicago), pp. 250-61.

WALMSLEY, D.J. (1974) 'The Simple Consumer Spatial Behaviour System', *New England Research Series in Applied Geography*, 38.

WALTERS, C.G. (1974) *Consumer Behavior: Theory and Practice* (Irwin, Homewood).

WASSON, C.R. (1969) 'Is It Time to Quit Thinking of Income Classes?', *Journal of Marketing*, 33, pp. 54-6.

WEBSTER, F.E. (1969) 'Industrial Buying Behavior: a State of the Arts Appraisal' in B.A. Morin (ed.), *Marketing in a Changing World* (American Marketing Association, Chicago), pp. 256-60.

WEIDENBAUM, M.L. (1968) 'Concentration and Competition in the Military Market', *Quarterly Review of Economics and Business*, 8, pp. 16-22.

WEIMAR, J., and P. STEVENS (1974) *Consumers' Preferences, Uses, and Buying Practices for Selected Vegetables* (US Department of Agriculture, Washington, DC).

WELLS, W.D., and G. GUBAR (1966) 'The Life Cycle Concept in Marketing Research', *Journal of Marketing Research*, 3, pp. 355-63.

WILMOTT, P., and M. YOUNG (1957) *Family and Kinship in East London* (Pelican, Harmondsworth).

WILSON, A.G. (1974) *Urban and Regional Models in Geography and Planning* (Wiley, London).

WOLD, H., and L. JUREEN (1952) *Demand Analysis* (Almquist & Wiksells, Uppsala).

WOLGAST, E.H. (1958) 'Do Husbands or Wives Make Purchasing Decisions', *Journal of Marketing*, 23, pp. 151-8.

WOOD, L.J. (1974) 'Spatial Interactions and Partitions of Rural Market Space', *Tijdschrift voor Economische en Sociale Geografie*, 65(11), pp. 23-34.

WYCKHAM, R.G. (1967) 'Aggregate Department Store Images: Social and Experimental Factors' in R. Moyer (ed.), *Changing Marketing Systems* (American

Marketing Association, Chicago), pp. 333-7.

YNEU, Y. (1964) 'An International Comparison of Consumption Functions', *Review of Economics and Statistics*, 46,(3), pp. 279-94.

ZALTMAN, G., and R. STIFF (1973) 'Theories of Diffusion' in S. Ward and T.S. Robertson (eds), *Consumer Behavior, Theoretical Sources* (Prentice-Hall, Englewood Cliffs), pp. 416-68.

ZWICK, C. (1957) 'Demographic Variation: its Impact on Consumer Behavior', *Review of Economics and Statistics*, 39, pp. 451-6.

4 THE ORGANISATION OF RETAIL DISTRIBUTION

Within the European Economic Community there are 2.5 million shops. In the USA there are a further 1.75 million. Numbers in the developing countries are more difficult to estimate as few countries have undertaken retail censuses, but estimates by Lakdawala *et al.* (1963) for Bombay, in the early 1960s, suggest around 100,000 shops which suggests, for India alone, shop numbers far in excess of those for the EEC (NEDO, 1973). These figures relate only to shops. There is also a wide range of other types of retail establishment both fixed and moving. Hong Kong has at least 50,000 hawkers and pedlars (Tse, 1974; McGee, 1970, 1974); the market in Tananarive, capital of the Malagasy Republic, has in excess of 3,000 stall holders (Donque, 1965). Ukwu, in studies in Nigeria, estimates that in Onitsha main market there are around 3,000 stalls, with many used by more than one trader, and when non-stall traders are included the market has at least 8,000 sellers (Hodder and Ukwu, 1969). Generally, national estimates of the *total* number of all types of retail establishments are not available, even in Western industrialised countries. A probable underestimate is provided in the USA with almost 20 per cent of registered firms being classified as in the retail trades. Farmers sell produce at the farm gate, automatic vending machines are becoming common in public places and mail order supplies account for an increasing share of retail trade in many countries. In considering the retail institutions in the market channel, therefore, there appears a great variety of business types. The total numbers involved are simply not known but they are extremely large compared with other economic sectors.

Functions of Retailing

One reason for the large numbers is that retail businesses are usually small. The Bolton Committee (1971) on small firms suggested that in Britain 96 per cent of all retail establishments could be classified as small. Retailing is a refuge for small firms in all economies, even in the closely controlled economies of China and USSR. Only in a few Western industrialised countries have large firms developed in or moved into retailing and even in the USA where this process is most advanced they operate only between 15 and 20 per cent of fixed shops although they are responsible for a much larger percentage of retail sales. Many of the major retail companies have grown from very small shop origins (Ferry, 1960; Mahoney, 1955).

Large businesses are few in number. In Great Britain in the mid 1970s there were fewer than 200 retail firms with a turnover in excess of £10m. In many industrial sectors these firms would only be classified as of moderate size. The majority of retail firms have only one or two workers who own and operate the retail enterprise. Almost all retailing in the market places in developing countries is carried on by enterprises with only one or two workers. Retailing is 'based upon small-scale supply units reaching small-scale demand units with minimal accumulation in between' (Belshaw, 1965, p. 64). One reason behind the small scale of operation is the general ease of entry and exit from retailing. Little capital is involved in starting trading and closure can take place at a moment's notice. Consequently while the overall numbers of firms involved in retailing changes only slowly there is a constantly changing membership of the retail sector. There are several analyses pointing to the extent of business openings and closures in Western societies but few from the developing world. Classic studies in the USA in the 1930s, several of which are reviewed in Dawson and Kirby (1979), showed how, in many cities, the life expectancy of a shop was quite low with fewer than 10 per cent of shops operating for ten years or more. Studies also showed how the stable total population changed; for example Greer (1936) indicates that from 1920 to 1933 in Chicago and out of a total of just over 6,000 butchers' shops, an average of 1,169 meat stores opened each year but each year 1,164 closed. More recent evidence suggests that birth, death and survival rates are not much less in present day conditions (Schell, 1964; National Commission on Food Marketing, 1966; McEvoy, 1972).

It is quite possible that in retailing in the developing world, birth and death rates of retail businesses are even higher and survival rates lower for there is often need of even less capital to enter the retail system in such countries. A Bombay study of fixed shops, which are probably the most capital intensive sector of retailing in the city, shows that fixed capital represents only 18 per cent of total capital compared with figures of over 60 per cent for manufacturing industry (Lakdawala and Sandesara, 1957; Lakdawala *et al.*, 1963). Total capital per firm was a factor of 12 times lower in retailing than in manufacturing. A sample of hawkers showed that virtually no capital was needed by this group with an average capital per firm (in 1963) of 167 rupees compared with 7,157 rupees for retailing and 88,966 for manufacturing industry. In rural markets several studies, for example in the survey provided by Bohannan and Dalton (1962) of Africa, and the older Guatemalan studies by Tax (1953), attest to the low capital commitment to retailing and with many part-time traders in periodic markets the only capital is the working capital accounted for by the articles on sale.

The retail component of the marketing system consists of a large number of small firms practising a wide range of business activities. The main feature which differentiates retailing from other parts of the marketing system is that it is the part of the channel where consumers do most of their purchasing. Retail institutions are intermediate between final household consumer and either wholesaler, manufacturer or producer. The consumers most in contact with retailers are household consumers although occasionally government and industry buy from retail institutions, but the main functions of retailing lie in servicing households. For most consumers the retail institution is their direct connection into the marketing system.

The functions of the retailer, as seen by North American Marketing Scientists (Bearchell, 1975; Markin, 1971; Dalrymple and Thompson, 1969) are buying, selling, storage, bulk breaking, risk sharing, display, information, credit extension and service. The central function is the aggregation of assortments of goods to make them available, in small lots, for the consumer. It becomes necessary to anticipate consumer demand and to have available what Baronoff (1964) terms a *concentrated variety* of goods for the convenience of consumers. It must be pointed out that the variety of goods on sale varies considerably from institution to institution. At one extreme is the general merchandise department store while at the other is the part-time marketeer selling personal agricultural supplies in a periodic market. The function of selling in small lots is illustrated by Belshaw (1965): 'Peasant market places facilitate trading in small lots, so small indeed that at one time, when currencies were introduced into West Africa, special coins were struck subdividing the penny into tenths' (p. 77). While the retailers' primary function is to provide a service to consumers they also serve producers and wholesalers by storing goods until they are needed, assuming credit risks and providing a product service.

There is an inevitable cost of these functions and the cost is usually paid by the consumer as the primary beneficiary. The extent of retail costs varies considerably both in respect of type of retail institution and commodity on sale. Some institutions do not perform many of the traditional retail functions and provide minimal levels in respect of the others. The cost of retailing is reduced. A hypermarket in a Western society performs fewer functions than a department store and consequently can reduce prices for the consumer. In a developing country a market trader provides fewer functions than a fixed shop and is similarly able to reduce the costs of retailing and pass on a price advantage to the consumer. The central difference between retail institutions is often the mix of retail functions each performs. There was much debate in the 1930s on the costs of distribution, including retailing, with some argument that retail costs were excessively high (Stewart and Dewhurst, 1939; Lengyel and Beecroft, 1949). The proliferation, in the last 20 years, of different types of retail institutions has reduced the debate as different institutions have widely differing cost compositions depending on the selection of functions each performs. The gross margin, which is the difference between purchase and sale price, in retailing is approximately an overall 30 per cent in the USA and Britain but the figure varies considerably for different commodities and for different selling methods (Hughes and Pollard, 1957; Douglas, 1975; Gardner, 1969) as well as for different regions. In the Republic of Ireland Census, statistics show that the gross margin of fixed shops in the Dublin area was 25 per cent but in Connacht in the West it was 5 per cent lower. There are many reasons for such differences but regular spatial patterns of gross margin do occur. Within many retail sectors there exists a mix of retail institutions offering a broad range of functions and consumers can decide the relative value of using the different retail types.

Retail Organisations and Selling Methods

In fulfilling the function of retailing, institutions place themselves relative to a number of axes of variability. First is a scale axis with poles of the large retail business and the small. Poles on other axes are store and non-store retailing, urban and rural, and general and specialist. A large, urban, fixed store general retailer is typified by Harrods department store in central London. At the other extreme is a farmer's wife selling surplus bananas laid on the ground in rural periodic market in Uganda. Most other institutions lie somewhere between these extremes.

In considering retail businesses as part of the marketing channel it is important to distinguish between the organisational form of the business and the method of selling. In almost all economies it is usual to distinguish three forms of retail organisation, *consumer co-operatives, multiple retailers* and *independent retailers.* Changes in the last 15 years in the independent organisations mean that this broad group has split into two. There remain the independent retailers but there are also *voluntary group retailers.* If the Soviet bloc is also considered then *government controlled retailers* provides a fifth group.

The consumer co-operative movement originated in the late eighteenth and early nineteenth centuries in Britain. The history of the movement is well documented (Holyoake, 1875; Gide, 1921; Smethurst, 1974; Harrison, 1969) and co-operative stores were operating in Hull, Brighton and Chatham before 1830. Present-day consumer co-operation philosophy stems from 1844 and the Rochdale Pioneers Society in Lancashire. The essence of consumer co-operatives lies in the ownership and management responsibility of the shop residing with members of a society of consumers. Profits from retail sales are distributed by the consumer society which often decides to pay the profits, in some way, to members of the society. So the consumers effectively control this form of organisation. The precise form this control takes and the responsibilities of consumer members differs from country to country where consumer co-operatives are allowed to operate. Consumer co-operatives in the Soviet Union, for example, are mainly confined to rural areas (Liniichuk, 1965; Samsonov, 1972) and have an executive structure quite different from British or Swedish consumer co-operatives, but control is retained in all cases by the consumer. Consumer co-operative retail organisations are well developed and comprise sizeable sections of retailing in many European countries and particularly in the United Kingdom, where in the mid 1970s they account for 7 per cent of sales, Sweden (18 per cent), Denmark (11 per cent) and Finland (35 per cent). They represent virtually the only form of retailing throughout most of the rural areas of Eastern Europe and the Soviet Union. In many of the developing countries, notably those with former colonial links with Britain, important consumer co-operative sectors have developed in the retail trades (Lombard, 1971; Hawkins, 1965). In North America and Australia there is an almost total absence of this form of retail organisation.

The second form of organisation comprises the multiple retailer business type. This form is limited to capitalist economies, and mainly to the industrialised nations. The organisational form consists of firms operating through several retail outlets (Lebhar, 1963). Many countries have rule of thumb definitions. For example in 1961 in Britain multiple retailers were defined as businesses operating through five or more retail establishments, but in the 1971 Census the critical number became ten. Control of the organisation resides in the hands of persons who may or may not be producers or consumers of the goods handled. A chain of stores may be controlled by one person or through a group of shareholders. The chain may be part of a large commercial/industrial conglomerate or it may itself comprise the total business of the firm. The aims of the firms included in this form of organisation are very varied but creating profit is usually high on the list of company aims.

The third form of organisation consists of the independent retailer.

While making a profit is certainly an aim of this group, other aims, such as creating employment for the owner operator, are often important. In most non-communist countries independent retailers comprise the dominant form of retail organisation. Frequently they are smallscale and operate through one, or a very small number, of outlets with the owner(s) taking direct and personal control of retail operations. In many instances this represents a type of worker control of the firm.

A variant on the independent retailer occurs when several of these firms co-operate for certain specialist activities (Fullop, 1962). Groupings of independent retailers, voluntarily made, have emerged in North America and Europe, as a significant organisational form. These associations, like the multiple retailers, are virtually limited to the capitalist based industrial nations and have a variety of organisational structures sometimes even with wholesalers having part control (see Chapter 5). The emergence and development of this form is largely a response to the competitive conflict between independent and multiple forms and represents action taken by independents to resolve conflict in their favour.

The final form of organisation is the state controlled retailer. The government store network in the USSR is.the single most important example of this organisational form (Goldman, 1963). Within the USSR there is a wide selection of stores, both specialist goods shops and department stores, for the consumer to visit. Within the urban areas everyday control of the store network resides with the local city trade department (*torg*) but this committee is ultimately responsible to the Republic Ministry of Trade. The state effectively operates the urban shop network. The Ministry of Trade is also responsible for wholesale distribution and, in theory, this overall control of distribution makes for more efficient marketing.

Distinct from the form of organisation is the selling technique adopted in the retail business. Some examples of different selling techniques are supermarketing, department store retailing, hawking, automatic vending, market stall retailing, door to door retailing and mail order. Probably the most common selling method is counter retailing which is the technique adopted in the majority of fixed shop premises. A firm in any type of organisation can use any selling technique. Within the British Consumer Co-operative movement mobile shops, counter service and selfservice stores, hypermarkets and supermarkets are all used to retail goods. Conversely supermarkets are operated by firms of every organisational type and this is true even within Britain if supermarkets in camps and depots of the armed services are classified as a state controlled organisation form. Similarly, in the large urban street markets in cities in the developing world the traders may belong to consumer co-operatives or to multiple retail organisations or may be completely independent. The latter are undoubtedly the most common but other organisations are present although stall layout, selling method, even the goods on sale do not differ over the organisation types.

It is important to distinguish between selling technique and organisational form because the patterns of conflict in retailing and optimal locations for firms differ depending on these two variables. Conflict occurs among selling methods and organisation forms but the conflict differs in the two cases. Two supermarkets may be in competition with each other and may resolve their conflict by giving trading stamps, promotions, price cutting or any of a number of other methods (Holton, 1957; Holdren, 1960; Udell, 1964; Markin, 1965; Cassady, 1962). Similarly, there may be conflict between different selling techniques. Supermarkets, traditional stores and hypermarkets, in the last few years in France, for example, have been in strong competition and conflict (Liepman, 1972; CRPC, 1973). The conflict between organisational forms is at a rather broader level with, for example, independent traders in conflict with chain stores in the USA or state trading conflicting with independent traders in Eastern Europe. This type of conflict can be resolved outside retailing by reference to legal procedures or the imposition of governmental policies, such as Resale Price Maintenance on the retail sector (Palamountain, 1955) (see Chapter 8).

Locational criteria differ by selling technique and organisational form. The criteria used in the market trader's decision as to where to locate in a periodic market are quite different from those of a potential hypermarket operator but both traders aim to maximise sales. Clearly then, locational decisions are individual to selling technique (Nelson, 1958; Kane, 1966; Kornblau, 1968). Equally organisational form affects the decisions locating retail operations. State controlled stores networks have different preferred locations to independent retailers. The decisions involved in optimising the location of one shop are quite different from those necessary to optimise a network of shops. The different responsibilities of the varied organisations also create different locational pressures. Within the consumer co-operative movement, for example, often the philosophy of consumer control leads to a location convenient to members of the society of consumers responsible for the shop. The Italian consumer co-operative sector consists of a large number of small convenience stores operated through over 4,000 societies because direct local control is written into the constitution of the Italian Consumer Co-operative Union (Ravazzi, 1967). Alternatively, the multiple retailer

sector in Italy seeks locations in the centres of large cities or in key suburban sites in the industrial cities of the North. The locational requirements and patterns differ for the various organisational forms.

Neither organisation nor selling technique is a static concept. Both
change constantly. The emergence of the voluntary association organisation form has already been noted as a response to conflicts between
existing organisations. The forms of organisation tend to change slowly,
taking several decades to evolve. Selling techniques exhibit a more
revolutionary pattern. Change occurs with the successive appearances
of new techniques which individually are almost completely evolved.
For example, mail order retailing has not changed fundamentally since
its emergence as an acceptable method of retailing. On appearance new
techniques often diffuse through a culture and even through several
cultures. It is sometimes useful to distinguish between selling techniques
which are restricted to a particular society and others which can be
termed megacultural. The supermarket transcends many cultures and
operates in Accra, Bangkok, Caracas, Denver or Exeter in much the
same fashion, although inevitably there are local, socially, economically
and politically derived variations. As such it is an institution of a world
wide megaculture. In distinction hawkers operate extensively in Asian
cities but hardly at all in urbanised Europe, North America or Australia.
Automatic vending has the opposite distribution pattern while techniques
such as rack-jobbing are even more culturally circumscribed.

The pattern of retailing in a society results from economic competition
and other forms of conflict among the organisations and selling techniques represented in the society. The evolution of organisations or the
introduction of new techniques creates a disruption in the equilibrium
of the retail subsystem of the marketing system. The disruption is
resolved in some way and equilibrium returns. The remainder of this
chapter is concerned with these conflicts and their resolution.

Evolution of Retail Organisations

The majority of firms in retailing are independent organisations. Within
the countries of Western Europe there is a mixture of organisation types
with the balance of power among the three major types (consumer co-
operative, multiple and independent) changing slowly but steadily in
favour of the multiple retailers. In Britain in 1900, Jefferys (1954)
estimates that 90 per cent of retail sales through fixed shops were accounted for by independent retailers. By 1975 this proportion had fallen to
almost half and the multiple retailers, from having 4 per cent of sales in
1900, accounted for 45 per cent of sales in 1975 (Economist Intelligence

Unit, 1976). Figure 4.1 shows the changes which have taken place since 1900. The graph underestimates the extent of change in respect of the multiple sector. In 1961 definitions changed and a stricter definition of the multiple retail firm was introduced. Applying the earlier definition (five or more branches) to 1971 figures shows multiples to be accounting for 48 per cent of sales. Using this definition it would be estimated that well over half retail sales in Britain pass through the multiple retail organisations who are fewer than 2 per cent of all retail firms.

The rise to power of the multiple retailer has been the outstanding feature of the changing organisational structure of retailing in Britain. Although the notion of a chain of stores was not unknown to British business, for firms such as the Hudson's Bay Company had utilised the chain store idea for many years, it was not until the mid nineteenth century that multiple retailers began to operate to any degree in British cities. Furthermore it took them until the 1920s to establish themselves fully in all trades and for effective trading to occur through a national network of stores. Alexander (1970) points out that lock-up shops in Victorian Britain were rare and that retail managers operated their own shop rather than managed one for someone else.

> But tradesmen with shops in big towns very often extended their operations to neighbouring towns and villages, if only temporarily and from a market stall or the back of a wagon. The most common multiple shop concern in this period (i.e. 1850) consisted of a main shop in a market town or large village with satellite shops in surrounding villages. The satellite shops were staffed by relatives, partners and trusted shopmen, and were supplied from the central shop in order that the system might be under direct control of the tradesman. (p. 103).

Organisationally, therefore, these shops differed little from the independent trader and it is hard to argue for them having a radically different organisational structure. Even the few companies which operated non-local branches, usually high class retailers with branches in several Spa towns, remained firmly under the executive control of the owner and were supplied from the main shop and not directly from wholesaler or manufacturer (Adburgham, 1964).

In the late nineteenth century the railways opened up the possibility both of maintaining effective control over a chain of spatially separated shops and of supplying several shops with essentially the same stock. Thus, W.H. Smith and Son and J. Menzies began to build a chain of

Figure 4.1: The Changing Shares of Retail Sales by Organisational Type in Britain

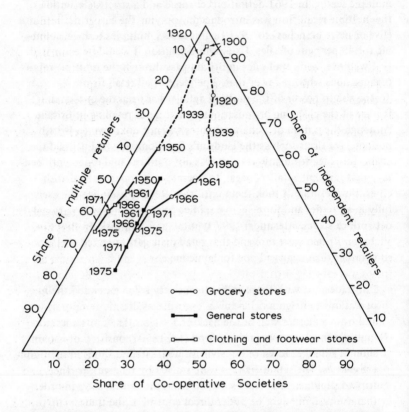

bookstalls, many actually on railway stations. The policy of multiples to hold a relatively narrow range of goods in shops at strategic locations is well typified by the early newsagent and bookseller chains. Jefferys (1954) estimates that by 1875 there were, at a minimum, 29 firms operating just under 1,000 shops.

The extension of the built up area of most British cities in the last quarter of the nineteenth century provided a base for multiple store growth. Fixed shop retailing and market stall retailing (Blackman, 1963; 1967) in the early nineteenth century had become concentrated in central city locations with consumers having to travel increasingly longer distances to visit shops. Wild and Shaw (1974) suggest almost 60 per cent of shop premises were in the central area of Hull in 1823. With suburban expansion, 'The multiples took the shops outwards to the consumers . . . The multiples were largely concerned with the narrow and relatively inflexible demands of the working classes and price and convenience were of great importance' (Stacey and Wilson, 1965, p. 43). Inevitably multiple retailers developed in the convenience goods trades particularly food, tobacco, chemist preparations and footwear products.

A third factor responsible for the establishment of multiple retailer organisations and one seen by Braithwaite and Dobbs (1932) as of major importance was the standardisation of products and the supply, in bulk, of cheap mass produced, sometimes imported, factory products. In the late nineteenth century Joseph Hepworth of Leeds began a regional network of men's clothes shops and other essentially regional networks of specialist stores developed in the early years of the twentieth century; so, for example, Scotch Wool and Hosiery Stores Ltd had over 200 branches by 1910.

In Britain by 1914 the multiple retailer sector was established but was not constituting any major threat to either the consumer co-operative stores or the independent retailers. Within cities multiple retailers operated a very small proportion of shops (Whysall, 1974) and overall accounted for a small fraction of total trade. Consumer spending in almost all trades was growing sufficiently strongly to allow chains to develop without impinging on the trading patterns of the independent sector. While there was competition among the three organisational forms it was not until the 1920s and 1930s that it became aggressive and caused conflict (Hough, 1949). The emerging multiples, at the turn of the century, were in potential conflict as insecure new entrants attempting to break into an established market. The potential for conflict among firms in the multiple sector was considerable. Boswell (1969) details a typical situation around 1900 and its resolution in respect of Sainsbury's, the grocery chain:

> In the climate of trading it was natural for firms to make mutual defence arrangements to protect their interests . . . Their [i.e. 8 small multiples] pact included the mutual benefits of bulk buying and an understanding that they would not encroach upon each other's territory by opening branches in close proximity.

This type of collusion, together with agreements to offer shops to fellow members of the pact should one multiple decide to sell out, protected emerging multiples from organised competition.

The interwar years in Britain constitute the period of major expansion of the multiples and the first serious signs of conflict among organisational types. Many of the smaller chains expanded by obtaining stock market raised finance and attempting a national coverage. Often this was achieved by amalgamation and takeover within the multiple shop sector. The large firms so created had considerable bargaining power in negotiations over supplies and McClelland (1967) points out that the power of the large multiple retailer to buy at low prices lies as much in withholding large orders from wholesalers and manufacturers as it does in placing the large orders. The increase in numbers of stores operated by chain retailers created a more extensive network and so increased the amount of competition between multiple retailers and other organisations. Scott (1970) describes the diffusion pattern of several non-food firms and Thorpe (1963) has shown the extent to which particular multiple retailers gained representation in almost all major British town centres. Unlike the early multiple traders who opened branches in centres close to the main shop and office, the expansion policies in the 1920s and 1930s sought a saturation cover (Mathias, 1967). With a wide representation multiple retailers became a major competitive element in high street retailing. The presence of Woolworths, Smailes (1953) remarked, was so critical as to determine whether a town had full urban status within the Smailes hierarchical scheme.

A second source of conflict stemmed from the attempts of multiple retailers to move 'up market'. Conflict particularly with independent retailers occurred with 'the widening of the appeal of multiple shop retailers so that this type of retailing was effective in a number of different markets instead of being concentrated as in the pre-1914 period on the working class market' (Jefferys, 1954, p. 88). The fall off of earlier increases in retail sales also meant that there was less opportunity for retail expansion, yet expansion occurred in the multiple sector. Again, many independent retailers began to feel the impact of multiple competition and began to lose custom (Smith, 1937). A loss of competitive strength, retail power and status led to conflict. Despite the depressed nature of trade, independent shopkeeping remained an economic sector with a very high birth rate. The ease of entry allowed many smallscale operators to open stores. The majority traded for only a few months yet there were just as many openings as closures. Many of these marginal entrepreneurs were unwilling to accept that they were responsible for their own failure and blamed the expanding, and obviously successful multiple store sector.

A fourth factor brought multiples into conflict with the consumer co-operatives. The multiple retailer organisation developed extremely flexible operating methods and, with its primary aim of optimising profitability, was able to close branches and open at a new site, or shift stock to operational branches. Poor selling lines in one branch could be moved to other branches where sales were more likely. The consumer co-operative sector, in contrast, had a responsibility to its members to trade at a particular location and in many cases the Management Committee and members could insist on a certain level of provision and even a particular mix of stock. The element of social responsibility implicit in consumer co-operatives often made them slow to respond to changes (Carr Saunders, Florence and Peers, 1938). In providing shopping facilities in new suburbs, for example, the co-operatives were often slow off the mark and key sites had already been taken by multiples before co-operatives made a decision to open a store. The traditional co-operative approach contrasted and conflicted with the aggressive management methods of the chain store organisation.

The major result of the conflicts involving multiple retailers in the 1920s and 1930s was an increase in their industry power and market share. Most conflicts were resolved to the benefit of the multiple retailer sector. The basic strength of the multiple became the realisation of economies of scale with the multiplication of standard retail units with centralised buying. With the large orders placed by multiples special rates could be negotiated and chains were able to exert considerable influence on suppliers, without actually owning them. In some cases, notably in the chemists, grocery and footwear trades, vertical integration occurred both forward by manufacturers and backwards by the retailers themselves (Levy, 1942). Partially as an attempt to stop the passing on of price concessions resulting from preferential purchasing rates by the multiples, price fixing became common. Although Resale Price Maintenance (RPM) blunted the competitive edge of the multiples it allowed them to increase profits and so their financial power (Yamey, 1966). This enabled them to expand the store network. While RPM protected prices and enabled the independent store parity of price competition with the multiple, the power base of the independent retailer was weakened by the growing multiples. It was inevitable, at least with hindsight, that once the multiples became strong enough they would seek the abolition of RPM. The advocacy of RPM by independent retailers as a method to resolve the conflict with multiples was partially successful with in 1939 around 30 per cent of all consumer goods sold in Great Britain having fixed prices (Jefferys *et al.*, 1950). Kuipers (1950) estimates that at the same time 20 per cent of grocery goods sales were subject to RPM. As well as protecting the independent trader, however, RPM also protected the multiple retailer from price cutting competition.

The continued growth of multiple retailing resulted in the same inter-organisational conflicts occurring in the 1960s and 1970s as were present in the 1920s and 1930s. Again the contrast is between small independent retailers with little individual purchasing power and the large central buying facilities of multiple retailers. The larger firms with more capital were able to introduce retail innovations designed to cut costs and increase profits. The independents lacked both capital and the ability to tap the scale economies realised by the multiples (Dawson and Kirby, 1979). The attempts to resolve the conflicts have been rather different in the last 20 years.

The gradual abolition of RPM, speeded by the 1964 Act, allowed increased competition in retailing and encouraged new retail techniques to develop. The search for lower costs and higher profits, mainly through price competition, allowed selfservice shops, supermarkets, discount stores and hypermarkets to open and flourish. Competition among these institutions, many of which are operated by multiple retailers, has been a major feature of retailing in the 1960s and 1970s. Both the increased number of multiple branches and the legal freedoms to engage in price wars have resulted in price and non-price based conflicts among the various multiple retail firms. The introduction and extension of trading stamps as a means of competition serves as an example (Fullop, 1964; Coldstream, 1963). Scrambles to obtain key sites have been common-place notably in the multiple sector. The conflicts over location have been controlled, to some extent, by land use planning legislation, so the availability of optimal sites for some institutions have been carefully controlled (Mills, 1974). Out-of-town locations have been particularly carefully controlled. The value of the M4-M5 intersection close to Bristol as a possible hypermarket or shopping centre location brought forth five major applications for permission at the one site which event-ually, after a long planning appeal, resulted in the Carrefour Company obtaining permission and opening their Patchway Store (Steen, 1972).

To improve their own market position multiple retailers have pur-sued a number of quite different policies. All are aimed, however, at improving their competitive position. Thorpe and Rhodes (1966) have shown how in the Tyneside conurbation different grocery multiples operate contrasting locational policies. Some seek key sites in major centres and aim to offset the high site costs with sophisticated operating techniques. Other multiple retailers locate in the smaller shopping centres of the conurbation and operate through a chain of smaller stores. It seems likely that this spatial rationalisation of competition occurs in other con-urbations with regional chains operating in the smaller centres and national chains, with their larger capital backing, locating in the major centres. A second policy followed by many of the multiples has been the closure of the smaller branches and the concentration of activities into existing or new large units. Expansion of a multiple by the takeover of another firm often means a closure of the small, less profitable shops. Table 4.1 shows figures for the numbers of stores operated by Tesco which is one of the major grocery chains in the UK. Proportionally and absolutely

Table 4.1: Number of Stores, by Size, Operated by Tesco Company in the UK

		Gross floor Area (ft^2)			
	2000	2000-4999	5000-9999	10000-19999	20000
1966	270	131	63	31	0
1972	274	245	180	69	23
1978	138	204	171	102	65

there are fewer small stores in the chain in 1978 than in 1966. This pattern is repeated for most multiple retailers. A third policy, which is partly tied to the increase in store size, is the product diversification of many multiple retailers. Nielsens (1976) estimate that 84 per cent of British multiple grocery shops sell ladies' tights while 76 per cent sell light bulbs. Limited lines of many non-food products are sold increasingly in grocery shops as multiples seek a competitive advantage over other multiples and other organisations.

The conflict between multiples and independents has resulted in many independents attempting to copy the selling methods of the multiples. Selfservice, supermarkets and hypermarkets are all operated by independent traders. Shop size has increased and stock distributions have been widened. In addition, a major response has been the growth of formal and informal associations of retailers for special functions. Mention has already been made of the growth of voluntary chains of retailers linked to wholesalers. These organisations seek to obtain similar types of scale economies to the multiples in providing the wholesaler with the combined buying power of many, perhaps several hundred, retailers. The retailer members of the organisation lose some of their independence but are able to enter price competition with the multiples.

The independent trader has tried to resolve the conflict with the multiple in other ways. Non-price competition has been increased. The independent frequently is able to offer higher levels of service by open-

ing longer hours, providing a social function for customers, allowing
credit and organising deliveries. A survey of small retailers in three
British cities in 1976 showed the considerable extent to which independents compete in this way. (Berry, Dawson, Kirby and Mair, 1976).
Some retailers seek to bring back RPM or request government help in
other ways through preferential taxes or assisted exit schemes. Public
policy makers have been slow, perhaps deliberately, in acting as referees
in the current bout of independent-multiple conflict.

The net result of the growth in power of the multiple retailer is shown
in Figures 4.1 and 4.2. Multiples have increased their market share but
not to the same extent in all parts of the country. Chain store expansion
is associated with twentieth century urban growth. Almost two-thirds
of grocery sales in South East England are accounted for by the multiple
sector while the figure is less than 40 per cent in the North West. Urban
population increase is only a part of the reason behind the distribution
of relative market shares. Some recent changes in market shares have
been considered by Kirby (1974, 1975). Hall, Knapp and Winsten (1961)
in their analysis of the 1950 census of distribution showed how multiple
shop sales share varied systematically with total size of town. The larger
the town, the larger the sales share of the multiple retailer organisation.
The national generalisation breaks down when regional systems of cities
are analysed. If a broadly similar analysis for 1971 is attempted, then
the relationship is absent even at a national level. Since 1950 the multiple
sector has grown in strength and has become important in some small
towns; consequently the systematic association between town size and
multiple sales is no longer present. Figure 4.3 shows the scattergram for
a sample of 127 towns with a population above 20,000. The wide scatter
of values for percentage of sales through the multiple sector is readily
apparent. The correlation coefficient r is 0.18. The mean value for the
percentage is 37.2 and the standard deviation is 14.2. Even in 1971 a
few small towns had no multiple retailer representation but in some
small towns well over half of sales were through the multiple sector.
While the New Towns have a high figure for multiple penetration there
is no apparent general pattern to the scores and local factors seem all-
important in determining the extent of the multiple retailer involvement
in a town.

The emergence and development of multiple retailer organisations in
Britain has been dealt with at some length here as it highlights a number
of typical sources of conflict in retailing. The emerging power of a new
organisational concept creates a disruption of the *status quo*. The conflicts often are resolved only partially. When the relative power bases of

Figure 4.2: The Proportion of Retail Shop Sales through Multiple, Independent and Co-operative Shop Sectors in Britain, 1974

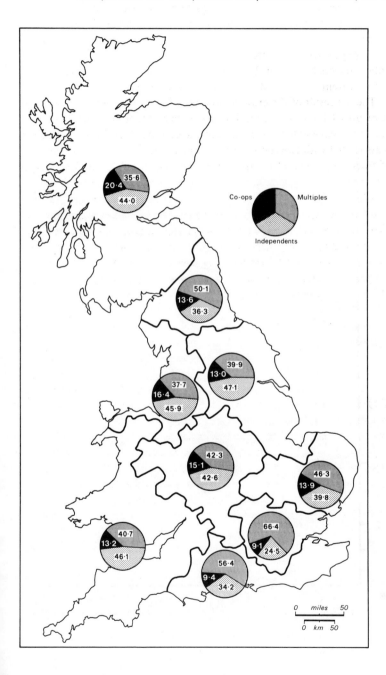

Figure 4.3: Proportion of Sales in the Multiple Sector and Town Size for a Sample of British Towns—1971

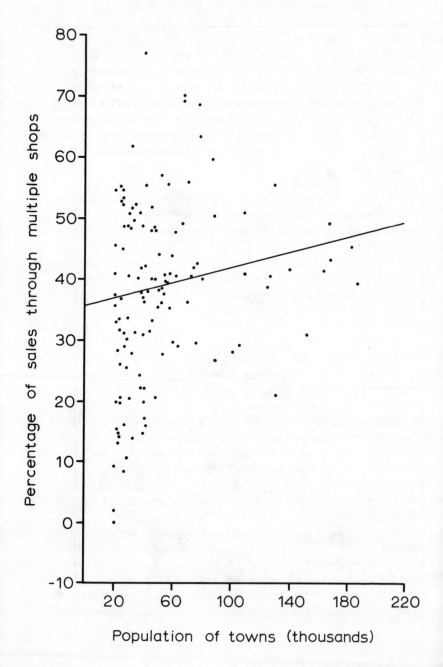

the organisations change yet again, often the same type of conflict arises and new compromises have to be found. Imperceptibly, and over the long term, permanent changes occur in the relative power of different organisational groups.

These broad patterns, as well as many of the detailed causes and resolutions of conflict seen in respect of British multiple retailers, are apparent in the development process of multiple retailers in other countries. There is a full literature on the independents' fight against the chain store in 1930s America (Beckman and Nolen, 1938; Converse, 1931; Furst, 1932; Schmulz, 1931; Vaile, 1932). There is also extensive documentation of the rapid pace of chain store growth as major firms emerged after takeover programmes (Federal Trade Commission, 1935, 1948; Nystrom, 1930; Nichols, 1940; Lebhar, 1963). Again in North America the independent traders sought RPM type legislation and regressive chain store taxation and Palamountain (1955) provides a classic study of public policy resulting from interorganisation conflict. The parallel with Britain remains with the movement into voluntary association type organisations (Federal Trade Commission, 1966; Cohen, 1961; Swann, 1970; Hansen, 1965), increases in operating scale and the shedding of small outlets (Wingate and Corbin, 1956; Gross, 1969; Mueller, 1973) and the locating of shops for particular market segments (Applebaum, 1964, 1965; Kinney, 1969; Green, 1961; Sexton, 1973; Brown, Applebaum and Salmon, 1970).

Throughout Europe in the 1930s there was distrust of chain stores and even positive legislation against them. In Denmark retailers were not allowed to establish more than one store in the same city or community and this law restricted severely chain store development (see Chapter 8). Limited growth occurred over most of Europe but the independent retailer organisation can be argued to have been stronger than the chain stores in several countries (Jefferys and Knee, 1962). Boddewyn (1971) shows how in Belgium the collective action of independent retailers effectively resolved chain store conflicts in favour of the independent sector. In the second phase of development in the 1960s and 1970s the chain stores have fared better and have been able to use their capital raising powers to invest in the new retail techniques. In several countries independent retailers have turned to voluntary associations (OEEC, 1960) or have sought help from legislators. Generally, they have not achieved antichain store legislation but have obtained help for themselves in other ways (Boddewyn and Hollander, 1972) and in particular in capital loan, accelerated closure (Roy, 1971) and even direct subsidy schemes (Kirby, 1976C). Detailed discussion of governmental rôles in this type of conflict is left until Chapter 8. The discussion on the previous few pages has centred on conflicts central to the emergence of multiple retailer organisations but a comparable type of analysis is possible for the consumer co-operative sector in most Western free enterprise economies.

Throughout the richer countries of the world the independent retailer has lost market share consistently over the last 50 years. In the developing world independent traders dominate retailing. In a few countries since about 1960 other organisations have emerged but they are still of a very secondary nature. Within the independent sector, however, there is considerable competition between retailers and particularly between different selling methods.

A good example of the strength of independent traders in retailing is provided in many of the Caribbean retail systems. Within Haiti, with a 3.5 million population, there are at least 65,000 independent market traders as well as several thousand part-time traders who are peasants producing and selling surplus goods. Mintz in a series of studies (1957, 1959, 1961, 1964) has analysed in detail the internal marketing system in Haiti. The professional market traders, termed *revendeuses*, often take on regular customers for whom they perform particular retail services or to whom they will give price concessions. The Haitians term this trading partnership concept *pratik* and this forms one of the strengths of the system and provides defence against competition from other organisational forms. Within a situation of apparent complete competition with many buyers seeking to purchase a small amount from one of many small sellers, *pratik* effectively ties particular consumers to individual traders and so allows the trader to be sure of some sales. Pure competition is limited in this fashion. Competition is still keen but some of the inherent risks of pure competition are reduced.

Several studies have shown the similarities in retailing over several Middle American economies and in all cases independent traders are dominant. (Nash, 1961; Foster, 1948; Kaplan, 1965). Even in the urban areas (Pyle, 1970; Waterbury, 1970) where a range of retail techniques operate, it is independent traders who have introduced and now manage the new methods. In Haiti there is an important Syrian and Lebanese minority who engage in trading; in Jamaica, Chinese traders have a similar role (Mintz and Hall, 1960). Essentially similar patterns are apparent elsewhere. Lawson (1971) points to the importance of Lebanese traders in technical innovation in retailing in Accra and in particular in the introduction of supermarkets to the city while Van der Laan (1975) and Bayley (1962) provide other examples of the minority group elsewhere in West Africa. In many Asian communities Chinese minorities are important in retailing (Cameron and Sutherland, 1975). In all these cases it is the independent trader, sometimes from immigrant stock, who holds the majority of the market share.

Change is occurring slowly in the developing countries with the introduction of both state operated retailing and multiple retail organisations. Norton and Symanski (1975) describe how in Jamaica the state sponsored Agricultural Marketing Corporation is developing a chain of retail stores on the island. In the last six months of 1974 the number of stores in the chain increased from nine to 23. Little attention is being paid to the impact this new organisation is having on the traditional independent retail sector but the chain's growing retail power will create conflicts within the established channels of the retail and wholesale system (Katzin, 1959, 1960). The availability of relatively large amounts of capital to chains, compared with the independent trader, means that expansion is inevitable and equally inevitable will be a reduction in number and market power of small traders. When and how they will react will become apparent over the years. In Accra the state shop network is both smaller and more specialised. In 1966 there was a chain of 16 fish shops operated by the State Fishing Corporation but this represents a very small section of the fixed shop sector of only 400 shops and an even smaller element when compared with the 15,000 or more independent market and street traders. The large size of the independent sector reduces the potential for conflict.

While the state network has become established in some countries, in others multiple retailers have prospered in rather similar fashion to North America in the early years of the century. A detailed study of marketing reform in Puerto Rico (Riley *et al.*, 1970A) provides a history of the development of retail grocery chains on the island: 'Harold Toppel, a U.S. citizen, visited Puerto Rico in late 1954 and became interested in opening a supermarket. He returned to open his first store in 1955, and to establish the Pueblo Supermarket chain' (p. 95). By 1965 the chain had 12 stores and had negotiated special agreements with wholesalers and had secured its channels by vertical integration. The parallel with chain store development in the USA is clear. Subsequently a second American financed chain has moved to the island. There appears to have been little reaction from independent traders owing probably to the lack of organisations to voice their comments. In 1970 a voluntary chain type organisation began trading but this was mainly an attempt by middle sized independent fixed shop retailers to come to terms with supermarket competition and its value to the small trader is minimal.

So far competition is essentially between the different retail techniques rather than among the different organisations involved in retailing.

The introduction of the new organisational forms in Puerto Rico was a result partly of the activities of government in encouraging their birth. The governmental blessing bestowed on chain store development contrasts with the situation in the developed countries. Carson (1967) points to governments elsewhere encouraging chain store growth. The Turkish government in 1955 invited the Swiss food chain Migros to enter the Turkish grocery market. By the end of 1964, Migros were operating 16 selfservice food stores. In rather similar fashion, Carrefour, the French hypermarket company, have opened new stores in Brazil and were involved in establishing a hypermarket in Gabon. While not operating a major chain in any single developing country they have introduced mass retail techniques and multiple retail organisations to several places. The hypermarket in Libreville, Gabon, was opened in 1975 but is now owned by another French based multiple (Libre Service Actualité, 1976). The store does not impinge much on the main body of independent retailing but does provide a possible glimpse of future developments. The spread into the developing world of the Euro-American pattern of retail evolution could take place before the end of the century and it is conceivable that the now well established independent trader organisation will be gradually superseded by chain stores and state operated store networks. The chain store is well on the way to becoming a *megacultural* organisation.

A one world orientation in the retail structure is also predicted by those who point out that consumers in developing economies gradually evolve the same needs and desires as their more advanced neighbours. These observers also remind us that vendors require the same conditions in all countries; in fact, the same international firms are the vendors in many different countries. Basic data for predictions about comparative retailing structures around the world are very meagre; but it is probable that retailing in severely underdeveloped nations will take thirty or forty years to reach the present stage of retailing in western countries. (Crawford, 1969, p. 77).

Retail Technique and Society

No area of marketing reveals as much about a people as retailing. Habits of living, thinking, eating, working, dressing and behaviour are all reflected in these aspects of retailing: types of retail outlets, size, location, and appointments . . . ; assortments, quality, and prices of merchandise and services, kinds and quality of advertising, sales promotion, and selling; and sales services. In almost all nations there is some representation of the most advanced retail institutions and methods, such as department stores, supermarkets, self-service, and vending machines. Yet in many parts of the world these forms of retailing are restricted to a small segment of the population, typically urban elite, and, in some places, confined largely to foreign enclaves. (Carson, 1967, p. 309).

The techniques of retailing are closely related to many aspects of society. Shopping behaviour often is an extremely stylised social activity as was shown in the previous chapter. Whether we are concerned with an economy with very peripheral marketing activity, for example the Australian aborigine, or with a totally market orientated society as in the USA, shopping institutions are stylised and retailing can take on almost ceremonial functions. The weekly evening produce market in rural Northern Nigeria, the department store in nineteenth century British cities or the supermarket in the USA each provoke action-reaction type behaviour similar to ceremonial activities in connection with religion or sport or any other fundamental activity in society. The society, in its attitude to the shopping act, effectively creates retail techniques. As society changes so also does retail technique. Within the Western capitalist style development model, techniques change from highly personalised ones in which retailing takes place in the house of the seller and involves face to face contact and a high degree of social interaction to techniques such as automatic vending in which retailing is depersonalised and involves the absolute minimum of social interaction.

Within a society there appear to be two major factors involved in establishing the mix of retail techniques. The first can be termed economic and the second cultural. The economic factor differentiates retailing techniques by the comparative spending power of the consumers and the closely related phenomenon of the level of personal mobility. Economies of high mass consumption and high levels of mobility—typified by the USA—are able to sustain techniques requiring both major capital spending and a large number of people to support them (Bucklin, 1972). The particular balance between spending power and mobility is important; one without the other creates a particular mix of techniques. The mobile shop, serving for example housebound young marrieds with small children in suburban Britain or the dispersed agricultural population in parts of Switzerland, shows how a technique may be successful in subcultures with a high spending power but low mobility. Low available spending power creates techniques requiring scant fixed or working capital so that a high proportion of the margin is effective profit. The daily and periodic markets and part-time retailers in the developing world may be considered in this fashion. The low mobility coupled with low spending potential can mean that periodic markets, operating on a market ring (effectively moving markets), allow a retailer moving in the ring both to have access to enough potential sales and to reduce the mobility needs of consumers (Stine, 1962).

The second fundamental variable in the society has been termed culture. In considering segmentation of consumers in the previous chapter it was pointed out that different culture groups exhibited different consumption patterns and shopping habits. Within plural societies contrasting retail techniques have developed to serve the culture groups. Lawson (1971) shows how the development of supermarkets in the early 1950s in Accra essentially was to cater for non-African households. Within South Africa governmental policies have related particular retail types to specific ethnic groups, for example, the Bantu trading stores (Wales, Winkie and Bak, 1963; Thorelli, 1968). Baker (1965) points out that in Lagos department stores and supermarkets carry a product range designed to appeal to the expatriate population. These cultural contrasts are not limited to developing countries because in America or Britain there is considerable contrast between retailing in urban and rural areas and between the inner city and suburbs. Techniques suited to urban culture may fail totally in rural areas.

Increasingly, however, individual retail techniques are multicultural in nature but the relative importance of different techniques still has an important cultural dimension. The Hudson's Bay Company general store in Northern Canada is not technically different from the Booker McConnell store in the Caribbean islands. Supermarkets have diffused around the world in basically the same form but the supermarket's importance varies considerably. Arndt (1972A) maintains that there is a sequence of technical development in retailing with societies placed somewhere in this sequence. Over time the society's mix of retail techniques develops in a fashion preconditioned by what has happened previously in other societies. Based on studies in Norway, Arndt (1972B) further claims that it is possible to predict many of the likely changes in retailing by direct application of what happened elsewhere earlier. Wadinambiaratchi (1972) after studying retailing in Ceylon similarly argues for a deterministic developmental model of retailing with six stages. First is a tribal stage when there is little infrastructure and monetary economies are virtually non-existent: 'During this stage consumer needs are rudimentary, and the predominant retail outlets are itinerant traders' (p. 397). A second stage encompasses peasant societies with basic consumer needs and often quasifeudal social organisation. 'During this stage the predominant retail outlets are exchange markets, with a few itinerant traders, and fewer country storekeepers' (p. 397). The third stage is termed early commercial. Commerce is organised barter and cash exchange and expatriate groups operate in imports, exports and retailing. Urbanisation remains low and 'During this stage country storekeepers predominate with a few itinerant traders and a lesser number of general stores' (p. 397). These first three stages correspond to the threefold categorisation by Bohannan and Dalton (1962) into 'market-less economies, economies with peripheral markets and economies in which the market principle is dominant' (p. 16). The remaining stages of Wadinambiaratchi are: a highly commercial stage where fixed general stores and a few specialist stores dominate retailing, an early industrial stage in which specialised stores develop, and a highly industrialised stage when 'mass merchandising stores become the predominant outlets with few product specialized stores' (p. 398).

While Arndt and Wadinambiaratchi may outline successfully a framework which describes the emergence of new methods, the models do not account for the actual mix of techniques which operate. In some societies there remains apparently a considerable legacy from earlier development stages; in others, the new techniques displace almost totally former practices. Paris, for example, has 16 covered markets and 52 open markets, compared with only 13 official markets (and additionally 30 private markets) in London. London on the other hand has a far higher number (about 8,000) of itinerant traders, operating in designated streets, than has Paris (approximately 1,200). Both market and street trading are techniques, which, according to Wadinambiaratchi, are more typical of peasant or early commercial stages of retail development. None the less, in Paris they account for an estimated 45 per cent of greengrocery sales in the city. Kirk, Ellis and Medland (1972) suggest that one reason behind the difference between conditions in London and Paris is the quite different political and legal background to retailing in the two cities. In many industrial societies the retailing of fish, fruit and vegetables is often carried on in traditional market situations. In the larger Italian towns over half the sales of these three commodities pass through street trading or market stall retailers (Moss, 1958). Other examples could be taken to show that the mix of techniques in societies broadens with economic development and as new techniques diffuse through societies. But the operational mix and relative importance of retail techniques within a society is related probably more to cultural, including political, factors than to purely economic ones.

Further criticism may be made of the developmental models of Wadinambiaratchi and others (Cundiff, 1965; Douglas, 1971; Coolsen, 1963) in their suggestions that the early stages of development are characterised by simple market structures. Many studies of 'primitive' marketing systems in peasant societies show retailing practices to be far from simple. Recent literature on periodic markets has shown a highly complex set of retail institutions (Smith, 1976; Symanski and Bromley, 1974; Tinkler, 1973; Wood, 1975).

In North East Brazil the traditional retail network within food retailing consists of three types: periodic markets, legal and illegal permanent markets, and permanent and temporary fixed stores. More recent innovations include company stores on sugar plantations, selfservice stores in the larger towns and specialist shops (Forman and Riegelhaupt, 1970; Slater *et al.*, 1969B). If non-food retailing is included the list of operating retail techniques becomes longer. The range of techniques is not untypical of many agriculturally based societies. The integration of these many techniques creates a very complex retail system.

The periodic markets are collections of itinerant sellers using nonpermanent structures and operating in a designated place at a set time. Three types occur in North East Brazil and similar forms are seen elsewhere:

> *The feira de consumo* is a rural Market Place in which goods and services are distributed in areas of poor access among rural populations with limited capital. Each *feira* is a cyclical market which meets once a week, the day depending largely upon the primary economic activity of the area it serves. For example, fairs in the coastal lowlands are usually scheduled on Saturdays and Sundays in order to take advantage of Friday paydays at the sugar mills. (p. 195).

There are three major groups of retailers at these markets. A few peasants sell their own produce and with the cash purchase their own consumer needs. Secondly, peasants sell their own produce and goods bought from others. A third group are full-time retailers who sell products purchased elsewhere. This mixture of occasional and regular, full- and part-time traders is typical of many periodic market networks in Africa (as described, for example, by Bohannan and Dalton, 1962; Hodder and Ukwu, 1969; and Jackson, 1971); or in Asia (Folke, 1967). There is, therefore, more than one type of retail institution represented in a periodic market. Just as town centres in Western cities contain a mix of retail institutions, particularly in respect of retail technique, so in periodic markets several selling techniques are represented. Clearly they will not be the same techniques present in periodic markets as in town centres and it would be sensible to expect that a different mixture of selling techniques would be present in North East Brazil from that in West Africa or Melanesia. There may be techniques common to all periodic market systems—as, for example, the family operated small counter service food store supplied by a traditional wholesaler is a common retail technique to most Western town centres. Locations of retailers within the consumer market in North East Brazil is well ordered, again a typical feature, with specific areas assigned to specific goods. There is a relatively rapid turnover of stock with most of the stock sold in a single day. The professional retailer may carry stock from market to market but for many sellers stocks are cleared on the market day. The periodic consumer market in North East Brazil, in common with many other areas, persists and this, in part, is owing to lack of mobility of the rural population. Absence of access roads to peasant holdings means that produce has to be brought out on foot and consequently is transported a limited distance.

The second type of periodic market is the distribution fair from which professional retailers purchase some of their stock, but many retailers also sell goods in these large markets. These markets, therefore, are combined wholesale and retail markets and are located in the larger cities. Good (1970) in a study of Uganda also found that some periodic markets sold direct to consumers and also acted as wholesale markets, in Good's case, for retailers from a nearby large town. Within North East Brazil both urban and rural retailers purchase from this second group of markets.

The third type of periodic market is the urban consumer market which meets on specific days of the week and is appended to a permanent market (*mercado*). On market days many small retailers, but also a few peasant producers, join regular retailers in the permanent market. A similar situation of enlargement of permanent markets is found in most large cities elsewhere in Latin America (Bromley, 1974; Slater *et al.*, 1969A; Riley *et al.*, 1970B) and in tropical Africa and Asia. The periodic market system in North East Brazil shows many features common to other systems but it also exhibits differences and a mix of markets and institutions not exactly the same as in other areas.

In contrast to many systems there is no real hierarchical structure to the market network. Goods do not move specifically from market to market and hierarchically through markets from peasant producer to urban consumer. Producers tend to supply each market level direct rather than through wholesalers collecting from the smaller markets, bulking, and then moving goods to larger markets. The markets in Java studied by Dewey (1962) exhibit a well developed intermarket whole-sale movement and this is often thought typical of periodic market systems (Donque, 1966). The feature is absent from North East Brazil. This shortening of channels, direct purchasing and bypassing the whole-saler is typical more of industrial societies than of traditional ones. Within North American marketing, for example, retailers increasingly purchase direct from the producer.

A feature not explained in North East Brazil by Forman and Riegel-haupt (1970) is the spatial pattern of periodic market cycles. The basis of a periodic market system is that markets operate on different days of the market cycle, so eliminating direct competition and allowing some retailers to travel a regular sequence of markets. This travelling retailer, operating on a fixed cycle, is considered by some authors as the only selling technique present in periodic markets. Skinner's (1964) analysis of markets in China outlines a distinct cycle of markets

in which a merchant can move between the central market and a pair of standard markets in a ten-day cycle divided into units of three: the central market (day 1), first standard (2), second standard (3), central (4), first standard (5), second standard (6), central (7), first standard (8), second standard (9), and central on day 10, when no business is transacted. (Berry, p. 95).

Figure 4.4 shows this pattern diagrammatically. These market traders operate a 10 day week with each market visited three times per week. Market traders' periodicity varies considerably and Fagerland and Smith show how periodicity in West Africa varies from two-day markets to eight-day markets in a relatively small area (Figure 4.5). Within the area covered by this map there appears to be little relation between periodicity and such factors as forest and savannah areas. Hill (1966) suggests that 'in earlier times, before the introduction of the northern Islamic week, it would have happened that the market-week gradually lengthened as northerly latitude increased' (p. 306). The reason for market weeks of different length is still largely unknown.

Within different societies periodic marketeers operate both from dif-ferent types of premises and according to different retail procedures. In

Figure 4.4: The Market Cycle Described by Skinner in China

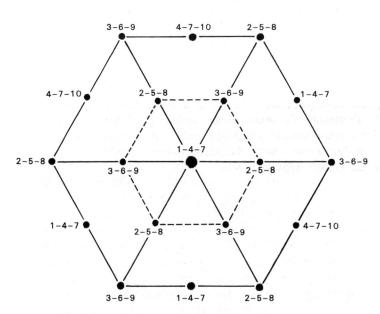

numbers represent market days within a 10 day cycle

much of East Africa the rural markets are located at transport inter-sections usually outside villages. There are few, if any, buildings. Good (1970) describes Rugando market in Uganda:

> The actual dimensions of the market measure approximately 40 yards long by 35 yards wide . . . Along the rear of the enclosure is a small building of pole-frame and mud-daub construction that is covered with a corrugated iron roof. It is infrequently used by market officials as an office, its greatest utility being a place for parking bicycles . . . Another simple grass-covered structure in the northwest corner of the market shelters a trader who visits Rugando regularly with a few shop goods and other items . . . In the rear of the market space is reserved for the sale of goats, and four of five salt sellers display their product on temporary tables made of saplings lashed together with banana fibre . . . [Vegetables, of many kinds] are typically displayed on burlap bags which serve as ground covers. (pp. 42-3).

In contrast is Popandetta market in Papua; again this is a periodic

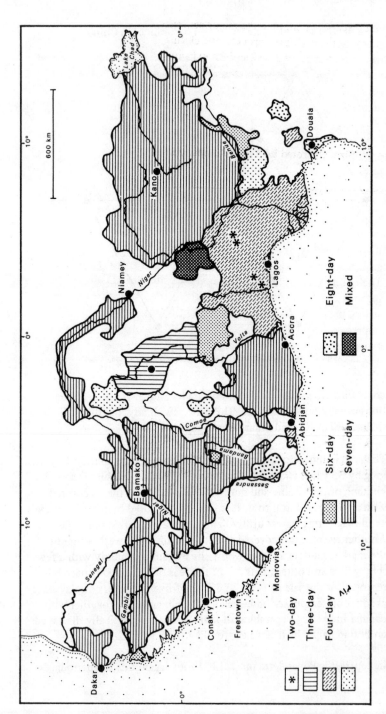

Figure 4.5: Market Periodicity in Part of West Africa

market supplying basic foodstuffs to a rural population (Dakeyne, 1969). Much of the activity takes place in a large concrete floored, tin roofed shelter shed. There are few traders who have come any distance. Dakeyne points out, 'There may be found one or two people who have come very long distances to sell relatively high priced commodities . . .' (p. 27). Some of this group are probably professional traders, similar to the salt sellers, etc. in the previous example. Part-time traders are more usual within each of the villages around the market: 'a small nucleus of families who depend heavily on the market for their cash earnings, but most families sell produce only when they need the money to buy some specific item or pay tax' (p. 32).

> Sellers usually operate in groups of related kin which I shall call family groups. A characteristic group might include a man, his wife, their two teen-age daughters and one of his brother's daughters. These groups are predominantly female, thus most sellers are women . . . The family group system results in a large number of people standing about at the backs of the stalls, giving the impression of many sellers, each having a very small amount of products on sale. This impression is strengthened by the fact that any member of the family group may apparently quote a price for an item when asked by a prospective buyer; she may also accept payment. (p. 30).

This method of selling is quite distinct from that of the full-time traders in the same market and from that of peasant sellers in markets in other societies, as in East Africa for example. Equally apparent are differences in the operations of full-time traders in different societies. Riddell (1972) points out that in Sierra Leone traders operate from fixed bases to which they return each night. In respect of North Eastern Ghana McKim (1972) states that: 'Traders who travel to several markets in the Yendi area average approximately 25 to 50 miles a day, with a round trip totalling 100 miles on some days for certain traders. No matter what the distance, most traders in this area return home each night' (p. 341). A similar situation occurs in most British periodic markets with market stall holders returning, after trading in a different market each day, to a home base. In other societies, however, full-time market operators are itinerant and this view is essential to Skinner's (1964) and Stine's (1962) theoretical treatments of market place systems.

Since the early 1960s there has been considerable interest, by geographers and anthropologists, in periodic marketing systems (Bromley, 1974B; Smith, 1972). A great deal of the work has concentrated on the markets as entities, their spacing, periodicity and system organisation. There have been relatively few studies of the retail processes operating within the market and the diversity of retailing techniques in the market. Notable exceptions are Epstein's (1961) study of Rabaul market, Harding's (1967) detailed analysis of a market system in New Guinea and many of the contributions in Bohannan and Dalton (1962). The early influence of central place theory, with its concentration on pattern not process, on periodic marketing studies is probably responsible for the unbalanced approach of many studies (Smith, 1976). Hodder and Lee (1974) point to the central place theory links of many studies. Until this imbalance is corrected and the detailed retail processes within markets in different societies are studied there is little hope of achieving meaningful general statements of how periodic markets operate. The limited evidence currently available suggests that retail techniques and methods are closely related in detail to local social conditions, but that there may be retail practices and techniques broadly common to several culture groups. A few studies have been concerned with price formation in periodic markets (Ilori, 1970; Dean, 1963) and some with kinship and related features in the seller mix in the market (Sinha, 1968; Fox, 1967; Knuri, 1965; Anthonio, 1970; Dakeyne, 1969). While recent research has extended considerably knowledge on market location and overall function, there is still relatively little known about relationships and conflicts among traders within periodic markets. Hill and Smith (1972) advocate analysing traders operations in Northern Nigeria on the basis of trader mobility:

> At one extreme there is the trader who visits one market weekly . . . and who farms or engages in craft activities during the remainder of the market week. At the other extreme there is the travelling trader who moves around a network of periodic markets, returning to his home at the end of the market week. (p. 550).

Trader mobility, however, is only one dimension of retail technique so that with a single periodic marketing system there are likely to be several conflicting retail techniques.

This section has shown some ways in which retail techniques are related to structures in society. It has concentrated on groups of marketing environments—namely the periodic market. Comparable studies are possible of Western style town centres, growing suburbs, cities in the developing world or in any one of several other distinct marketing environments. In each case the retail techniques used by retailers would be seen as related to the society in which they operate.

Emergence and Diffusion of New Retail Techniques

The crosscultural development models of retailing suggest that all retailing in any society may be considered to be on the path towards a North American retail pattern. The contrasts outlined above, of different retail institutions within a society, suggest that these development models provide, at best, partial explanations of the operation of a retail economy (Shapiro, 1965). Hodder and Lee (1974) argue that there is evidence which 'suggests strongly that all types and operations of markets may be seen as intermediate stages on a single, albeit many stranded continuum from the most elementary to the most complicated economies' (p. 142). There is, however, considerable evidence to suggest otherwise. While some aspects of American culture are strong in producing a world culture, with McLuhan's *global village* decidedly North American in outlook, retailing in many ways remains closely tied to the society in which the retailers operate (Dichter, 1962). Just as we no longer expect all cities to look like New York or pass through its growth phases, so it is feasible to assume that all societies will not pass through the same stages as American society in respect of retail development.

Recently developed institutions such as the hypermarket indicate some truth in this assertion. The hypermarket is essentially a French institution which has spread through Northern and Western Europe. In many technological aspects it is at the frontier of retail development. The institution is virtually absent from North America yet has diffused to some developing countries. There are more hypermarkets in Brazil than there are in the USA. It is quite inadequate to suggest that Brazil follows the American model of retail development.

Most change in retailing may be related to three axes of development. These are:

(1) a structural axis along which are arranged the different methods of retailing together with the relative economic viability of the different techniques;
(2) a locational axis along which lie the many different types of location suitable for retailing; and
(3) an administrative axis along which the extent of public (governmental) control varies.

The retail economy of a society may be related to each of these interdependent axes. The changes in location of retailing are discussed in the next section while public policy intervention in retailing is discussed in Chapter 8. The concern in this section is to consider the changing structural factors of retailing. In particular, four aspects will be discussed.

The operating scale of retail institutions is a major component in determining overall retail structure and in this respect there have been two significant but related developments in recent years. These are an increasing polarity in the size distribution of retailing firms and also the emergence of very largescale operations, both retail outlets and firms. A second aspect of retail structure is the extent of non-store retailing. A third is the time it takes for institutions to pass through a life cycle. The extent to which retailing institutions can be typified by the mix of goods on sale is a final variable in retail structure.

It is important as a first step, in a consideration of scale related variations in retail operations, to distinguish between the size of a firm and the size of establishment. In most organisation types a firm may operate several establishments. The establishments may be small or large. Similarly a one-establishment firm may operate a store of any size. Much of the immediate conflict in retailing arises from interestablishment competition rather than interfirm competition.

It is generally acknowledged that larger establishments are economically more efficient (Stigler, 1963; Pratten, 1971). Economies gained from mass production methods in manufacturing industry mean that increased plant size results in lower unit product cost. Within retailing the relationship between economic efficiency (see Chapter 8) and size is much more complicated (Douglas, 1962; Tilley and Hicks, 1970). As establishment size increases, so the form of establishment changes and no longer is like compared with like. Most studies ignore the changing technique of retailing and point to the large shops having both relatively high profit levels and high levels of labour productivity (Rowe, 1956; McClelland, 1966; Bellamy, 1946; Tucker, 1975; McAnally, 1971; Economist Intelligence Unit, 1972). Furthermore, owner-operator involvement tends to decrease with increasing size, the proportion of part-time workers decreases, and both sales and gross margin per unit of floorspace usually increase. While these broad relationships are the same for most types of shop and for most organisations, differences in actual values are considerable. The differences have been explored by a number of authors for the different shop types (McAnally and Scott, 1958; Tilley and Hicks, 1970; Dawson and Kirby, 1977) and forms of organisation (Roberts, 1955; Hall and Knapp, 1956; Skillcorn, 1956; Bamfield, 1976; McNair and May, 1963). There are relatively few studies of particular retail techniques and their scale related economic processes.

McClelland (1964) compares selfservice with counter service grocery shops for co-operative and multiple retailer organisations. He suggests that wage costs are higher in the very small selfservice store than in counter service shops with comparable sales level. Wage costs, however, then decrease considerably with size and are consistently lower in self-service than in counter service stores. Henksmeier (1960) in a similar study of counter and selfservice stores in Western Europe found wage costs in selfservice stores consistently lower than in counter service shops but rather more variable over the size distribution. The broad pattern was the same whether size was measured by sales volume, sales area or numbers employed.

There is considerable evidence, much of it summarised in Douglas (1975), that when individual techniques are considered, diseconomies of scale begin to occur above critical size levels. Employee productivity begins to fall, wage costs increase, rates of stock turnround stabilise, etc. Most retail techniques have an optimal size of operation. Retailers in search of higher profits consistently have devised new techniques which have a larger optimal operating size. Within the grocery trade in Western Europe, for example, the supermarket (of around 1,000 m^2) followed the selfservice store, then came the discount store (around 1,500 m^2), the superstore (2,500 m^2) and the hypermarket (7,000 m^2). There are critical differences other than size among these techniques but the more recently evolved technique has always been larger than existing ones. If operating ratios at the typical size level of each technique are compared then a higher economic return (sales/profit and capital/ profit ratios) would be expected for each new technique. It is difficult to test this hypothesis rigorously as both organisation and location will offset the economic return on specific shop units. The regular analyses of supermarkets and hypermarkets presented by the selfservice institutes in France and Germany and statistics on discount and supermarket industries in USA are suggestive that, generally, the newer techniques yield a higher financial return. Table 4.2 shows some typical figures for samples of supermarkets and hypermarkets in France in 1976. The figures show a consistently higher potential economic return for the average hypermarket than for the typical supermarket.

The development of a new, larger, store inevitably creates conflict between the new technique and existing techniques and the new store and existing establishments. The birth of a new large store in a district almost inevitably means either the rapid death of some existing stores or closure of the new store itself unless, within the district, consumer spending power is increasing extremely rapidly. The more efficient

Table 4.2:   Operating Characteristics of Stores, Supermarkets and Hypermarkets in France, 1976

A. Typical Supermarkets and Hypermarkets

Size range (m^2)	Supermarket 800-1200	Hypermarket 4000-6500
Number in sample	515	90
Average size	973	5157
Gross margin per m^2 (F)	2386	3117
Operating costs as % sales	13.32	11.92
Labour costs as % sales	7.33	6.17
Operating costs per m^2 (F)	2169	2519
Sales per employee ('000F)	526	536

B. Stores operated by 1 retail group

	Small shop (selfservice)	Superette	Supermarket	Hypermarkets
Size range (m^2)	Less than 120	120-400	400-2,500	Over 2,500
Number of stores	40	137	257	17
Average size (m^2)	70	225	327	3,785
Sales per m^2 (F)	11,900	15,700	15,300	23,700
Sales per checkout ('000F)	800	1,432	2,133	3,878
Sales per employee ('000F)	448	446	501	571

operation of the new store in this situation means that it begins operation from a more powerful economic position than existing competitors.
Often, then, this conflict is resolved in a drastic fashion with the closure
of stores using older retail techniques.

The development and growth of hypermarket retailing typifies this
conflict. A hypermarket is a food and general merchandise store of at
least 2,500 m^2 selling on selfservice principles and operating a mass
merchandising policy including direct purchasing from manufacturers.
The store is open long hours and provides large areas of customer car
parking. A hypermarket often contains a small number of specialist
'boutiques' within the store, a cafeteria/restaurant, garden centre and
car service station (Dawson, 1976B; Langeard and Peterson, 1975). Such
stores typically have a sales figure in excess of that expected of all shops
in a small town of 10,000-12,000 population. The potential for conflict
when such a store is placed in a medium sized city is considerable. These
stores have developed rapidly in France and many other Western Euro-

pean countries with over 1,000 coming into existence in the decade prior to 1976 (MPC, 1973; Henksmeier, 1977).

The impact of a hypermarket on existing retail provision has been studied widely (Thorpe and McGoldrick, 1973; Pickering, 1972; Dawson, 1975; Wood, 1976; CRPC, 1973). Thorpe and McGoldrick (1973) found in South Wales that the retail group most seriously affected after a hypermarket opened were small and medium sized supermarkets. Dawson and Kirby (1976) noted that the level of perception among retailers of the impact of hypermarkets was very varied. Similar surveys of stores in the North of England (Thorpe, 1977) found that small independent corner shops survived by providing a service at very convenient locations. Studies in France have shown the impact as rather more subtle and suggest that the immediate reduction in sales in supermarkets can be as large as 30 per cent but that it is eventually usually less than 10 per cent, in the supermarkets that survive (Liepmann, 1972; Bibaud, *et al.*, 1972). It would seem that the opening of a hypermarket can create the trigger mechanism for marginal or near marginal enterprises to close (Coquery, 1970; Reynaud, 1972). Some supermarkets attempt non-price competition and change opening hours, product mix and other customer services (such as delivery). It is generally these stores which continue in existence. The research in France has shown also that small counter service corner shops are affected adversely by hypermarket opening and again closures occur particularly among shops having a relatively old owner operator. The sudden appearance of conflict in the retail system is met by a totally capitulative response (Roy, 1971). Not all small shop operators have responded in this way and political lobbying has resulted in governmental intervention and the limiting of the growth of the hypermarket technique (Dawson, 1976C; see Chapter 8).

This pattern of conflict and response is common throughout Europe. Hypermarkets are prepared to retail goods at low prices to large numbers of consumers and the existing retailers respond in a variety of ways but rarely, if ever, through price competition. An appeal for governmental intervention is common either through national government limits on hypermarkets or local government limits on land use permissions for hypermarkets (Lee and Kent, 1976). The rapidity of diffusion of hypermarket retailing through much of Western Europe has resulted in a related diffusion of conflict between the new large store and existing retail practices.

Alongside the emergence and growth of these very large stores there are also signs of an increased retail importance of small stores. Activity at the two ends of the size distribution has polarised much of the newer retail development in Western capitalist society. There are several reasons for the renewed development of small shops. The most important is their convenience value. As major stores become larger they require a larger catchment population in order to be successful and so have to locate relatively distant from each other and from a considerable number of their customers. There is scope therefore for much smaller stores to operate at a profit, convenient to customers and providing services not available at the large mass merchandising stores. Many local shops provide delivery, cash cheques, or give credit or other extra customer services. The American convenience store has grown in importance in this way (Kirby, 1976A; 1976B). From a few hundreds in the late 1950s this type of shop, defined as a small compact selfservice store open long hours but providing basic convenience goods at locations close to consumers, now numbers in excess of 30,000 in the USA (*Progressive Grocer*, 1978). Convenience stores are also becoming common in Europe and this is so particularly in those countries (notably France, West Germany) where large scale retailing is well established. The convenience store offers essential food and non-food goods at places and times attractive to consumers and so fills a considerable consumer need.

A second area of small store development is in meeting the demand for specialist goods. Such 'boutique' type shops carry a deep assortment of a very specialised line. Antique shops, specialist clothes shops or hobby shops are of this type and all three are increasing in number in the USA and Western Europe.

By adjusting either their location or their product mix large and small shops can complement one another rather than be in conflict. In some cases the two retail techniques are operated by one firm. The major hypermarket group in Britain (Wheatsheaf Holdings), which trades through Carrefour hypermarkets, also controls, through a wholesale group, a voluntary chain of affiliated small grocers usually located in residential areas or in small centres. The two retailing techniques have been developed so that conflict does not arise. It is the shops of intermediate scale and the smaller ones which have not adjusted their product mix for which the outlook looks bleak.

The increased polarity of retailing affects only the fixed shop sector. A second major change occurring in retailing lies in non-store retailing. The two major forms are automatic vending and mail order and both are increasing in importance as groups of consumers are less willing to spend time travelling some distance both to and from the shops and finding their way around large stores. Mail order, particularly, has grown in importance in recent years throughout Europe (Economist Intelligence

Unit, 1966, 1967). Location costs are low as a warehouse may be sited at extremely low cost sites. Operating costs consist mainly of labour and postage items. In Britain, mail order in 1975 accounted for 5 per cent of retail sales compared with 2.5 per cent in 1971 (Gower Press, 1976). This can be compared with the 7.5 per cent of consumer co-operative societies in 1975. There are three main types of mail order retailing. The most common is agency mail order where goods are sold by catalogue with a part-time sales force working on commission. The second type is the fastest growing and combines mail order with fixed store retailing. Heavy promotion is made in the national or regional press and goods can be bought by mail or through fixed shops often in secondary locations in shopping areas. The third form is direct mail selling with goods displayed in a catalogue or leaflet and purchase is made direct through the post.

Much of the strength of mail order lies in the service it provides to rural populations in both small towns and dispersed farmsteads and in the credit facilities it provides (Stacey and Wilson, 1965). American mail order is particularly strong in these rural areas where potential competition, for comparison goods, from fixed shops is weakest (Emmet and Jeuck, 1950). In Britain mail order retailing has its main strengths in lower-middle income areas where credit is a necessary aspect of purchasing of non-food items. Mail order provides retail facilities to populations unable to use fixed shops either because of their relative inaccessibility or because of the relatively low mobility of consumers and those consumers being unwilling to seek credit at local stores. With the trend to larger, more widely spaced shops, mail order retailing now is growing in importance in the suburbs of large metropolitan areas. Johnson (1971) has suggested a number of reasons for the growth of mail order in Britain, including the consumer's increasing disenchantment with the shopping environment. Perhaps the single most important reason for the success is their relative lack of conflict with other retail institutions. The service provided by mail order precludes them from entering into direct competition with retailers operating fixed shop techniques.

Each retail technique has a life cycle. The techniques pass through an introductory phase as innovation occurs. There then occurs a period of growth and the reaching of maturity. Other new innovatory techniques then begin to compete seriously with the established institutions. Maturity leads to saturation which is followed by decline. A marked trend in retailing is the shortening of the time span from innovation to maturity for each successive innovation. It took 50 years, at least, for department stores to achieve maturity. Pasdermadjian (1954) shows how their development was a gradual evolutionary process and only since about 1970 has there been evidence of serious decline. Supermarkets have developed more rapidly. Markin (1968) and Zimmerman (1955) suggest they have taken about 25 years to reach maturity. Although the antecedents of franchising can be traced back for several decades in its present day form and on North American experience it may be expected to reach maturity in less than 20 years (Izraeli, 1972). Similarly, hypermarkets are close to a mature position and it has taken them barely a decade to reach this stage.

The implications of this shortening in life cycle are many, not least those associated with the rapid outdating of the physical structures housing the techniques. Many department stores operate in buildings 100 years old. Some supermarket buildings are already coming to the end of their economic life. Will hypermarket structures have an economic life of more than 25 years? It seems doubtful. The physical life of the structure will be far longer than its economic life.

During the growth phases of the life cycle there is an increase in the numbers of retail outlets utilising the particular technique. There is also a spatial diffusion of the technique. The combination of greater numbers and widespread diffusion creates a situation of increasing conflict between the maturing techniques and those already established. As maturity is reached, so conflict is resolved and the new technique becomes part of the equilibrium pattern of relationships. But, almost inevitably, as a technique reaches maturity so new innovations emerge which again create conflict. The concept of conflict is therefore central to the life cycle process of institutions.

Spatial diffusion studies have tended to ignore the innovations occurring in retailing but many of the general principles suggested by Hagerstrand (1952) and Rogers and Shoemaker (1971) are applicable to retail innovations. There are, however, a few studies. The gradual spread of selfservice retailing has been mapped in Ireland (Dawson, 1970). From the initial innovation nodes of Belfast and Dublin the technique diffused both hierarchically to other large towns and spatially westwards. To understand the dynamics of the innovation it is necessary to consider the organisational forms in Irish retailing. In Belfast the co-operative society was an important innovator of selfservice methods and initial growth occurred in Belfast and its suburbs. In the Republic of Ireland voluntary chains have been instrumental in spreading the technique from the initial urban innovatory sources to the more rural areas. The interrelationship of organisation and technique is also apparent in selfservice diffusion within a city. Within Nottingham four phases of diffusion have been identified (Dawson, 1973). In the early 1950s there was a innovatory phase when the technique was pioneered by the Nottingham Co-operative Society. A second phase saw the adoption of selfservice by multiple retailers particularly in respect of inner suburban locations. Thirdly, there was an increase in scale of operation. This feature is characteristic of the approach of maturity in most retail techniques. In the third phase there was growth in the outer suburbs. The fourth stage included considerable growth in the outer suburbs, with a rationalisation of selfservice shops in favour of larger operations (Giggs, 1972). From introduction to saturation will have taken about 25 years in the Nottingham case. Supermarkets, which were introduced about two years after selfservice, will reach the saturation stage at about the same time as selfservice. It appears that discount houses will reach maturity and saturation in considerably less than 20 years. The life cycle of retail techniques has both a numerical and spatial dimension and the acceleration of life cycle processes results not only in a more rapid increase in numbers but also in a faster operation of spatial diffusion processes.

The shortening of life cycles also has implications for what has been termed the *wheel of retailing*. The idea of the *wheel of retailing* was suggested by McNair (1958) who argued that new retail techniques begin with crude facilities, little prestige, and a reputation for cutting prices and margins. As they mature, they often acquire more expensive buildings, provide more elaborate services, impose higher margins, and become vulnerable to new competition. Hollander (1961) has reviewed this idea critically and examined possible explanations for the changes that occur. There is evidence that not every technique follows this pattern and it is safer to limit its application to Western capitalist society. But given these limitations, there is considerable evidence to support McNair's hypothesis.

One criticism of the approach is that it ignores the reactions of established retailers to the changes occurring in the emerging technique. It ignores the conflicts and reactions which occur as the wheel 'turns'. Established techniques borrow and adapt particular aspects of newly emerging methods, and new techniques sometimes are 'a new combination of already known factors and an elaboration of existing retailing methods and principles' (Nielsen, 1966, p. 105). The incorporation of this mutual influence of new and old into the wheel concept has been advocated by Nieschlag (1959). He argues that as a technique develops not only trading up occurs as McNair argues but also assimilation takes place through a borrowing by established techniques of certain features of the new method. Conflict within the wheel type of development is reduced by these assimilation processes. A second extension to the wheel concept has been suggested by Agergard, Olsen and Allpass (1968). They argue that as living standards improve successive innovations are not quite as basic and crude, in marketing terms, as previous innovations. Instead of a wheel, therefore, they compare retail development to a spiral.

The acceleration of life cycles means that the wheel, or spiral, revolves increasingly faster. There is consequently less time for adaptation and assimilation, so the potential for conflict is greater. The spatial processes in the wheel idea, which are tied to the changing locations of evolving techniques, also have less time to operate. The movement from lower rent to higher rent sites means a more rapid turnover in low rent property, which often means a more rapid rate of physical deterioration. The acceleration of the life cycles of retail institutions can be seen to have widespread implications.

A common feature of retailing in Europe and North America is the increasing extent to which *lines of trade* conventions have been abandoned since the early 1960s. It is estimated that in the USA more than one shop in four sells automotive products of some type and 40 per cent of grocery stores sell motor oil. In Britain the Nielsen survey (Wallis, 1976), mentioned earlier, showed that 87 per cent of grocery stores sell ladies' tights and 77 per cent sell light bulbs. Neither of these items is a traditional grocery item. Between 1961 and 1971 the percentage of multiple grocers selling fresh meat increased from 11 per cent to 36 per cent and for cosmetics the comparable figures are 6 per cent and 36 per cent. It is not only in the grocery industry that product mixes have expanded. By 1971, 13 per cent of multiple tobacconists were selling records, 60 per cent of multiple grocers sold chocolate and sugar confectionery, over 30 per cent of greengrocers sold frozen meat and approximately the same percentage of butchers sold frozen fruit and vegetables. In the USA independent traders are purchasing the smaller less economic branches of multiples, closed through rationalisation schemes, are extending the merchandising mix, particularly with bakery and delicatessen departments, and are operating the stores profitably (Love, 1976). This extension of product lines beyond traditional boundaries is termed *scrambled merchandising.* Large stores are extending their product range and seeking high profit or rapid turnover lines which previously were the stock-in-trade of specialist stores. Many grocery stores sell a limited range of records, paint, chemist's preparations, convenience clothing and even books. These items were once the main profit earners of small specialist shops. As the most profitable lines are pirated from these specialist stores they find it increasingly difficult to operate. A study of the changing mix of shops in a small town in South Wales (Dawson and Morgan, 1976) suggested that this expansion of non-food and specialist food sales of general grocers was a major factor in the decreasing number of specialist shops.

The four trends isolated in this section do not operate independently of each other. The movement to scrambled merchandising is closely related to the increased operating scale of shops and to the emergence of new retail techniques. There are also other trends which are affecting the structure of retailing. The growth of vertical integration in marketing channels has been discussed in an earlier chapter, and the benefits of horizontal integration have been considered in an earlier part of this chapter. Many of the structural changes that have taken place have resulted in locational changes in retailing with different retail institutions having different optimal locations.

Location of Retail Institutions

The increase in scrambled merchandising has resulted in the development of different types of institution and operating method. It has also raised questions on the future validity of central place theory and classical urban rent theory as models of retail location. Central place theory has been, for many years, the main explanatory model for retail location. Refinements to the theory have been legion and the central place model has been used to explain existing locational patterns and to plan the location and the future provision of retailing. As described in Berry (1967), basic to central place theory is the definition of retail and service *functions* and the grouping of these on the basis of the amount of consumer sales required to support their provision. The details of this hierarchical grouping procedure is described in detail in widely available sources. The problems arising when scrambled merchandising becomes widespread stem from defining what constitute central place functions, functional units and business types. If a garage sells newspapers, bread and coal, as many in Britain now do, does the garage have one function or four functions? Central place theory has been derived in a period of specialist retailing with the few general merchandise stores carrying a deep assortment of a rather limited mix of products. This is no longer the case and to suggest that the provision of a few, rapid-turnover record stands in a supermarket should be treated in the same way as a specialist record shop is to fail to appreciate how retailing really operates. Recent studies, particularly in urban areas, have come up against this problem but have failed to solve it. Berry's arguments (Guy, 1976) for the incorporation of central place theory into planning models and for its value in locating new drugstores in North American suburbs were valid and acceptable with the retailing processes of the 1950s but though retailing has changed central place theory has failed to respond. Whilst the theory serves to describe and, in part, explain locational patterns developed prior to the 1960s it can no longer be used as a basis either for the explanation of present patterns or the planning of future patterns. Central place theory, because of these measurement difficulties, disintegrates and merely states that some places are more important than others.

Much the same arguments can be used to refute the applicability of urban rent theory to the present-day location of retailing in intraurban sites. The ubiquity of comprehensive planning and managing of new retail facilities casts doubt on rent theory's use in these cases and in the unplanned centres the changes in retailing make it very difficult to differentiate retail functions as Garner (1966) did in Chicago. Furthermore the very different profit returns at different scales of operation mean that shops of the same type but of different size have different rent paying capacities. Again, with the shortening of institutional life cycles the rent paying capacity for a shop type will change as it passes through its life cycle. The changes in rent capacity can be far more rapid than the ability either to change location or to renew rents. With the rapid changes, examples of suboptimal locations, owing to inertia, increase in number.

Since the 1940s and 1950s there has been a systematic decline in the importance of rural and small town locations for retailing and a corresponding increased prominence of locations in the larger towns and their immediate urban fringes. This change results partly from the trends occurring in the economic structure of retailing and partly from the shift in the rural/urban population and the increased mobility of the rural population. The newer retail methods usually require sizable capital investment and an adequate return is potentially available only at sites with a large catchment population. Urban locations, and a few exceptional rural sites, meet this condition. The rural/urban growth differential is not just a feature of developed Western society. A similar process is occurring in the developing world with smaller settlements unable to sustain the smallscale and traditional retail institutions.

Within the rural areas the generalisation of a relative decline of activity masks some important locational changes. There has been a considerable reduction in the numbers of convenience food and general stores in rural areas. In Britain the number of shops in villages of less than 2,500 population has fallen from 25,000 in 1950 to approximately 20,000 in 1975 (Dawson, 1976A). In the Netherlands there are 1,100 villages, accounting for over 15 per cent of the population, which have no food shop. This decline has been occurring steadily for several decades and is associated with the increased mobility of the rural population. Lively (1932) and Landis (1933) point out the importance of a railway to retail survival in villages in North America in the early part of this century. In the 1920s and 1930s improved rural roads and greater availability of automobiles resulted in further declines in village general trading (Morrison, 1927). Mitchell (1939) shows that of 168 retailers questioned in villages in rural Illinois 67 per cent said that a cause of decreased sales was increased personal mobility and 40 per cent said it was the *primary* cause.

> Village stores located at greater distances from *primary trading centers* held their own better from 1926 to 1938 than those closer to such centers. At the present time (*i.e. 1938*), however, the effects of increased automobile ownership and improved roads seem to be reaching out further from *primary trading centers*, with the result that many stores formerly not affected very much by these factors are not feeling the effects of increased mobility of trade. (p. 54).

A follow-up study in 1950 shows that stores in very small villages with 400-1,000 population continued to decline in numbers and sales penetration but that some larger villages were able to support branches of regional chain stores which allowed them to compete, effectively, with the larger country towns (Scotton, 1953). More recently still, Johansen and Fuguitt (1973) claim, 'That improved access to larger centers has caused a restructuring of the retail system with a decline in functions for nearly all places in this size class' [i.e. villages] (p. 2167). Comparable changes have occurred in Britain for many of the same reasons (Hampshire County Council, 1966; Lindsey County Council, 1973; Norfolk County Council, 1976).

While general stores have closed, more specialist stores have begun operation. Antique shops, craft shops, picture shops and garden centres are all found increasingly in rural areas in Britain. Martin (1976) estimates that in North Wales, the number of craft shops increased by almost a third between 1970 and 1974 with the majority in rural areas. Many operate at locations within a half-day's driving distance from a large metropolitan centre while others have flourished in tourist and holiday areas. Many of these new specialist non-food shops have taken over premises formerly used by retailers supplying the local population. The net effect of these changes in a village may even be an increase in retail activity with more shops and larger sales volume. None of these new shops are typically associated with low order central places, and this change again provides evidence for the rejection of central place theory as a model for retail planning.

A third feature of the locational change in rural retailing has been the differential growth of village centres consequent on planned development. Many local physical planning agencies, not only in the developed countries as Johnson (1970) points out, use growth centre and key village development policies. These policies aim to concentrate new infrastructure capital such as new public housing schemes into a few specified villages. New potential retail sales, therefore, become similarly concentrated with consequential increases in retail capital expenditure. Key villages, in becoming suitable sites for supermarkets, effectively cause the closure of village stores in surrounding small settlements.

Locational change in retailing in rural areas is not a simple one of small shop decline. In some ways the problems of adaptation facing retailing in village communities are more intractable than these faced by urban retailers.

There have been a number of attempts to determine why retail sales volumes vary by urban area. The studies based on central place theory argue that the amount of aggregate buying power in the town and its trade area is the sole determinant of size of retailing. Attempts have been made to group cities into hierarchies on the basis of the amount of sales (Price, 1970; Thorpe, 1968). Other, hardly more convincing studies, have attempted to model variations in retail sales among cities by cross-sectional correlation of sales volume and gross income levels. Not unexpectedly big cities have large volumes of retail sales and large populations providing large volumes of gross income. High intercorrelations result. When attempts are made to remove crude size factors, the statistical evidence for a relationship between income and sales becomes conflicting. Russell (1957) found virtually no correlation between per capita sales and median family income among 78 cities in the USA. Ferber (1958) in an analysis among 51 Illinois cities also found that 'the simple correlation between per capita sales and per capita income reveals a virtual absence of correlation for all types of retail stores studied' (p. 299). When per capita income is placed in a multiple regression model with per capita sales as the dependent variable and independent variables such as stores per 10,000 population and percentage of families earning over $7,000 (1950 data), then 'contrary to the previous findings income turns out to be highly significant in every instance. The elasticity of sales with respect to income is in fact higher than the elasticity for any other variable' (p. 300). Ferber's conclusions suggest income, number of stores relative to the population and distance to nearest larger town as 'major determining factors in the intercity variation in per capita sales' (p. 300). No attempt is made to assess the extent of multicolinearity in the multiple regression model.

More recent studies by Tarpey and Bahl (1968) and Liu (1970) show high levels of intercorrelations among a wide range of potential descriptor variables. Tarpey and Bahl conclude that population size and town spacing are the primary determinants of total urban retail sales. This view lends support to the traditional central place view but it only shows, once again, that bigger cities have higher retail sales – which is hardly unexpected. In respect of per capita sales there is a higher degree of correlation with per capita income but other socioeconomic variables are not significant as explanatory variables. Liu extended the analysis to consider changes in sales volume and introduces other variables such as local government finance into the model. Most of these attempts to model sales volume and per capita sales fail to appreciate that the urban population is responsible for only part of retail sales in the city which renders ratios such as city retail sales/city population extremely suspect.

An alternative hypothesis, which has implications for the variations in retail sales among towns, is that

> in any regional system of towns, there exist groups of towns which are similar in respect of the functioning of their urban retail economies. The groups need have no relation to the hierarchies of central place theory. The suggested grouping is based on the working of the economies; it is not based on a simple description of the size of an urban economy. The groups, however, do have to be 'discrete' in terms of size and structure relationships for it is these which define the processes at work in the urban retail economies. In such a hypothesis it is conceivable that economic processes in a particular small town may be the same as those in a particular large town and also that these processes may be distinct as between two small towns. (Dawson, 1972, p. 26).

The hypothesis has been tested, and shown worthy of more detailed testing, in Ireland, Denmark and representative regions of England. Towns have been grouped into discrete clusters on the basis of a multivariate analysis of a wide range of measures of retail activity. Relationships among these measures are shown to be individual to each of the defined discrete groups, which suggests the possibility of different processes operating in the different groups. There also seems to be some correspondence of group relationships between different systems of towns. Some common group relationships are evident to both the Danish and Irish urban systems. The approach suggests the study of aggregated retail location, an approach which is unrelated to central place theory. Studies of interurban location of retailing other than those based on central place theory have tended to be descriptions of present or changing patterns (Forrest, 1968; Carruthers, 1967) rather than analyses of the processes of change. It is possible that multivariate analyses of operational measures could provide an adequate basis for an alternative approach which considers, among others, the productivity, labour, shop size and organisational form of interurban retail aggregates.

Within studies of intraurban locational change one major trend emerges – the suburbanisation of retail activity. A wide variety of conflicts and potential conflict situations arise in the differential growth of retailing which favours suburban locations at the expense of inner city sites. Some of these conflicts will be considered in more detail in later chapters as suburbanisation entails broader land use conflicts (Chapter 7) and conflicts created and resolved by politicians and their bureaucracies (Chapter 8).

The causes of the suburbanisation process in most Western capitalist cities are the decentralisation of demand, increased personal mobility, central area decay, and the availability of suitable sites. The speed at which the process operates is largely a result of the urban planning policies and their interpretation by the land use planners. The wide applicability of these causes in North America, Europe, Japan and Australia has been shown elsewhere (Dawson, 1974). The suburbs not only have been the areas of most rapid population growth but they also house the higher income groups in the city. Levels of personal mobility are also high in the suburbs and together with increased congestion in the city centre these factors have deterred would-be car travelling shoppers from using city centre stores. Suburban locations become both more profitable to the retailer and more attractive to the consumer. The increased scale of retail operations means that new developments require particular types of building. Physical decay in city centres, partly caused by the suburbanisation of retailing, means such buildings are not available except at high cost and the space limitations of the city centre also means the absence of sufficiently large sites to be attractive to retail investment

(Dent, 1978; see Chapter 7).

The extent of the shift of retail sales from the city centre to the suburbs is remarkable. In the 1930s in Chicago and Los Angeles the process occurred rapidly. Hoyt (1933) and Mayer (1942) describe the shifts that took place in the 1920s and 1930s and Berry (1963) indicates how the trends continued through to the 1960s. Cassady and Bowden (1944) show how in 1929 the city centre of Los Angeles accounted for 75 per cent of department store sales. By 1939 this share had fallen to 54 per cent. The process has continued to the 1960s with, in 1963, only 3 per cent of the Standard Metropolitan Statistical Area (SMSA) retail sales accounted for by Los Angeles CBD (Ullman, French and Meyers, 1967). Many North American cities and all cities outside the USA have some way to go before reaching the extreme position of Los Angeles. In British cities about half of retail sales is accounted for by suburban retailing but this varies by city size, with the smaller cities having more sales concentrated in the central areas.

While there is an extensive literature on the causes and overall results of the suburbanisation process there are few studies of the process as it affects individual retailers. How does the operation of a supermarket, for example, differ in an inner urban area compared with a suburban shopping centre? Jonassen (1953) and many others have compared overall patterns but none has considered whether retail processes differ in contrasting urban locations. Also in North America, Foster (1967) has suggested that shop birth processes are different in city centre and suburbs and although this view is likely to be upheld elsewhere it appears not to have been studied. Kinnard (1964) and Kinnard and Malinowski (1960) suggest that although the process may differ there is no reason why birth rates or life expectancy of shops should differ from suburbs to CBD.

Suburbanisation is the major locational change to have occurred in retailing. There are many broadscale studies of the implications for land use planning and change. Surprisingly, few studies have been undertaken of how suburbanisation affects retail processes. Here is a major area of potential conflict between competing groups of retailers – increasingly successful suburban located operators and increasingly less successful city centre retailers. There have been few, if any, attempts by the latter to halt the expansion of the former. The contrast with the conflict between chain and independent store is particularly notable. There are perhaps two reasons why the apparent basis for conflict has never created serious conflict. In North America much of the suburban expansion has taken place as branch store expansion by city centre based operators. All the early suburban shopping centre developments in Chicago had strong relationships with city centre department stores. Similarly the expansion of suburban retailing in the 1960s in most Australian cities was directed, to a large extent, by city centre department store groups. Any conflict between the two locations in this instance was internal to a firm and so easily resolved. The second likely reason, at least in Europe, is the strength and acceptance of government as a control in the suburbanisation processes. Many policies of central area renewal, for example, in Britain have resulted in interest focusing on central area locations and the suburbanisation process has occurred gradually. Retailers in potential conflict situations have been unaware of the true extent of suburbanisation. Although the suburbs now dominate retailing, it is widely believed in British land use planning that shopping facilities are concentrated into central areas. Davies (1976) states: 'There is no other country in Western Europe which has sought to contain the process of decentralisation to the same degree as in Britain' (p. 177). Perhaps when reality dawns outcry will occur.

There are two other important processes in retail location but both are secondary to the suburbanisation process. They relate to microlocation within the city or market. The first has been reviewed in detail by both Scott (1970) and Davies (1976) and is the process by which, in certain cases, the same and related types of business (irrespective of organisational form) group together within a city. A similar process occurs in periodic and fixed markets in developing countries where traders selling similar products locate together. The process creating these grouped locations appears to be very general. Scott (1970) provides numerous examples of the spatial clustering of particular retail trades.

The process does not operate for all types of shop because some shops, by their operating method, seek spatial monopolistic positions. Many convenience type stores are of this kind (Schell, 1968). It must also be remembered that the process is a general one and ceases to operate within specific organisational forms. All firms having more than one outlet seek to minimise competition between their own outlets. Point pattern analysis of the location of co-operative stores or of the stores of a multiple retailer in any large city will show a distribution with a strong uniform component. Membership of voluntary associations and groups is often limited to non-competing retailers. A further situation in which the process does not operate is in the totally planned shopping centre environment. An increasing proportion of shopping in urban areas is accounted for by these centres both in suburban and central locations (see Chapter 7). The mix of shop types allowed in these centres is closely controlled by centre managers and developers and it is often centre policy to reduce competition and allow representation by only one or two shops of each type of trade. In this way individual shop sales are increased and rents, which are often tied to turnover, rise accordingly. It becomes more profitable to retailers and developers to over-ride the natural process which associates together similar trades.

The process has operated for many centuries with similar types of retailers located in the same street. Streets where butchers, fishmongers, or water sellers congregate were often named after the type of trade carried on there. The same street names are present in many modern cities but the traders have moved on. Waterbeer Street in Exeter is a typical example. More recently the process seems more applicable to stores selling comparison rather than convenience goods. The cause of the process is largely the consumer. In comparison goods shopping (meat, fish, etc. were comparison goods before the mass merchandising revolution of the early twentieth century) a consumer may wish to visit several stores before making a purchase. By locating together competing shops allow the consumer to choose from a wide variety of stock:

> Shops retailing certain goods varying in style and price but unable to compete successfully when located some considerable distance apart may increase their sales sufficiently to become supramarginal when located in close proximity. The specialisation thereby made possible provides a higher class of service or a greater variety of merchandise at lower prices. More potential customers are attracted, a higher proportion make purchases, and probably more return to make further purchases. Customers are thus given greater opportunities for choosing their requirements within a given expenditure of time and money. (Scott, 1970, pp. 26-7).

Furthermore, within market places where retailers are free to fix their own prices there are advantages to being aware quickly of any price changes made by competitors. The theoretical economic rationale for the clustering process rests in trade area maximisation and the extensively documented problem of the location of ice cream sellers on a beach and other related trade area optimisation problems as collected in Dean, Leahy and McKee (1970).

There are several retail trends which make the clustering process less forceful than formerly. Scrambled merchandising allows shoppers to save time by buying several types of good in the same shop and so dis-

count the time and effort saved against the slight price or quality difference obtained by visiting specialist shops. The general movement away
from specialist shops results in a decrease in importance of specialist shop
clusters. While this is present in Western style town centres, the traditional market in developed and developing countries is still based on specialist traders and here the clustering process shows no diminution, as shown
by many of the studies mentioned above. Again in Western cities the
larger stock range, wider or deeper, carried by stores means that the
customer's comparisons can be made within the one shop. The demand
for clusters of similar retailers is declining in Western city centres.

The second locational process has emerged in response to the changing
nature of the first. There is now frequent location of shops within shops.
This occurs at a number of levels but most frequently associates a relatively large space user and one or more small space using retail types.
The shop types complement rather than compete with each other. At
one extreme is the very familiar rural general store with post office. This
comprises two distinct retail outlets—even in this case with different
forms of organisation—within the one unit. Specialist jewellers, and
other retailers selling fashion items, often locate within department stores
and operate a small high margin establishment. Within hypermarkets
there is often a gallery of small specialist shops marketing services or goods.
A florist is typical of many French hypermarkets. The space for the small
units is usually leased to independent traders who have their main branch
elsewhere. In 1977, 62 per cent of the 337 French hypermarkets con-
tained groups of independent retailers operating in conjunction with
the hypermarket. A case study of the origins of some small independent
retailers associated with a hypermarket is provided by Labat (1972). In
Italy the Citta Mercato hypermarket in Bergamo is typical of many in
Western Europe and has a main store area of 8,000 m^2 and a further
3,000 m^2 set aside for a group of independent retailers and service units.
The location of the smaller units is governed completely by the location
of the main hypermarket.

Retail location and the processes involved may be considered at three
scales. At a microlevel the linkages between individual shops and between
particular shops and particular consumers generate location processes.
Parker (1962) has suggested 12 types of linkage. The strength of links
varies through time and in some instances particularly powerful institutions can nullify the linkage effects. These microprocesses control the
location of a unit within a retail cluster, for example, a town centre or
market place. At a second level are processes generated by broad associations in urban economies which include not only associations between

retail institutions. The operation of the urban economy creates differential advantages at particular locations for specific components of the urban economy. Manufacturing industry thus has preference at certain locations. The suburbanisation of retailing is a response to the more general urban processes. At a third level are macroprocesses which allocate inter-regional and interurban differentials in retail location. In order to develop a workable planning structure for retailing it is imperative to take account of location at the three levels and to be aware of the vastly different processes at each level.

The Next Retail Revolution

With the rapid changes that have occurred in retailing since the early 1960s a number of studies have attempted to forecast likely future change. Some, notably the Distributive Trades EDC (NEDO, 1971) in their report on *The Future Pattern of Shopping* are content to extrapolate the trends of the last 10 years—larger units, increased suburbanisation, scrambled merchandising, etc. (McNearnie, 1975; Gross, 1969). Others, of which Crawford (1969) is a good example, have sought to discover the revolutionary as well as evolutionary changes. Almost all these crystal ball gazers see an increasing divergence of convenience and comparison shopping—or the chore of shopping for necessities and the pleasure of shopping for specialist items. It is in the convenience shopping sector that the most radical changes seem likely to occur. It is worthwhile to outline some of the more outstanding likely changes but the following discussion is meant only as a cursory survey and is in no way exhaustive.

First, there will be far-reaching changes in the technology of retailing which will affect store size, layout and even location. The application of computer technology to checkout, store ordering and materials handling will become widespread in the 1980s. Almost all major computer manufacturers have designed point-of-sale systems to integrate customer checkout and store stock control. By the late 1970s 'scanner' methods of automating checkout methods are operational in over 100 stores in the USA, and in 1976 the first fully operational system in Europe began working in an Irma supermarket in suburban Copenhagen. These systems are only one aspect of the movement of retailing out of the mechanical and into the electronic era (Segaud, 1978; Dawson, 1978) with resulting labour productivity increases (O'Neill, 1977).

A second easily forecastable trend is the expansion of non-store retailing. Bogart (1973) believes that 'by the end of the century as much as a third of all general merchandise business will be done outside the store, perhaps as early as 1984' (p. 26). While telephone shopping, mail order, catalogue stores and the like will all increase, it will also become necessary for stores to allow consumers to shop outside the building, at all hours, for items like bread, milk, rapid preparation foods, common clothing items and other basic convenience goods. Some form of automatic vending machines will be necessary. Small groups of these machines could replace corner stores quite easily. The short-term reply to these developments is a more flexible approach to store design and there are already indications of this in North America (*Chain Store Age*, 1977).

A third possible change will also integrate increased non-store retailing and electronic retailing technology. Doody and Davidson (1967) argue that much of the convenience shopping a family needs to do will be carried out at home in front of a display terminal and keyboard connected to a large computer system. Orders will be made, subsequent to questions being asked on price, quality, availability, etc., through the console and the goods will be delivered next day. The technology for this type of retailing is already available and as households increasingly become linked into computer communication networks for banking, local tax purposes, etc., so push-button shopping will occur. The implications of this revolution are enormous, not just for retailing but for the whole concept of shopping and town centres. The location of the retail warehouse is such that deliveries can be made to households within a few hours. Shops effectively disappear. Clearly it will be a few years before such a system takes over but perhaps by the 1990s it could be creating conflict with the established traditional supermarkets and hypermarkets.

In the shorter term a fourth change will be the provision of increased customer services in stores. Not only will more information have to be provided about the goods on sale but provision for delivery will have to be made, even creches and nurseries provided in the larger stores. Stores will have to provide a pleasanter environment for the shopper than they do now. In the short run this change will be most apparent in convenience stores but in the longer run the speciality stores will have to fall into line. With the increase in consumer leisure time shopping for specialist goods will have to compete with other leisure time activities. Hensel (1973) argues that the specialist stores such as sports, and home furnishings shops will not only carry deeper assortments of goods but will also provide electronic aids to simulate product use and testing. Systems of overlaying colour slides will allow customers to view various combinations of styles and colours of furnishings, for example.

A further longer term future trend is an organisational one and contrasts with the previous one (Starling, 1971). Increasingly, retailing will be controlled by conglomerate organisations with a wide range of horizontally managed and vertically integrated businesses. Food, for example, will be controlled from farm to consumer via a whole range of different distribution channels. The aim of organisations will be maximisation of total organisational profit, which might mean a reduction in the traditional service role of retailing. Services would be provided only if they were cost effective. A delivery system would operate only if it was discovered that the costs of the system were covered by the increase in sales profit generated. The free services provided by many retailers, effectively out of their own pocket, will disappear. The corner grocery shop operator who not only sells light bulbs but also will close the shop for five minutes to go out to mend a fuse has no place in the conglomerate dominated retail sector of the future.

References

ADBURGHAM, A. (1964) *Shops and Shopkeeping, 1800-1914* (George Allen & Unwin, London).

AGERGARD, E., P.A. OLSEN and J. ALLPASS (1968) *The Interaction between Retailing and Urban Centre Structure: a Theory of Spiral Movement* (Institute for Centre Planning, Lyngby).

ALEXANDER, D. (1970) *Retailing in England during the Industrial Revolution* (Athlone Press, London).

ANTHONIO, Q.B.O. (1970) 'Distributors in Foodstuffs Markets in Nigeria', *African Urban Notes*, 5, pp. 86-108.

APPLEBAUM, W. (1964) 'Store Location Research – a Survey by Retailing Chains', *Journal of Retailing*, 40, pp. 53-6.

—— (1965) 'Store Performance in Relation to Location and Other Characteristics', *Chain Store Age*, 41, pp. E14-17.

ARNDT, J. (1972A) 'Temporal Lags in Comparative Retailing', *Journal of Marketing*, 36, pp. 40-5.

—— (1972B) *Norsk detaljhandel frem til 1980* (Johan Grandt Tanum, Oslo).

BAKER, R.W. (1965) 'Marketing in Nigeria', *Journal of Marketing*, 29, pp. 40-8.

BAMFIELD, J. (1976) 'Economies of Scale in Retail Scieties', *Co-operative Marketing and Management*, Nov., pp. 27-30.

BARANOFF, S. (1964) 'Retailing as an Operating System' in R. Cox, W.A. Alderson, and S.J. Shapiro (eds), *Theory in Marketing* (Irwin, Homewood).

BAYLEY, R.B. (1962) 'The Lebanese in West Africa', *Comparative Studies in Society and History*, 4(3), pp. 296-303.

BEARCHELL, C.A. (1975) *Retailing: a Professional Approach* (Harcourt-Brace-Jovanovich, New York).

BECKMAN, T.N., and H.C. NOLEN (1938) *The Chain Store Problem* (McGraw-Hill, New York).

BELLAMY, R. (1946) 'Size and Success in Retail Distribution', *Bulletin, Oxford University Institute of Statistics*, 8, pp. 324-39.

BELSHAW, C.S. (1965) *Traditional Exchange and Modern Markets* (Prentice-Hall, Englewood Cliffs).

BERRY, B.J.L. (1963) *Commercial Structure and Commercial Blight* (University of Chicago Department of Geography, Research Paper, 85).

BERRY, B.J.L. (1967) *Geography of Market Centers and Retail Distribution* (Prentice-Hall, Englewood Cliffs).

BERRY, R.K., J.A. DAWSON, D.A. KIRBY and G.I.U. MAIR (1976) *Survey Method and Codebook of a Questionnaire of Small Unit Retailers in Derby, Exeter and Port Talbot* (St David's University College, Lampeter).

BIBAUD, B.P. *et al.* (1972) *Grandes surfaces et commerce preexistant* (Institute of Business Administration, Bordeaux).

BLACKMAN, J. (1963) 'The Food Supply of an Industrial Town', *Business History*, 5, pp. 83-97.

—— (1967) 'The Development of the Retail Grocery Trade in the Nineteenth Century', *Business History*, 9, pp. 110-7.

BODDEWYN, J.J. (1971) *Belgian Public Policy toward Retailing since 1789* (Michigan State University, East Lansing).

BODDEWYN, J.J., and S.C. HOLLANDER (1972) *Public Policy toward Retailing* (Lexington Books, Lexington, Mass.).

BOGART, L. (1973) 'The Future of Retailing', *Harvard Business Review*, 51, pp. 16-32.

BOHANNAN, P., and G. DALTON (1962) (eds), *Markets in Africa* (Northwestern University Press, Evanston).

BOLTON COMMITTEE (1971) *Small firms. Report of the Committee of Inquiry on Small Firms* (HMSO, London).

BOSWELL, J. (1969) *JS 100. The Story of Sainsbury's* (J. Sainsbury, London).

BRAITHWAITE, D., and S.P. DOBBS (1932) *The Distribution of Consumable Goods* (Routledge, London).

BROMLEY, R.J. (1974A) 'The Organization of Quito's Urban Markets: towards a Reinterpretation of Periodic Central Places', *Trans. Inst. Brit. Geog.*, 62, pp. 45-70.

—— (1974B) 'Periodic Markets, Daily Markets and Fairs: a Bibliography', *Monash Publications in Geography*, 10.

BROWN, M.P., W. APPLEBAUM, and W.J. SALMON (1970) *Strategy Problems of Mass Retailers and Wholesalers* (Irwin, Homewood).

BUCKLIN, L.P. (1972) *Competition and Evolution in the Distributive Trades* (Prentice-Hall, Englewood Cliffs).

CAMERON, R.C., and A.M. SUTHERLAND (1975) 'The Rôle and Significance of Overseas Chinese in Asian Marketing', *European Journal of Marketing*, 9(1), pp. 52-8.

CARRUTHERS, W.I. (1967) 'The Major Shopping Centres in England and Wales, 1961', *Regional Studies*, 1, pp. 65-81.

CARR-SAUNDERS, A.M., P.S. FLORENCE and R. PEERS (1938) *Consumers' Co-operation in Great Britain* (Allen & Unwin, London).

CARSON, D. (1967) *International Marketing: a Comparative Systems Approach* (Wiley, New York).

CASSADY, R. (1962) *Competition and Price Making in Food Retailing* (Ronald Press, New York).

CASSADY, R., and W.K. BOWDEN (1944) 'Shifting Retail Trade within the Los Angeles Metropolitan Market', *Journal of Marketing*, 8, pp. 398-404.

CHAIN STORE AGE (1977) 'Retailers Probe the Unknown', *Chain Store Age*, 53 (10), pp. 23-7.

COHEN, S.B. (1961) 'Location Research Programing for Voluntary Chains', *Economic Geography*, 35, pp. 1-11.

COLDSTREAM, P. (1963) 'The Stamp War', *New Society*, 28 November.

CONVERSE, P.D. (1931) 'Business Mortality of Illinois Retail Stores from 1925-1930', *University of Illinois, Bureau of Business Research Bulletin*, 41.

COOLSEN, E.G. (1963) 'Marketing and Economic Development' in W.S. Deeker (ed.), *Emerging Concepts in Marketing* (American Marketing Association, Chicago), pp. 26-37.

COQUERY, M. (1970) *Recherches sur la mobilité des commerçants* (Centre National de la Recherche Scientifique, Paris).

CRAWFORD, C.M. (1969) *The Future Environment for Marketing* (University of Michigan, Bureau of Business Research).

CRPC (1973) *Grandes surfaces et petite commerces: mythe et realités* (Centre de Recherche et de Prospective Commerciale, Paris).

CUNDIFF, E.W. (1965) 'Concepts in Comparative Retailing', *Journal of Marketing*, 29, pp. 143-62.

DAKEYNE, R.B. (1969) 'The Small Market at Popondetta, Northern Papua' in H.C. Brookfield (ed.), *Pacific Market-places* (Australian National University Press, Canberra), pp. 25-34.

DALRYMPLE, D.J. and D.L. THOMPSON (1969) *Retailing: an Economic View* (The Free Press, New York).

DAVIES, R.L. (1976) *Marketing Geography* (Retailing and Planning Associates, Corbridge).

DAWSON, J.A. (1970) 'The Development of Self-service and Supermarket Retailing in Ireland', *Irish Geography*, 6, pp. 194-9.

——— (1972) 'Retail Structure in Groups of Towns', *Regional and Urban Economics*, 2(1), pp. 25-65.

——— (1973) 'The Development of Self-service Retailing in Nottingham', *East Midland Geographer*, 5, pp. 355-60.

——— (1974) 'The Suburbanization of Retail Activity' in J.H. Johnson (ed.), *Suburban Growth – Geographical Processes at the Edge of the Western City* (Wiley, London), pp. 155-75.

——— (1975) 'Hypermarket Happening', *Geographical Magazine*, 48(2), p. 118.

——— (1976A) 'The Country Shop in Britain: Objectives and Background to a Research Project' in P. Jones and R. Oliphants (eds), *Local Shops: Problems and Prospects* (Unit for Retail Planning Information, Reading), pp. 63-71.

——— (1976B) 'Hypermarkets in France', *Geography*, 61, pp. 259-62.

——— (1976C) 'Control over Large Units in France', *Retail and Distribution Management*, 4(6), pp. 14-18.

——— (1978) 'Speed at the Checkout', *Geographical Magazine*, 50(9), p. 589.

DAWSON, J.A. and D.A. KIRBY (1976) 'Retailer's Reactions to Cwmbran's Superstore', *Estates Gazette*, 239, p. 113.

——— (1977) 'Shop Size and Productivity in British Retailing in the 1960's', *European Journal of Marketing*, 11, pp. 262-71.

——— (1979) *The Small Shop in Britain* (Teakfield, Farnborough).

DAWSON, J.A. and R.H. MORGAN (1976) *Shopping in Carmarthen* (University of Wales, Department of Geography, Lampeter).

DEAN, E.R. (1963) 'Social Determinants of Price in Several African Markets', *Economic Development and Cultural Change*, 11, pp. 239-56.

DEAN, R.D., W.H. LEAHY, and D.L. McKEE (1970) *Spatial Economic Theory* (Free Press, New York).

DENT, B.D. (1978) 'The Challenge of Downtown Shopping', *Atlanta Economic Review*, 28(1), pp. 29-33.

DEWEY, A. (1962) *Peasant Marketing in Java* (Free Press of Glencoe, New York).

DICHTER, E. (1962) 'The World Customer', *Harvard Business Review*, 40, pp. 118-21.

DONQUE, G. (1965) 'Le zona de Tananarive. Etude geographique d'un marche urbain', *Madagascar Revue de Géographie*, 7, pp. 93-227.

DOODY, A.F., and W.R. DAVIDSON (1967) 'The Next Revolution in Retailing', *Harvard Business Review*, 45, pp. 4-20.

DOUGLAS, E. (1962) 'Size of Firm and Structure of Costs in Retailing', *Journal of Business*, 49, pp. 158-90.
____ (1975) *Economics of Marketing* (Harper & Row, New York).
DOUGLAS, S.P. (1971) 'Patterns and Parallels of Marketing Structures in Several Countries', *Business Topics*, 19, pp. 38-48.
ECONOMIST INTELLIGENCE UNIT (1966) 'Mail Order in France', *Marketing in Europe, Special Report*, 1, pp. 21-7.
____ (1967) 'Mail Order in Germany', *Marketing in Europe, Special Report*, 3, pp. 31-41.
____ (1972) 'Economies of Scale in Retailing', *Retail Business*, 175, pp. 14-24.
____ (1976) *Retail Distribution in Britain* (EIU, London).
EMMET, B. and J.E. JEUCK (1950) *Catalogues and Counters* (University of Chicago Press, Chicago).
EPSTEIN, T.S. (1961) 'A Study of Rabaul Market', *Australian Journal of Agricultural Economics*, 5, pp. 1-18.
FEDERAL TRADE COMMISSION (1935) *Chain Stores: Final Report on the Chain Store Investigation* (Government Printing Office, Washington, DC).
____ (1948) *The Merger Movement. A Summary Report* (Government Printing Office, Washington, DC).
____ (1966) *Economic Report on the Structure and Competitive Behavior of Food Retailing* (Government Printing Office, Washington, DC).
FERBER, R. (1958) 'Variations in Retail Sales between Cities', *Journal of Marketing*, 23, pp. 295-303.
FERRY, J.W. (1960) *A History of the Department Store* (Macmillan, New York).
FOLKE, S. (1967) 'Central Place Systems and Spatial Interaction in Nilgiris and Coorg (South India)', *Geografisk Tidsskrift*, 66, pp. 161-78.
FORMAN, S. and J.F. RIEGELHAUPT (1970) 'Market Place and Marketing System: toward a Theory of Peasant Economic Integration', *Comparative Studies in Society and History*, 12, pp. 188-211.
FORREST, J. (1968) 'Retail Activity in New Zealand Towns, 1958-63', *New Zealand Geographer*, 24, pp. 61-75.
FOSTER, G.M. (1948) 'The Folk Economy of Rural Mexico with Special Reference to Marketing', *Journal of Marketing*, 13, pp. 153-62.
FOSTER, J.R. (1967) 'The Effect of Shopping Center Financing on the Opportunity for Occupancy by Independent Retailers', *Southern Journal of Business*, 2, pp. 25-37.
FOX, R.G. (1967) 'Family, Caste and Commerce in a North Indian Market Town', *Economic Development and Cultural Change*, 15, pp. 297-314.
FULLOP, C. (1962) *Buying by Voluntary Chains* (Allen & Unwin, London).
____ (1964) 'The Role of Trading Stamps in Retail Competition', *Institute of Economic Affairs, Eaton Papers*, 3.
FURST, R.L. (1932) 'Relationships between the Numbers of Chain and Individually Owned Grocery Stores in Fort Wayne', *Journal of Business of University of Chicago*, 5, pp. 335-45.
GARDNER, G.G. (1969) 'Distribution Cost Analysis' in B.A. Morin (ed.), *Marketing in a Changing World* (American Marketing Association, Chicago).
GARNER, B.J. (1966) 'The Internal Structure of Retail Nucleations', *Northwestern Studies in Geography*, 12.
GIDE, C. (1921) *Consumers Co-operative Societies* (George Allen & Unwin, London).
GIGGS, J.A. (1972) 'Retail Change and Decentralization in the Nottingham Metropolitan Community', *Geographia Polanica*, 24, pp. 173-88.
GOLDMAN, M.I. (1963) *Soviet Marketing* (Free Press of Glencoe, New York).
GOOD, C.M. (1970) *Rural Markets and Trade in East Africa* (University of Chicago, Department of Geography, Research Paper, 128).

GOWER PRESS (1976) *Retail Trade Developments in Great Britain* (Gower Press, Chelmsford).
GREEN, H. (1961) 'Planning a National Retail Growth Program', *Economic Geography*, 37, pp. 22-32.
GREER, H.C. (1936) 'Business Mortality among Retail Meat Stores in Chicago between 1920 and 1933', *Journal of Business of the University of Chicago*, 9 (3), pp. 189-209.
GROSS, W. (1969) 'Retailing in the Seventies', *Baylor Business Studies*, 79, pp. 19-31.
GUY, C. (1976) 'The Location of Shops in the Reading Area', *University of Reading, Geographical Papers*, 46.
HAGERSTRAND, T. (1952) 'The Propogation of Innovation Waves', *Lund Studies in Geography*, B4.
HALL, M. and J. KNAPP (1956) 'A Note on Labour Productivity in Capitalist and Co-operative Shop Trading', *Journal of Industrial Economics*, 5, pp. 68-74.
HALL, M., J. KNAPP and C. WINSTEN (1961) *Distribution in Great Britain and North America* (Oxford University Press, London).
HAMPSHIRE COUNTY COUNTIL (1966) *Village Life in Hampshire* (The Council, Winchester).
HANSON, R.W. (1965) 'The Growth and Development of Co-operative Retail Chains and their Marketing Significance' in L.G. Smith (ed.), *Reflections on Progress in Marketing* (American Marketing Association, Chicago).
HARDING, T.G. (1967) *Voyagers of the Vitiaz Strait* (University of Washington Press, Seattle).
HARRISON, J.F.C. (1969) *Robert Owen and the Owenites in Britain and America* (Routledge & Kegan Paul, London).
HAWKINS, H.C.G. (1965) *Wholesale and Retail Trade in Tanganyika* (Praeger, New York).
HENKSMEIER, K.H. (1960) *The Economic Performance of Self-service in Europe* (OEEC, Paris).
___ (1977) *Self-service in 1977* (International Self-service Organization, Cologne).
HENSEL, J.S. (1973) 'Environmental Change and the Future Structure of Retailing', *Arizona Business*, 20, pp. 14-20.
HILL, P. (1966) 'Notes on Traditional Market Authority and Market Periodicity in West Africa', *Journal of African History*, 7(2), pp. 295-311.
HILL, P. and R.H.T. SMITH (1972) 'The Spatial and Temporal Synchronization of Periodic Markets: Evidence from Four Emirates in Northern Nigeria', *Economic Geography*, 48, pp. 345-55.
HODDER, B.W. and R. LEE (1974) *Economic Geography* (Methuen, London).
HODDER, B.W. and U.I. UKWU (1969) *Markets in West Africa* (Ibadan University Press, Ibadan).
HOLDREN, B.R. (1960) *The Structure of a Retail Market and Market Behavior of Retail Units* (Prentice-Hall, Englewood Cliffs).
HOLLANDER, S.C. (1961) 'Measuring the Cost and Value of Marketing', *Business Topics*, Summer, pp. 17-27.
HOLTON, R.N. (1957) 'Price Discrimination at Retail: the Supermarket Case', *Journal of Industrial Economics*, 6, pp. 61-8.
HOLYOAKE, G.J. (1875) *The History of Co-operation in England* (2 vols, Trubner, London).
HOUGH, J. (1949) *Co-operative Retailing 1914-45* (International Co-operative Alliance, London).
HOYT, H. (1933) *One Hundred Years of Land Values in Chicago* (University of Chicago Press, Chicago).
HUGHES, J.D. and S. POLLARD (1957) 'Gross Margins in Retail Distribution',

Oxford Economic Papers, 9, pp. 75-87.

ILORI, C.O. (1970) 'Price Formation and Profit Margin in the Traditional Food Markets in Western Nigeria', *African Urban Notes*, 5, pp. 109-28.

IZRAELI, D. (1972) *Franchising and the Total Distribution System* (Longman, London).

JACKSON, R.T. (1971) 'Periodic Markets in Southern Ethiopia', *Trans. Inst. Brit. Geog.*, 53, pp. 31-42.

JEFFERYS, J.B. (1954) *Retail Trading in Great Britain* (Cambridge University Press, London).

JEFFERYS, J.B. *et al.* (1950) *The Distribution of Consumer Goods* (Cambridge University Press, Cambridge).

JEFFERYS, J.B., and D. KNEE (1962) *Retailing in Europe* (Macmillan, London).

JOHANSEN, H.E., and G.V. FUGUITT (1973) 'Changing Retail Activity in Wisconsin Villages: 1939-1954-1970', *Rural Sociology*, 38, pp. 207-18.

JOHNSON, E.A.G. (1970) *The Organization of Space in Developing Countries* (Harvard University Press, Cambridge, Mass.).

JOHNSON, P. (1971) 'The Development of British and American Mail Order Trading', *British Journal of Marketing*, 10, pp. 220-5.

JONASSEN, C.T. (1953) 'Downtown versus Suburban Shopping', *Ohio State University Bureau of Business Research, Special Bulletin*, X58.

KANE, B.J. (1966) *A Systematic Guide to Supermarket Location Analysis* (Fairchild Publications, New York).

KAPLAN, D. (1965) 'The Mexican Market Place, Then and Now' in J. Helm (ed.), *Proceedings of the 1965 Annual Spring Meeting of the American Ethnological Society* (American Ethnological Society, Seattle), pp. 80-94.

KATZIN, M. (1959) 'The Jamaican Country Higgler', *Social and Economic Studies*, 8, pp. 421-40.

—— (1960) 'The Business of Higgling in Jamaica', *Social and Economic Studies*, 9, pp. 297-331.

KINNARD, W.N. (1964) *The Mythology of Business Displacement in Urban Renewal* (University of Connecticut, Institute of Urban Research).

KINNARD, W.N., and Z. MALINOWSKI (1960) *The Impact of Dislocation from Urban Renewal Areas on Small Businesses* (Institute of Urban Research, University of Connecticut).

KINNEY, W.R. (1969) *Measuring Performance in Multi-outlet Businesses* (Michigan State University, East Lansing).

KIRBY, D.A. (1974) 'The Decline and Fall of the Smaller Retail Outlet', *Retail and Distribution Management*, 2(1), pp. 14-18.

—— (1975) 'The Small Shop in Britain', *Town and Country Planning*, 43, pp. 496-500.

—— (1976A) 'The North American Convenience Store: Implications for Britain' in P. Jones and R. Oliphant (eds), *Local Shops: Problems and Prospects* (Unit for Retail Planning Information, Reading).

—— (1976B) 'The Convenience Store Phenomenon', *Retail and Distribution Management*, 4(3), pp. 31-3.

—— (1976C) 'Planning and the Small Shop – the Scandinavian Example', *Retail and Distribution Management*, 4(5), pp. 41-2.

KIRK, J.H., P.G. ELLIS, and J.R. MEDLAND (1972) *Retail Stall Markets in Great Britain* (Marketing Department, Wye College, Ashford).

KNURI, F.I. (1965) 'Kinship, Emigration, and Trade Partnerships among Lebanese in West Africa', *Africa*, 35, pp. 385-95.

KORNBLAU, C. (1968) (ed.) *Guide to Store Location Research: with Emphasis on Supermarkets* (Addison-Wesley, Chicago).

KUIPERS, J.D. (1950) *Resale Price Maintenance in Great Britain with Special*

Reference to the Grocery Trade (Drukkerij Vada, Wageningen).
LABAT, G. (1972) 'Contribution a l'étude de la modernisation du commerce: le magasin collectif d'independants. Le cas d'Hypercosmos', *University of Bordeaux, Institute of Business Administration, Report*, 30.
LAKDAWALA, D.T., V.N. KOTHARI, J.C. SANDESARA and P.A. NAIR (1963) *Work, Wages and Wellbeing in an Indian Metropolis – Economic Survey of Bombay* (University of Bombay Press, Bombay).
LAKDAWALA, D.T., and J.C. SANDESARA (1957) 'Shops and Establishments in Greater Bombay', *Journal of University of Bombay*, 25(4), pp. 15-28.
LANDIS, P.H. (1933) 'The Growth and Decline of South Dakota Trade Centres, 1901-33', *South Dakota Agricultural Experiment Station Bulletin*, 279.
LANGEARD, E., and R.A. PETERSON (1975) 'Diffusion of Large-scale Food Retailing in France', *Journal of Retailing*, 51, pp. 43-63, 80.
LAWSON, R.M. (1971) 'The Supply Response of Retail Trading Services to Urban Population Growth in Ghana' in C. Meillassoux (ed.), *The Development of Indigenous Trade and Markets in West Africa* (Oxford University Press, London), pp. 377-98.
LEBHAR, G.M. (1963) *Chain Stores in America, 1859-1962* (Chain Store Publishing Corporation, New York).
LEE, M. and E. KENT (1976) *Planning Inquiry Study* (Donaldsons, London).
LENGYE, S.J., and R.M. BEECROFT (1949) *The Cost of Distribution of Consumption Goods in Australia and Elsewhere* (University of Melbourne Press, Melbourne).
LEVY, H. (1942) *Retail Trade Associations* (Kegan Paul, London).
LIBRE SERVICE ACTUALITE (1976) 'Mbolo ou la reússite du hypermarche´ africain', *Libre Service Actualité*, 590, pp. 49-50.
LIEPMANN, C. (1972) *Hypermarches contre supermarches. Trois années de concurrence* (Institute Français du Libre Service, Paris).
LINDSEY COUNTY COUNCIL (1973) *Communities in Rural Lindsey* (The Council, Lincoln).
LINIICHUK, I. (1965) 'Some Problems of Internal Rural Trade Turnover', *Voprosy Ekonomiki*, 7, pp. 45-52.
LIU, B-C (1970) 'Determinants of Retail Sales in Large Metropolitan Areas, 1954 and 1963', *Journal of American Statistical Association*, 65, pp. 1460-73.
LIVELY, C.E. (1932) 'Growth and Decline of Farm Trade Centers in Minnesota 1905-30', *University of Minnesota, Agricultural Experimental Station, Bulletin*, 287.
LOMBARD, C.S. (1971) *The Growth of Co-operatives in Zambia, 1914-71* (Institute for African Studies, Lusaka).
LOVE, B. (1976) 'Independents Score with Stores Bought from Large Chains', *Supermarketing*, 31,(10), pp. 1, 12, 34.
McANALLY, P. (1971) *The Economics of the Distributive Trades* (George Allen & Unwin, London).
McANALLY, P. and M.E. SCOTT (1958) 'Labour Productivity in Department Stores', *Journal of Industrial Economics*, 8, pp. 216-20.
McCLELLAND, W.G. (1964) 'Economics of the Supermarket' in W.G. McClelland (ed.), *Studies in Retailing* (Blackwell, Oxford).
—— (1967) *Costs and Competition in Retailing* (Macmillan, London).
McEVOY, D. (1972) 'Vacancy Rates and the Retail Structure of the Manchester Conurbation' in B.D. Clark (ed.), *The Retail Structure of Cities* (Inst. Brit. Geog. Occasional Publication, 1), pp. 59-67.
McGEE, T.G. (1970) *Hawkers in Selected Asian Cities* (Centre for Asian Studies, University of Hong Kong).
—— (1974) *Hawkers in Hong Kong* (Centre for Asian Studies, University of Hong Kong).

McKIM, W. (1972) 'The Periodic Market System in Northeastern Ghana', *Economic Geography*, 48, pp. 333-44.
McNAIR, M.P. (1958) 'Significant Trends and Developments in the Postwar Period' in A.B. Smith (ed.), *Competitive Distribution in a Free, High Level Economy and Its Implications for the University* (University of Pittsburgh Press, Pittsburgh), pp. 1-25.
McNAIR, M.P., and E.G. MAY (1963) *The American Department Store* (Harvard University Press, Cambridge, Mass.).
McNEARNIE, H. (1975) 'Retailing in the 1980's', *Estates Gazette*, 26 July, pp. 281-5.
MAHONEY, T. (1955) *The Great Merchants* (Harper, New York).
MARKIN, R.J. (1965) 'Dimensions of Supermarket Pricing: Attitudes and Behavior', *Business Review*, 24, pp. 75-85.
—— (1968) *The Supermarket: an Analysis of Growth, Development, and Change* (Washington State University Press, Pullman).
—— (1971) *Retail Management* (Macmillan, New York).
MARTIN, I. (1976) 'The Changing Pattern of Tourism in North Wales', *Cambria*, 3, pp. 65-9.
MATHIAS, P. (1967) *Retailing Revolution: a History of Multiple Retailing in the Food Trades Based upon the Allied Suppliers Group of Companies* (Longman, London).
MAYER, H.M. (1942) 'Patterns and Recent Trends in Chicago's Outlying Business Centers', *Journal of Land and Public Utility Economics*, 18, pp. 8-16.
MILLS, E. (1974) 'Recent Developments in Retailing and Urban Planning, *PRAG Technical Paper TP*, 3.
MINTZ, S.W. (1957) 'The Role of the Middleman in the Internal Distribution System of a Caribbean Peasant Economy', *Human Organization*, 15, pp. 18-23.
—— (1959) 'Internal Market Systems as Mechanisms of Social Articulation' in V.F. Ray (ed.), *Proceedings of the 1959 Annual Spring Meeting of the American Ethnological Society* (University of Washington Press, Seattle), pp. 20-30.
—— (1961) 'Pratik: Haitian Personal Economic Relationships' in *Proceedings of the 1961 Annual Spring Meeting of the American Ethnological Society* (University of Washington Press, Seattle), pp. 54-63.
—— (1964) 'The Employment of Capital by Market Women in Haiti' in R. Firth and B.S. Yamey (eds), *Capital, Saving, and Credit in Peasant Societies* (Aldine Publishing Co., Chicago).
MINTZ, S.W. and D.H. HALL (1960) 'The Origin of the Jamaica Internal Marketing System', *Yale University Publications in Anthropology*, 57.
MITCHELL, R.V. (1939) 'Trends in Rural Retailing in Illinois, 1926-38', *University of Illinois, Bureau of Economics and Business Research, Bulletin*, 76.
MORRISON, V.G. (1927) 'The Influence of Automobiles and Good Roads on Retail Centers', *University of Nebraska, Studies in Business*, 18.
MOSS, L. (1958) *The Consumer's Food-buying Habits* (OEEC, Paris).
MPC (1973) *The Changing Pattern of Retailing in Western Europe* (MPC and Associates, Worcester).
MUELLER, R. (1973) 'U.S. Retailers go for Bigger Stores and Bigger Profits', *Grocery Management*, October.
NASH, M. (1961) 'The Social Context of Choice in a Small-scale Society', *Man*, 61, pp. 186-91.
NATIONAL COMMISSION ON FOOD MARKETING (1966) *Organization and Competition in Food Retailing* (Technical Study, 7, Washington, DC).
NATIONAL ECONOMIC DEVELOPMENT OFFICE (1971) *The Future Pattern of Shopping* (HMSO, London).
—— (1973) *The Distributive Trades in the Common Market* (HMSO, London).

NELSON, R.L. (1958) *The Selection of Retail Location* (F.W. Dodge, New York).

NICHOLS, J.P. (1940) *The Chain Store Tells Its Story* (Institute of Distribution, New York).

NIELSEN, O. (1966) 'Developments in Retailing' in M. Kjaer-Hansen (ed.), *Readings in the Danish Theory of Marketing* (North-Holland, Amsterdam), pp. 101-15.

NIELSON, A.C. Co. Ltd (1976) 'Grocery Trading in 1975', *Nielson Researcher*, 17 (2), pp. 1-5.

NIESCHLAG, R. (1959) 'Binnenhandel und binnenhandelspolitik' in A, Weber, *Volkswirtschaftslehre*, IV, pp. 148-60.

NORFOLK COUNTY COUNCIL (1976) 'Thresholds for Village Food Shops' in P. Jones and R. Oliphants (eds), *Local Shops: Problems and Prospects* (Unit for Retail Planning Information, Reading), pp. 73-80.

NORTON, A., and R. SYMANSKI (1975) 'The Internal Marketing Systems of Jamaica', *Geographical Review*, 65, pp. 461-75.

NYSTRON, P.H. (1930) *Economics of Retailing* (Ronald Press, New York).

OEEC (1960) *Voluntary Chains: Origins, Definitions, Development, Conditions of Success and Prospects* (OEEC, Paris).

O'NEILL, R. (1977) 'Why Scanning is Picking up Speed', *Progressive Grocer*, 56 (12), pp. 56-8.

PALAMOUNTAIN, J.C. (1955) *The Politics of Distribution* (Harvard University Press, Cambridge, Mass.).

PARKER, H. (1962) 'Suburban Shopping Facilities in Liverpool', *Town Planning Review*, 33, pp. 197-223.

PASDERMADJIAN, H. (1954) *The Department Store: Its Origins, Evolution and Economics* (Newman Books, London).

PICKERING, J.F. (1972) 'Economic Implications of Hypermarkets in Britain', *European Journal of Marketing*, 6, pp. 257-69.

PRATTEN, C.F. (1971) *Economies of Scale in Manufacturing* (Cambridge University Press, London).

PRICE, D.G. (1970) 'An Analysis of Retail Turnover in England and Wales', *Regional Studies*, 4, pp. 459-72.

PROGRESSIVE GROCER (1978) 'Annual Report of the Grocery Industry', *Progressive Grocer*, 57(4), pp. 38-198.

PYLE, J. (1970) 'Traditional Supply in a Modern Context: the Public Markets of Mexico City', *Proceedings of the Association of American Geographers*, 2, pp. 115-8.

RAVAZZI, G. (1967) *Le strutture commerciali in Italia* (Franco Angeli, Milan).

REYNAUD, P. (1972) *Les petits commerçents face a la cessation d'activité* (Centre de recherche et de documentation sur la consommation, Paris).

RIDDELL, J.B. (1972) 'A Note on the Origin and Conditions of Periodic Marketing Systems', Paper to International Geographical Union Congress, Montreal.

RILEY, H. *et al.* (1970A) *Food Marketing in the Economic Development of Puerto Rico* (Michigan State University, East Lansing).

—— (1970B) *Market Coordination in the Development of the Cauca Valley Region – Colombia* (University of Michigan, East Lansing).

ROBERTS, C. (1955) 'Labour Productivity and Utilization in Capitalist and Co-operative Shop Trading', *Journal of Industrial Economics*, 4, pp. 78-80.

ROGERS, E.M., and F.F. SHOEMAKER (1971) *Communication of Innovation* (Free Press, New York).

ROWE, J.W. (1956) 'Productivity and Size of Establishment in New Zealand Distributive Trades, 1953', *Economic Record*, 32, pp. 148-52.

ROY, M. (1971) *Les commerçants* (Seuil, Paris).

RUSSELL, V.K. (1957) 'The Relationship between Income and Retail Sales in Local Areas', *Journal of Marketing*, 21, pp. 329-32.

SAMSONOV, L. (1972) 'Problems in the Development of Retail Trade', *Problems in Economics*, 15, pp. 61-79.

SCHELL, E. (1964) *Changes in Boston's Retail Landscape* (National Retail Merchants Association, New York).

—— (1968) 'Geographic Factors Affecting the Distribution of Drug Stores in Boston' in C. Christians (ed.), *Colloque international de géographie appliquée* (Report of 3rd meeting of IGU Commission on Applied Geography), pp. 265-76.

SCHMULZ, C.N. (1931) 'Independent Stores vs. Chains in the Grocery Field', *Harvard Business Review*, 9, pp. 431-2.

SCOTT, P. (1970) *Geography and Retailing* (Hutchinson, London).

SCOTTON, D.W. (1953) 'Trends in Rival Retailing in Two Illinois Districts 1938 to 1950', *University of Illinois, Bureau of Economic and Business Research, Bulletin*, 76.

SEGAUD, J-P. (1978) 'La symbolisation: une revolution en marche', *Libre Service Actualité*, 681, pp. 74-6.

SEXTON, D. (1973) *Groceries in the Ghetto* (Lexington Books, Lexington, Mass.).

SHAPIRO, S.J. (1965) 'Comparative Marketing and Economic Development' in G. Schwartz (ed.), *Science in Marketing* (Wiley, New York).

SINHA, D.P. (1968) *Culture Change in an Inter-tribal Market* (Asia Publishing House, London).

SKILLCORN, M.D. (1956) 'The Measurement of Efficiency in Co-operative Retailing', *Co-operative College Papers*, 5.

SKINNER, G.W. (1964) 'Marketing and Social Structure in Rural China' (part 1), *Journal of Asian Studies*, 24, pp. 3-43.

SLATER, C. *et al.* (1969A) *Market Processes in La Paz, Bolivia* (University of Michigan, East Lansing).

—— (1969B) *Market Processes in the Recife Area of Northeast Brazil* (Michigan State University, East Lansing).

SMAILES, A.E. (1953) *The Geography of Towns* (Hutchinson University Library, London).

SMETHURST, J.B. (1974) *A Bibliography of Co-operative Societies' Histories* (Co-operative Union, Manchester).

SMITH, C.A. (1976) (ed.), *Regional Analysis – Economic Systems* (Academic Press, New York).

SMITH, H. (1937) *Retail Distribution: A Critical Analysis* (Oxford University Press, London).

SMITH, R.H.T. (1972) 'Periodic Markets in Africa, Asia and Latin America', *Council of Planning Librarians, Exchange Bibliography*.

STACEY, N.A.H., and A. WILSON (1965) *The Changing Pattern of Distribution* (Pergamon, Oxford).

STARLING, J.M. (1971) 'Contemporary and Prospective Future Developments in Retailing', *Business Studies*, 10, pp. 14-19.

STEEN, E.J.L.C. (1972) *Cribbs Causeway Out-of-town Shopping Centre Enquiry* (City Planning Department, Bristol).

STEWART, P.M., and J.F. DEWHURST (1939) *Does Distribution Cost Too Much?* (Twentieth Century Fund, New York).

STIGLER, H.O. (1963) *Profitability and Size of Firm* (Institute of Business and Economic Research, University of California, Berkeley).

STINE, J.H. (1962) 'Temporal Aspects of Tertiary Production Elements in Korea' in F.R. Pitts (ed.), *Urban Systems and Economic Development* (University of Oregon Press, Eugene), pp. 66-88.

SWANN, J.E. (1970) 'Parsons and Smelser's Model of Social Change Applied to the Emergence of Contractually Integrated Chains in the Grocery Trade', *South-*

ern Journal of Business, 5, pp. 167-74.
SYMANSKI, R., and R.J. BROMLEY (1974) 'Market Development and the Ecological Complex', *Professional Geographer*, 26, pp. 382-8.
TARPEY, L.X., and R.W. BAHL (1968) 'Intercity Variations in Retail Sales: Some Hypotheses Revisited', *Southern Journal of Business*, 3(4), pp. 1-10.
TAX, S. (1953) *Penny Capitalism – a Guatemalan Indian Economy* (Institute of Social Anthropology, Smithsonian Institute, Washington, DC).
THORELLI, H.B. (1968) 'South Africa: its Multi-cultural Marketing System', *Journal of Marketing*, 32, pp. 40-8.
THORPE, D. (1963) 'A Geographical Study of the Retail Trade – a Study of Regional and Urban Variations' (Unpublished Ph.D. thesis, University of Durham).
—— (1968) 'The Main Shopping Centres of Great Britain in 1961: Their Locational and Structural Characteristics', *Urban Studies*, 5, pp. 165-206.
—— (1977) (ed.), *Co-op Society Superstores* (Manchester Business School, Manchester).
THORPE, D. and P.J. McGOLDRICK (1973) *Caerphilly – Consumer Reaction* (Manchester Business School, Manchester).
THORPE, D. and T.C. RHODES (1966) 'The Shopping Centres of the Tyneside Urban Region and Large Scale Grocery Retailing', *Economic Geography*, 42, pp. 52-73.
TILLEY, R.P.R. and R. HICKS (1970) 'Economies of Scale in Supermarkets', *Journal of Industrial Economics*, 19, pp. 1-5.
TINKLER, K. (1973) 'The Topology of Rural Periodic Market Systems', *Geografiska Annaler*, 55B, pp. 121-33.
TSE, F.Y. (1974) 'Street Trading in Modern Hong Kong' (Unpublished Ph.D. thesis, University of London).
TUCKER, K.A. (1975) *Economies of Scale in Retailing* (Saxon House, Farnborough).
UDELL, J.G. (1964) 'How Important is Pricing in Competitive Strategy?', *Journal of Marketing*, 28, pp. 44-8.
ULLMAN, E.L., V.O. FRENCH and C.S. MEYERS (1967) *Trends in CBD and SMSA Retail Sales 1948 to 1963* (Washington Center for Metropolitan Studies, Washington, DC).
VAN DER LAAN, H.L. (1975) *The Lebanese Traders in Sierra Leone* (Mouton, The Hague).
VAILE, R.S. (1932) *Grocery Retailing with Special Reference to the Effects of Competition* (University of Minnesota Press, Minneapolis).
WADINAMBIARATCHI, G.H. (1972) 'Theories of Retail Development', *Social and Economic Studies*, 21(4), pp. 391-403.
WALES, H.G., F.F. WINKIE and C. BAK (1963) 'Marketing in South Africa', *Journal of Marketing*, 27, pp. 42-47.
WALLIS, C.J. (1976) (ed.), 'The Grocery Trade in 1975', *Nielsen Researcher*, 17 (2), pp. 1-6.
WATERBURY, R.G. (1970) 'Urbanization and a Traditional Market System' in W. Goldschmidt and H. Hoijer (eds), *The Social Anthropology of Latin America* (Latin American Center, University of California, Los Angeles).
WHYSALL, P.T. (1974) 'The Changing Pattern of Retail Structure of Greater Nottingham, 1912-71' (Unpublished Ph.D. thesis, University of Nottingham).
WILD, M.T., and G. SHAW (1974) 'Locational Behaviour or Urban Retailing During the Nineteenth Century: the Example of Kingston-upon-Hull', *Trans. Inst. Brit. Geog.*, 61, pp. 101-18.
WINGATE, J.W., and A. CORBIN (1956) *Changing Patterns in Retailing* (Irwin, Homewood).
WOOD, D. (1976) *The Eastleigh Carrefour: a Hypermarket and Its Effects* (Department of the Environment, Research Report, 16).

WOOD, L.J. (1975) 'The Functional Structure of a Rural Market System', *Geografiska Annaler*, 57B, pp. 109-18.

YAMEY, B.S. (1966) 'United Kingdom' in B.S. Yamey (ed.), *Resale Price Maintenance* (Weidenfeld & Nicolson, London).

ZIMMERMAN, M.M. (1955) *The Super Market: a Revolution in Distribution* (McGraw Hill, New York).

5 CONFLICT AND RESPONSE IN THE WHOLESALE SECTOR

Between the retailer and the mass manufacturer is the buffer of the wholesaler. At home in sixteenth-century Venice or twentieth-century Detroit, the merchant performs the sorting functions of the marketing channel. Articles are purchased in bulk, broken into smaller lots and made up into different mixes to meet the demands of individual retailers. In many marketing channels the wholesaler is a critical institution. Through ten wholesalers a food retailer, for example, has access to several hundred producing firms. Conversely a single manufacturer, again through ten wholesalers, is able to get his product to several hundred supermarkets. Inevitably, the wholesaler charges for the services to retailer and manufacturer. Within a capitalist economy, in many instances, the wholesaler can exert a stranglehold on a market channel and wield considerable power over the retailer on one side and the manufacturer on the other. In such a power relationship there is considerable potential for conflict. Retailer and manufacturer are likely, if they view the wholesaler as too powerful, to find ways to bypass wholesalers within the marketing channel. This removal of the need for wholesalers currently is occurring in channels for some goods in North America and Western Europe. Not unnaturally wholesalers respond strongly to this erosion of their power base and seek new ways to create and influence markets.

The Pivotal Position of Wholesaling

The strength of wholesalers within a national marketing system reflects the complexity and extent of internal integration in the particular national economy. It has been shown earlier that peasant producer-retailer economies operate through the local distribution of small amounts of goods and consequently have no need for wholesalers. Goods are not produced in sufficient quantities to ever be bulked and distribution is local so the primary wholesale functions of breaking bulk and transport are absent from the marketing system. Belshaw (1965) with reference to Port Moresby and Fiji, states that, with the beginnings of marketing,

> In both places the first suppliers were peasant producers who brought handicrafts and crops to the market place, remained there until they had sold their supply or reached the end of demand. (p. 73).

213

Such societies, without any wholesale function, are rare. Examples have been provided in Chapter 2 showing the increasing complexity of whole-saling institutions as inter-regional and international trading links are created. In some instances individual wholesale institutions characterise the trade in a specific commodity. Cohen (1966) has shown, for example, that the trade in kola nuts in Nigeria, which requires an inter-regional marketing channel, has resulted in a tribal monopoly, by the Hausa, in wholesaling the product. Disputes have arisen between Yoruba farmers and the Hausa but the effective power has remained with the wholesalers.

The domination of wholesaling in these societies by a tribal group or by a particular ethnic group has parallels with the influence of particular families in the development of wholesaling in Europe and North America. The merchant guilds in North European cities and the London companies of 300 years ago represent attempts to control wholesale functions by small elite groups. Thrupp (1933), describing the work of German historians, states that in the fifteenth century, 'The leading merchants of Augsburg were chiefly engaged in wholesale trade. Again, Des Marez proved the existence of a superior class of wholesale cloth merchants in Ypres'. While in London, 'There was undoubtedly a class of merchants mainly engaged in wholesale trade' (p. 273). In the eighteenth century development of domestic commercial institutions in North America Schlesinger (1957) shows how merchant power was concentrated into a few families. The Whartons, Pembertons and Willings of Philadelphia, four families in Boston and a further four in New York dominated the wholesale institutions in these towns in the late eighteenth century. Similarly in parts of West Africa where national economic integration is poorly developed, wholesaling is dominated by a few large European based trading organisations.

At this stage of development of wholesaling it is difficult to separate wholesale and retail functions for while the functions were separate and distinct often the wholesaler carried on a small retail business. In fifteenth-century London,

> it is clear that among the grocers and other leading London merchants there was a class of wealthy merchants mainly engaged in wholesale trade. At the same time there was no line of demarcation between the wholesaler and retailer; retail trade formed a regular part of the business of the greater men. (Thrupp, 1933, p. 277).

Other examples are provided by Chartres (1977). In the present-day dis-tribution system in South Dahomey, the distinction made between wholesalers and retailers is obviously linked to the scale of the trade, but 'the boundary between wholesale and retail can easily be stepped over' (Tardits and Tardits, 1962, p. 92). While the wholesale sector is clearly developed as an intermediate stage between production and retailing, the economic units in the channel operate, unknowingly, a policy of vertical integration. Similarly Mukwaya (1962) in describing the distribution of staple foods in Kampala points to the presence of a complex set of wholesale institutions. Some transport goods, others bulk material, others sell to retailers, others are agents but 'few wholesalers are engaged exclusively in wholesaling; most of them are willing on occasion to sell direct to the consumer . . .' The only clear distinction which can be made between retailer and wholesaler 'is that few of the women and boys in the market engage in anything but retail trade while few of the men confine themselves to retail trade' (p. 659). Also in East Africa, Hawkins (1965) states, 'There is no clear-cut distinction between importers, wholesalers, sub-wholesalers and retailers in Tanganyika. [*sic*] Most importers are also wholesalers and very often retailers as well. Only a few of the largest wholesalers do not also sell retail . . .' (p. 23). It is further estimated that at least a third of retail sales are handled directly by wholesalers. Although the functions of wholesaling are present there is no demand for specialist wholesalers.

As national economic integration progresses, so wholesale functions are enlarged and the wholesale sector becomes larger and specialist wholesale firms emerge. Firms specialise in respect of function with some concentrating on transport, some on selling to retailers and some on importing/exporting commodities. Specialisation also occurs by type of commodity, so jewellery wholesalers, clothing wholesalers, greengrocery wholesalers all become established as the overall economy expands and specialist manufacturers and retailers become necessary to supply more specialised consumer demands. In nineteenth-century British and North American cities markets came to be differentiated into wholesale and retail with the consumer rarely purchasing directly from the producer. Alexander (1970) points out that in Britain this situation characterised most provincial large towns by 1850. Buchanan's directory of Derby for 1867, for example, lists the addresses of nine grocery wholesalers. In North America from about 1840 onwards wholesaling began to develop in the interior cities. Prior to this, wholesaling was based in the Eastern seaboard cities where shipping merchants and importers effectively controlled the wholesale trade (Jones, 1937; Vance, 1970; Revzan, 1965).

The expansion of demand for the services offered by the wholesaler allowed entry into the trade of smaller scale operators than previously.

The large merchant houses still prospered but within the burgeoning cities numerous small wholesalers set up business. Wholesaling in these economies becomes concentrated into urban areas with many small traders in operation. In situations of rapidly growing demand wholesaling increases its position of power in the marketing channel. Manufacturers are seeking to distribute goods rapidly and the collection/redistribution function of wholesalers provides for a rapid and relatively efficient movement of goods through channels leading small but growing manufacturers to an increasingly large number of small retailers.

This level of development is typified by Turkey in the 1960s (Stirling, 1965; Samli, 1964; Oluc *et al.*, 1963) when the wholesaler held the key channel rôle in distribution. Wholesaling is concentrated in the cities, particularly in and around the dispersed CBDs of Istanbul (Tümertekin, 1968), with retailers from small towns and rural areas visiting wholesalers, at particular seasons, to buy their goods. The functions of the wholesaler in this situation are to provide credit for retailers and obtain goods, required by retailers, both from manufacturers and by import. There is no need to engage in the sophisticated functions of advertising, branding, providing consultancy services for retailers, etc. that are a prerequisite for the modern wholesaler in an economy of abundance. 'In this respect the Turkish wholesaler resembles the American wholesaler of the 1800s or early 1900s when the American economy was not one of abundance' (Samli, 1964, p. 58). The small scale of operation and the concentration of activity into major urban centres is shown also by the wholesaling institutions in Thailand (Anderson, 1970). Here, although the 120 municipalities account for only 14 per cent of population they account for over 90 per cent of wholesale sales. The Bangkok metropolitan area in 1966 accounted for 83 per cent of the nation's wholesale sales. Within the city there were 1,300 wholesale establishments employing an average 11.4 persons. Similarly, in Peru all but 500 of the 3,500 wholesalers in the country operate in Lima-Callao. Although there is some dispute over the absolute values of these figures because of multiple listing of firms in the 1963 economic census, the concentration within the major city is undisputed (Glade *et al.*, 1970). As in countries with more complex economies, the power structure in wholesaling is changing in countries such as Turkey, Thailand and Peru. In Thailand, 'Historically, in the flow of imported goods the channel members downstream from the rural or urban retailer have seen one or more levels of Chinese wholesaler and western trading firms' (Anderson, 1970, p. 141). These firms have the functions, similar to comparable firms in Turkey, of import, warehousing, break of bulk, shipment to retailers and provision of credit.

The firms are general wholesalers providing a range of functions. With a growing market, foreign manufacturers take an increasing interest in the marketing or products, so pressures are created which restrict the activities and power of the traditional wholesalers.

Types of Wholesale Trade

Throughout Europe wholesaling is a clearly established sector of distribution. Individual wholesale functions have become the focus of distinct types of wholesaler. Wholesalers also have specialised in particular types of good with electrical goods, for example, developing as a specialist type of hardware wholesaling.

Within capitalist Western style economies it is usual to distinguish five types of wholesale trade. The largest group are merchant wholesalers. In the USA, according to the 1967 Census of Business, 213,000 of the 311,000 wholesale establishments were operated by merchant wholesalers. This group, at the same census, accounted for 45 per cent of all wholesale sales. Merchant wholesalers take title to the goods they handle. They are concerned, therefore, in buying and selling merchandise on their own account. The source and destination of goods varies from wholesaler to wholesaler. Some specialise in importing and exporting goods, others buy from manufacturers, some buy from other wholesalers. Merchant wholesalers operate through a variety of premises but most commonly through some form of warehousing. Further variety is introduced into this group by the organisational form of the firm. Co-operatives, private companies, public corporations and even government organisations operate successfully. Merchant wholesalers' operations are influenced particularly by their location for they are actively concerned with receiving, storing and despatching large volumes of goods.

The second type of wholesaler is less concerned with transport orientated locations. Merchandise agents and brokers do not take title to the goods but perform other wholesaling functions. They may act as a sales force taking commission on sales made, some sell goods by auction on an agency basis, others act as import and export agents. This type of wholesaling requires a high level of communication among agents, buyers and sellers. Traditionally these wholesalers have been located in major cities in order to obtain this high level of communication (Alexander, 1979). The growth of mass electronic communication makes location in central business districts less important but most of these wholesalers remain tied to the financial centres of major cities. Since they are engaged in buying and selling for others, the physical space demands of agents and brokers are very small.

The third type of wholesaler is the manufacturer's sales branch and sales office. This is the wholesale arm of the manufacturer involved in direct selling to final consumers. In this case the functions of the wholesaler become the responsibility of a division of the manufacturing company. There are around 30,000 such sales offices in the USA, located in direct consequence of the location of the final consumer. It might be considered that these sales branches are not truly in the wholesale sector but form part of the manufacturer's marketing network (see Chapter 6).

In the USA a further 30,000 wholesale establishments are classified as petroleum bulk stations and terminals. The location of these establishments is related to the market and transport facilities. Again many of these establishments are part of an integrated marketing channel for oil products in which one organisation performs almost all the marketing functions.

A final wholesaling group recognised by the Department of Commerce in the USA comprises the 11,000 assemblers of farm products. Assemblers combine the relatively small output of individual farms into economically useful quantities for transport to consumers including food processors. The whole topic of agricultural marketing will be considered in Chapter 6 and agricultural wholesaling will be discussed in this context.

There is a further form of wholesaling present in Euro-American society and which falls outside the five types outlined above. This is wholesaling by chain stores. Again, as with manufacturers' sales branches, the wholesale functions are performed by a non-wholesale institution. Chain store organisations, particularly in the grocery trades, frequently operate their own warehouses and purchase stock direct from manufacturers. Hypermarket developments in Europe usually follow a similar pattern in obtaining their stock. This trend has caused considerable anguish among merchant wholesalers who have lost sales volume with this trend to retailer initiated direct purchasing. In North America the movement towards chain store wholesaling gained momentum in the 1930s amid a storm of protest from small retailers and merchant wholesalers. Chain stores used their size as a negotiating lever and became powerful institutions within the wholesale structure. Palamountain (1955) in his analysis of the conflicts arising from this situation points out that chain store power can be checked: 'The size and control over supply possessed by many manufacturing processing concerns grants them sufficient power to balance, with varying outcomes, the power of chains' (p. 74). Chain store wholesaling is relatively small when compared with the overall merchant wholesaler group — it represents a small fraction (12 per cent in the USA where it is probably most developed) of total merchant wholesale trade. The difficulties arise in its concentration within the grocery sector where ratio of sales volume through chain store wholesalers and merchant wholesalers in the USA would seem to be around 1.4:1.0 (Beckman, 1965).

Location of Wholesale Activities

Before considering in more detail the responses of merchant wholesalers to the shifts in channel relationships it is worthwhile to look at the broad locational patterns of all wholesale types. There are few studies of wholesaling outside the USA but within North America there are a number of important analyses. Bucklin (1972) using data from the 1963 Census of Business carried out a cross-section analysis by state of the market share held by the three major forms of wholesaling. The three forms studied were merchant wholesalers (wm), manufacturers' sales offices and branches (wb), and agents and brokers (wa). Using multiple regression techniques with the dependent variable (MS) as the market share held by a particular wholesale type the following three regression equations modelled the data.

$$MS_{wm} = 0.984 - 0.067Z - 0.828C - 0.003Fc - 0.010E \quad (R = .66) \ldots 5.1$$
$$\phantom{MS_{wm} = } (0.019) \quad (0.355) \quad (0.001) \quad (0.006)$$

$$MS_{wb} = -0.268 + 0.071Z + 1.121C + 0.12E \quad (R = 0.77) \qquad \ldots 5.2$$
$$\phantom{MS_{wb} = } (0.19) \quad (0.239) \quad (.005)$$

$$MS_{wa} = 0.087 + .034Z + 0.270C + 0.002FC \quad (R = 0.80) \qquad \ldots 5.3$$
$$\phantom{MS_{wa} = } (0.009) \quad (0.161) \quad (0.0003)$$

where

    Z is a measure of market size (wholesale sales per capita);

    C is the ratio of chain store sales to total retail sales;

    Fc is farms per 1,000 persons; and

    E is customer density (manufacturers and retailers per square mile).

The market size variable is positively associated with both manufacturers' agents and agents and brokers, which suggests that these forms of wholesaling are important in states with large wholesale centres. Vance (1970) shows that the large wholesale centres ring the North East manufacturing belt lying between industrial and agricultural areas. Gottmann (1961) in his study of Megalopolis shows that there is also a concentration of wholesaling in the North Eastern seaboard states. The negative coefficient for Z in respect of merchant wholesalers (equation 5.1) suggests that their strength lies in the smaller market centres. The more general nature of merchant wholesaler sales means that they can operate effectively in smaller markets than manufacturers' agents who by definition wholesale specialist product lines and so require a large potential market in order to be efficient.

The second variable common to all three equations is the chain store share of the retail market. The competition between chain store and merchant wholesaling is shown in the negative coefficient in the first of the three equations. The association of chain stores with major markets in some way accounts for the large positive coefficient for C in equation 5.2 but also manufacturers' agents and chain store operation complement each other. A first step in direct buying by chain stores is a movement from using merchant wholesalers to using manufacturers' agents. The second step is then to cut out the manufacturers' agent.

The penultimate variable in the equations shows both the merchant wholesalers' small share of farm goods wholesaling and the agents' and brokers' relative strength in this connection. The final variable indicates, 'that where wholesale customers were highly dispersed (few per square mile), they were served by a merchant wholesaler rather than a manufacturers' sales branch or office' (Bucklin, 1972, p. 236).

While there is a concentration of wholesaling into urban areas and particularly large centres, this process affects merchant wholesalers less than either manufacturers' agents or brokers. This generalisation has to be qualified slightly for particular product groups such as agricultural machinery and supplies. Of the other types of wholesaler it might be expected that petroleum bulk plants would be located in the smaller urban centres and agricultural assemblers will undoubtedly be based in rural market centres. Limited confirmation of Bucklin's results is possible by study of the Australian Wholesale Census of 1968-9 which uses a similar division of wholesaling to that adopted by the US Census of Business.

From Table 5.1, which lays out some basic calculations from the Australian Wholesale Census, it appears that the two most populous states account for over two-thirds of wholesale sales. In these states wholesaling is highly concentrated into Sydney and Melbourne respectively but not in the central business districts in these cities. Wholesaling is traditionally a CBD frame activity from where in recent years it has been affected strongly by suburbanisation processes. These pressures have been felt most strongly by merchant wholesalers whose space requirements are high compared with the other urban concentrated wholesale groups. In the two most highly urbanised states in Australia merchant wholesalers represent 68 per cent of all wholesale establishments and approximately the same percentage of sales volume. The distribution of manufacturers' offices contrasts with the USA where the states with large markets have a concentration of manufacturer's office type wholesaling.

Table 5.1: Wholesale Activity in Australian States, 1969

	Percentage of national sales	Percentage of establishments in capital-city	Percentage of establishments in city CBD	Percentage of establishments which are Merchants	Manufacturers' offices	Agents/brokers	Petroleum distributors	Primary produce and agricultural dealers
New South Wales	36.1	67.0	12.4	68.3	3.7	10.2	6.0	11.8
Victoria	32.2	71.2	13.1	68.5	3.8	9.5	6.2	12.0
Queensland	13.4	47.1	8.0	57.1	7.3	9.2	10.1	16.3
South Australia	7.8	70.1	22.0	57.8	8.1	13.1	6.0	15.0
Western Australia	8.0	63.3	11.6	57.2	7.2	13.2	10.5	11.9
Tasmania	1.9	44.1	16.8	59.8	11.0	11.5	6.2	11.5
Northern Territory	0.2	64.5	49.5	59.8	7.5	13.1	9.3	10.3
Australian Capital Territory	0.3	NA*	8.1	69.9	12.3	10.6	3.0	4.1

NA = not applicable.

The reverse appears to be the case in Australia where many of the manufacturers' offices deal with agricultural products and so tend to be in the less industrialised states.

Although Australian definitions are not exactly comparable with those of the USA it is interesting to compare market shares among wholesale types. Within the USA the variation among states is larger than in Australia but if the 300,000 wholesalers in the USA are compared with the 35,000 in Australia, then merchant wholesalers in both cases account for around two-thirds of establishments but only 40 per cent of sales in the USA compared with over 65 per cent in Australia. The manufacturers' sales branches account for a slightly greater share of establishment numbers in the USA but a considerably greater share of sales. The respective sales shares are over 30 per cent and less than 10 per cent. The remaining three groups are broadly comparable in market share between the two economies. The difference in the two cases appears to hinge on the rôle played by the direct selling divisions of manufacturing enterprises with a wider range of commodities wholesaled in this way in North America.

Revzan (1966) by the use of wholesale/retail sales ratios has shown, for the USA that wholesaling is heavily concentrated in the large cities. In 1963, for example, Table 5.2 indicates the variation in wholesale/retail

Table 5.2:   Wholesale/Retail Sales Ratios for 1963 by City Size Groups in USA

City size	Ratio
500,000 and over	4.41
250,000-499,999	1.76
100,000-249,999	1.19
50,000-99,999	0.92
25,000-49,999	0.96
10,000-24,999	0.49
2,500-9,999	0.25
Remainder of US	0.83
US average	1.47

sales ratio by city size groups. Within Europe wholesaling is similarly concentrated. Figure 5.1 shows the extent of concentration within the Oslo area in respect of the Norwegian economy in 1973. From Danish statistics for 1958 it appears that almost 55 per cent of wholesale sales volume was

Figure 5.1: Wholesale Sales in Norway — 1973

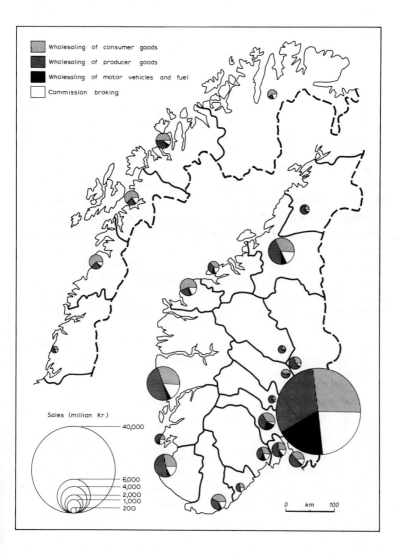

Wholesaling of consumer goods
Wholesaling of producer goods
Wholesaling of motor vehicles and fuel
Commission broking

Sales (million Kr.)

40,000

6,000
4,000
2,000
1,000
200

0   km   100

accounted for by establishments in Copenhagen. In 1966 in the Republic of Ireland out of the wholesale sales volume of £328m, establishments in metropolitan Dublin represent £180m. Similarly in Japan in 1970 the two largest cities of Tokyo and Osaka, taken together, accounted for 55 per cent of Japanese wholesale sales volume. The wholesale/retail sales ratio of Tokyo is 10.9 and of Osaka 14.9. Clearly then wholesaling is a large city activity.

Changing Channel Relationships of Wholesalers

The figures for Japan, cited above, are considerably higher than comparable ratios for almost all cities in North America and Europe. The reason for this lies in the very powerful position that merchant wholesalers hold in marketing in Japan. There is a long history of wholesalers undertaking ingenious collusive actions to prevent competition and to consolidate their power base (Sheldon, 1958). A marketing system developed in which wholesalers financed other firms both forward and backward in the distribution channel (Glazer, 1970). The small scale of production and retailing meant that few firms had sufficient working capital to be efficient and consequently sought loans. Banks were unwilling to extend credit to small firms, so allowing wholesalers to take up a pivotal position in channel finance and effectively dominate channel relationships. Wholesalers tended to specialise by function, by product and regionally. The consequence of this is that the distribution system has become highly fragmented and complex. Some wholesalers specialise in negotiating with producers, others with transport, others in inter-regional sales, others in dealing with retailers. Added to this functional complexity, which can involve three levels of wholesalers, are specialist wholesalers for particular goods. Processed food wholesalers and their channel relationships are quite distinct from those handling frozen foods, for example. Add again the dimension of regionally circumscribed areas of operation and it becomes possible for goods to pass through eight or ten institutions between producer and consumer. Figure 5.2 shows the distribution channel for domestically produced pharmaceutical products. Over 7,000 wholesalers distribute products from 1,100 producers to 56,000 retailers and a variety of clinics and hospitals. Imports into the economy pass through a different wholesaler structure. Studies of Japanese marketing such as those by Yoshino (1975, 1971), Elgass and Dowd (1963), JETRO (1972) and Dowd (1959) all point to the high costs involved in this complex wholesale network. Given smallscale producers and small shops, the heavy use of wholesalers is the most efficient method of distribution:

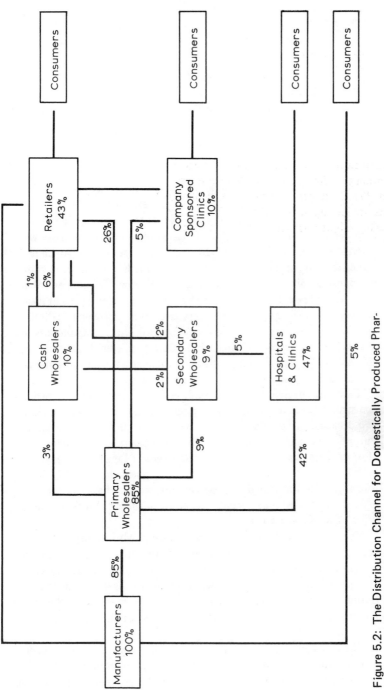

Figure 5.2: The Distribution Channel for Domestically Produced Pharmaceutical Products in Japan

For these smaller producers, in particular, wholesalers provide certain important functions, such as supplying them with information on market size and potential markets, in some cases with technical information and almost always with financing to assure product flows from factories to retail stores. While the role of wholesaler as financier for the manufacturer and retailer has declined in recent years, for the majority of small retailers the wholesaler is still important and supplies a function that is indispensable. (JETRO, 1972, p. 21).

The division of wholesale functions among several types of wholesaler has resulted in a plethora of small wholesale establishments. In 1972 almost 72 per cent of wholesale establishments had fewer than 10 employees. It must be remembered that wholesaling is an activity with a dominance of small units and although the 72 per cent in Japan is higher than in North America and probably the larger European countries it is considerably below economies such as Norway, Belgium and Denmark where fewer than 15 per cent of wholesalers employ 10 or more employees. There are, however, a very large number (over 180,000 in 1972) of wholesalers in Japan employing fewer than 10 employees. A relatively small number of large wholesalers, long complicated wholesale channels and a commanding position in the marketing channel all characterise the traditional wholesale sector in Japan.

To a lesser degree these same features exist in the traditional wholesale structure of most developed capitalist economies. Within the last two decades considerable changes have occurred in North America and Europe which have changed, radically, wholesalers' channel relationships. Most of these changes are becoming apparent in Japan and changes, even in this most traditional economy, are taking place quite quickly. The forces creating the changing wholesale processes are basically the same in Japan as in Western societies. The result of these changes is a diminution of wholesaler power.

The fundamental process creating change in wholesaling is the economic growth of manufacturing industry in response to the creation of a mass-consumption economy. In most capitalist countries within the last 20 years manufacturers have experienced increasing industrial concentration with the growth of large corporate enterprises. These changes in the productive sector have had an effect on the marketing system:

These changes include (1) the extensive development of consumer industries, (2) active entry of large firms into consumer fields, (3) the widespread adoption of the mass production system in consumer industries, (4) the rapid growth of output and (5) the introduction of numerous new products. (Yoshino, 1971, p. 31).

Although this relates to the Japanese situation, the comment is applicable to most Western countries. The rapid growth in output has created stresses in traditional wholesale institutions and manufacturers have sought ways to improve their access to the consumer.

Alongside the changes in the manufacturing sector have been changes in retailing which has taken much of the direct impact of increased demands from emerging mass-consumption societies. In the previous chapter the revolution in retailing method was discussed. Larger units and larger organisations have come to power in the retail sector with important consequences for wholesaling.

Between the changing retailers and manufacturers the traditional wholesale sector was slow to respond to the new environments of the marketing channel. Consequently both manufacturers and retailers sought non-traditional methods to satisfy the wholesale function. The most common response was for manufacturer or retailer to take on, themselves, the wholesale function. The development of chain store warehousing has been mentioned already. Many grocery chains operate both as retailers and wholesalers for many of their products and negotiate direct with manufacturers. The functions and costs of wholesaling are borne by the retailers. Wholesale institutions have no rôle to play. The large retail companies sometimes, initially, have difficulty obtaining supplies from manufacturers who fear harming their relationships with wholesalers. As both manufacturers have become larger and more powerful in their own right and mass merchandising retailing has become established, so negotiations for direct sales have become easier. Again specifically in respect of Japan but describing a more widely existing state of affairs, Yoshino (1971) writes:

the newly emerging mass merchandising firms can now buy whatever they desire from almost any sources at their own terms. Not only do they now enjoy access to a wide variety of the well-known national brands but they enjoy considerable freedom in determining at what price they can be sold by manufacturers. (pp. 157-8).

This position of Japan in the early 1970s typifies much of Europe in the mid 1960s and North America, initially in the 1930s, but to a considerable degree in the 1950s.

While the wholesaler has been cut out by vertical integration initiated by the retailer, he has also been bypassed by integration forward by the manufacturer. Manufacturers have adopted policies of exclusive dealership and also have invested in larger and more efficient distribution facilities. While manufacturer sponsored direct distribution has been common in industrial marketing for many decades it has become part of consumer goods distribution. From small beginnings in North America in the 1920s and 1930s the concept has become widespread in North America (Thorp, 1939; Alderson, 1949; Wedding, 1952; Converse, 1957; Webster, 1967) and in Europe (Mills, 1972). In Japan,

> in many industries large manufacturing firms have taken away the initiative that was once vested with large primary wholesalers. In a number of key consumer industries, manufacturing firms clearly have emerged as captain of the channels . . . There is every indication that this trend is likely to continue and probably to be intensified in the future. (Yoshino, 1971, p. 25).

Wholesaler Responses

Despite a slow response to the possibilities created by mass-consumption societies, wholesalers have reacted to being eased out of their key position in market channels. Their loss of power in some trades, for example the grocery trade in the USA, was rapid (Cassady and Jones, 1949). But, by evolving new types of organisation and technique, wholesalers have regained some of the wholesaling functions lost to retailers and manufacturers.

The wholesalers' first reactions to being bypassed by retailers, particularly chain stores, was to seek legal protection from the *unfair practice* of direct buying. They also sought to bring pressure on manufacturers who sold direct to retailers or to non-wholesaler sponsored buying groups. In 1918, for example, the Los Angeles Grocery Company, a retailer buying group, came in conflict with the Southern California Wholesale Grocers' Association. The association warned all manufacturers that any who sold to the retailer group would receive no orders from members of the wholesale association. After a number of legal actions and counteractions the courts directed the wholesalers to stop their discriminatory action but by this time the Los Angeles Grocery Company had gone bankrupt (Cassady and Jones, 1949). Many of the restrictive activities of the Wholesale Grocers' Association ended in court battles—St Louis Association in 1923, Wisconsin in 1924, North Dakota in 1925, Arkansas in 1926 and many others during the 1920s and early 1930s (Palamountain,

1955). Wholesalers inevitably lost these cases. Attempts at concerted protective action were abandoned in favour of attempts to adjust individual operations to the changed marketing environment.

Although some individual wholesalers have changed in very particular ways there are four major responses which have emerged as positive wholesaler policy. These are, first, a change in operating scale usually to create larger companies with more purchasing muscle. There is also evidence for success among small specialist wholesalers. Thus the first response is a polarisation of firm size. Second is the creation of voluntary chains. Third is the introduction of cash-and-carry wholesaling and fourth is a change in preferred location within the urban area.

The increased returns to scale in wholesaling appear to be related to organisation size in a different way from establishment or depot size. As in retailing, it is important to distinguish between the organisation and the establishment. A merchant wholesaler may operate through a number of wholesale establishments. Bucklin (1972) has shown that wholesale establishments have increased in average sales volume slower than retailers' sales volume in North America as wholesalers have sought particular supply niches. Between 1929 and 1967 sales per establishment on an inflation corrected basis increased by 81 per cent. Average cost as a percentage of sales is shown to decrease for merchant wholesalers, but not very steeply, in respect of increased establishment size. In respect of wholesale firms, Douglas (1975) shows that, again in North America, net profit as a percentage of sales shows a trend to increase with firm size. The increase is not regular over the size bands considered but the trend to higher profitability is present. Increased firm size and larger establishment size usually go together. An OECD report (1970) provides evidence from Sweden and the USA that large firms and large establishments have significantly higher employee productivity than small firms. The report concludes: 'Evidence that large wholesalers are more efficient than small ones is limited but convincing' (p. 72).

The advantages of increased size of firm come through the acquisition of greater purchasing power. Only by becoming larger can wholesalers obtain greater purchasing and negotiating power with manufacturers. In 1976 in Britain the merger took place between the Warriner and Mason's APT and the Alliance wholesale groups, both large grocery wholesalers. Effectively the two groups combined their organisational and buying resources to increase their purchasing muscle. Warriner and Mason, which is an associate company of a large conglomerate company, and three other companies merged at the same time as the major link between the two larger concerns. The new umbrella marketing organisation, called

National Food Distribution, operates 130 establishments including over 100 cash-and-carry units (see below). It has also about 2,000 retailers contractually linked to the wholesalers by means of voluntary retail chains.

The success of wholesaling in large, diversified multinational companies is shown by the success of the wholesale division of the British based Booker-McConnell organisation. In 1976 after tax, profits of the food distribution (including retailing and wholesaling) division rose 64 per cent to almost £2m. Diversification into wholesaling, from a base as a Caribbean sugar producer which had expanded into engineering and pharmaceuticals, began in 1957 and by 1976 it was the largest private wholesale group in Britain. Since 1976 the group has acquired the large grocery wholesaler, Kinloch, which had 1,800 affiliated retailers. Also it has bought the Oriel Foods Group, bringing another 1,000 retailers into the organisation's list of customers as well as gaining control over a further 28 wholesale depots. Not only is the group able to negotiate with manufacturers from a very strong position but the acquisition of the several companies has provided national coverage for the wholesale division of Booker-McConnell. Larger organisations provide greater purchasing power and a wider geographical coverage (Beaumont, 1977).

With returns to scale in establishments provided by lower proportional capital costs, land costs, etc. in larger units together with the ability to obtain goods competitively through large purchasing operations, some merchant wholesalers in recent years have increased their market share of wholesaling functions. This has been the case particularly in the grocery trades. The increasing concentration of activity through larger establishments operated by larger companies is shown again by the changes taking place in Japanese wholesaling. Table 5.3 shows the number of establishments of different size. The relative importance of small wholesale establishments has declined while the larger ones have increased numbers considerably. Only in the smallest group have actual numbers declined in the past few years. The large units also have increased their sales share with establishments with 50 and more employees accounting for 43.6 per cent of sales in 1960 and 56.7 per cent in 1970. Furthermore sales per employee show considerable increases with larger scales of operation. For an establishment with approximately 50 workers the average sales per employee is twice that of one with 10 employees. As large operations increase their size even more they find their efficiency increases and so the trend towards increasing size becomes a cumulative one.

Many small wholesalers in Japan have failed to adapt to the changed

Table 5.3: Distribution of Wholesale Establishments by Size in Japan

Number of employees	Number of establishments as percentage of total		
	1956	1964	1972
1-2	27.8	24.8	20.3
3-4	25.3	21.4	23.0
5-9	28.4	27.2	28.5
10-19	13.0	15.6	16.0
20-29	2.9	4.7	5.2
30-49	1.6	3.3	3.8
50-99	1.0	1.9	2.2
100 or more		1.0	1.0
Total establishments		229,248	259,863

marketing situation and have either closed or become increasingly marginal. A few have taken on specialist functions and supply small stores. They benefit from their personal contacts with both small shop and larger, primary, wholesaler. Much of the market for consumer goods remains in neighbourhood stores and these retailers prefer to deal at a personal level with small wholesalers. Increasingly, however, these small wholesalers are coming under pressure as a shake-out occurs in retailing. Larger wholesalers are organising small secondary wholesalers into a closely coordinated network of affiliates and so are creating increased polarisation in operating scale. The large primary wholesalers, believing a place still exists for the small secondary wholesaler, offer financial and managerial help to the affiliated small firms. There comes a point at which it becomes more profitable for this type of network to be centrally organised by one company operating through several depots. The type of organisation operated by Booker McConnell then becomes the most rational and streamlined form of wholesale distribution.

A second response of wholesalers to the erosion of their power is the formation of voluntary chains. This policy response is a common one through North America and Europe. It has been rather slow to develop in Japan where, although chains are present in the food trades, textiles, bedding and pharmaceutical goods, only about 20,000 retailers are members out of the total of almost 1.5 million shops. The voluntary chain movement is likely to expand considerably in Japan through the 1980s.

The voluntary chain policy response of hard pressed merchant wholesalers rests on the idea that they must establish a basic market if they are to compete effectively with other institutions carrying out whole-saling functions. Mention has been made in Chapter 4 of the advantages to independent retailers of membership of a voluntary chain but bene-fits also accrue to the sponsors of the chains. The basis of a voluntary chain is an agreement between a wholesaler and several retailers where-by the retailers

> agree to take all, or a stipulated proportion of their supplies from the wholesaler and to follow the direction of the wholesaler with regard to store layout, display merchandise methods and the identification of the retail store as a member of the chain or group by the use of the standard facia or sign. (Stacey and Wilson, 1965, p. 152).

By being assured of regular orders from a number of retailers the whole-saler can gain customers by mass purchasing from manufacturers.

The wholesaler, by concentrating on a smaller number of retailers who buy most of their stock from the wholesaler, reduces supply costs and rationalises supply services. The larger voluntary groups become sufficiently large to launch their own brands of goods. Their purchasing power is such that they can negotiate with manufacturers to purchase 'own label' goods. The wholesaler thus competes directly with the chain store who similarly market 'own label' products. The wholesaler in the voluntary group concentrates on wholesaling, while the retail members concentrate on selling to the consumer. Fullop (1962) in a comprehen-sive study describes the advantages of the method to wholesalers and the many variations possible on the basic idea. Some of the largest wholesaler sponsored chains are now beginning to develop their own chains of whole-saler owned and managed shops. With chain stores integrating backwards to cut out the wholesaler, the wholesaler is now integrating forward into retailing. A second, very common extension of the scheme is the joining together of regionally based wholesalers, operating chains, to create a national coverage of a particular chain. Even multinational chains have been created in that way. The advantages of increasing the scale of operation are as relevant to a voluntary chain wholesaler as to any other wholesaler.

Grocery wholesalers were the first to adopt voluntary group methods as a way of recovering their loss of market share. Consequently in this commodity group development has gone further. The earliest attempts to create voluntary chain type operations appears to have been in 1919 in the USA (Centre d'Étude du Commerce, 1955) but the first main period of growth was in the 1920s and 1930s after which the idea spread

to Europe. The Spar group was formed in the Netherlands in 1932 and
grew steadily for about five years and again after World War 2. The
movement had a second phase of growth, this time in Europe, during
the 1950s when it spread to France (1950) and Britain (1954) and
became established firmly as a successful policy for grocery wholesaler
growth. Between 1955 and 1965 the number of affiliated retailers in
Europe more than doubled to over 400,000 shops. The voluntary group
wholesaler is now widely established throughout Europe, North America
and Australia where its growth pattern is similar to that outlined above
(Briggs and Smyth, 1967) and is emerging as a major force in Latin
America (Guthrie, 1974). In being accepted in the grocery trades it
became apparent that the concept could be applied equally well to
salvage the declining wholesaler sectors in other trades. Most branches
of trade now have well established voluntary chains and it seems likely
to continue to grow in importance as a wholesaler response to attempts
to shorten marketing channels.

After some early setbacks voluntary chains developed rapidly in North
America. Grether (1930) and Cassady and Jones (1949) point to initial
failures in California owing to sectional differences of opinion in the
chain and to competition from retailer co-operatives which were particularly strong in the Los Angeles area. A case study of the changing
wholesale sector in Des Moines, Iowa is provided by Volpp (1956). By
1939 voluntary group wholesalers accounted for almost one-third of
the general grocery trade in the USA not controlled by chain stores.
Brown, Applebaum and Salmon (1970) provide a case study of a wholesaler who, in 1935, 'in an effort to compete with the corporate chains'
(p. 592) joined a national voluntary chain. The company concentrated
on supplying members of the chain and, by 1959, the 95 chain members
serviced by the wholesaler accounted for 81 per cent of sales and the
remaining 74 retailers accounted for less than one-fifth of sales. By a
process of mergers and linking together informally of wholesalers, nation-
wide chains were created. By 1958 the Independent Grocers Alliance con-
sisted of 53 wholesalers, the Red and White group had 23,000 retailers
and 40 wholesalers and the Clover Farm chain had 28 wholesalers. By
the mid 1960s over half the grocery wholesaling sales passed through
voluntary chain wholesalers. Affiliated retailers, buying most of their
stock from the voluntary chain wholesalers, accounted in 1972 for 44
per cent of grocery sales in the USA, compared with 49 per cent by the
chain stores and 6 per cent by unaffiliated independents. By a policy of
encouraging voluntary chain development wholesalers have recovered,
albeit slowly, their decline in market power lost so rapidly in the 1920s

and 1930s. Grocery wholesaling is proving a model for other merchandise groups. Lopata (1969) sees further development of voluntary chains and McKeon (1972) states: 'The wholesalers' latest strategies in the drug and hardware channels have been the establishment of wholesaler-sponsored and retailer-sponsored co-operatives' (p. 43). The loosely integrated wholesale groups have the size, capital, management resources and organisational structure that allows them to market goods as efficiently as the corporate retail chain.

Within Europe major competition hit the wholesalers in the 1950s and during the decade voluntary chain formation was extensive. The movement was instrumental not only in modernising wholesalers but also in acting as a catalyst for the conversion of shops to selfservice. Henksmeier (1960) suggests this function of the voluntary chain was particularly important in Austria, Denmark, West Germany, Sweden and Switzerland. While in the USA associations of wholesalers created national coverage for voluntary chains, within Europe multinational coverage was achieved in the same way.

The Spar group had developed into a European-wide organisation by the early 1960s and has since moved to Africa and also Japan. The group originated in 1932 in the Netherlands with a wholesaler modelling his operation on the Red and White chain in the USA. Table 5.4 shows the size of linked national associations of Spar in 1977. Other groups operate in several countries. There are also signs of a regrouping of chains leading to closer co-operation between existing chains. In West Germany, for example, Ifa, Vivo and Végé groups have combined some buying functions within an umbrella organisation – Central Marketing. The larger wholesalers have become larger in this way and many of the smaller ones have failed to respond and have closed down. Between 1961 and 1973 the number of wholesale enterprises in France fell from 78,000 to 67,000, the number of establishments over approximately the same period fell from 107,000 to 99,000 but employment in the remaining firms increased from 574,000 to 812,000. The creation of voluntary chains is seen as an integral part of the modernisation of wholesaling within French national plans (Buissan and Morice, 1966; Commissariat Général du Plan, 1976). Future voluntary chain expansion is anticipated in Europe as a means both of modernising wholesaling and also as an aid to the independent retail sector (Delville, 1970; Tietz, 1971; Distributive Trades EDC, 1973).

The adoption of cash-and-carry wholesaling techniques is a further common response to the conflict situation in which wholesalers found themselves. Again wholesalers in the USA were the first to exploit the

Table 5.4: Wholesale and Retail Operations of Spar

	Year of establishment	Number in 1976 Wholesalers	Retailers	1975 Sales in £m (est.) Wholesale	Retail
The Netherlands	1932	7	975	170	280
Belgium/Luxembourg	1947/1960	5	587	21	45
West Germany	1953	38	7,220	895	1,610
Denmark	1953	2	79	80	45
Austria	1954	1	1,248	100	260
France	1955	26	2,497	115	114
United Kingdom	1956	19	3,887	350	390
Spain	1959	25	4,890	102	423
Italy	1959	26	3,252	92	190
Finland	1961	6	723	127	115
South Africa	1962	7	400	56	125
Ireland	1963	4	284	29	33
Rhodesia	1966	2	90	—	—
Greece	1970	1	19	9	8
Japan	1977	1	1,000	—	—
Data for Portugal not available					

potential of cash-and-carry in which the wholesale services offered are considerably limited. In most large North American cities, by 1925, at least one major wholesaler was operating a cash-and-carry depot as a subsidiary part of their wholesaling enterprise. So, for example, the first cash-and-carry in San Francisco opened in 1925, and in Los Angeles in 1922 with expansion taking place in 1924 after the wholesaler had seen the Toledo operation of the Berdan Company who were pioneers in cash-and-carry development (Cassady and Jones, 1949). As with the other adoptions of wholesalers, cash-and-carry spread to Europe and has proved a successful part of the wholesale trade.

The basis of cash-and-carry wholesaling is the adaptation, by the wholesaler, of a warehouse such that retailers can select articles them-selves (in similar fashion to selfservice retailing), collect them together, pay at a checkout and deliver the goods themselves to their own shop. The technique lifts from the wholesaler the responsibility and costs of a delivery service, of collecting and packing orders and of many of the service functions such as providing information on new products. Whole-saling costs are reduced and this cost saving can be passed to the retailer in the form of lower prices, so allowing the smaller shop to retail goods

at prices competitive with chain stores. The cash-and-carry system is
geared to the specific needs of small businesses – both retail and service.
Consequently it is favoured by independent retailers as a means of
obtaining their supplies. (Kirby, 1974). As with voluntary chains the
technique emerged and grew in the grocery trades but has since spread
to clothing, hardware and other non-food trades.

The adoption of cash-and-carry techniques complements the other
structural changes taking place within wholesaling. With larger enterprises it is possible to co-ordinate a chain of cash-and-carry depots with
warehouses serving as bases for a traditional, full-service, delivered trade.
It is also possible to co-ordinate voluntary group wholesaling (involving
a delivered service) with cash-and-carry depots to service retailers who
are not members of the group.

A series of surveys by the Manchester Business School (Thorpe, 1971;
Thorpe and Thorpe, 1976; Thorpe, 1975) have described the integration
of cash-and-carry methods into wholesalers' operations in Britain. Numbers of depots increased to a peak of around 650 in late 1969, since
when numbers have fluctuated but have shown a tendency to decrease.
The reason for this decrease in numbers is the search for scale economies
with small depots closing and giving way to a smaller number of larger
units. Table 5.5 shows the change in the size distribution between 1971
and 1975. The same process has occurred elsewhere in Europe as shown
by the figures for France and Belgium in the lower part of the table.
Depots in excess of $10,000 \, m^2$, and even a few over $20,000 \, m^2$, are now
not unusual features of peripheral industrial estates around large European cities. Thorpe and Thorpe (1976) also point to the more even
spread of centres throughout Britain, with most key locations already
having a depot by 1975. Replacement of existing units by larger depots
then becomes more important than expanding the network of sites.

First, with the increase in numbers and more recently the increased
depot size, sales of cash-and-carry operations have increased substantially.
An Economist Intelligence Unit (1976) report suggests that the top
eleven operators in Britain in 1975 accounted for 88 per cent of sales
and operated 485 out of the 640 depots. From sales of about £400m in
1970 the sector had grown to deal with £1,400m worth of goods in
1975. In Britain for some grocery wholesalers, at least, cash-and-carry
depots have enabled them to halt their decline in market power and
even to improve their position.

The same success story is evident elsewhere in Western Europe with
a few large companies gradually accounting for more depots and more
sales. For the small wholesaler cash-and-carry has often allowed the

Table 5.5: Size of Cash-and-Carry Warehouses in Great Britain, France and Belgium

Size (m^2)	Percentage of warehouses		Percentage change in number
Great Britain	1971	1975	1971-5
over 4,600	3.3	10.0	191
2,800-4,599	7.8	17.6	126
1,800-2,799	24.0	26.0	8
900-1,799	39.5	29.5	-27
less than 900	25.4	16.9	-35
Total number	658	640	
France	1973	1976	1973-6
over 2,500	12.4	14.2	23
2,000-2,499	6.8	11.3	77
1,500-1,999	9.6	8.1	10
1,000-1,499	24.2	23.6	4
750-999	11.2	10.5	0
500-749	13.6	11.1	−14
less than 500	22.3	21.2	0
Total number	323	344	
Belgium	1971	1977	1971-7
over 4,000	7.1	14.8	80
3,000-3,999	4.3	8.2	67
2,000-2,999	7.1	18.0	120
1,000-1,999	31.4	26.2	-27
500-999	21.4	19.7	-20
less than 500	28.6	13.1	-60
Total number	70	61	

wholesaler to stay in business a little longer but it has not proved a panacea as it has for a few large companies. In France the number of depots has increased rapidly from 12 in 1960 to 131 in 1965, 209 in 1970 and 349 in 1976. One company operates 128 depots. There seems to be still room for more depots but already some small depots are closing and larger ones are replacing them. Rapid growth characterises Italy (100 in 1972 and 226 in 1975) and Spain (112 in 1975) but numbers have stabilised in West Germany, Belgium and the Netherlands. In West Germany the number of depots had fallen from a peak of 681 in 1972 to 652 three years later but over the same period floor space rose 12 per cent to over 2 million m². From the evidence of growth patterns in several European countries there appears to be a limit to the extent wholesalers can use cash-and-carry methods. As this limit, for a particular trade group, is reached so the larger wholesale enterprises, through mergers and larger depots, take an increasingly larger share of the trade.

A fifth common response of wholesalers to their conflict with chain store and manufacturers is to move to suburban sites. The demand for sites for the large units, central area redevelopment, the need for cash-and-carry units to be close to their customers (independent retailers tend to be concentrated in suburban areas) and the desirability for depots to be linked easily with the inter- and intraurban road network means that suburban wholesale locations have to become preferred to the traditional CBD frame locations. Traditional models of urban structure, substantiated by empirical studies related to 1950 and earlier (William-Olsson, 1960; Firey, 1947; Hoyt, 1933) all suggest wholesaling as a central area use located on the fringes of the CBD. The pattern is changing drastically and relatively quickly. Table 5.6 shows the change in floorspace in the London metropolitan region over the three years 1967-9. New warehousing has located in outer London and the outer

Table 5.6:   Warehouse Floorspace in Metropolitan London, 1967-9

	Increase in warehouse floorspace	
	Net ('000 m²)	Percentage
Central London	-39.0	-1.3
Rest of Inner London	-15.2	-0.4
Outer London	500.5	12.8
Outer metropolitan area		
East	127.0	19.8
North	157.9	16.3
West	103.7	11.0
South West	53.8	10.2
South	21.6	5.7
South East	58.0	9.8

metropolitan area. From a situation in 1967 when 47 per cent of metropolitan warehouse space was located in inner London the situation had changed by 1969 to only 43 per cent in these inner areas — a very con-

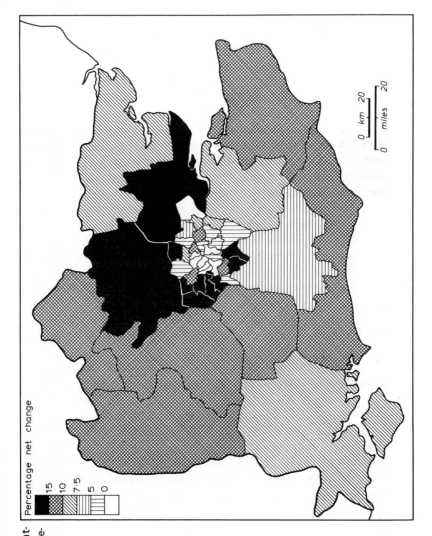

Figure 5.3: The Percent-
age Net Change in Ware-
house Floorspace in
South East England
1967-9

Percentage net change

15
10
7·5
5
0

0 km 20
0 miles 20

siderable fall in only two years. Figure 5.3 shows the shift in wholesaling growing not in town centres in the outer metropolitan areas but in industrial estates in the suburbs of these towns. The shift to suburban sites has occurred at all levels of urban centre.

The move to the suburbs began earlier in the USA than in Europe. Cassady and Jones (1949) in describing the activity of the major cash-and-carry operator in Los Angeles point out that, 'The 37 branch stations in Los Angeles County are strategically situated so that the average distance from any retailer's location to a Smart and Final branch is less than two and a half miles' (p. 37). Customer convenience is the key to suburban location in this case. Redevelopment of city centre areas has also been a factor in encouraging suburbanisation. In this case the redevelopment process sometimes has proved beneficial to the wholesaler in forcing the firms from inertial locations to more optimal sites. A conclusion in Zimmer's (1966) study of small businesses was 'that while non-survivors were largely small food-related retail, neighbourhood-type businesses, the units that moved to the suburbs were predominantly those in the manufacturing, wholesale, and construction category' (p. 387).

The suburbanisation of wholesaling occurred alongside the structural changes in wholesale business in many American cities. Cain (1966) has studied the pattern in Washington DC, Lewis (1952) in Minneapolis; St Paul and Harmston (1970) show how in St Louis, Missouri wholesale sales increased from $3.1 to 4.5 billion between 1948 and 1967 but over the same 20 years sales in St Louis County increased from $0.2 to 3.1 billion. The dispersion of wholesaling in North America has largely gone unstudied. Vance (1970) in a very brief and inadequate section attempts to contrast the rôle of transport costs and customer access in creating wholesaling districts. He suggests that central locations will occur for wholesaling of the 'will call' type. The growth of cash-and-carry wholesaling in the suburbs negates this argument. The suburbanisation of wholesaling is a more complex process than a balancing of physical distribution costs and consumer access.

The suburbanisation process is international. While the processes began earlier in the USA than in Europe the same locational changes are now becoming apparent in Japan and Australia. Yoshino (1971) discussing Japan argues that traffic congestion, outdated buildings, expensive land costs and lack of space for expansion have forced wholesalers to the suburbs where purpose built wholesale centres have been developed:

These newly created wholesale centres have a number of common facilities that serve the entire group, including warehouses, distribution terminals and even a common computer centre. Particularly notable is the construction of major wholesale merchandising marts in Tokyo and Osaka. (p. 189).

Between 1963 and 1968, 54 such centres have been built or actively planned (see Chapter 7). The creation of these trade centres is still at an early stage (Nakanishi, 1973) but it is likely to increase in importance not just in Japan but also in Europe:

Location cooperation is based on the consideration that it is not· necessary for every firm to perform all functions itself, but that certain work processes can be more rationally carried out via joint facilities such as typing and correspondence pools, forwarding offices, loading and storage depots, central data processing plants, sample and show rooms, etc. Decisive for the success of trading is a careful selection of the members, exact planning of location, building layout, technical installations and a dynamic cooperation management. Only this form of relocation of firms in agglomerative structures facilitates modernisation and a far-reaching rationalisation and decreasing trend in costs. (Commission of the European Communities, 1976, p. 32).

Central area congestion has affected merchant wholesalers to a considerable extent but Alexander (1976) has shown that agent/broker wholesalers are also moving out of the CBD. In an analysis of movements of over 200 such firms in Sydney CBD in 1965 over 34 per cent had moved to suburban sites by 1975. The majority of these firms have relocated to sites outside the suburban office centres around Sydney. This important aspect of suburbanisation has not been considered elsewhere.

The search for cheaper, more accessible and less congested sites has led wholesalers to the suburbs. The change in locations together with various structural and technical changes initiated by wholesalers has enabled them to recover some of their marketing status. Most of these changes have centred on the merchant wholesaler sector. The move to the suburbs has had wider effects particularly in respect of the wholesaling of perishable foods. City wholesale markets for fruit and vegetables have been relocated in many cities and often account for sites of 100 ha or more in the suburbs. The changes in this wholesale institution will be considered in more detail in Chapter 7.

Changing Wholesale Costs

The broadscale changes in wholesaling discussed in this chapter have resulted in increasingly complex wholesale operations. Increased operating scale has created higher levels of capital expenditure with critical decisions required on the allocation of this expenditure. Increased depot size means a greater quantity of goods which in turn means a greater concentration of transport activity at depot sites. The increasing variety of goods associated with economies of high mass consumption creates a greater demand for transport and more vehicle trips. In a case study of Associated Wholesale Grocers of Kansas City, Coyle (1976) shows how these developments affect a particular firm. The company carries around 10,000 grocery lines (much increased in recent years) and offers a delivery service within 450 km of the depot. By automated warehousing, computer control and efficient vehicle selection the company can distribute goods to allow independent retailers to be price competitive with chain stores. Most of these changes result in increased costs of distribution coupled with greater efforts to minimise these costs. The control of distribution costs can even lead to company mergers (Hannington, 1973). Not only in the USA has the growth of cost consciousness spawned attempts to view distribution as a total event; in Europe, Japan and Australia the same trend is apparent (Wills, Magrill and Cooper, 1972; Ikeda, 1974; Gilmour, 1974). The controlling of this event is termed physical distribution management (PDM). Physical distribution management in Britain accounts for 20 per cent of Gross Domestic Product. 'It is concerned both with movement and storage of raw materials and finished goods. It is, therefore, a cumulative cost, commencing during the processing and transportation of raw materials, and increasing continuously until the sale of the finished article is made'. (Bream, 1976, p. 74). The three major costs are transportation, warehousing and stockholding, all of which are wholesaling functions. Wholesalers are constantly attempting to reduce the costs of physical distribution.

Cost control is possible in a number of ways. Strict inventory control, protective packaging, effective financial management, efficient material handling techniques and a well designed information processing system all help. Several texts are available on these aspects of PDM (Smykay, 1973; Magee, 1968; Mossman and Newton, 1965). Probably the single most important cost area—accounting for around 40 per cent of PDM costs—is transportation and cost effective transport techniques are central to *the new wholesaling*. Within warehouses there is need to plan and manage the physical movement of goods. Only in this way can the full economies of scale be achieved. Automated warehousing techniques increasingly are being applied but there is still considerable interfirm variation in materials handling costs within depots or warehouses (Williams, 1974).

Costs associated with transport external to the warehouse account, in Britain, for approximately 20 per cent of the wholesalers gross margin (Edwards, 1969). Again this cost varies considerably from firm to firm depending both on the commodity dealt with and the location of the depot facilities. The whole field of PDM is one in which mathematical methods, particularly those associated with operations research, have been applied in attempts to create optimal distribution systems and so reduce costs. The siting of depots is a particular case in point. The differences between optimal and suboptimal locations for depots is most apparent in terms of transport costs.

Watson-Gandy (1972) identifies five aspects of the depot location problem. These are

(1) How many depots?
(2) Where should they be located?
(3) What areas should these depots serve or to which depots should customers be allocated?
(4) How big should these depots be with particular reference to the economies of scale interest in warehousing operations?
(5) When should the depots be opened?

Figure 5.4 provides a very simple illustration of the first question. The total cost function comprises the sum of four elements which are the fixed costs of having warehouses (F), stock holding or inventory costs (I), the costs of truck transport to the depot (T_1) and the costs of local deliveries (T_2). With more depots the first three rise but more depots mean lower delivery costs. For different commodities different costs functions of the four variables result and different optimal numbers of depots ensue. One feature of the total cost function is that as warehouse numbers increase so the total cost function becomes shallower. The difference between 3 or 4 warehouses and 23 or 24 is considerable and usually this benefits the larger firm and provides a greater degree of flexibility in depot location in the larger firm.

The whole field of depot location has been reviewed by Eilon, Watson-Gandy and Christofides (1971) and a briefer review is presented by Stasch (1968). Watson-Gandy and Christophides concentrate on the various technical approaches available to model depot location. Although they,

Figure 5.4: Cost Patterns in Depot Location

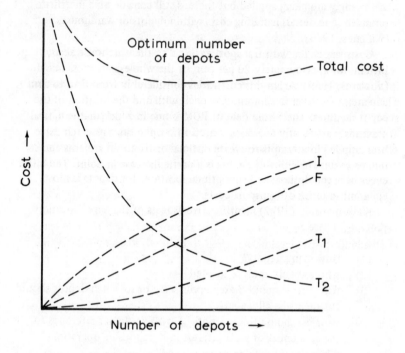

and the workers they review, consider a large variety of variables relevant to locational decisions, there still remain others exogenous to the economics of warehouse operation. Taff (1972) working in the slightly different North American context lists over 200 variables to be considered in planning a distribution centre. To build any model relating together so many variables is almost impossible and so to some degree depot location must remain outside the strict analyses of operations research (Mole, 1975). This is not to say that the incomplete models are not useful. The mathematical model will indicate possible locations at which different specific sites can be explored. Operating costs can be reduced substantially in this way and the models of Ballou (1968), Eilon and Deziel (1966), and Haley (1963) are much superior to the market area analyses with flags and maps characteristic of the 1940s market analyst's attempt to reduce transport costs (Rasmussen, 1943; Peterson, 1940). Future enhancements in wholesaler power lie in the adoption of strict PDM methods (Walters, 1975; Comité Belge de la Distribution, 1976; Heskett, 1973).

Discussion in this chapter has concentrated on the responses of the wholesale sector, and the firms in this sector, to growth within capitalist economies. The need for wholesaling is also present in communist economies but expectedly the institutions are responding to change in different ways from those discussed above. Within China and the USSR there appears to be considerable concern over the apparent low productivity in wholesaling and the long channel needed to fulfil wholesale functions. There are few studies in English of wholesaling in China. Chou's (1963) study relates to the 1950s and shows how most products pass through at least three levels of wholesale institution but the economic reforms of the last 20 years have streamlined the channels at least for food products. Skurski (1972) similarly points to a shift in the USSR from concern with the administration of wholesaling to devising more efficient commercial methods. Particularly important has been the separation of wholesale and retail functions so that the direct purchasing conflict, which occurred in capitalist economies and was in danger of occurring at an administrative level in the USSR, is defused. A scheme of centralised deliveries to wholesalers has been devised with the wholesaler then taking responsibility for subsequent delivery.

> This arrangement has enabled several cities to transfer the warehouses of retail trade organizations to wholesale bases, to consolidate inventories, and to lower costs. This process also eliminates the conflict between wholesale and retail warehouses existing in the same city. (Skurski, 1972, p. 63).

It is generally anticipated that changes such as this are forerunners to a more drastic reform of wholesaling. The necessity for wholesale functions to be performed is a feature of capitalist and communist economies; the contrast is in the institutions involved in wholesaling and in the resolution of interinstitution conflict within the marketing channel.

References

ALDERSON, W. (1949) 'People and Places of Wholesaling in the United States', *Journal of Marketing*, 13, pp. 149-55.

ALEXANDER, D. (1970) *Retailing in England during the Industrial Revolution* (Athlone Press, London).

ALEXANDER, I. (1976) 'The Suburbanization of Private Sector Office Employment: Fact or Fiction' in G.J.R. Linge (ed.), *Restructuring Employment Opportunities in Australia* (Australian National University, Canberra).

—— (1979) *Office Location and Public Policy* (Longmans, London).

ANDERSON, D.A. (1970) *Marketing and Development. The Thailand Experience* (Michigan State University, East Lansing).

BALLOU, R.H. (1968) 'Dynamic Warehouse Location Analysis', *Journal of Marketing Research*, 5, pp. 271-6.

BEAUMONT, P. (1977) 'Wholesalers – Not Well Known but Getting Bigger Just the Same', *Grocer*, 12 November, pp. 79-83.

BECKMAN, T.N. (1965) 'Changes in Wholesaling Structure and Performance' in P.D. Bennett (ed.), *Marketing and Economic Development* (American Marketing Association, Chicago), pp. 603-18.

BELSHAW, C.S. (1965) *Traditional Exchange and Modern Markets* (Prentice-Hall, Englewood Cliffs).

BREAM, R. (1976) 'Distribution Costs Hit £17 billion', *The Grocer*, 5 June, p. 74.

BRIGGS, D.H., and R.L. SMYTH (1967) *Distribution of Groceries* (University of Western Australia Press, Nedlands).

BROWN, M.P., W. APPLEBAUM and W.J. SALMON (1970) *Strategy Problems of Mass Retailers and Wholesalers* (Irwin, Homewood).

BUCKLIN, L.P. (1972) *Competition and Evolution in the Distributive Trades* (Prentice-Hall, Englewood Cliffs).

BUISSON, J., and G. MORICE (1966) 'La revolution silençieuse de commerce de gros en France', Supplement to *L'economie*, 1034, pp. 6-9.

CAIN, J.L. (1966) 'Changes in the Structure of Retail and Wholesale Food Marketing in Maryland and the District of Columbia 1929-1963', *University of Maryland, College of Agriculture, Agricultural Economics Information Series*, 36.

CASSADY, R., and W.L. JONES (1949) *The Changing Competitive Structure of the Wholesale Grocery Trade* (University of California Press, Berkeley).

CENTRE D'ETUDE DU COMMERCE (1955) *Les entreprises pilotes – les chaines volontaires* (Paris).

CHARTRES, J.A. (1977) *Internal Trade in England, 1500-1700* (Macmillan, London).

CHOU, Y. (1963) 'Wholesaling in Communist China' in R. Bartels (ed.), *Comparative Marketing-Wholesaling in Fifteen Countries* (Irwin, Homewood), pp. 253-70.

COHEN, A. (1966) 'Politics of the Kola Trade', *Africa*, 36(1), pp. 20-30.

COMITE BELGE DE LA DISTRIBUTION (1976) *Methodes nouvelles de réduction des couts dans la distribution physique* (Comité Belge de la Distribution, Brussels).

COMMISSARIAT GENERAL DU PLAN (1976) *Commerces, services et artisanat* (Le Documentation Française, Paris).

CONVERSE, P.D. (1957) 'Twenty Five Years of Wholesaling', *Journal of Marketing*, 21, pp. 152-8.

COYLE, J.S. (1976) 'Inside Associated Wholesale Grocers of Kansas City', *Progressive Grocer*, 55(9), pp. 56-89.

DELVILLE, M.C. (1970) 'Tendances quantitatives et qualitatives a l'horizon de 1980 dans les chaines volontaires' in *La distribution en 1980* (vol. 2) (Office Belge pour l'Accroissement de la Productivité, Bruxelles), pp. 74-82.

DISTRIBUTIVE TRADES EDC (1973) *The Distributive Trades in the Common Market* (HMSO, London).

DOUGLAS, E. (1975) *Economics of Marketing* (Harper & Row, New York).

DOWD, L.P. (1959) 'Wholesale Marketing in Japan', *Journal of Marketing*, 23, pp. 251-60.

ECONOMIST INTELLIGENCE UNIT (1976) 'Cash and Carry Wholesaling', *Retail Business*, 225, pp. 19-24.

EDWARDS, S.C. (1969) 'Transport Costs in the Wholesale Trades', *Journal of Transport Economics and Policy*, 2, pp. 272-8.

EILON, S., and D.P. DEZIEL (1966) 'Siting a Distribution Centre – an Analogue Computer Application', *Management Science*, 12(6), pp. B245-54.

EILON, S., C.D.T. WATSON-GANDY and N. CHRISTOFIDES (1971) *Distribution*

Management: Mathematical Modelling and Practical Analysis (Griffin, London).

ELGASS, G.A. and L.P. DOWD (1963) 'Wholesaling in Japan' in R. Bartels (ed.), *Comparative Marketing-Wholesaling in Fifteen Countries* (Irwin, Homewood), pp. 156-68.

FIREY, W. (1947) *Land Use in Central Boston* (Harvard University Press, Cambridge Press).

FULLOP, C. (1962) *Buying by Voluntary Chains* (George Allen & Unwin, London).

GILMOUR, D. (1974) (ed.) *PDM in Australia* (Cheshire, Melbourne).

GLADE, W.P., W.A. STRANG, J.G. UDELL and J.E. LITTLEFIELD (1970) *Marketing in a Developing Nation* (Heath-Lexington, Lexington, Mass.).

GLAZER, H. (1970) 'Japan's Marketing Structure', *Sophia University, Socio-economic Institute, Bulletin*, 23.

GOTTMANN, J. (1961) *Megalopolis: the Urbanized North-eastern Seaboard of the United States* (Twentieth Century Fund, Cambridge, Mass.).

GRETHER, E.T. (1930) 'Trends in the Wholesale Grocery Trade in San Francisco', *Harvard Business Review*, 8, pp. 443-50.

GUTHRIE, C.B. (1974) 'Economics of Voluntary Chains in Latin America' in D. Izraeli *et al.* (eds), *Marketing Systems for Developing Countries* (Wiley, Chichester), pp. 160-71.

HALEY, K.B. (1963) 'The Siting of Depots', *International Journal of Production Research*, 2(1), pp. 41-5.

HANNINGTON, B.G. (1973) 'The Case of the Frozen Merger', *Management Today*, December, pp. 108-11.

HARMSTON, F.K. (1970) 'Wholesaling Activity in Missouri – Trends and Shifts 1948 through 1967', *University of Missouri-Columbia, Business and Government Review*, 11(5), pp. 3-13.

HAWKINS, H.C.G. (1965) *Wholesale and Retail Trade in Tanganyika* (Praeger, New York).

HENKSMEIER, K.H. (1960) *The Economic Performance of Self-service in Europe* (OEEC, Paris).

HESKETT, J.L. (1973) 'Sweeping Changes in Distribution', *Harvard Business Review*, 51, pp. 123-32.

HOYT, H. (1933) *One Hundred Years of Land Values in Chicago* (University of Chicago Press, Chicago).

IKEDA, M. (1974) 'The Progress of Physical Distribution in Japan', *Transportation and Distribution Management*, 14, pp. 41-4.

JETRO (1972) *Planning for Distribution in Japan* (Japanese External Trade Organisation, Tokyo).

JONES, F.M. (1937) 'Middlemen in the Domestic Trade of the United States', *Illinois Studies in the Social Sciences*, 21(3), pp. 1-81.

KIRBY, D.A. (1974) 'Shopkeepers Go Shopping', *Geographical Magazine*, 46(10), pp. 526-8.

LEWIS, E.H. (1952) *Wholesaling in the Twin Cities* (University of Minnesota Press, Minneapolis).

—— (1961) *Marketing Electrical Apparatus and Supplies* (McGraw-Hill, New York).

LOPATA, R.S. (1969) 'Faster Pace in Wholesaling', *Harvard Business Review*.

McKEON, J.C. (1972) 'Conflicting Patterns of Structural Change in Wholesaling', *Economic and Business Bulletin*, 24(2), pp. 37-53.

MAGEE, J.F. (1968) *Industrial Logistics* (McGraw-Hill, New York).

MILLS, G. (1972) 'The Analysis of European Distributive Systems', *International Journal of Physical Distribution*, 3, pp. 21-42.

MOLE, R.H. (1975) 'An Appraisal of Warehouse Location Models', *International Journal of Physical Distribution*, 5(1), pp. 31-5.

MOSSMAN, F.H., and M. NEWTON (1965) *Logistics of Distribution Systems*

(Allyn & Bacon, Boston).

MUKWAYA, A.B. (1962) 'The Marketing of Staple Foods in Kampala, Uganda' in P. Bohannan and G. Dalton (eds), *Markets in Africa* (Northwestern University Press, Evanston), pp. 643-66.

NAKANISHI, C. (1973) 'Physical Distribution in Large Cities', *The Wheel Extended*, 3(2), pp. 12-20.

OECD (1970) *Food Marketing and Economic Growth* (OECD, Paris).

OLUC, M., N. NEYZI, E. CONENSOY and E.J. ENRIGHT (1963) 'Wholesaling in Turkey' in R. Bartels (ed.), *Comparative Marketing. Wholesaling in Fifteen Countries* (Irwin, Homewood).

PALAMOUNTAIN, J.C. (1955) *The Politics of Distribution* (Harvard University Press, Cambridge, Mass.).

PETERSON, E. (1940) 'Solving Wholesalers' Problems through Trading Area Research', *Journal of Marketing*, 4(2), pp. 39-45.

RASMUSSEN, E.G. (1943) 'Hardware Wholesale Trading Centers and Trading Territories in Nine South Eastern States', *Journal of Marketing*, 8(2), pp. 165-71.

REVZAN, D.A. (1965) 'Some Evolutionary Aspects of the Wholesaling Sector' in D.A. Revzan (ed.), *Perspectives for Research in Marketing* (University of California, Berkeley), pp. 101-34.

—— (1966) *The Marketing Significance of Geographical Variations in Wholesale/Retail Sales Ratios* (Institute of Business and Economic Research, Berkeley).

SAMLI, A.C. (1964) 'Wholesaling in an Economy of Scarcity: Turkey', *Journal of Marketing*, 28, pp. 55-8.

SCHLESINGER, A.M. (1957) *The Colonial Merchants and the American Revolution* (F. Ungar Pub. Co., New York; originally published 1917).

SHELDON, C.D. (1958) *The Rise of the Merchant Class in Tokugawa, Japan 1600-1868* (J.J. Augustin, Locust Valley, NY).

SKURSKI, R. (1972) 'Wholesaling of Consumer Goods in the U.S.S.R.', *Quarterly Review of Economics and Business*, 11, pp. 53-67.

SMYKAY, E.W. (1973) *Physical Distribution Management* (Macmillan, New York).

STACEY, N.A.H., and A. WILSON (1965) *The Changing Pattern of Distribution* (Pergamon, London).

STASCH, P. (1965) 'Distribution Systems Analysis: Methods and Problems', *The Logistics Review*, 4, pp. 7-34.

STIRLING, P. (1965) *Turkish Village* (Weidenfeld & Nicolson, London).

TAFF, C.A. (1972) *Management of Physical Distribution and Transportation* (Irwin, Homewood).

TARDITS, C., and C. TARDITS (1962) 'Traditional Market Economy in the South Dahomey' in P. Bohannan and G. Dalton (eds), *Markets in Africa* (Northwestern University Press, Evanston), pp. 89-102.

THORPE, D. (1971) *The Density of Cash and Carry Wholesaling, 1971* (Manchester Business School, Retail Outlets Research Unit, Research Report 4).

—— (1975) (ed.), *Cash and Carry Wholesaling and Town Planning* (Manchester Business School, Retail Outlets Research Unit, Research Report 17).

THORPE, D., and S. THORPE (1976) *The Density of Cash and Carry Wholesaling 1976* (Manchester Business School, Retail Outlets Research Unit, Research Report 14).

THORPE, W.C. (1939) 'Changing Distribution Channels', *American Economic Review*, 29, pp. 75-84.

THRUPP, S. (1933) 'The Grocers of London: a Study of Distributive Trade' in E. Power and M.M. Postan (eds), *Studies in English Trade in the Fifteenth Century* (Routledge, London), pp. 247-92.

TIETZ, B. (1971) 'The Future Development of Retail and Wholesale Distribution

in Western Europe', *British Journal of Marketing*, 5(1), pp. 42-55.
TÜMERTEKIN, E. (1968) 'Central Business Districts of Istanbul', *Review of Geographical Institute of University of Istanbul*, 11, pp. 21-36.
VANCE, J.E. (1970) *The Merchant's World: the Geography of Wholesaling* (Prentice Hall, Englewood Cliffs).
VOLPP, L.D. (1956) 'The Changing Functions of the Grocery Wholesaler', *Iowa Business Digest*, 27, pp. 21-9.
WALTERS, D. (1975) 'Physical Distribution Futures for the U.K. Food Industry', *Retail and Distribution Management*, 3, pp. 42-7, 57.
WATSON-GANDY, C. (1972) 'Warehouse/depot Location' in M. Christopher and G. Wills (eds), *Marketing Logistics and Distribution Planning* (George Allen & Unwin, London), pp. 209-41.
WEBSTER, F.A. (1967) 'Model of Vertical Integration Strategy', *California Management Review*, Winter, pp. 49-54.
WEDDING, N. (1952) *Vertical Integration in Marketing* (Bureau of Economics and Business, University of Illinois, Urbana).
WILLIAMS, J.M. (1974) *Food Distribution Costs* (National Materials Handling Centre, Cranfield).
WILLIAM-OLSSON, W. (1960) *Stockholm: Structure and Development* (Almquist & Wiksell, Stockholm).
WILLS, G., L. MAGRILL and A. COOPER (1972) 'The Analysis of European Distribution Systems', *International Journal of Physical Distribution*, 3, pp. 21-42.
YOSHINO, M.Y. (1971) *The Japanese Marketing System: Adaptations and Innovations* (MIT Press, Cambridge, Mass.).
____ (1975) *Marketing in Japan* (Praeger, New York).
ZIMMER, B. (1966) 'The Small Businessman and Relocation' in J.Q. Wilson (ed.), *Urban Renewal: the Record and the Controversy* (MIT Press, Cambridge, Mass.).

6 MARKETING BY PRODUCERS

Although it is usual to divide an economy between those institutions which produce goods and those which market them the distinction is not clearcut. Firms whose dominant function is production must nevertheless sell the goods they produce. Farms must market their agricultural products; manufacturing firms must sell goods either to other manufacturers or to specialist marketing institutions who pilot the goods into a marketing channel; mining concerns have to market the ore they produce. Productive firms perform marketing functions although these firms are not primarily marketing organisations. Within most manufacturing firms there is a sales or marketing department. In some firms the department has a very low status while in others it is a key department of the company and has equal status with production management (Hise, 1965). Whatever the status of industrial marketing it still exists. Similarly within agriculture, farmers perform marketing functions themselves or, because of the small scale of production, specialist agricultural marketing institutions have evolved and do it for them.

Industrial Marketing

Within industrial marketing there is also evidence for the growth of specialist marketing institutions. Revzan (1961) points to the close connections necessary between wholesaler and producer in the markets for industrial goods. He goes on to point out that specialist services such as transport, materials handling, market research, etc. are increasingly being carried out by 'facilitating functional agencies' which 'act as auxiliaries to almost every aspect of the basic functions of marketing strategy, buying and selling, and physical distribution' (p. 587). Many of these specialist agencies themselves act as buyers for industrial goods. The marketing function itself thus stimulates the productive function. For example, materials handling equipment has to be manufactured and data processing and computing equipment have to be developed and produced to meet the demands of marketing institutions. The post-industrial society of Bell (1976) is essentially a marketing based society. Despite the obvious importance of industrial marketing it is a much less well developed field than consumer marketing and has been ignored almost totally, by many social science disciplines, including geography.

It is worthwhile to consider, briefly, the characteristics of industrial marketing and how these differ from consumer marketing. The relative roles and power positions of the participants then become clearer and the likelihood of conflict occurring can be assessed (Cassel *et al.*, 1954).

A considerable part of the demand for industrial goods is derived demand from consumer goods and services while a further part is demand from government, defence and war purchases. Because demand is a derived demand interindustry input-output analyses are important tools in industrial market research. By using input-output tables a manufacturer can obtain a general picture of the market segments for the products of his industry. The derived nature of demand also causes considerable fluctuations in industrial marketing activity. In boom periods, consumer goods manufacturers work to expand production rapidly and market power tends to gravitate to the supplier of industrial goods. 'Many of the buying considerations such as price and quality are outweighed by shorter delivery dates. If the seller's output is relatively limited, his problem is how to allocate it between old and new customers'. Here is a clear likely source of conflict. 'New firms will spring up in those portions of the industrial market where entry costs are not formidable . . . When consumer-goods demand slackens, the opposite situation develops . . . Production of consumer goods is at a lower level, inventories of both consumer and industrial goods are reduced, and no new capital expenditures are made' (Dodge, 1970, p. 24). While specialist marketing services and institutions emerge in periods of high business activity when industrial firms concentrate on production, in slump conditions marketing activities become an integral part of the manufacturing firm in order to absorb management no longer fully employed in organising production. The specialist marketing services create tertiary employment in city offices and also transport based employment. The fluctuating, usually cyclical, demand for these services produces difficulties in providing balanced employment opportunities in urban areas. Employment generation in industrial marketing activities, therefore, fluctuates much more than in consumer marketing institutions.

One marketing policy which has been adopted in coming to terms with these fluctuations is more accurate market forecasts through market segmentation analyses. The use of segmentation methods is widely accepted in consumer goods marketing (see Chapter 3) but until the late 1960s was rarely used as a tool in industrial marketing (Ames, 1971; Cardozo, 1968). Wind and Cardozo (1974) argue that market segmentation 'is at least conceptually as applicable in industrial marketing as it is for the marketing of consumer goods' (p. 153).

A market segment is simply a group of present or potential customers with some common characteristic which is relevant in explaining
(and predicting) their response to a supplier's marketing stimuli. For
example, a market segment may consist of all firms whose annual
purchases of steel exceed $5 million, but are less than $10 million.
(p. 155).

The contrast with consumer segmentation is that there is less likelihood
of members of industrial segments being in any way spatially related to
each other. The geographical element in industrial marketing policies
based on market segmentation is often minimal. While it would be possible to segment the industrial market on a spatial dimension it would
be of little value because the product dimension is fundamental in
industrial marketing.

Because of the rapid changes that can take place in industrial market
relationships, marketing policies, *per se*, have had little effect on industrial
location. The attractiveness of a location close to a large general market
(both consumer and industrial) is one reason for the concentration of
industrial plant into metropolitan areas but this concentration of industry
is not a response to the industrial marketing policies of individual companies. Frequently, it is not clear whether a preferred industrial location
is accepted because of market proximity or because of reduced transport
costs (Greenhut, 1960). Dodge (1970), for example, points out that 75
per cent of the industrial goods market of California is located in the Los
Angeles and San Francisco metropolitan areas but he neither draws a
conclusion from this concentration nor provides a reason for it. While
this concentrated location is an advantage in reducing transport costs,
particularly if the market is local, it will not of itself create sales.

For most firms supplying the industrial market the number of buyers
is relatively small. This is in clear contrast to consumer goods marketing.
The rational behaviour pattern of industrial buyers has already been
mentioned as a characteristic of industrial purchasing patterns (Chapter
3). The small number of participants in industrial marketing often leads
to a close relationship between buyer and seller. Fisher (1976) quotes
a study by Hokansson and Östberg which suggests, 'The actual purchase
transaction is . . . an interaction system between two active counterparts
rather than merely a relationship between one active component and a
passive market.' This leads (they argue) to a power-dependence relationship. 'This relationship may well be progressively strengthened by mutual
adaptation between the firms concerned' (pp. 17-18). Given the development of this negotiated relationship, which is also stressed by Marrian

(1965), conflicts are resolved quickly and without the creation of *channel leaders.* Corey (1962) stresses, in a series of case studies, that successful industrial marketing policies are based on close supplier-customer relationships, often at a personal level.

Although industrial marketing is a vital part of the total marketing system industrial marketing relationships are of limited relevance for the purpose of this book. The relatively short channels used for industrial goods and the increasingly common forward integration of production orientated firms to encompass marketing functions within the present organisation (Stevens, 1963) make it difficult to isolate variations in industrial marketing characteristics. The major cause of variations appears to be product line although Diamand (1963), in a study of 156 manufacturers in the USA, found substantial similarity in channel patterns and relationships over a wide range of industrial equipment and machinery type products.

Agricultural Marketing

If industrial marketing can be typified by the similarities in channel structure, agricultural marketing is characterised by the variety of its channel relationships. Dodge (1970) suggests that agricultural marketing is a branch of industrial marketing because most of farm output passes through an industrial process before final consumption. Farm production, he argues, is therefore for industrial purposes. This represents a rather narrow view of the agricultural marketing system. The market for farm produce is only one of many variables in agricultural marketing and it would seem to be the only one worthy of comparison with industrial marketing. There are far more contrasts than similarities between agricultural and industrial marketing practices.

Regular estimates from the United States Department of Agriculture show that the farmer's share of retail cost of all farm food products has been around 40 per cent since the early 1950s. Thus 60 per cent of the retail price of these products is taken up in marketing (40 per cent) and processing (20 per cent) costs. These percentages vary considerably from product to product with the farmer's share falling to less than 10 per cent on biscuit type products which have a relatively high processing cost but rising to 70 per cent on butter and eggs. In these products, marketing costs account for most of the difference between farm-gate and retail prices.

A large marketing share of final costs does not necessarily mean an inefficient structure to the market channel. Marketing costs are affected by the spatial gap between production and consumption and if these distances are large marketing costs will be high even if the distribution system is efficient. Sheppard and Futrell (1969) show how marketing costs on lettuce in the USA are high at 66 per cent of retail price but this high cost results from transporting a bulky, perishable product from production areas in California to markets on the Atlantic seaboard. But the costs of production in the highly efficient producing areas in California plus the marketing cost still total to less than the combined costs from potential production areas close to the consumers in the east.

The data from the USA on marketing costs allow analysis of costs by year for a wide range of farm products. Such analyses have led to a general awareness of the importance of agricultural marketing procedures in the overall agricultural economy. There are consequently a large number of standard texts available on agricultural marketing in the USA. Typical are those by Thomsen (1951), Brunk and Darrah (1955) and Moore and Walsh (1966), with perhaps the best two in the present context being those of Shepherd and Futrell (1969) and Kohls and Downey (1972). Most provide an overview of the agricultural marketing system in the USA coupled with case studies of marketing procedures for individual products. These texts are widely available and there is little advantage here in summarising their contents.

A feature of agricultural marketing which differentiates it from both consumer and industrial marketing is the presence of many small production units. In developed and underdeveloped free enterprise economies agriculture is dominated by smallscale activity. In economies with collectivised agriculture the whole marketing system is quite different, for several reasons, including the larger size of agricultural units. In capitalist countries the small scale of agricultural production has two major implications for marketing. First, individual agricultural producers have little effect in price making processes. A producer may find great difficulty in obtaining information on current prices at the various alternate sales places available to him. Radio broadcasting of market information can be a big help but the producer, even when prices are known, often remains in the position of having to accept a posted price. In order to resolve this difficulty a variety of channel institutions have developed and the farmer may choose one of several selling methods; for example direct to processor, through auction market, to government agency, etc. The second implication of the small scale of production is the low amount of negotiating power resting with the producer. In general the processors are large units with considerable market power. Misuse of this power can result in conflict with the producers.

A further distinct feature with implications for marketing is the scattered distribution of production units. Although specific crop production is often concentrated regionally within a country individual producers are scattered through the region. The transport element in marketing a product becomes critical under these circumstances. Marketing institutions, in order to operate, have to draw on several sources of supply. The scattered nature of these sources in the case of agricultural goods often results in high transport costs in the marketing operation, while changes in transportation infrastructure have implications for marketing costs (Smith, 1975). Problems of transport arise not only in capitalist marketing systems. Even when agriculture is state controlled and farm sales are directed to specific food processing factories, problems arise both in the allocation of market areas for the food processing plants and in the minimisation of farm transport costs when several crops are produced.

Krajkó *et al.* (1974) describe some of these difficulties in state and co-operative farm marketing operations in Southern Hungary. Even with a relatively simple marketing system, as in wheat production, difficulties arise. The capacity of the processing plants (wheat mills) is greater than that of local granaries, so grain has to be transported to the mill from both farm storage and warehouse storage facilities. Some wheat is transported twice, from farm to warehouse and then to mill; other wheat, sometimes even from the same farm, is taken direct to the mill. Figure 6.1 shows the movement in wagons from granary to mill. There is additional movement from farm to warehouse/granary and from farm to mill. The dispersed pattern of production and the centralised pattern of mills creates a complex transport pattern, which is far from optimal. The reallocation of warehouses to mills particularly in the south western part of the district shown and the increase of storage facilities at some mills could provide a more efficient distribution system. The marketing of wheat in Southern Hungary is relatively simple compared with both wheat marketing in a capitalist society and with the marketing of other products in this part of Hungary.

Marketing systems have responded to the various conflicts created by the presence of many small producers and the dispersed nature of production. Before considering these responses it is necessary to consider the difficulties for marketing stemming out of the character of the product rather than the characteristics of production. The perishable and bulky nature of much agricultural produce is perhaps the most important characteristic. In Chapter 2 it was suggested that perishable products have short marketing channels as the time in the system is an important marketing (and price formation) variable. The two characteristics of production,

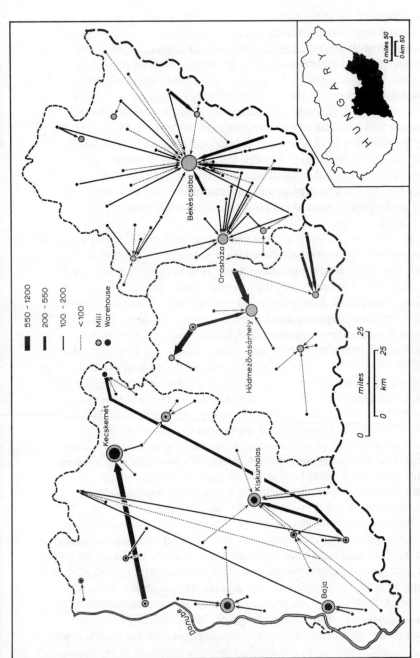

Figure 6.1: The Allocation of Wheat from Granaries to Mills in South Hungary in 1970

outlined above, inhibit the development of direct marketing. None the less, either rapid movement to market is necessary or else produce has to be treated to allow it to withstand a longer time in the marketing system. Drying, cooling, freezing and chemical treatments are all used to allow produce to spend a longer time in the marketing channel. Specialist transport technologies have been devised for the same purpose. There have been relatively few attempts to redesign marketing channels to allow the more efficient flow of goods.

The bulk of the product influences marketing functions concerned with physical handling of products. Transport and storage costs are high per product unit with high bulk products. It might be expected, therefore, that channels for such goods will seek to minimise the transport and storage functions. For many reasons, but particularly owing to the regional specialisation of production mentioned above, this is not the case. Thus there is a considerable intercontinental transport element in the marketing of meat, grain, fibre and even fruit and vegetables. The traditional Von Thunen type view of fruit and vegetable production around city fringes supplying local markets is shown to be a rather abstract view of the real world when marketing channels are studied. In greengrocers in British cities there are temperate vegetables from the Mediterranean countries, most countries in the EEC and even from Eastern Europe (Smyth, 1959). There are also more specialist subtropical and tropical products available to meet consumer demands. Thus, although agricultural products are perishable and bulky this has not inhibited the development of long, and complex, marketing channels.

Annual and seasonal variation in quantity of production coupled with fluctuations in quality add another variable in determining the channel structures for agricultural goods. The implications of this variable are that channels have to be designed to allow for surplus production either to pass through efficiently or in some way to be stored. This increases the complexity of channel structure. Similarly quality variation may mean that end uses for a product change with quality, so again channels have to allow for the interactions of these different consumer groups depending on the quality of the produce.

Alongside the characteristics of production and the character of the product there are also traditional features of the marketing channel which are causes of potential conflict. Agricultural producers are, in general, conservative in outlook and any change in marketing channels is slow to be established — new institutions are slow to be accepted. This inherent conservatism means that inertial structures in marketing channels operate long after new institutions and relationships have become accepted.

At any one time there are usually several methods of marketing a particular crop and the choice of a particular channel reflects the attitudes of the farmer as well as the relative efficiency of alternative channels. So, for example, in livestock marketing in Wales (Bateman *et al.*, 1971; Williams, 1972) or Scotland (Carlyle, 1975) farmers sell at auction animals on the hoof, to dealers, individual butchers, agents for multiple retailers and wholesalers, as well as arranging slaughter of the animals to sell direct to institutional and individual consumers. The same farmers may also sell animals directly, not through an auction market, to other farmers, to representatives and to dealers. Finally, farmers may if they choose belong to co-operative or group marketing schemes. Each of these methods of farm sales results in the meat passing along a different marketing channel. This situation of eight or ten different channels for some (domestically produced) agricultural goods is fairly typical of many products and there are sometimes additional channels associated with imports. This situation is not unique to Wales and occurs in most countries (Williams and Stout, 1964). The institutions within these channels are frequently in potential, if not actual, conflict. Dealers buying direct from a farm reduce the amount of stock passing through the auction market and are consequently in conflict with the auctioneers operating the market. Auction markets can be in conflict with each other in their temporal and spatial relationships, in similar fashion to the discontinuity that can occur in periodic markets in developing countries. There are, in agricultural marketing, several competing methods of sale each of which supports its own series of marketing institutions.

From this brief discussion of the characteristics of agricultural marketing it might appear surprising that the system works at all. The potentialities for conflict are considerable. That agricultural goods reach final consumers is owing to a number of responses by those concerned with marketing to the difficulties inherent in the marketing system. These responses can be classified for convenience into those of the producer, those of middlemen, those of the consumer and those of outside regulators. It is not proposed here to consider all the changes that are taking place in agricultural marketing but to present examples of each of these types of response. A response of agriculturalists is to form co-operatives; industrial consumers have attempted to introduce the methods of industrial marketing to the agricultural sector; the middlemen have developed specialist facilities for particular products; and government, as an outside regulator of the system, has intervened in price mechanisms and has created specific institutions such as marketing boards (Moore, 1966).

Agricultural Marketing Co-operatives

Agricultural co-operative organisations have been set up both to supply farmers with their agricultural requirements and to sell their produce. Within communist countries the term has a slightly different meaning and implies a co-operative production function in addition to co-operative marketing. Within capitalist economies it is commonplace for farmers, despite their traditionally independent viewpoint, to join together to increase both their buying and selling power (Oldenstadt and Call, 1964). In the late 1960s in the USA (USDA, 1970) there were 7,940 agricultural marketing co-operatives. Of these 4,929 were primarily concerned with marketing farm products, 2,835 with supplying agricultural requirements and 176 with providing services. In addition were many other co-operative groups dealing with insurance, credit, rural telephones, livestock improvement and irrigation. In Britain at the same time about 200,000 farmers belonged to one of the 70 agricultural supply co-operatives and/or one of the 83 marketing societies. It is probable that many more farmers used the facilities of these co-operatives without being formal members. Although co-operatives in Britain account for only some 5 per cent of the total produce handled, in individual product groups, such as wool, they are responsible for marketing about one-third of production. In Denmark agricultural co-operatives are even more important in farm operations, as Figure 6.2 shows. (Webster, 1973). Here the co-operative marketing groups have extended their operations into food processing and supply associations provide for almost all the agricultural needs of the farmer. The Internal Co-operative Alliance estimates show that globally the 612,000 agricultural co-operatives (purchasing, selling and processing) had a combined membership of 230 million farmers even when the USSR and China are excluded. The world distribution shows around a third of the membership in Europe and a further 50 per cent in Asia. Most of the remainder is accounted for by Brazil and the USA. Within Asia, India and Japan each have around 7 million members in agricultural co-operatives. These global estimates are far from complete and are probably underestimates of the real situation. Reports in the Yearbook of Agricultural Co-operation testify to the world wide development of co-operatives with, for example, the 1974 issue providing a survey of agricultural co-operation in South East Asia. Most of the marketing societies are related specifically to individual crops, while the requirements societies are of a more general nature.

Although there has yet to be a study of the diffusion of co-operative principles, the origins of agricultural co-operation rest in North West Europe, notably in Switzerland and Ireland, with the idea spreading

Figure 6.2: The Structure
of Danish Agricultural
Co-operation

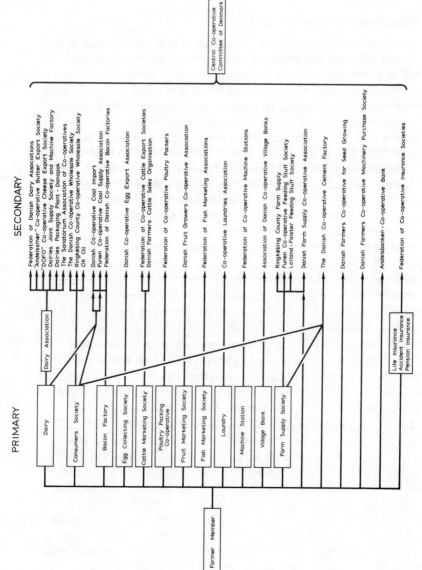

throughout Europe in the nineteenth century. Subsequently the concept has become a major component first in the agricultural exploitation and later in the planned development of agriculture in the developing countries:

> Some countries concentrated at a very early stage on distinctly agri-
> cultural types of co-operation – the co-operative loan and savings
> bank in Germany, for example, the Danish creamery or, rather later,
> the Canadian Elevator Company. The whole agricultural co-operative
> movement grew rapidly and became more diverse, each country
> making its own contribution. The method, by which men of moderate
> means banded together to carry through commercial and financial
> operations which none of them would have the knowledge or the
> funds or the standing to undertake alone, proved extra-ordinarily
> fruitful in many lands and among farmers of the most diverse types.
> (Digby, 1968).

Hewlett (1967), in a review of agricultural co-operatives in Europe, suggests that the strength of the movement is related to the level of agricultural prosperity. In periods of low prosperity co-operation is strong while when agricultural conditions improve interest in co-operatives wanes. Such a hypothesis is in line with the view, suggested earlier, that agricultural co-operation is one of the farmer's responses to conflict in the marketing channel. From the farmer's viewpoint conflict will be most severe in periods of depression. Conflict is also likely to occur in situations of monopoly or near monopoly when power relationships easily become distorted. The bulk production of a single crop over large areas is in some ways a monopoly situation, with the producers individually having little market power. These areas also often are affected heavily in periods of agricultural depression. Not unexpectedly, therefore, 'co-operatives are generally most successful in areas of bulk production of single crops' (Tarrant, 1974, p. 223). A third general situation when co-operatives are strong is when governmental intervention encourages co-operative activity. The establishment of agricultural marketing co-operatives is often seen as a tool in agricultural planning and rural development in the lesser developed countries. Government sponsorship may result in co-operative institutions taking a prominent role in agricultural marketing.

An agricultural co-operative is a distinct marketing organisation in a number of ways. In most countries co-operatives have to be registered under the provisions of some Act of Government which usually defines the trading methods of co-operatives in the particular country (Valko, 1954). There are some almost universal rules which apply to co-operative marketing institutions and other nationally applied rules. It is these rules which distinguish co-operatives from joint-stock or private companies. The almost universal characteristics are:

(1)   Membership of the co-operative organisation is voluntary and open to anyone within the organisation's sphere of operations.

(2)   Contributions to the capital of the undertaking are spread through all members with no individual able to obtain a controlling interest.

(3)   Financial shares in the co-operative can not be bought or sold but may be repaid by the co-operative.

(4)   Each member has an equal interest and rights in the co-operative with each member having one vote, irrespective of financial or other stake in the co-operative, at meetings.

(5)   Any net profit realised by the co-operative is distributed among the members in proportion to the business they have done with the co-operative.

In some countries membership of a co-operative implies that members must do all their business with the society. In other cases co-operatives may only do business with members. There are many other *house* rules of national co-operative organisations such as cash trading or specific educational contributions. The central idea, however, is that agricultural producers carry out some marketing functions in association with other producers. In this way an individual producer increases his buying or selling power within a particular marketing channel without loss of control over productive functions. The major reasons why farmers use supply co-operatives were claimed, by the farmers themselves in a survey in Indiana, to be advantages in price, service, quality of goods and convenience. The social philosophy of co-operation rates well below economic advantage in the apparent success of a co-operative institution (Downey, Kohls and Wilson, 1965). Thus there is a germ of truth in Babcock's assertion: 'I regard a farmer owned, farmer controlled co-operative as a legal, practical means by which a group of self-selected, selfish capitalists seek to improve their individual economic positions in a competitive society' (Babcock, 1935).

The catalyst for co-operative development is often a disruption of established relationships in the marketing channel. A catastrophic fall in marketing margins, a usurping of monopoly power or protection against dishonest suppliers are all typical stimulants (Solbraa and Sundby, 1961). Typical is the origin of Aspatria Agricultural Co-operative Society

which celebrated its centenary in 1970. In 1869 a group of Cumberland
farmers were victims of a fraud in connection with the purchase of
fertiliser. The farmers grouped themselves co-operatively and decided
to form their own society for the supply of fertilisers and feeding stuffs.
In 1870 the Aspatria Agricultural Co-operative Society was registered.
A number of other, regionally based, co-operatives followed, notably
Cheshire, Shropshire and North Wales Farmers (later to become North
Western Farmers) in 1873. By 1908 there were 114 societies, the main
aim of most being the protection of producers from sales of substandard
fertilisers, seeds, etc. With the 1930s came a change in function with
more societies concentrating on the selling function than the supply
function. Since 1950 a number of large multipurpose societies have
emerged through merger and rationalisation schemes. By the early
1970s the largest dozen societies, which accounted for three-quarters of
national membership of co-operatives (Morley, 1975) existed alongside
a large number of small, economically marginal, co-operatives (Jones,
1967).

The same enlargement and diversification processes have occurred
throughout Western Europe. Marketing co-operatives in France have
become processors of tinned fruit and vegetables in the Eastern Pyrenees,
and cider and fruit juice producers in the West. Alongside the large societies searching for economies of scale through vertical integration the
long established small supply co-operatives still exist in France, particularly in the West, the North and the Paris Basin. About half the
agricultural requirements of farmers pass through these supply organisations (Nicholas, 1973; Berthelot, 1972).

The extension of functions of supply and selling co-operatives is also
well illustrated in Denmark (Webster, 1973; Pedersen, 1973). Dairy and
bacon co-operatives have extended their functions and developed creameries and milk product processing plants on the one hand and slaughter-
house and a wide variety of processing plants on the other. In the first
eight years of growth to 1890, 679 co-operative creameries were opened
in Denmark. The number rose to over 1,200 by 1910 and remained
about this level, with a slight peak in the mid 1930s, until 1962 when
the first of a series of rationalisation plans was introduced. By 1972 the
number of dairies had been reduced to 370. From a situation in which
small villages had their own dairy the pattern is changing to large regionally based milk processing plants. In Bornholm, for example, 17 of the
18 co-operative dairies operating on the island in 1963 amalgamated to
develop a single, multifunctional, dairy plant. In 1970 the remaining
dairy joined the larger society. Similarly in Funen in 1968 most of the

dairies merged to form two large groups. The tendency is for even larger co-operatives to develop as the processing of milk for butter, cheese, yoghurt, tinned milk, etc. becomes susceptible to increasing economic returns to scale.

Co-operation among Danish dairy producers shows a further purpose of co-operatives. Efforts have been made by the co-operatives to improve the quality of the product. Laboratories are common in the larger dairies and regular quality testing of butter and cheese are carried out. Grading, control and branding of dairy products also has been introduced and this has raised general standards with payment to the farmer depending on the quality of the milk delivered. Within milk marketing similar developments have occurred in the co-operative sector of a dozen or more countries (OECD, 1973; Ward, 1975).

The vertical integration, the larger scale of operation and the concern with quality are changes which are widespread in the agricultural co-operative movement in Denmark and other Scandinavian countries. Bacon co-operatives have been amalgamating rapidly such that between 1968 and 1972 the 62 co-operatives, each operating a single factory, were reduced to 27 operating 43 factories. There were still 19, mostly in North Jutland, operating single processing units but since 1972 a number of these have amalgamated. Vertical integration, followed by increases in operating scale, has been shown in the last two chapters to be a common process operating in the marketing channel: 'Ever-changing technological developments will almost inevitably require continuing adjustments to economies of scale' (Larzelère, 1964, p. 214). Agricultural co-operatives are following this general process of marketing development.

Alongside the structural changes have been spatial changes. Three tiers of institution have developed. The first tier comprise, 'Locals which cover such activities as retailing fertilisers or manufactured feed stuffs, the primary assembly and resale of grain or milk' (Allen, 1973, p. 8). Regionals are a second tier and these have developed integrated selling and processing functions and as the name suggests operate over sub-stantial areas. Farmland Industries, operating in Kansas, Missouri, Iowa and Nebraska, is typical of this tier. The highest level are Apex co-oper-atives which are large, often national, operations which usually are con-trolled by regional level institutions. Often there is considerable vertical integration and Apex organisations are sometimes more concerned with processing and production than with marketing. Central Farmers (USA), probably the largest fertiliser producer in the capitalist world, is jointly owned by 21 regional co-operatives and may be seen as an example of an Apex level institution. This pattern has evolved in many countries and

NATIONAL ASSOCIATIONS FOR:	REGIONAL ORGANISATIONS	LOCAL ORGANISATIONS	NUMBER OF MEMBERS
Milk	6 milk pools	195 dairies	53,500
Meat and pork	11 slaughter co-operatives		64,000
Eggs and poultry	13 district pools		4,400
Horticultural products	10 regional divisions		5,300
Potato distillery	8 potato distilleries		2,000
Potato flour	8 potato flour factories		3,000
Honey			3,400
Fur, skins	32 regional divisions		2,900
Timber	20 regional divisions	465 locals	54,600

8 National associations in purchasing, banking, insurance and animal breeding co-operatives

Central Federation of Agricultural Co-operatives

Figure 6.3: The Structure of Norwegian Agricultural Co-operation

Figure 6.3 shows the organisational structure in Norway which in this respect is typical of many countries (Sagelumo, 1976; Digby, 1961).

With the increased scale of agricultural co-operative activity so management structures have evolved (International Co-operative Alliance, 1965). The three tiers of institutions have management as well as operational implications, with traditional co-operative democracy being most evident at the local level. The Apex type organisation, however, is able to initiate change and development according to an overall plan, and as such has found favour in developing countries using agricultural co-operation as a method of rural development (Flores, 1971; Izraeli, Izraeli and Meissner, 1974; Surridge, 1967; Worsley, 1971).

Technological Change in Agricultural Marketing

The development of co-operative forms of activity is not the only response of farmers to conflict within marketing channels. As with small retailers, many small farmers have moved out of farming altogether because of marketing difficulties, others have changed their style of operations and altered production methods. The marketing problems associated with agricultural production are not problems just for the farmers. The special character of agricultural production (its small scale, seasonality, high bulk perishable products, etc.) has implications for the middlemen in agricultural marketing. In common with middlemen elsewhere the rôle of agricultural marketing intermediary institutions has changed to compensate for efforts by farmers and processors to reduce marketing margins. Such efforts often mean the shortening of marketing channels as for example described above in the growth of vertically integrated production-processing co-operatives. Similarly, middlemen institutions have changed in several ways in response to the activities of the other institutions. It is proposed here to consider only one response. Middlemen and intermediate institutions have increased the standards of the services they offer within the marketing channel and by technological innovation have succeeded, to some extent, in limiting the process of vertical integration (De Loaoch, 1958).

In the two functions of storage and transport middlemen have been particularly active in adopting new technologies. The use of refrigeration units and bulk transport are two examples of new technologies which have been adopted widely. The extent to which technology is available, which is to some extent outside the control of the middlemen, affects the market channel structure.

In cotton production and marketing, for example, technological research has tended to be concentrated on improving production and manufacturing methods with market channels remaining traditional in outlook. Vertical integration with the bypassing of middlemen has become an important process. The middlemen's functions are carried out within the integrated firm but the numbers of specialist marketing institutions and firms are being reduced. In cotton marketing in the USA, where it might be expected that technology would be at a high level, there is a complex channel structure between producer and processor but it has changed little, other than declining in importance (Sinclair, 1968).

The majority of the cotton crop in the United States is produced in the South West and the West, with processing concentrated in the South East. There is also a considerable export of unprocessed cotton. The marketing system serves to transfer the crop several hundred kilometres from producer to processor or to export warehouse. The short product-ive harvest season coupled with year round processing operation adds storage as a further major function in the marketing system. The flow of cotton is from farms (about 100,000) to cotton gins and then either direct to the processors or to warehouses (about 1,000) with subsequent movement to processors or to an export warehouse. Involved in this marketing operation are about 1,500 merchandising firms and several thousand firms in secondary institutions which finance, insure, and transport the crop from farm to processor.

Transport to the cotton gin is usually the responsibility of the pro-ducer. There are considerable scale economies to be achieved in cotton ginning (Covey and Hudson, 1963) and the number of gins is less than 5,000 compared with 25,000 60 years ago (Cleveland, 1976). This has meant that many farmers must take their crop further at their own expense than formerly, but this increase in costs has been offset by larger trailers and innovations in farm machinery. It is after ginning that the farmer usually sells his product.

> Most cotton is sold by farmers in local markets or placed in the government loan. The primary function of these farmers' markets is to provide a ready outlet for cotton in odd lots consisting of a vary-ing number of bales of mixed quality. Local markets vary widely in terms of organisation, number and kinds of buyers, physical facilities and services performed, and practices followed by merchandising agencies. (Fowler, 1966, p. 299).

The government loan scheme effectively pledges cotton as collateral on a government loan and by the mid 1960s about half the cotton crops were absorbed by the government loan scheme. The remainder of the crop was bought by a variety of types of merchandising firms who traditionally have been

> specialists, concentrating primarily on one method of operation. However, in the early fifties, as a matter of survival, many of them adjusted to the changing marketing conditions by diversifying their operations. As a result, by the early sixties over a fifth of the active central market firms were multitype businesses. If present competition and lines of cotton movement continue, the trend to multitype operations is likely to continue. (Cable, 1966, p. 118).

A key marketing institution is the shipper who provides the major link between farm and processing plant. Brokers, local merchants and commission agents help shippers obtain supplies. Brokers, formerly a more important group than now, are agents who sell, on commission, for producers. Local merchants buy at gin or local markets and sell to shippers or processors' agents at central markets. The number of these firms has declined owing to the increase in direct movements of cotton from producer either to government loan store or to processor. The number of commission agents also has fallen for similar reasons. This group makes purchases at local markets and gins on behalf of shippers or processors. They are similar to the brokers but action is initiated by the buyers in the case of commission agents and by the sellers with brokers. All three of these marketing institutions have declined in importance with the increased activity of co-operative marketing associations who perform the full range of marketing functions, even competing with the shippers.

Shippers generally operate out of central markets. Fifteen of these are *designated spot cotton markets* and each issues cotton price quotations. The central market thus becomes the main price forming body in the marketing channel. Shippers, the traditional controllers of central markets, have been a key group in pricing policy but again their numbers are declining:

> With the growing volumes of a few large farmer co-operative marketing associations, the increase in direct mill buying, and the loan program of the government, the number of bona fide shippers and other firms in central markets will probably continue to decline. (Cable, 1966, p. 119).

In general, the middlemen institutions within cotton marketing have failed to adapt to the relationships in marketing channels and their functions have been taken over by vertical marketing organisations. The above example shows a typical traditionally orientated marketing system in which technological change has been minimal and middlemen have been bypassed.

In sharp contrast within North American agriculture is grain marketing. A market system has evolved incorporating middlemen who, despite the pressures of vertically integrated organisations, continue to perform key channel functions. The middlemen have been able to sustain their position through a number of technological changes in their operating methods (Wills, 1972).

The grain marketing system consists of a series of storage facilities. Within the channel each successive facility bulks grain from a larger area than its predecessor (Vosloh, 1966; Heid, 1961). The lowest level in the chain is the country grain elevator which receives grain from the farmer by truck; there they grade, store, blend and bulk the grain before forwarding it, usually by rail, to subterminal or terminal elevators (Wright, 1965). Around two-thirds of wheat entering the market in the USA passes through country elevators. Figure 6.4 shows the channel diagram for the mid 1960s. For other grain products an even greater proportion passes through country elevators. The majority of the elevators are owned and operated by small independent companies or co-operatives. The network of elevators developed in the period of horse-drawn transport when a farmer may well have had two elevators within 15 km of his farm.

With the advent of motor transport and more recently advances in trucking technology which allow much larger loads to be taken long distances, so the need has diminished for a closely spaced network. The larger supply areas in turn mean more grain so the country elevators have increased in size and become more widely spaced (Richey and Johnson, 1952). A study in Montana of 48 co-operative grain elevators showed the average radius of supply areas to be over 30 km, with some elevators considerably in excess of this (Yager, 1959). The number of country elevators has fallen by over 20 per cent from the 9,000 operating in 1939. The thinning out process has been particularly active in the traditional grain areas of the North Central Region. The initial response of the country elevator sector was to increase the size of elevator and increase their spacing. The larger ones also installed newly available machinery to handle high moisture grain and to dry the grain before bulking. The size and functions of country elevators have been extended

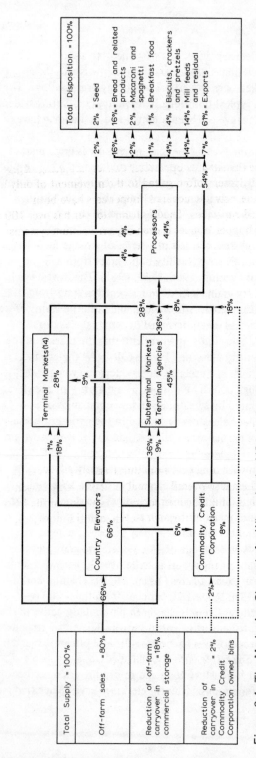

Figure 6.4: The Marketing Channels for Wheat in the USA in the mid 1960s

to combat potential direct selling to subterminal facilities.

Subterminal elevators are located away from metropolitan areas and provide large scale grain handling facilities. Grain is railed or, increasingly, trucked to subterminal facilities from where it passes to terminal elevators, processors and exporters (Farris, 1970). The cost competitive position of subterminal facilities rests on transport and handling costs of incoming and outgoing grain (Corley, 1964). Here again changes in technology have come to the aid of the elevator operators. Carriers are using larger and more specialised equipment often suited to the movement of only a few commodities. On the railways, covered hopper cars have been designed with larger load capacities. The Big John Hopper has over 100 ton capacity and the Whopper Hopper is even bigger. Vacuum systems aid unloading of the large hoppers. Specialised freight rates are available for grain movement in these large hoppers with rates for multiple car (usually around 25 hoppers) movements frequently around half those of single hopper rates. These innovations in transport have resulted in more specialised handling equipment being installed in subterminal elevators but it also means that middlemen have been able to sustain a key rôle in grain marketing.

Terminal elevators operate at even larger distribution points and are heavily involved in the export trade. The terminal elevators on the Great Lakes for example deal in grain by the shipload. Again improvements in grain handling technology have allowed these terminals to stabilise their channel position. Within this physical marketing channel of three tiers of elevator operations there are other institutions such as brokers and agents whose activities complete the financial relationships in the channel. Vertical integration with direct off-farm purchasing by processors has remained a small element in overall channel structure. One reason for the continued strength of middlemen in grain marketing in the USA has been their willingness to adapt, through technological innovation, to changing supply conditions.

Middlemen in grain marketing in the USA are not alone in utilising technology to consolidate their channel position. There are many studies of meat and vegetable marketing which show the willingness of middlemen to adapt to changing market situations (Snitzler and Byrne, 1959; Ulrey, 1964; National Commission on Food Marketing, 1966). New materials handling technologies have been particularly important in this adaptation process and a consequence of these new techniques has been the change in optimal locations of middlemen and first-stage processing plants (Yli-Jokipii, 1971; Wills, 1952; Ferguson and McCarthy, 1970). Management methods, unlike in the retailing and wholesaling of consumer goods, appear to have changed only slightly. Within the marketing of many agricultural commodities in both North America and Europe, middlemen have been successful in at least slowing the rate of their decline.

In many underdeveloped countries the middlemen's position has yet to come under attack. Lele (1971) has shown, for example, that in wheat marketing in the Punjab there can be as many as five primary middlemen institutions between producer and processor. Marketing of other grain crops also effectively is controlled by middlemen. 'Despite the similarities in the marketing of grain throughout India, there are differences not only from one region to another but from one grain to another that are both complex and interesting' (p. 44). But in all cases the middlemen hold a powerful position. In Thailand, according to Anderson (1970) although the number of middlemen is fewer, their power is paramount in rice marketing. Abbott (1970) shows that this situation, in respect of fruit and vegetables, is repeated throughout the developing world. In these marketing systems there is little chance of the process of vertical integration becoming established in agricultural marketing.

Marketing under Contract

In the previous pages mention has been made of processor sponsored vertical integration schemes. These activities, it has been pointed out, are developed poorly or even are absent from the indigenous agricultural systems of developing countries but within Western developed economies the process is an important one in stimulating change in agricultural marketing systems. There is a long history of manufacturing based companies integrating backwards into agriculture to secure their sources of raw materials. Plantation cultivation of sugar cane and rubber within the tropics in some cases was initiated and developed within a vertically integrated company. In such companies the functions of agricultural marketing still have to be performed, although specialist marketing institutions are reduced to a department within the company structure. Britton (1969) has shown the growing degree of vertical integration in cereal production in the UK, with middlemen companies being taken over by processing firms. The fully integrated company is only one aspect of the overall vertical integration process.

Contract farming is a more common expression of the integration process. In recent years contract farming has become widespread as food processors anxious to reduce marketing costs have shortened channels. The Barker Report on contract farming reserves the term *vertical integration* for situations where production and marketing are under overall

common management, and uses the term *vertical co-ordination* for contract farming. The bases of contract farming are verbal or written agreements between producers and processors, or producers and feed suppliers,
in which the market for a product is agreed prior to its availability. There
are many variations on this basic theme and most of these are discussed
in the Barker Report (Barker, 1972) and by Guiton (1967) and Allen
(1972). In Eastern England sugar beet production and vegetables for
freezing are grown extensively under contract and processor and producer share the marketing functions. Over 40 per cent of fat pig marketing in Britain in 1970 was under contract schemes (Coppock, 1971;
Watts, 1971; Dalton, 1971). In the USA the broiler chicken industry
was one of the earliest to accept contract farming methods. By the early
1960s almost two-thirds of the producers (involving over 90 per cent of
production) were on contract to processors. Almost all processors used
contract methods. In these extreme positions the channel power lies
firmly with the processor who initiates the contract. Standard contracts
are offered and the producer either accepts the terms or is unable to
find a market for his output (Roy, 1963).

Price determination in this form of marketless marketing becomes
difficult, and conflicts can arise very easily. Furthermore, Weller (1967)
has pointed to the imbalance in investment which can occur as the
result of contract farming with ultimate concentration of power in a few
firms. Thus, a change designed to reduce conflict involved in operating
through middlemen produces conflict of a different type at a different
level. The producer then has to seek an alternative method of resolving
the conflict and increasingly contract farmers are forming groups, or co-
operatives, to negotiate contracts with processors. Fewer firms become
involved in channel decisions. 'With this integration of functions, the
precise separation of producing, input-supplying and marketing roles
has been blurred' (Rogers and Conley, 1966, p. 361); 'but contract farming is a suitable mechanism for processing the standard commodities in
large volume which make up the bulk of consumption' (Barker, 1972,
p. 73).

The various changes in agricultural marketing practice are interrelated. As vertical co-ordination progresses, for example, so there is
pressure for producers to act co-operatively. In some instances the action
and reaction bargaining in the marketing channel is not left to those
directly involved. Government can step in to direct the formation of
marketing relationships and, in some cases, to create marketing institutions which can have monopoly power in the marketing channel. Even
in capitalist *free market* economies governments are able to act in a wide

variety of ways to influence, indirectly, agricultural marketing and to improve its efficiency. In many countries governments take an active and direct rôle, for example in the operation of marketing boards.

The Rôle of Marketing Boards

Marketing boards are

> public bodies set up by government action and delegated legal powers of compulsion over producers and handlers of primary or processed agricultural products. They include advisory and promotional boards whose only compulsory feature may be a levy on sales to meet their expenses, boards which are empowered to regulate individual producers' and traders' marketing operations and provide facilities for their use, and boards empowered to stabilize prices by various administrative methods. They also include boards which buy and sell on their own account, either with a monopoly or in competition with other trading enterprises (Abbott and Creupelandt, 1966, p. 1).

While marketing boards are only one form of governmental intervention into agricultural marketing processes they have proved popular tools by which farmers can increase their own channel power. Butterwick and Neville-Rolfe (1971) in an analysis of intervention within Western Europe suggests that British Marketing Boards, despite their chequered histories, have come to be regarded as 'an enviable model by many continental farmers' (p. 16). But they conclude that the boards have cushioned farmers from the impact of changing market processes and as such may have hindered the search for improved marketing methods.

The general aim of boards is to protect the producer from particular, detrimental, marketing situations. Specific powers allow individual problems to be tackled, for example quality and packing standards may be imposed, prices equalised over the whole market, or producers sheltered from sharply fluctuating prices. In many countries boards developed out of the conflicts created by the world depression of the early 1930s. The difficulties experienced in maintaining prices with excess supplies led Australia, New Zealand, Canada, the UK, the USA and South Africa to introduce compulsory marketing schemes. There are several studies of the development of market boards. For example in Britain, Giddings (1974) provides a general study while specialist studies of milk marketing have been produced by Simpson (1959), Milk Marketing Board (1965) and Straus and Churcher (1967). A variety of price support methods were administered by statutory marketing organisations in their early years.

The fluctuations in world prices in the 1930s meant the prolongation of the list of the statutory agencies and the Second World War produced further marketing management problems responsive to this type of regulatory treatment. During the war marketing boards were introduced into developing countries which in their postwar independence phase used the boards to control export marketing and as agencies to promote agricultural development such as crop production in new areas (Morley, 1967). Marketing boards, in their various forms, are now widespread throughout the world. The key feature which separates marketing boards from other marketing authorities is that boards emphasise producer control with governmental intervention. Other non-board authorities also may have governmental backing but often involve a sharing of control between two parties, for example producer and processor. The marketing board, therefore, unashamedly is aiming to improve the marketing position of the producer, usually the smallscale farmer.

This induced bias towards producer interests has been called, euphemistically, the development of *more orderly* marketing arrangements. The farmers' political parties usually use this rallying call in periods of price instability. In the early 1970s there was a renewed rise of interest in marketing boards in Canada and Australia (Hiscocks and Bennett, 1974; Campbell, 1973). In Canada, national legislation provided for the interprovincial co-ordination of the many provincial based boards. More than 80 commodity based marketing boards operate in Canada; 15 deal with milk marketing, 11 with eggs and a further 16 with vegetable marketing. Hiscocks and Bennett (1974) conclude a summary of the functions of various boards by stating that 'the operation of marketing boards has ensured that farmers receive equal treatment at the hands of buyers and that through pooling, farmers can get the same price throughout the season' (p. 22). In contrast, Campbell (1973) concludes his analysis of the value of boards in Australia by suggesting that, 'If government assistance to increase the market power of farmers is required, the evidence does not suggest that the producer monopoly' (i.e. the marketing board) 'is the only, most effective or the most socially acceptable way of providing such help' (p. 188).

Within Australia, in 1970, there were ten marketing boards operating across the whole country and at least a further 50 operating under state government legislation. The major agricultural products of wheat, dairy products, meat, eggs, canned fruit, apples, pears and dried fruit each had their own national boards, as did the lesser products of wine and honey. Additionally, a control board with no trading function operates in marketing wool. Alongside the Australian Wool Board is the Australian Wool

Commission which became operational in 1971 in response to a drastic fall in wool prices. The Wool Commission acted as a trading board and its functions were to operate a reserve price system, to set product standards, to set conditions for the control of auctions and to develop a range of market research activities. Within Australia 'orderly marketing' has been achieved by marketing boards and the producers' position has been strengthened, but 'orderly marketing has been viewed solely as a means of obtaining higher prices for farm products' with consumer (both final and processor) interests a secondary consideration (James, 1971, p. 147).

The protectionist function of marketing boards is also shown in Baldwin's (1970) review of marketing board operations in East and West Africa. In East Africa marketing boards have been set up on the one hand to oversee exports from the largescale agricultural operations and on the other to aid small farmers and protect them from middlemen. The Malawi Farmers' Marketing Board is of this latter type and operates buying points never more than a few miles from a small farm so that the farmer can travel easily to the site and obtain a guaranteed price, so making it not worthwhile for the middleman to intervene. In West Africa there has been a more critical examination of the success of marketing boards. Bauer (1954) argued that their success in price stabilisation in Nigeria and Ghana had limitations and the more recent study by Ogunsheye (1965) suggested that while prices might be stabilised this did not necessarily reduce violent fluctuations in producer incomes. Further criticism also comes from Hay (1970) who maintains that marketing boards in Nigeria have not used their market power at all effectively in promoting transport development. As with the other developments in agricultural marketing discussed in this chapter, marketing boards have created, with their sectional interest, just as many conflicts as they have resolved.

In most of this chapter the concern has been with agricultural marketing as a means of moving products from the farm to the processor. Developments have been pointed out and the suggestion made that conflict and conflict resolution are fundamental to the evolution of channel structure. It must not be forgotten, however, that farm enterprises are also consumers and that there is a flow of products from factory to farm. The design of efficient channels of distribution for fertiliser is a prime concern in agricultural programmes in the developing world. De Guia (1972) has shown, for example, quite different channel structures in Chile, Egypt, Mexico, the Philippines and Ivory Coast and it is evident that the institutional structure of each national channel determines the relative efficiency of the distribution system. Within Egypt, for example, fertiliser distribution is a government monopoly while in the Philippines the distribution is not regulated by any central or co-ordinating agency. In contrast again are the farm service centres which have been set up in North America by major fertiliser companies (Farm Chemicals, 1969). These sites, of which there were in excess of 1,000 in the Mid West in 1969, sell a range of farm goods from bulk fertiliser to spray nozzles and stuffed teddy bears. In some ways they could be seen as the retail outlets of the agricultural procurement industry. Farmers are also consumers of farm machinery and channels of distribution for machinery probably vary considerably both nationally and regionally but there are very few studies of farmers as consumers (Phillips, 1956; Agri-marketing, 1977). Little is known of the buying behaviour of farmers. Do they fit the models outlined in Chapter 3 or are other decision making processes active? Studies in agricultural marketing have tended to concentrate on the channels moving products off the farm and have tended to ignore the distribution patterns and problems of agricultural inputs.

References

ABBOT, J.C. (1970) *Marketing Fruit and Vegetables* (FAO, Rome).

ABBOT, J.C. and H.C. CREUPELANDT (1966) *Agricultural Marketing Boards; Their Establishment and Operation* (FAO, Rome).

AGRI-MARKETING (1977) 'How Farmers Make Buying Decisions', *Agri-marketing*, January, pp. 26-33.

ALLEN, G. (1973) 'Agricultural Co-operatives in the Marketing of Agricultural Produce and Inputs', *Yearbook of Agricultural Cooperation*, pp. 7-26.

ALLEN, G.R. (1972) 'An Appraisal of Contract Farming', *Journal of Agricultural Economics*, 33, pp. 89-98.

AMES, C.B. (1971) 'Dilemma of Product/market Management', *Harvard Business Review*, 49, pp. 66-74.

ANDERSON, D.A. (1970) *Marketing and Development* (Michigan State University, East Lansing).

BABCOCK, H.E. (1935) 'Cooperatives, the Pace-setters in Agriculture', *Journal of Farm Economics*, 17, pp. 153-6.

BARKER, J. (1972) *Contract Farming. Report of the Committee of Inquiry on Contract Farming* (HMSO, London).

BATEMAN, D.I. *et al.* (1971) *The Structure of Livestock Marketing in Wales* (University College of Wales, Department of Agricultural Economics, Aberystwyth).

BELL, D. (1976) *The Coming of Post-industrial Society* (Basic Books, New York).

BERTHELOT, J. (1972) *Les co-operatives agricoles en économie concurrentielle* (Cujas, Paris).

BRITTON, D.K. (1969) *Cereals in the United Kingdom* (Pergamon, Oxford).

BALDWIN, K.D.S. (1970) 'Marketing Boards in East and West Africa' in A.H. Bunting, *Change in Agriculture* (Duckworth, London), pp. 535-43.

BAUER, P.T. (1954) *West African Trade* (Cambridge University Press, London).

BRUNK, M.E. and L.B. DARRAH (1955) *Marketing Agricultural Products* (Ronald, New York).

BUTTERWICK, M. and E. NEVILLE-ROLFE (1971) *Agricultural Marketing and the EEC* (Hutchinson, London).

CABLE, C.C. (1966) 'Marketing Cotton and Cotton Textiles' in Marketing Economics Division, *Agricultural Markets in Change* (USDA, Washington), pp. 112-49.

CAMPBELL, K. (1973) 'The State Marketing Board – Relic or Prototype', *Australian Journal of Agricultural Economics*, 25, pp. 179-88.

CARDOZO, R.N. (1968) 'Segmenting the Industrial Market' in R.L. King (ed.), *Marketing and the New Science of Planning* (American Marketing Association, Chicago).

CARLYLE, W.J. (1975) 'Livestock Markets in Scotland', *Annals of Association of American Geographers*, 65, pp. 449-60.

CASSEL, E.C. *et al.* (1954) 'Fundamental Differences between Industrial and Consumer Marketing', *Journal of Marketing*, 18, pp. 152-7.

CLEVELAND, O.A. (1976) 'Optimal Organization of Gins and Warehouses for Marketing Cotton in Oklahoma-Texas Plains' (Ph.D. thesis, Oklahoma University).

COPPOCK, J.T. (1971) *An Agricultural Geography of Great Britain* (Bell, London).

COREY, E.R. (1962) *Industrial Marketing* (Prentice-Hall, Englewood Cliffs).

CORLEY, J.R. (1964) 'An Analysis of Grain Transportation in the Northwest', *U.S.D.A. Economic Research Service Report*, 200.

COVEY, C.D. and J.F. HUDSON (1963) 'Cotton Gin Efficiency as Related to Size, Location and Cotton Production Density in Lousiana', *Louisiana Agricultural Experiment Station Bulletin*, 577.

DALTON, R.T. (1971) 'Peas for Freezing: a Recent Development in Lincolnshire Agriculture', *East Midlands Geographer*, 5, pp. 133-41.

DE GUIA, E.O. (1972) *A Comparative Study of Fertiliser Distribution Systems* (OECD, Paris).

DE LOACH, D.B. (1958) 'Adapting Marketing Organization to Changing Requirements', *Journal of Farm Economics*, 40(5), pp. 1525-40.

DIAMOND, W.M. (1963) *Distribution Channels for Industrial Goods* (Ohio State University, Bureau of Business Research, Monograph 114).

DIGBY, M. (1961) *The Structure of the Norwegian Co-operative Movement* (Plunkett Foundation, Occasional Paper 22).

——— (1968) *Agricultural Cooperation in the United Kingdom* (Plunkett Foundation, Occasional Paper, 34).

DODGE, H.R. (1970) *Industrial Marketing* (McGraw-Hill, New York).

DOWNEY, W.D., R.L. KOHLS and R.B. WILSON (1965) 'Purchasing Behaviour of Co-operative Members', *Indiana Experiment Station Research Bulletin*, 797.

FARM CHEMICALS (1969) 'Farm Service Centers', *Farm Chemicals*, October, p. 1528.

FARRIS, P.C. (1970) *Truck Shipments of Grain from Indiana Country Elevators 1968-9* (Purdue University, Research Progress Report, 376).

FERGUSON, D.C. and W.O. McCARTHY (1970) 'A Spatial Analysis Approach to Size and Location of Australian Wool Selling Centres', *Review of Marketing and Agricultural Economics*, 38, pp. 153-65.

FISHER, L. (1976) *Industrial Marketing* (Business Books, London).

FLORES, X-A. (1971) *Agricultural Organisations and Economic and Social Development in Rural Areas* (International Labour Office, Geneva).

FOWLER, M.L. (1966) 'The Cotton Industry' in J.R. Moore and R.G. Walsh, *Market Structure of the Agricultural Industries* (Iowa State University Press, Ames), pp. 287-323.

GIDDINGS, P.J. (1974) *Marketing Boards and Ministers* (Saxon House, Farnborough).

GREENHUT, M.L. (1960) 'Size of Markets versus Transport Costs in Industrial Location Surveys and Theory', *Journal of Industrial Economics*, 8, pp. 172-84.

GUITON, N.F. Le H. (1967) 'Contracts in Agricultural Marketing' in T.K. Warley (ed.), *Agricultural Producers and Their Markets* (Basil Blackwell, Oxford), pp. 505-13.

HAY, A. (1970) 'Crop Marketing Boards and Transport Policy in Nigeria, 1950-64', *Journal of Transport Economics and Policy*, 3, pp. 171-80.

HEID, W.G. (1961) 'Changing Grain Channels', *USDA, Economic Research Service Report*, 39.

HEWLETT, R. (1967) 'Status, Achievements and Problems of Agricultural Co-operatives in Europe' in T.K. Warley (ed.), *Agricultural Producers and Their Markets* (Blackwell, Oxford), pp. 311-21.

HISCOCKS, G.A. and T.A. BENNETT (1974) 'Marketing Boards and Pricing in Canada', *Canadian Farm Economics*, 9(3), pp. 15-22.

HISE, R.T. (1965) 'Have Manufacturing Firms Adopted the Marketing Concept?', *Journal of Marketing*, 29, pp. 9-12.

INTERNATIONAL COOPERATIVE ALLIANCE (1965) *Structural Changes in Co-operatives* (ICA, London).

IZRAELI, D., D.N. IZRAELI and F. MEISNER (1974) (eds), *Agricultural Marketing for Developing Countries* (Wiley, Chichester).

JAMES, P.G. (1971) *Agricultural Policy in Wealthy Countries* (Angus & Robertson, Sydney).

JONES, W.D. (1967) *Agricultural Co-operative Trading in Wales* (Department of Agricultural Economics, University College of Wales, Aberystwyth).

KOHLS, R.L. and W.D. DOWNEY (1972) *Marketing of Agricultural Products* (4th edn, Macmillan, New York).

KRAJKO, G. *et al.* (1974) 'Determination of Economic Microregions in the Southern Great Plain', *Acta Geographica*, 14(2), pp. 1-21.

LARZELERE, H. (1964) 'Cooperatives in Agricultural Marketing' in V.L. Sorenson (ed.), *Agricultural Market Analysis* (Michigan State University, East Lansing), pp. 205-16.

LELE, U.J. (1971) *Food Grain Marketing in India* (Cornell University Press, Ithaca).

MARRIAN, J. (1965) 'Marketing Characteristics of Industrial Goods and Buyers' in A. Wilson (ed.), *The Marketing of Industrial Products* (Hutchinson, London).

MILK MARKETING BOARD (1965) *The Structure of Dairy Farming in England and Wales* (Thames Ditton).

MOORE, J.R. (1966) 'The Causes and Consequences of Major Changes in the Organization of Agricultural Marketing Activities', *Journal of Farm Economics*, 48, pp. 148-61.

MOORE, J.R. and R.G. WALSH (1966) (eds), *Market Structure of the Agricultural Industries* (Iowa State University Press, Ames).

MORLEY, J.A.E. (1967) 'Marketing Boards' in T.K. Warley(ed.), *Agricultural Producers and Their Markets* (Basil Blackwell, Oxford), pp. 341-51.

—— (1975) *British Agricultural Co-operatives* (Hutchinson, London).

NATIONAL COMMISSION ON FOOD MARKETING (1966) *Food from Farmer to Consumer* (Government Printer, Washington, DC).

NICHOLAS, P. (1973) 'Specifité et role de la cooperation agricole dans la complexe agro-alimentaire français', *Institut de Science Economique Appliquée en Economies et Societiés*, 8(11, 12), pp. 2307-31.

OECD (1973) *Changes in the Processing and Distribution of Milk and Milk Products* (OECD, Paris).

OGUNSHEYE, A.O. (1965) 'Marketing Boards and the Stabilization of Producer Incomes in Nigeria', *Nigerian Journal of Economic and Social Studies*, 7, pp. 131-43.

OLDENSTADT, D. and D. CALL (1964) 'Group Action in Agricultural Marketing' in V.L. Sorenson (ed.), *Agricultural Market Analysis* (Michigan State University,

East Lansing), pp. 190-204.

PALMER, C.M. (1975) *Distributive Margins for Meat in Great Britain* (University of Exeter, Agricultural Economics Unit, Report, 194).

PEDERSEN, A. (1973) 'Agricultural Co-operative Marketing and Production with Special Reference to the Changes in Denmark', *Yearbook for Agricultural Co-operation*, pp. 120-36.

PHILLIPS, W.G. (1956) *The Agricultural Implement Industry* (University of Toronto Press, Toronto).

REVZAN, D.A. (1961) *Wholesaling in Marketing Organization* (Wiley, New York).

RICHEY, P.S. and T.W. JOHNSON (1952) 'Factors to be Considered in Locating, Planning and Operating Country Elevators', *USDA, Marketing Research Report*, 23.

ROGERS, G.B. and F.M. CONLEY (1966) 'Marketing Poultry and Eggs' in Marketing Economics Division, *Agricultural Markets in Change* (USDA, Agricultural Economic Report 95), pp. 329-68.

ROY, E.P. (1963) *Contract Farming. U.S.A.* (Interstate, Daneville).

SAGELUMO, O. (1976) 'Agricultural Marketing Co-operatives in Norway', *Yearbook of Agricultural Cooperation*, pp. 159-69.

SHEPHERD, G.S. and G.A. FUTRELL (1969) *Marketing Farm Products* (5th edn, Iowa State University Press, Ames).

SIMPSON, E.S. (1959) 'Milk Production in England and Wales: a Study in Collective Marketing', *Geographical Review*, 49, pp. 95-111.

SINCLAIR, J.L. (1968) *The Production, Marketing and Consumption of Cotton* (Praeger, New York).

SMITH, V. (1975) 'Marketing Agricultural Commodities in Pichincha Province, Ecuador', *Geographical Review*, 65, pp. 353-63.

SMYTH, R.L. (1959) *The Distribution of Fruit and Vegetables* (Duckworth, London).

SNITZLER, J.R. and R.J. BYRNE (1959) 'Interstate Trucking of Frozen Fruits and Vegetables under Agricultural Exemption', *USDA Marketing Research Report*, 316.

SOLDBRAA, A. and C. SUNDBY (1961) *Farmers Marketing Organisations* (OECD, Paris).

STEVENS, T.L. (1963) 'Here Comes Vertical Marketing', *Industrial Marketing*, 47, September, pp. 123-7.

STRAUS, E. and E.H. CHURCHER (1967) 'The Regional Analysis of the Milk Market', *Journal of Agricultural Economics*, 18, pp. 221-40.

SURRIDGE, B.J. (1967) 'The Role of Co-operative Apex Organizations Overseas' in T.K. Worley (ed.), *Agricultural Producers and Their Markets* (Blackwell, Oxford), pp. 589-96.

TARRANT, J.R. (1976) *Agricultural Geography* (David & Charles, Newton Abbot).

THOMSEN, F.C. (1951) *Agricultural Marketing* (McGraw-Hill, New York).

ULREY, T.W. (1964) 'Problems and Issues in Transportation Policy and Implications for Agriculture', *Journal of Farm Economics*, 46(5), pp. 1281-9.

USDA (1970) 'Statistics of Farmer Co-operatives 1967-8', USDA, *Farm Cooperative Service Report*, 11.

VALKO, L. (1954) *International Handbook of Cooperative Legislation* (State College of Washington, Pullman).

VOSLOH, C.J. (1966) 'Grain Marketing' in Marketing Economics Division, *Agricultural Markets in Change* (USDA, Washington), pp. 215-57.

WARD, A.H. (1975) *A Command of Cooperatives* (New Zealand Dairy Board, Wellington).

WATTS, H.D. (1975) 'The Location of the Beet-sugar Industry in England and Wales, 1912-36', *Transactions of the Institute of British Geographers*, 53, pp. 95-116.

WEBSTER, F.H. (1973) *Agricultural Co-operation in Denmark* (Plunkett Foundation, Occasional Paper, 39).

WELLER, J. (1967) *Modern Agriculture and Rural Planning* (The Architectural Press, London).

WILLIAMS, O. (1972) 'The Role of the Auctioneer in the Livestock Trade of South Wales', *Geography*, 57(1), pp. 18-23

WILLIAMS, W.F. and T.T. STOUT (1964) *Economics of the Livestock Meat Industry* (Macmillan, New York).

WILLS, W.J. (1952) 'Livestock Market Location Theory', *Journal of Farm Economics*, 34, pp. 253-8.

––– (1972) *An Introduction to Grain Marketing* (Interstate, Daneville).

WIND, Y. and R.N. CARDOZO (1974) 'Industrial Market Segmentation', *Industrial Marketing Management*, 3, pp. 153-64.

WORSLEY, P. (1971) (ed.), 'Two Blades of Grass', *Rural Co-operatives in Agricultural Modernisation* (University of Manchester Press, Manchester).

WRIGHT, B.H. (1965) 'Changes in Transportation Used by Country Grain Elevators in the North Central Region', *USDA Marketing Research Report*, 724.

YAGER, F.P. (1959) 'Cooperative Country Elevators in Montana', *USDA, Farmer Cooperative Service Report*, 64.

YLI-JOKIPII, P. (1971) 'The Spatial Characteristics of the Livestock and Meat Trade in Finland with Special Reference to Slaughterhouses', *Fennia*, 110, pp. 1-35.

7   LAND USE COMPLEXES—TWO EXAMPLES

Marketing Land Use Complexes

Conflicts, both real and imagined, are commonplace among firms comprising the broad sectors of the marketing system. As has been indicated in earlier chapters, conflict increasingly is occurring on an intersectoral basis, for example, with the contrasting corporate aims of largescale retailers and merchant wholesalers. One result of attempts to resolve some of these many conflicts has been the spatial aggregation of firms trying to achieve economic and social benefits consequent on explicit or implicit co-operation. It is not surprising therefore that areas of land exist which are devoted to a particular marketing activity but provide locations for many firms. Just as many firms may occupy a single office block, so many retailers may occupy a shopping centre or many wholesalers locate in a distribution centre. Marketing firms operating from these complexes impinge on each other but relationships have tended to become ordered and formalised as the complex has evolved. None the less, conflicts do occur not just among the constituent firms but also between the total complex and other land users in the urban area.

The processes creating these blocks of marketing land uses are not new. It is possible to argue, although it is an extreme position, that the town centre, with its collection of retailers, is such a land use block. Acceptance of this extreme case means aggregating a variety of marketing functions into a single land use complex and it would seem more manageable to define these blocks of marketing land use as areas with a single broad function. Within the urban area the marketplace with many smallscale retailers operating from stalls or off the floor would certainly be typical of the idea of a land use complex. In Chapter 4 it has been shown that these market areas exist from Accrington and Ahamadabad to Zeebrugge and Zaria and while there are many types each has an ordered relationship among its participants. Although in the Third World these markets are often classified as the *informal* sector, they operate through a range of quite formal contacts and relationships. Within agricultural marketing the stock saleyards are similar in comprising many functionally similar or closely related firms operating at one site. Similar are distribution centres, shopping centres and wholesale produce markets.

Many of the general evolutionary processes apparent in most marketing institutions apply to these land use complexes. There is a general increase in scale of operation but also a bipolar pattern of development with both the very small and very large having most success. The functions taken on by operators in these complexes are increasing in variety and product lines are tending to be more varied. The innovation development life cycle is shortening. Vertical and horizontal integration of firms represented in the complexes is altering established relationships among the firms. All of these general changes have been discussed in earlier chapters and all, to various degrees, are applicable to marketing land use complexes. In the evolution of most of these complexes, there have been, as with many specific marketing institutions, strong pressures for the suburbanisation (or even removal from the town altogether) of these land use blocks. But in the last few years there have been signs with some types of land use complex, that central city locations are proving attractive. This is particularly so with shopping centres and the building of these complexes 'downtown' will be considered later in this chapter. Alongside these general features there are also conflicts and characteristics of change which are particular to individual land use types. Conflicts have arisen owing to the aggregation of firms and their operation in close proximity but there are also conflicts which have arisen in consequence of the allocation of relatively large areas to a single use. Although the many types of land use complex each have particular development processes resulting from the conflicts present, the urban wholesale produce market and the shopping centre provide good examples of both the general themes and particular determinants of change.

Urban Wholesale Produce Markets

> Wholesale produce markets are those central places in cities or major urban areas where the bulk of the fruit and vegetables, sometimes also meat, eggs and dairy produce, and fish, arrive daily from local producing areas or from abroad for display and sale to retailers. (Mittendorf, 1976, pp. 2-3).

The function of these markets is to break the bulk of agricultural production into small lots suited to retailers' needs and to provide the retailer with the variety of products needed to meet consumer demand. The importance of the produce market within the channel of distribution of fresh vegetables, fruit, etc. depends both on the general strength of the wholesale sector, which has been discussed earlier, and also on the size of the urban area served. It would seem that in many small urban areas retailers, through personal contact with local market-garden type producers, can buy some produce direct while in the larger cities a greater proportion of produce passes through the central market. The produce market at Nine Elms in London, Rungis in Paris and Hunts Point in New York constitute key points in the distribution network in the three cities. The rapid growth in recent years of Asian and Latin American cities coupled with their developing wholesale sector, resulting from general economic development producing a demand for a greater variety of goods, means that in cities such as Mexico City and Bangkok the urban wholesale market has increased in prominence. In such cities the need to provide efficient markets for the exapnding demand has often created land use planning problems and in some cases has led to the development of a system of wholesale markets within the city. The highly centralised nature of most produce markets in Western countries is less efficient in developing economies where transport modes are different and transaction size is much smaller. One refrigerated articulated trailer at Nine Elms is probably equivalent to several dozen trucks, motor trishaws, boats and barges at the Bangkok market. Thus although the function of the market remains the same in developed and developing countries, the patterns of provision can vary considerably and their layouts differ in response to dominant transport modes (Sherbini, 1966; Ueda, 1975).

In a broad fashion the function of the wholesale produce market is relatively clear and simple. In reality there are many different activities often related to specific characteristics both of the product and of the demand. A series of studies by the US Department of Agriculture of the major markets in cities of the USA showed that a series of specialist activities had developed in these markets. In Washington 64 firms of 14 distinct types operated in the market. The majority fell into the broad class of wholesale handler and included different types of jobbers, receivers, repackers, truckers and commission merchants. Goods passing through the market could pass through vastly different channels all within the one wholesale market (Bohall and Macomber, 1962). This pattern is repeated in all the studies in the series – in New York, Baltimore, Boston, Denver, Butte etc. Within North American markets the USDA studies identified 25 types of wholesale handler, 13 types of broker and agent and 6 types of retailer who could be operating in any single market. So, for imported produce, brokers could be involved with the goods before their being auctioned, with some passing through jobbers specialising in hotel provisions and some passing to a receiver who would pass the goods via a repacker and trucker to another wholesale market in a smaller centre where a jobber may sell to a wholesale grocer and finally to the retailer. It is not difficult to build up extensive and expensive chains of distribution when specialist functions are involved. It is small wonder therefore that the channels have come under close scrutiny by wholesalers and retailers alike with larger retailers attempting to enter into contracts with producers for the direct supply of produce (see Chapter 6).

Within the developing countries the patterns are no less complex though in general less well studied. The study of Cali in Colombia by Riley and others (1970) suggests that business in wholesale markets is not differentiated by function but by product. In the market there were, in 1969, 450 wholesalers of fruit and vegetables including 35 dealing in oranges, 40 in onions, 72 in tomatoes, etc. Functionally almost all the wholesalers acted as simple jobbers dealing directly with producers and retailers. A comparable study of La Paz (Henley *et al.*, 1970) shows 'three specific types of fruit and vegetable wholesalers . . . (1) potato wholesalers, (2) banana wholesalers, and (3) vegetable wholesalers' (p. 95), and again functionally they provide simply 'a consistent link between rural farmer and urban retailer' (p. 95). In both these examples it appears that unlike the USA or UK the other wholesale functions such as importing are carried out by firms not located within the urban wholesale produce market area.

Table 7.1 shows for several markets the number of wholesalers involved. The degree of concentration of trade affects these figures with, for example, large multifunctional firms operating in New York and London to a far greater degree than in Paris. Most of the markets included in Table 7.1 are all relatively recently established or relocated and are at suburban sites.

In most cities the produce market usually has developed at a central site but as conflicts have arisen so in the larger cities relocation has occurred. In Boston, for example, the Faneuil Hall market area dates back to 1742 and with subsequent extensions and additions became the main wholesale market by the mid nineteenth century. As the volume of trade grew, so the congestion in the market areas increased. The central location hindered expansion and the lack of railway access increased the traffic congestion with trucking necessary between the market and railway. In 1927, the New York, New Haven and Hartford Railroad built the Boston Terminal Market and with changes in ownership in 1953, truck shipments have been permitted to this formerly rail served market. The Boston Terminal Market has become the major wholesale market in Boston with only relatively minor sales at other specialist produce markets (Manchester, 1962). The Faneuil Hall area has been redeveloped into a downtown shopping centre with an emphasis on small-scale retailers selling craft type products in the renovated and conserved

Table 7.1: Selected Characteristics of Some Large Urban Wholesale Markets

	Year of opening	Area (ha)	Vehicles per day	Most common wholesale unit (m^2)	Number of wholesalers
New York (Hunts Point)	1967	50	2,300	242	70
London (Nine Elms)	1973	25	6,000	72,204 and 259	240
Paris (Rungis)	1969	204	13,600	80-150	930
Hamburg	1962	25	1,300	40, 80, 120	150
Barcelona	1971	33	NA	72 and 103	500
Milan	1965	45	7,500	315	240
Rotterdam	1969	12	NA	100	104
Bangkok[a]	1962	NA	NA	17 and 22	433
Manila	1971	125	5,000	180	500
Bogota	1972	40	3,350	10, 12	1,500
Brasilia	1972	62	NA	66	241
Kuwait	1962	15	3,500	75	40

a. Part of the activity takes place on barges and boats, so area and vehicle numbers have little meaning.
NA = not available.
Source: Mittendorf (1976).

market hall (Redstone, 1976). Although the reuse of the city centre market area is rather special to Boston the general development pattern shown by the Boston wholesale market is typical of many in urban North America and Europe.

The reasons for the need to move from city centre sites are not hard to find and may be seen as a method of resolving the conflicts created by the expansion of trade in produce markets caused by an urban population growth. As the number of ultimate consumers supplied by the market increases, so the number of active participants in the market tends to increase and the location may become less convenient for participants. It is widely accepted that 'A wholesale food distribution centre should be located at a point where a minimum of travel time is required both by buyers to shop and sellers to distribute commodities and return to their establishments' (Taylor and Miller, 1967, p. 42). By defining the location in terms of time, so suburban locations become favoured over central cities. A second reason for suburban locations is the reduction of conflicts between non-market and market traffic. Central city market areas are usually crossed by streets handling non-market traffic, so causing congestion and an increase in market operating costs. In the report assessing relocation possibilities for Covent Garden market, London, the Fantus Company (1963A) point out that with the growth in market activity after 1920 it became necessary to expand out of the previous market area and into surrounding streets:

> The loading and unloading of vehicles, parking of lorries and the disposal of empties on the street extend well beyond the area of the market premises, and cause acute congestion in most of the streets leading to the original market, causing traffic problems and delay in market operations. (p. 28).

The need for rail access is often a contributory factor to relocation at a suburban site. In many markets in the USA, Europe and Australia a third or more of produce enters by rail and if the market serves an extensive region produce is usually sent out by rail. In Perth, Western Australia, for example, an argument for a future relocation of the market from a CBD frame site to a location adjacent to the main rail freight terminal is the problem created by trucking produce to and fro from market to terminal. In this case the problem is particularly acute because the market serves the whole of Western Australia with retailers in Kalgoorlie (600 km away) buying through agents in the market. London provides a second example, where

> One of the major deficiencies of Covent Garden is the absence of railway tracks on which produce can be brought right into the market. All produce arriving at the railway terminals must be moved by lorry into and out of the market area. (Fantus, 1963B, p. 4).

The presence of a rail link played an important part in the evaluation of alternative sites. Efficient rail freight terminals, for the most part, are non-central city activities and consequently the advantage of linkage between terminal and market adds to the pressures for a decentralisation of produce markets. Convenience, transportation and accessibility considerations are of prime importance in determining the need for the relocation of facilities.

Land availability factors also favour suburban sites for enlarged produce markets. Mention has been made of how Covent Garden market spilled over into the surrounding streets. In central Paris the old market of Les

Halles covered 6 ha, but market facilities and operations, by the time of the market's removal to Rungis, covered 24 ha. The Rungis site is 204 ha. In Milan the market centred on a 2.5 ha. site in the city has been re-located to a 40 ha. site on the edge of the city. The space needs of modern markets in large cities inevitably mean a suburban site, for the costs of securing a sufficiently large central city site are prohibitive. (Horticultural Marketing Council, 1962).

The need for such large site areas of new markets is a response not simply to the increased volume of trade but also to changes in operation of markets particularly in commodity handling. Within markets in the wealthier countries pallet storage, mechanisation and specialised storage facilities have become commonplace in recent years. These technological changes all imply single-storey buildings and the horizontal rather than vertical movement of goods. Despite the increased efficiency of their operation and their relocation at convenient accessible sites, the increase in sales volume passing through produce markets has not kept up with the increases in retail sales of fruit and vegetables.

As retail companies and establishments increase in size, so order sizes of fruit and vegetables increase and direct buying occurs with producers contracted to particular companies (see Chapter 6). The produce markets therefore are particularly important in distributing products to smaller scale retailers. Inevitably, however, because of the complex structure of firms in these markets, prices for small retailers buying in small lots are higher than for the large firms both purchasing directly from the grower and also buying large discounted lots at the produce market.

The price differential between fruit in the supermarket/hypermarket and in the small fruiterer is in large part a result of the relatively high cost wholesale market within the channel of distribution for fruit. The large firm's response is not to trade at the market. A study by CTIFL (1976) of the firms from the Paris Region purchasing fruit and vegetables at Rungis showed that in 1975 small independent retailers purchased 57 per cent of their produce through Rungis but that hypermarket buyers bought only 18 per cent of their goods in that way. As hypermarket and other largescale retail trading increases, so there is a decline in the relative importance of urban wholesale markets in the channel for fruit and vegetables. Such a change may call into question the cost effectiveness of single large, expensive markets acting as the supplier for a whole metropolitan area. Suggestions for developing countries, where almost all participants are smallscale operators, indicate a possible series of smaller regional metropolitan markets which can be located closer to retailers than the large centralised market. In any case the convergence of many smallscale buyers at markets such as Rungis is forcing market planners to reconsider the operation of the markets which, on the whole, have been designed with largescale buyers in mind (LSA, 1978). A report by the FAO (Mittendorf, 1976) on planning wholesale markets concludes that because of small retailers and the need to distribute highly seasonal products:

> Investments in new wholesale markets in industrialised countries are therefore still justified although they will be smaller than they would have been if direct sales had not expanded so rapidly . . . The wholesale market, in these conditions, has more of a supplementary function . . . (p. 7).

The report goes on to argue strongly that with the different rôle of wholesale markets in countries at different levels of development it is important to design the market for its function to minimise conflict and to maximise distributional efficiency.

Shopping Centres

Shopping centres are a second complex of firms constituting an area of marketing land use. The shopping centre is a much more recent phenomenon than the urban wholesale market and contrasts with the produce market in being almost impervious to the host society. The shopping centre is a megacultural feature, with a centre in Kuala Lumpur being very similar to one in Copenhagen, Sydney, Tokyo, Tel Aviv or Cape Town (see Figure 7.1). In all these places many of the conflicts created by the shopping centre and inherent in its evolution are similar, as again are many of the responses to the conflicts. Although the shopping centre is a relatively recent feature of marketing activity, none the less it has undergone extensive evolution even in its short life and while the overall feature is a megacultural phenomenon such social imperviousness is not the case with its evolution.

Although there is an extensive literature on many varied aspects of shopping centres none of the major texts attempts to define what the term means. It is worthwhile before considering their evolution to attempt a definition and to differentiate the shopping centre from the shopping district or area. Often the term shopping centre is used very loosely to describe any cluster of shops but a stricter definition is much more valuable. A shopping centre comprises a group of businesses the majority of which are retailers, located in a unified architectural unit which may be a single structure or related group of buildings. The local

Figure 7.1: Some Common Types of Shopping Centre Layout

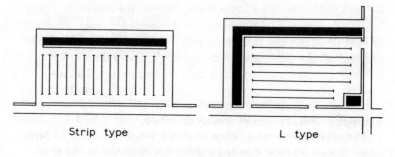

Strip type   L type

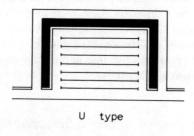

U type

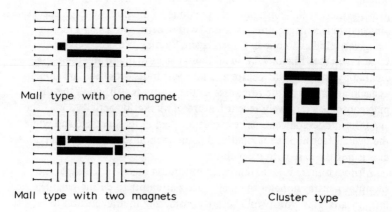

Mall type with one magnet

Mall type with two magnets   Cluster type

economic environment in which the retailers operate is controlled usually by the body responsible for the development of the centre. Shopping centres, therefore, are differentiated from shopping districts in respect of both their form and their operation. With the growth of shopping centres both in number and through space, there is a third aspect which differentiates the shopping centre and shopping district. This is the emergence of a shopping centre culture quite distinct from the culture associated with shopping districts (Kowinski, 1978). As the concept of a shopping centre evolves so does its definition.

The origins of shopping centres are hard, if not impossible to determine. McKeever (1953) suggests that centres developed in the early 1920s in Baltimore and Kansas City in the USA were among the first. These probably are early examples at suburban sites but in many British cities in the nineteenth century groups of shops were built by a single developer who rented the sites to retailers. The shops together would form a single architectural unit and the landlord/developer would influence the retailer's operations to a considerable degree. In the USA the Roland Park development of 1907 was along these lines. Such centres would be small and located in existing shopping districts but they were, and some still are, planned shopping centres. As urban areas have expanded so has the concept of the shopping centre, although half a dozen shops could still comprise a small centre but at the larger end of the size continuum centres over 100,000 m^2 are not unusual and contain over 300 shops together with a range of personal service enterprises and probably offices of government agencies. Even these large centres are developed as a single complex of buildings with a unified design and strictly controlled operating environment. With the range of types of shopping centre which have been developed it is not surprising that their number has increased from around 1,000 in 1955 to 20 times this figure 20 years later. On average this represents about three new shopping centres opening every day for 20 years. If we add figures for new openings elsewhere then it can be appreciated that shopping centres now represent a major land use complex with its own particular set of development problems. The Urban Land Institute has reviewed many of these problems in several of its publications, notably the Development Handbook published in 1976.

With such a rapid growth it would be expected that evolution would be similarly dramatic. Such has been the case with evolutionary change occurring, in part, as a response to the conflicts created by the shopping centre phenomenon. The evolutionary trends can be related to the criteria of definition. First, a number of changes have affected the form, design and technology of centres. Secondly, new locational requirements have emerged. Thirdly, the development process, organisation and operation of centres have altered; and finally, there is the emergence of a shopping centre way of life.

Changing Form of the Shopping Centre

The early shopping centres were small and were composed of small units suited to the retail technology of the time even to the extent of including, often over the shop, living accommodation for the shop operator. The beginnings of the boom in shopping centre births in 1930s North America coincided with the emergence of effective multistore retailing and changed operating methods which required larger shop premises. More recent developments in consumer mobility have produced further changes in centre form and layout and additionally have resulted in the establishment of discrete types of centre form.

The rise of the motor car dependent society has played a major part in the evolution of shopping centre form. The nineteenth-century centres were integrated into city centres and formed parts of pedestrian orientated shopping streets. With the rise of the car it has become necessary to provide parking space. First these were outside the store doors but congestion resulted so parking areas were provided behind the stores with customers entering the back doors of shops: 'the first planning step forward was taken when store buildings were moved back from the road and larger parking areas were provided in front' (Gruen, 1959, p. 103). As centres became more popular with customers, retailers and developers and as car ownership increased, so

> the depth of the parking lots had to be increased until it became impossible to construct shopping facilities within the narrow 150 to 200-ft deep strips which zoning laws [in North America] usually allowed for retailing . . . Instead of one strip, two parallel strips of stores were built, and parking was arranged outside both. (p. 104).

The stores still fronted the parking areas and the centre mall, for a long time, was underplayed. The Highland Park Shopping Village in Dallas was the first (1931) unified development to have its stores facing away from the access streets. Gradually pedestrians and traffic became segregated. Even delivery traffic was channelled underground below the stores, and centre layouts changed to freestanding designs with a totally pedestrian orientated shopping concourse. Vast parking areas have been provided around centres. In modern large centres the most striking visual feature is usually the area set aside for customer and employee parking.

Where new centres have been developed in city centres multistorey parking blocks have become integral to the centre and even overpower it, while in sites with lower land costs the shopping complex sits in the centre of tens of hectares of asphalt parking lots. For example, at the Northwest Plaza, a major centre in suburban St Louis, there are spaces for 7,500 cars, while the Eagle Centre in Derby's CBD has several multistorey parks crammed into the overall site. These two examples are typical of the many thousand such centres.

Even in newly developed small centres parking space around the centre is vital to its economic success and is thus a major component of the form. Estimates vary on the space norms necessary for car park provision, with Snaith (1959) suggesting a 4:1 ratio (10 car spaces per 100 m² of retailing) between car park and shopping space. The Urban Land Institute suggests 2.2:1, Welsh (1969) advocates 3:1 and Barton Aschman Assoc. Inc. (1977), after a large study of several major regional centres in the USA, suggest a *maximum* ratio of 2:1 and argue that many centres could reduce their car park provision. Jones (1969) and Darlow (1972), studying British centres, and the ITE Project Committee Report (1972) in the USA all showed that effective provision is around 2:1 or 5 cars per 100 m² of retail space. Much depends on the type of centre and the amount of non-retail space in the centre. If there is a large amount of office accommodation, parking ratios need to be higher to allow for the long-stay office workers. In general also, smaller centres usually have lower figures as the time a car space is occupied by each car is lower for these centres. After initial levels of provision, which were very high, there has been a reaction against possible overprovision of expensive car park space so that recent North American reports suggest around 5 car spaces per 100 m² of shopping and Northern and Haskoll (1977) suggest that for Britain 3.5 spaces per 100 m² 'is a more reasonable target' (p. 78). Clearly such a reduction affects costs for developers but traffic planners are unlikely, it is hoped, to be duped by demands to reduce parking provision to cater for something slightly over average demand when peak demands can be over three times average demand.

At first, the conflict between centre visitors and other road users led to congestion around shopping centres and the incorporation of shopper car parks in centre design. As mobility levels have risen, so continued conflict has occurred over parking space provision so that throughout the evolution of centre form, the car parking component is a dominant aspect and there have been numerous studies of parking plot design and circulation (Lipp, 1961; Welch, 1961; Douglass, 1958) as well as studies to quantify trip numbers and character (Miller, 1969; Highway Research

Board, 1966; Harding, 1968). It seems unlikely that in the short term, future shopping centres will have less parking provision, even if the developers, for cost reasons, would like this. Despite energy shortages and more expensive personal mobility almost all trips to centres are made by car. Single-car families in the USA in 1974 undertook around 200 shopping trips by car with 16 per cent of all car trips being for shopping purposes (Sansom, 1975). Not all these trips end at shopping centres but given an energy shortage, it is likely that more preplanning of trips will occur and one-stop shopping centres will increase their share of shopping trips.

The second major evolutionary trend in the form of shopping centres relates to the division of the retail floor space into shop units. Shop units have increased in size in both large and small centres. This trend is only to be expected given the overall changes in retailing and the higher levels of efficiency and profitability associated with the larger stores. In the USA in the 1930s the department stores gave a major impetus to shopping centre development. By developing branch stores in shopping centres in the suburbs, department store groups provided a change in emphasis in shopping centre form. Instead of a centre comprising a group of shops each of roughly the same size, it became commonplace to have a major store of perhaps 10,000 m² or larger, and a group of smaller units.

As centres have grown in size and status so the number of units has increased and so has the range of unit sizes. In large centres there are three or more large department stores of at least 20,000 m² each, a supermarket of, say, 3,000 m² and variety stores of about the same size. At the other extreme there are cigarette kiosks, fruit juice stalls, shoe repairers, etc. of only 5 m². Table 7.2 shows the size distribution of units in a shopping centre of 50,000 m² in South Canberra, Australia. There are seven units of less than 10 m² but also a department store and several large discount variety stores. This distribution is not untypical of larger centres. Also shown in Table 7.2 is the combined distribution of seven small, recently developed, centres in the same area. In this case the larger units are supermarkets but there is still a considerable spread in the size range (Alexander and Dawson, 1978). But it is only in recent years that a range of shop sizes has been introduced into centre development. Darlow (1972) states: 'the days of the "standard unit" in major shopping centre developments are numbered' (p. 19). For many years in Britain – and there are examples in housing areas throughout the country – small centres comprised a set of identical units. Consequent on the more flexible approach to the size mix of units demanded by retailers, the form and layout of centres has changed.

Table 7.2: Distribution of Shop Sizes in Shopping Centres in South Canberra, Australia, 1978

Size of unit (m^2)	Number of units	
	Regional centre	Seven neighbourhood centres
10 and smaller	7	0
11-25	20	0
26-50	31	17
51-75	41	10
76-100	24	4
101-125	15	12
126-150	11	0
151-200	6	2
201-300	2	3
301-400	3	0
401-4,000	3	0
over 4,000	4	0

A series of distinct centre layouts have evolved as demand for different sized units has been met and also as shopping centres have become more complex shop clusters. Typical layouts are shown in Figure 7.1:

There has been a steady evolution of shopping center design from its original concept as a strip with parking, through the L-shape, the U-shape, the mall, the cluster, and then the adaptation of these two latter forms to enclosure and air conditioning. Furthermore, there has been the innovation of *stacking* or double-level arrangements of the retail facilities. This treatment is a solution called for by site design to answer problems of extremes in walking distances otherwise imposed by a large, single-level regional center, by the steepness of topography, by the shape of a particular parcel of land or by a relatively small but high value parcel of ground. (McKeever, 1968, p. 321).

The *strip* type centre is essentially an integrated shopping street with its own parking plot. Often the pedestrian walk along the front of the stores is covered by a canopy. This basic type is easily adaptable to most site conditions. It is also common for a large store to be part of the strip and even to account for over 50 per cent of floor space. The strip layout is a common response to the demand for a small centre comprising convenience shops.

The 'L' and 'U' types are responses to the need for larger centres than is feasible with a strip layout. The maximum length of strip is around 130 m, beyond which shoppers are unwilling to use the whole centre. By turning the ends of the strip into an 'L' or 'U', the centre becomes larger without any major increase in walking distances. The location of large units, which act as magnets to pedestrian flows, is critical in the success of 'L' and 'U' type centres. Corner or end sites are important for these larger store units and have proved the most successful sites from the consumer viewpoint but can result in serious congestion in the service road which is usually at the rear of the centre. Again because of the un-willingness of pedestrians to walk more than around 130 m, in a small centre, there is a limit to the size of the 'L' and 'U' type centres. To overcome this problem the cluster layout has been developed.

The *cluster* type is comprised of groups of stores and store-blocks separated by pedestrian areas with the whole surrounded by car parking. The layout allows for the minimisation of walking distance between the centre and the furthermost parking plots. The degree of complexity of the cluster can be increased to take account of larger centre size and probably the only limiting factor is the size of the parking area needed to serve the centre. The *mall* is a pedestrian circulation pattern and is usually associated with a cluster type layout. At its simplest the cluster is two strips separated by a mall but this form rarely occurs. The cluster and mall combination provides greatest flexibility, of all types, for varied shop units and the creation of a coherent architectural form to shopping centres.

In all cases the central concern of shopping centre layout is to con-trol the shopper circulation system. This control is easiest in the cluster layout as entrances and exits to the mall are limited and the relative position of pedestrian spaces manipulates the flow of shoppers. The essence of shopping centre design is the creation of a totally controlled marketing environment and each advance in layout pattern has moved centre operators closer to this goal.

As the shopping centre concept has evolved, so centres have become more complex both in form and operation. The size of a centre has become a critical variable in determining its form. Most studies of centre development isolate three types of centre differentiated in respect of size. The crystalising of ideas on the neighbourhood, district (or com-munity) and regional shopping centre have been simultaneous with the evolution of the formal aspects of the shopping centre. The three types of centre are distinct in function and operation as well as in form but, for the moment, it is proposed to discuss only differences in form. The essential distinction is one of size.

The *neighbourhood centre* has a size range of 3,000-10,000 m^2 with an average gross leasable area of around 5,000 m^2 on a total site area slightly over 2 hectares. As suggested above, parking ratios can be well below 2:1 (5 cars per 100 m^2) but often the parking area is dependent on the size of the supermarket in the centre. With a superette or small supermarket of around 1,000 m^2 a lower ratio is possible than if a major store of 2,000-3,000 m^2 is integrated into the centre.

The *district centre* is larger and often more complex in layout even to the extent of being enclosed and having air-conditioned malls. Sizes usually range from 10,000 to 30,000 m^2 with an average around 15,000 m^2 on at least a 10 ha site. In addition to a large supermarket structure the layout of a district centre has to be capable of incorporating a variety/discount store or a small department store. When a hypermarket is incorporated into these centres, sometimes 60 per cent of the floor space is accounted for by the key tenant and parking ratios rise to 4:1 (Unit for Retail Planning Information Ltd, 1977).

The third type is the *regional centre* which has at least 30,000 m^2 of floor space and can have 150,000 m^2. Minimum site areas are about 16 ha. Usually between 30 and 50 per cent of the floor space is accounted for by department stores and in the large centres four or five such stores are common. Most new centres in this category have complex cluster layouts, many are multifloored and almost all will have an artificial climate in the shopping malls.

It must be stressed that the threefold division is as much related to function as form (Dawson, 1974). The Urban Land Institute (1966), for example, provides the following range of floor space figures for the centres in their survey of operating characteristics in the USA. There is considerable overlap between the centre types:

neighbourhood   1,250-14,000 m^2 gross leasable area;
district   6,600-40,000 m^2 gross leasable area;
regional   21,000-140,000 m^2 gross leasable area.

These ranges are derived from data on the operating characteristics of centres rather than their form and would tend to suggest that there is a continuum of shopping centres in respect of size and form rather than three discrete groups. More recent data suggest that although median sizes of the types has increased there is still considerable overlap in the floor space size among the categories.

Two new forms of centre are gradually appearing in the larger metropolitan areas. First is the multifunctional centre. Instead of consisting of the two aspects of parking area and retail space, some new centres have additional areas introduced into the centre building complex. A number of large regional centres have been designed with office buildings, entertainment areas and residential accommodation integrated with the shopping centre which also becomes an important intrametropolitan transport interchange. Redstone (1973) describes a number of plans for North American centres along these lines, such as the Cross Roads Centre in Oklahoma City which provides a mixture of shopping, office and residential space. In Australia two such centres have been developed in Canberra with the centres integral to larger town centre schemes which include offices, community services, clubs, sport and other recreational facilities. These land uses produce activity outside usual trading hours and would be impossible to fit into the rental structure of the traditional type centre.

The Woden Town Centre in South Canberra, 10 km from the city centre, contains over 46,000 m² of shopping space including a department store, two variety stores, two discount houses and a major supermarket together with over 150 other shops. This shopping provision is in an enclosed air-conditioned plaza while around 15,000 m² extra retail space is provided in a 'service trades area' which contains a mix of car sales and repair firms, garden and builders' supplies, hardware stores, household furnishers, restaurants, fast food retailers, wholesalers selling at retail and similar types of operation. Most of these operate outside usual trading hours and so are open when the main retail centre is closed. In addition to these two retail areas, offices for doctors, legal consultants, accountants, insurance agents, airlines, etc. are provided together with public and community service facilities. The plan is to create a town centre environment and economy at a suburban site and retail sales in this shopping district are now larger than those of the city centre. In the northern suburbs of Canberra at Belconnen, a second 'town centre' is under construction; the first major phase of shop provision opened in February 1978. The closely controlled nature of all development in Canberra makes the creation of such town centres more feasible than in *private enterprise* cities. But in Perth plans are active for the development of a major shopping centre within a similar multipurpose town centre in the northern suburbs at Joondalup and, 25 km south of Adelaide city centre, a new multipurpose centre is being developed at Noarlunga.

The Australian and American examples of multipurpose centres have built on experience gained from such centres in Europe. The planned decentralisation of Copenhagen, with multipurpose centres strategically placed along the corridors of development, and the creation of new centres around Paris (Beaujeu-Garnier and Delobez, 1970) have served

as guidelines for this type of suburban development in the USA and
Australia. Three basic relationships between centre and CBD have been
derived in European cities. They are summarised diagramatically in
Figure 7.2. All involve at least one ring of centres creating a decentralised
retail structure. These centres can be combined with other decentralised
town centre facilities as in Stockholm or Copenhagen or may be simply
shopping centres as in Liège (Sporck, 1972; Merrenne-Schoumaker, 1974,
1976). The *Lyngby storcenter* to the north west of Copenhagen, for
example, contains a theatre, cinema, housing, hotel, swimming pool and
offices (Architektur D.K., 1975) and other centres are at various stages
in the western fingers of development (Regional Planning Council, 1969).
In Britain there have been many attempts to introduce a range of community services into district shopping centres. Local government offices
and agencies for central government departments have been integrated
into the middle sized centres which also provide space for community
medical facilities (Duerden, 1977). There is, however, a considerable
difference in the variety of land uses in the full, multipurpose centre and
the district shopping centre with added community facilities and consequently in the overall form of the centre (Gern, 1970).

The search for ways to add soul to the shopping centre includes the
association of a specialist land use with the shopping centre, with consequent adaptations to centre form. In major metropolitan areas large
hotels are linked into shopping centres, centre and hotel being part of
one formal structure. Such centres occur both in Western style cities,
for example, the Hyatt Kingsgate Hotel and Centre in Sydney or the
Ilikai Hotel and Centre in Honolulu, but also in cities such as Hong
Kong, Singapore or Bangkok. Often the units in these centres are small
but this is not always the case, for a supermarket operates quite successfully
successfully in the Hyatt Kingsgate complex in Sydney. The idea of
having shop and customers in the same building is also behind the idea
of linking residential blcks with shopping centres. Again this is widespread, with examples in such contrasting cities as Budapest and Singapore (Lim, 1974).

A second new form is the specialist shopping centre. In some centres
a particular theme is developed to influence both form and operation
of the centre (Brown, 1976). Some developments contain only antique
shops, for example, others only specialist clothing shops. The overall
shell of such centres may well be similar to the traditional centre, but
the mix of units of different size, parking ratio, etc. is quite different.
While specialisation can occur by the type of the goods sold, other
centres specialise on the national or cultural origin of the goods on sale.

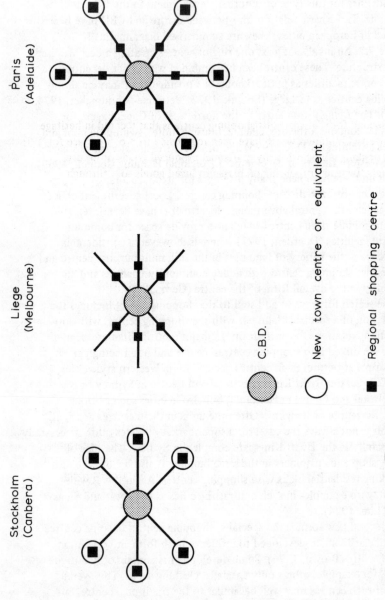

Stockholm
(Canberra)

Liege
(Melbourne)

Paris
(Adelaide)

C.B.D.

New town centre or equivalent

Regional shopping centre

Figure 7.2: Three Forms of Relationship between CBD and Regional Shopping Centre Systems

Perhaps the best example is the Japan Centre in San Francisco which is a multipurpose centre with a hotel, offices, theatre, etc. all linked around a shopping centre, but the shops sell Japanese products, the restaurants are Japanese, the offices are let to Japanese companies or the Japanese consulate, and in the hotel, as the brochure boasts, 'each of its 208 guest rooms – with shoji and fusuma screens and Japanese sunken baths – reflects the influence of Japan'. Not unexpectedly, the form of the centre reflects this influence even to the central Pagoda.

A second form of specialist shopping centre is that located in heritage or conserved buildings which have been redesigned to provide space for shops or stalls selling primarily craftsman produced goods or luxury products. Instead of focusing on mass-produced goods sold through large units by mass-merchandising methods, which is the strength of the traditional type centre, these 'alternative' centres highlight a high level of customer service by selling individually produced goods from very small floor areas. In Melbourne the centre based in Gordon House, originally built in 1884, comprises a basement devoted to specialist food and wine businesses and on the ground and first floors there are 50 small shops of around 30 m² and, in addition, eight studio apartments. The units are arranged around two central courtyards which are set aside for eating and entertainments with weekend food festivals, concerts, art shows, etc. In Sydney, the Argyle Centre consists of craft, antique, curio, art, etc. shops in a converted warehouse in the oldest part of the city next to the quay and almost under the Harbour Bridge. The centre depends to a considerable degree on tourist sales but provides space for individually designed small units retailing very specialised craft type products. In San Francisco, the Ghirardelli Square shopping centre is in buildings formerly used as a chocolate factory. Interiors of several buildings were gutted and laid out for small boutique type retailers and the space among the buildings was landscaped and made into pedestrian piazzas. Underground parking on approximately a 2:1 ratio has been provided. Less than a kilometre away is the Cannery which was the Del Monte Fruit Cannery but is now a three-level shopping centre, again designed for small units. The Faneuil and Quincy Market buildings in Central Boston were formerly a city commodity market (see beginning of chapter) but have been changed into a shopping centre with 21,000 m² of retail space and 13,000 m² of offices. The central building in Quincy Market opened in summer 1976 as a food hall with shops, kiosks, open stalls and pushcarts selling a wide variety of fresh, preserved and processed foods. The other two buildings concentrate on non-food goods but again small units are the norm. Canal Square, Washington and York

Square, Toronto are further examples of a growing trend in shopping centre design. Their form is a far cry from the windowless concrete block centred on a wide expanse of asphalt of the traditional type of shopping centre. Typical layouts are shown in Figure 7.3. Neither the multipurpose nor the specialist centre fits into the usual neighbourhood, district and regional shopping centre classification which has been established for the traditional type centre.

Locational Requirements of Centres

Before it is possible to explore the reasons for this increase in variety in the shopping centre species it is necessary to consider their locational needs. The development of shopping centres in this century is inextricably linked with the decentralisation of cities. The suburban branches of city centre department stores have formed early foci for largescale shopping centre development throughout North America and Europe (Rolph, 1933; J. Walter Thompson Co., 1954; Smith, 1952). Since the 1950s the vast tracts of residential suburbia in cities in Australia, Canada and the USA have proved particularly fertile areas for shopping centre growth (Moyer, 1973).

The reasons for the shift of retailing to the suburbs are well recognised (Dawson, 1974; Cox and Erickson, 1967). Population growth in the suburbs, coupled with increased personal mobility, has caused a decentralisation of consumer demand which has been met, in part, by a supply of shopping centres. The inner cities with their congestion, social problems, physical and economic blight and relatively low level of demand for most consumer products have not been attractive areas for investment and new investment, in shopping centres particularly, has been pushed out from the central area. Such was certainly the case in the 1950s and 1960s in the USA but generally in Europe with its stronger tradition of viable city centres this process has been less important. The interaction between businesses and the changing technology of business activity provides a third reason for suburbanisation. The general trend towards bigger business units has been made possible through improved communication and transportation. The Institute for Centre Planning (1966) argues that 'the present concentration of business establishments in the CBD is the result of an interplay between earlier periods business structure and communication technology' (p. 9) and as that changes so decentralisation takes place. Consequently, 'the traditional step-like hierarchical model for the centre structure, with the existing, highly concentrated CBD as the all dominating centre, where all the most important activities must be located, is unrealistic' (p. 17). A fourth important

Figure 7.3 A-E: EXAMPLES OF SHOPPING CENTRE FORM AND LAYOUT

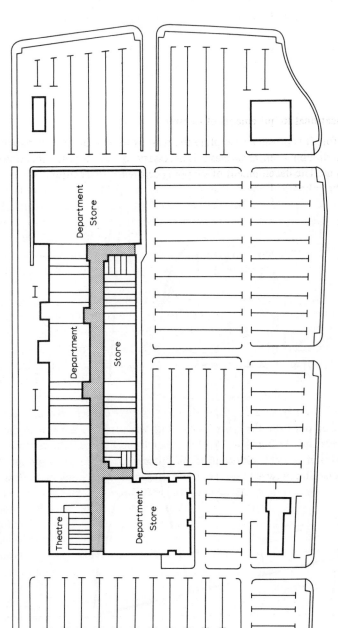

Pedestrian walkway

A: A Traditional Type Regional Shopping Centre—York Mall, York, Pennsylvania

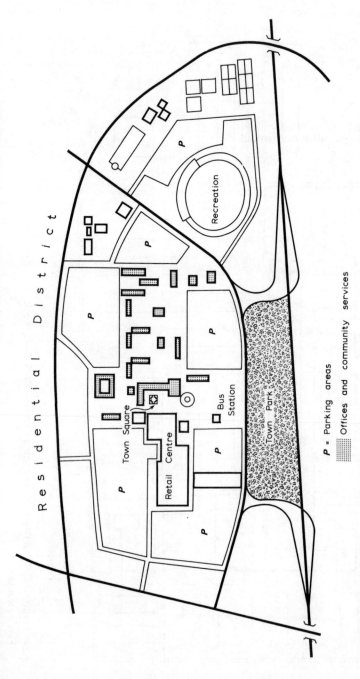

Residential District

Recreation

P

P

P

P

Town Square

Retail Centre

Bus Station

P

P

P

Town Park

P = Parking areas

Offices and community services

B: A Multi-purpose Centre—Woden Centre, Canberra

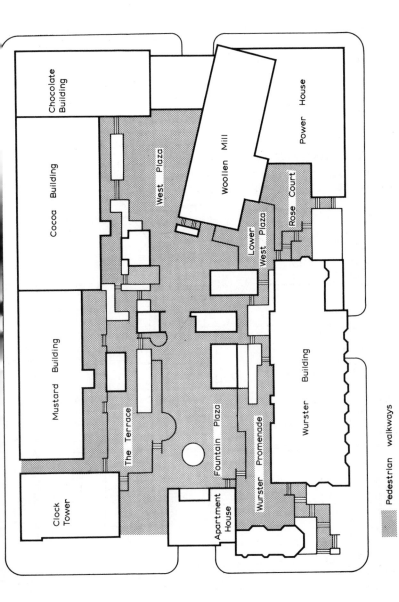

Chocolate Building

Cocoa Building

West Plaza

Woollen Mill

Power House

Mustard Building

Rose Court

Lower West Plaza

The Terrace

Clock Tower

Fountain Plaza

Apartment House

Wurster Promenade

Wurster Building

Pedestrian walkways

C: A Renovated Specialist Centre in Heritage Building—Ghiradelli Square, San Francisco

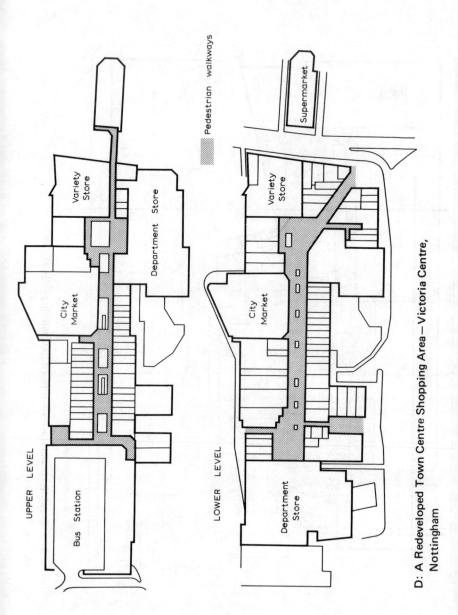

UPPER LEVEL

Bus Station

City Market

Variety Store

Department Store

LOWER LEVEL

Department Store

City Market

Variety Store

Supermarket

Pedestrian walkways

D: A Redeveloped Town Centre Shopping Area — Victoria Centre, Nottingham

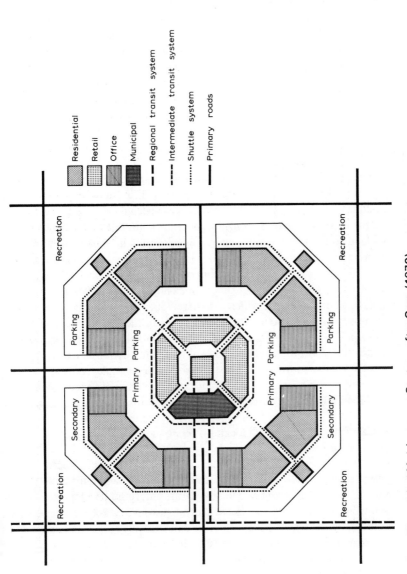

E: A Theoretical Multi-purpose Centre—after Gern (1970)

Residential
Retail
Office
Municipal

Regional transit system
Intermediate transit system
Shuttle system
Primary roads

Recreation
Recreation
Recreation
Recreation

Parking
Parking

Secondary
Secondary

Primary Parking
Primary Parking

reason underlining decentralisation is the availability and cost of shopping centre sites in the suburbs compared with the centre and inner parts of the city (Benett, 1971). Site area requirements over 20 ha are quite usual for the larger centres and obtaining such a site in the inner parts of the city is well nigh impossible without governmental intervention and compulsory purchase. Even small centres require 3 or 4 ha and the cost of such sites in cities is usually prohibitive for retail development. Thus only in the suburbs, and often on the urban fringe, are sites available for large centre developments.

While developers of large centres seek 40 ha of flat land at motorway intersections in high-income neighbourhoods in the suburbs, it would be false to assume that all centres have been located in this way. For the very large centres a single segment of suburbia is not large enough and land requirements cannot be met by a location in present suburbia or on its fringe. Centres of 150,000 m² and more may seek locations between major suburban tracts and in open agricultural land. Midway between Los Angeles and San Diego for example, work began in 1977 on a multipurpose centre which is to have 750,000 m² of retail and business space on a 190 ha site in the triangle formed by three freeways. Green-field and interurban sites are almost inevitable for developments of such size. Even for smaller centres, interurban locations have proved popular for some forms of centre. In France, for example, centres anchored by a hypermarket of 5,000-10,000 m² and with around ten small stores have been developed between small towns and often at strategic road intersections. The relatively close mesh of urban places in Western Europe makes such locations economically viable when car ownership is high.

In North America the development of shopping centres has been governed by free market processes. As consumer demand built up in the suburbs, so centres were provided by private enterprise developers. Gradually the suburban areas have become provided with centres and although by the late 1970s possibilities still exist the opportunities for suburban development have become limited. Alternative locations and alternatives to the traditional centre have been considered. The previous section has shown that various new types of centre have evolved after, sometimes excessive, provision of traditional centres in the suburbs. For example, Madison, a city of 300,000 people, has five major regional shopping centres in the suburbs and this degree of provision is not untypical of many North American cities. The second response is to re-consider city centre locations. Although there have been sporadic attempts at downtown renewal (Forman, 1959; Smith, 1954; Sternlieb, 1963) it was not until the mid 1970s that there was a significant movement to establish centres in the city centre, but this trend seems likely to grow through the 1980s (Redstone, 1976).

Four centres under construction in New Orleans typify the renewed interest in CBDs. Several years ago the city authorities and the Chamber of Commerce collaborated to develop a Growth Management Program which has served as a blueprint for the comprehensive planning of the CBD. A special tax district was created in which the central city taxes itself and income is used in the CBD. The four development schemes currently active will increase together central area retail floor space by at least 120,000 m² and despite the euphoria surrounding the projects there are nagging doubts over an expansion of this size in a metropolitan region of just over 1 million people.

Three of the projects are multiuse developments. The Canal Place development is on a 9 ha site bounded by the Mississippi River and will contain 230,000 m² of office space, 90,000 m² of retailing, two hotels, residential accommodation and a restaurant/entertainment complex. The office space and 23,000 m² of retailing are in the early phases of the scheme and construction started in the summer of 1977. The three-level shopping mall will be integrated into the pedestrian circulation system of the whole development. The International River Centre project is the second multiuse development and also abuts the Mississippi. The site area is much the same as the Canal Place and similarly includes office, hotel and recreation facilities. The retail section, opened in October 1977, is provided in a mall alongside the river with a half-kilometre shopping promenade attached to 18,000 m² of retail space. The building which houses the retailing is a former wharf property and interior work has restored its appearance to what it once was; beams, girders, etc. remain exposed and existing skylights are incorporated into the interior design. The aim in letting the centre is to attract high fashion and exclusive retailing and to cater for tourist and convention shoppers.

The third retail development is smaller and only a few blocks away from both Canal Place and International River Centres. This is the Piazza d'Italia which again will provide specialist stores but with a distinctly Italian flavour, for example an open Italian market is included. The retailing, some of which uses refurbished existing buildings, will be linked to a public open space which it is hoped will provide a place to meet and promenade. Poydras Plaza is the fourth project in downtown New Orleans and another multiuse development including hotel, sports facilities, office space and 20,000 m² retail complex. The feature of this centre will be the provision of specialist convention facilities. All four centres consciously are providing retailing for a specific segment of consumer demand and in this way they contrast with the new general purpose developments in the suburbs.

These large developments are mirrored by smaller developments in many small and medium sized towns throughout the USA. A report of the Annual Convention of the International Council of Shopping Centres (*Shopping Center World*, 1978A) quotes a leading industry spokesman as saying: 'Downtown is where the shopping center industry is going' (p. 34). Many of the specialist type centres are in the central city and even general purpose traditional type centres are returning to the CBD.

There is a very strong contrast here between development trends in North America and those in Europe. In North America developers have looked to central areas when suburbia has been provided for but in much of Western Europe, and outstandingly in Britain, political control of market forces has reversed the position. In Britain in 1977, 68 per cent of the major cities in Britain had a central city shopping centre operational or under construction (Schiller and Lambert, 1977). As opportunities in central areas have decreased so there has been increasing pressure on land use planners to allow suburban centres. The suburban centres that have been allowed rarely have been on green-field sites but have been redevelopments of minor suburban shopping districts. For the most part the growth of suburban shopping centres in residential areas in Britain has been restricted to neighbourhood type developments (Burns, 1959). Throughout much of Europe major redevelopment of central cities has been the rule rather than the exception. Lyon, Strasbourg, Newcastle upon Tyne, Brussels (Tuppen, 1977; Bennison and Davies, 1977; Gilian and Yvanoff, 1976) and many other major cities (Hubschmann, 1968; Smith, 1977), as well as a host of small towns, have shopping centres integral to their central business districts (Multiple Shops Federation, 1967). Davies and Bennison (1978) in a review of in-town shopping centres in Britain suggest a threefold classification into fully fledged regional shopping centres, core-replacement schemes and peripheral accretions. Certainly in Britain, and to a lesser extent elsewhere in Europe, local government investment in central areas was protected by land use planning policies of refusing permission for suburban centres. The government report on *The Future Pattern of Shopping* in Britain states that

> Discussions with a number of planning officers suggest that the programme of investment in many town centres has gone too far to be reversed and that those concerned with municipal planning would

view with grave disquiet any development which would channel off
a substantial proportion of the consumer spending which was reckon-
ed on, either explicitly or implicitly, when the development programmes
were started. (Distributive Trades EDC, 1971, p. 65).

The rôle of government in marketing will be explored in more detail in
Chapter 8 but a major factor determining shopping centre location
within Western Europe is the intervention of land use planning authorities in market processes (Comité Belge de la Distribution, 1964).

A concern of land use planners has been to ensure that a balanced
system of centres evolves without overprovision in some parts of a city
and underprovision elsewhere. This control of the market has been
absent from North America and, for the most part, Australia. In both
cases though the system of centres which has come into being has fundamental imperfections.

In North America, the developers of centres have attempted to seek
the economically most lucrative sites. High income suburbs are preferred
and overprovision has occurred here, while lower income areas have not
been provided with basic shopping facilities. From the early 1950s to
the early 1970s there was a phenomenal growth in the shopping centre
industry and over a 20-year period on average three new shopping centres
opened in the USA each working day. Cohen (1972) has shown admir-
ably how the shopping centre concept spread through the interurban
system and how its spread depended on the commercial expertise and
acumen of the businesses developing the centres in picking cities with
high per capita income but low enough gross income so that alternative
investment opportunities were not available. Such an analysis probably is
just as applicable to intraurban systems of centres. The location of
shopping centres in San Diego in 1970 shows a concentration of centres
in the higher income northern suburbs while the inner suburbs are almost
without centres, as can be seen from Figure 7.4.

The imperfections resulting from establishing a formal hierarchy of
neighbourhood, community and regional centres are of a different kind.
In the British new towns, for example, centre development has been
strictly controlled both in respect of type and location. While the welfare imperfections of the American system have been removed, commercial imperfections are introduced as the system is static and cannot
respond to changes in commercial viability of different types of centre;
nor can it adjust to the emergence of new types of retailing and centre.
The range of shopping environments available to the consumer is limited
and the retail technology at the time of development of the centres' con-

Figure 7.4: Shopping Centre Provision in the San Diego District in 1970

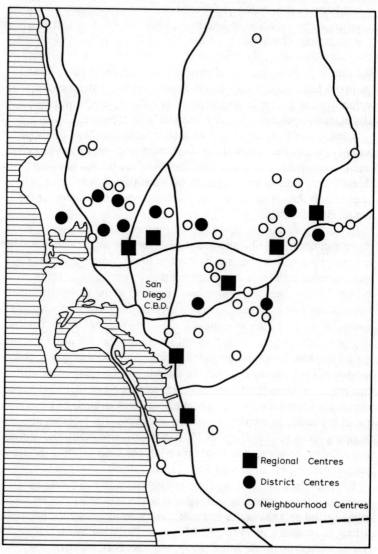

struction becomes fossilised in the centres and their locational system. The balance between total freedom and strict control is one of the major problems of retail planning which will be discussed in the next chapter.

Changing Shopping Centre Operation

The third major strand in the overall evolution of shopping centres, alongside the changes in their form and location, is the transformation that has occurred in development and operation. The following discussion refers only to shopping centres in capitalist economies where they now comprise one of the major forms of property investment. Change has occurred such that instead of being owned and leased by an individual, as with the early small developments, they may be in complex ownership let by a specialist company and with day-to-day operation delegated, for a price, to a shopping centre management company. The levels of investment return created by shopping centres have been a major factor in their growth, development and influence in retailing. It would be quite wrong to suppose that their rise to power is owing to any altruistic attitude of developers towards the creation of pleasant shopper environments. Most centres yield a high return on investment (Smith, 1959). There is ample evidence for assuming centre development to be related to the state of the money market. For example, the West Australian mineral boom in the mid 1960s created wealth which required investment. Once the office market had been saturated it was the turn of shopping centres and the plethora of shopping centres which opened in the early 1970s in suburban Perth was a response to this hot money. As well as providing capital the mineral boom also produced a rapidly expanding state economy, so 'the suburbs also attracted investors where opportunities existed to provide shopping facilities for many newly created suburbs' (Johnston and Assoc., 1974, p. 22). Cohen (1972) similarly points to local money markets as an important factor in the growth of regional shopping centres in the USA and this is confirmed by the numbers of American banks which produce detailed surveys of the local shopping centre market (for example First National Bank of Arizona, 1972, 1973). It can be argued, in similar fashion, that the emergence of shopping centres in the developing world is a response to investment opportunities in particular cities (Campbell, 1974). Available finance is one factor in the spread of shopping centre operations and probably the most important but there are others. Undoubtedly shifts in population create new investment opportunities with large investments following in the wake of population growth. In North America, 'corporate moves involve countervailing trends, with northern and national chains penetrating deeper into the Sunbelt while southern and western operations fuelled by rapid recent growth, push north and east into the Snowbelt' (*Chain Store Age*, 1978, p. 57). Developers with money are constantly searching for new potential sites.

Early centres were developed by individuals with private finance; the suburban centre of the 1930s in America and of the early 1960s in Australia were developed by large retail companies, often department store groups with public finance; modern centres often are developed by specialist property development companies using institutional finance. Important in the modern situation is the variety of forms of finance that may be used and the complexity of the financing process. Banks, property companies, insurance companies, oil companies, trade union pension funds, churches, government, even the retailers themselves are some of the groups involved in shopping centre financing. Large centres may have different parts effectively owned by quite different institutions although the centre has been developed as a single project by one development company. Lion (1976) describes six types of financing commonly used in the USA. These are the conventional mortgage, bond issue, participatory mortgage, sale and leaseback, tenant co-operative and real estate investment trust. While the terms are self-explanatory and describe the methods of finance each has different tax and investment return implications (Shinehouse, 1962). The range of methods in Britain or Hongkong is equally great. In centre finance, as in any other field, there are 'horses for courses' with particular firms specialising in different types of centre. In Britain, for example, the large life insurance groups tend to favour large city centre redevelopment projects while small property companies fund neighbourhood centres. Winston Estates, for example, concentrates on small centres with office or residential accommodation over the shops and most of its portfolio is in London and the South East. Other companies favour different forms of investment. Shopping centre finance and development has become a very complex sector of business finance.

This change has come about because of several characteristics of shopping centre investment. Cameron (1977) quotes the North American view of shopping centres as providing an investment with security and growth potential:

In general, security is provided and risk is reduced by the fact that, typically, a substantial percentage of a centre's space is leased to either national or regional chains with 'A' or better credit ratings . . . The growth potential of a shopping centre is derived from the ability of the owner to participate, either directly through average rents or indirectly through lease renewals at higher rents, in the ability of tenants to increase their sales. (p. 373).

Roberts (1973) also stresses the long-term growth potential of the investment but also points to the many tax shelters provided for centre investment in the USA. The growth of shopping centre numbers, their evolution in form and location must all be related, at least in North America, to the emergence of a type of real estate which provides an attractive investment to accountants. In Britain economic viability is also vitally important but the involvement of local government has introduced social costs and benefits into the overall balance sheet, so producing the emphasis on central city shopping centres rather than suburban centres along North American lines. By the late 1970s there were about 25,000 shopping centres in North America and, in the USA, such centres accounted for approximately 40 per cent of retail sales. Shopping centres represent a major form of property investment.

The financial success of a centre depends to a considerable degree on its tenant mix. In the larger centres,

the backbone of the entire project is its vertebrae of long term leases with strong national chain tenants which structure its financing. This basic strength, meat and potatoes, makes it possible for the developer/investor to enjoy the cake and ice cream of highly lucrative leases with smaller merchants. (Roberts, 1973, p. 624).

But, as many studies point out, even the smaller units tend to be let either to national or regional chain retailers or at least to retailers with a successful track record. The 'smaller merchants' of Roberts are not independent retailers but sizable chain store groups although not featuring in the list of the 100 largest companies. The 1972 issue of *Dollars and Cents of Shopping Centres* shows for the USA the tenant mix by centre type. Table 7.3 summarises the figures and adds some data from a census of centres in South Canberra, Australia (Alexander and Dawson, 1978) and from the 1961 Census of Canada (Moyer and Snyder, 1967). With the larger centres there are much higher levels of participation by chain retailers and conversely a smaller proportion of independent traders. Analysis of a sample of 13 centre schemes in Britain (Centre for Advanced Land Use Studies, 1975) showed that in a majority of the centres independent traders (with nine or fewer branches) accounted for between 30 and 35 per cent of establishments. Using either of the defin-

Table 7.3:   Percentage Distribution of Tenant Type in Shopping Centres

Type of tenant	Type of centre		
	Regional	District	Neighbourhood
A. USA, 1972			
National chains	37	27	20
Local chains[a]	28	25	22
Independents[b]	35	48	58
B. South Canberra, Australia, 1978			
National chains	22	2	2
Local chains[c]	34	26	12
Independents[d]	44	72	86
C. Canada, 1961			
Chains	49	46	28
Independents[e]	49	52	71
Department stores	2	2	1
Percentage of sales by tenant type USA, 1972			
National chains	62	57	55
Local chains	27	28	25
Independents	11	15	20

a. Operating in 3 or fewer metropolitan areas.
b. With not more than 2 outlets.
c. Head office in Canberra.
d. With not more than 1 outlet.
e. With not more than 3 outlets.

itions of Table 7.3 would decrease this independent share and it is some-what anomalous that in Britain where planning and local government control on shopping centre form and location is relatively strong, some extreme tenant mixes have resulted. The major shopping centre in Telford New Town has no independent traders. Chain store companies are more likely to be stable financially and are likely to remain in the centre longer than independent traders. Consequently, from an investment view-point the tenant mix policy of a development company can be vital to the financial success of a centre. This is clearly seen in various detailed case studies of individual centre development in the USA (Applebaum, 1970; Applebaum and Kaylin, 1974).

Because the total environment of the shopping centre is controlled, competition within the centre is often minimised. By limiting competition gross sales can be increased and higher profits for the centre achieved.

Retailers may be willing to pay high rent to be represented in a centre if they also buy the right to be the single supplier (or one of only two) of a particular group of goods. Department stores in large centres may be able to put pressure on the developer to restrict the number or type of clothing shops in the centre (Sturtevant, 1959). Frequently the number of, for example, shoe shops is closely controlled and it is not unusual for tenants to complain if their quasimonopoly is infringed by a new entrant to the centre.

There are a number of implications and conflicts to the strict control of tenant mix. Small business lobbies constantly complain that they are excluded from centres by either high rents or the provision of units of the wrong size (Foster, 1967; Liepmann, 1973; United States Senate, 1960). With centres acting as a magnet to consumers these small traders feel excluded from a 'fair' chance to compete. The unwillingmess of centre developers to provide space for new entrepreneurs often results in a very conservative approach to retailing by most retailers in the centre. Innovatory retail methods, if their source is outside large corporate organisations, are inhibited from locating in centre environments where, if they are successful, they ultimately will be adopted. For example, only as the discount industry has become legitimate has it moved into shopping centres. Retail methods, as well as retailers themselves, have to prove themselves before they are allowed to trade in shopping centres. Furthermore the high level of representation of national chain stores within shopping centres frequently means that similar mixes of goods are sold in many centres. The consumer entering a centre often is faced with the same names selling the same goods as in the centre down the road. If tenant mix policies become too extreme, consumer choice can be severely limited not only within a centre but also more broadly in society.

Passing mention has been made of the varied functions of the different types of centre. The distinctions between neighbourhood, district and regional centres are discussed at length by Jones (1969), Davies (1976), Chapin (1965) and Urban Land Institute (1976). All stress the notion of a functional hierarchy and certainly in Britain, where the philosophy of a functional hierarchy has determined the spatial allocation of centres through urban areas, there is empirical evidence substantiating the philosophy. Whether there was a hierarchy before the planners created one is another question. Certainly though, within traditional shopping centres at least, larger centres are functionally more complex but the integration of hypermarkets and discount warehouses into shopping centres can mean a functionally very simple centre with a floor space comparable to regional centres. The appearance of new types of shopping centre throws into disarray some of the supposed relationships between centre size, type of goods sold, number of units and consumer drawing power.

With the evolution of a series of shopping centres operating in an urban area, so increasingly their activities impinge on each other and on the other forms of retailing operating in the city (Johnston and Rimmer, 1976). It is a moot point as to which direction the causal arrow points in relating together city centre decline and suburban centre growth in most North American cities (Walker, 1957; Smith and Kelly, 1960) and in several European cities (Gantvoort, 1971). The shift to shopping centre retailing has occurred at the expense of particular types of shop. Berry Parsons and Platt (1968) show for a redevelopment area in Chicago how retailing becomes consolidated into centres from former shopping street locations but that it is rarely the existing retailers who move into the new centres. There is thus a decrease in net numbers of retailers and also a larger decrease in gross numbers. Extensive evidence suggests that it is branches of chain stores which relocate in the new centres and independent stores which die (Davidson, McMillan and Gladfelter, 1960). Shopping centre development adds a filter to the normal birth and death processes of retailers and effectively reduces the birth rate and increases the death rate of small firms in retailing. The overall result is similar, but for different reasons, whether the shopping centre is part of a city centre or inner city renewal scheme, a traditional suburban centre or is one of the newer types of centre. In some instances existing retail property is demolished and in others the retailers in the centres absorb the trade of existing retail firms (Davies and Bennison, 1977). The competitive success of shopping centres stems not only from the representation in them of branches of large firms (the reasons for the success of largescale retailing have been discussed in Chapter 4) but also from the creation of an environment which the majority of consumers find attractive and accessible. Problems arise for the minority of consumers who cannot or do not desire to use a centre because the range of alternatives is decreased. Not only is the number of other potential shopping places reduced but also they become more widely spaced. One of the minority groups who are unable to use shopping centres consists of those who have limited mobility, for either physical or economic reasons. The shopping centres themselves are often inaccessible to this group and as centre numbers increase so other shops become increasingly inaccessible. The evolving pattern of shopping centre operations poses a severe equity problem for society.

Shopping Centre Environment and Society

'The success of failure of a regional shopping center won't really be measured by the character of its architecture or the balance sheets of the center; it will be measured by what it does for the people it seeks to serve' (Rouse, 1963, p. 100). Such a view, instead of being held by a few 1960s prophets such as Rouse (1962) is now widespread among many of the more enlightened developers and land use planners. The caricature of the regional centre as a giant cash register in verdant suburbia may now be replaced by the image of the centre as a space station with a full life support system acting as a refuge for travellers through parlous urban space. Centre advertising often now stresses the totality of the shopping experience and environment in a centre (*Business Week*, 1971). This environment has been very carefully created with strict control over the various stimuli present. The large shopping centre has become a social laboratory in which participants react in controlled fashions to given stimuli. Whether the creation of such artificial environments is good or bad, whether they should be encouraged or rejected, becomes a moral question which society must answer. In the meantime a shopping centre culture is evolving.

The large centre is enclosed. The temperature, humidity – a microclimate without seasons – is designed to encourage shopper activity (Nevils, 1977). The climate is not bland but air conditioning creates variety. A slight breeze spreads the smell of newly baked bread, another recycles into the main mall the smell of leather from a shoe shop. Both these stimuli are encouragements to buy. The full grown palm tree overhangs the fountain in the centre plaza and close by will be a travel agent or airline office. Shop fronts are absent and the carpeting in the mall is the same as in the shop, again encouraging the visitor to enter and then to buy. Lighting intensities vary, so creating moods in different sections of the centre (*Shopping Centre World*, 1978B). While olfactory and visual senses are tantalised, so aural stimuli are also part of the new environment. Background music interspersed with carefully designed and modulated advertisements passes through speaker systems. There can be little doubt that the large centre can provide a physical environment unlike any other on earth.

Similarly a social environment is created. Places are provided for people to meet or sit and watch the world, albeit the very special shopping centre world, go by. Activities are generated. Vintage cars go on display, Miss World makes a visit, pancake sampling takes place on Shrove Tuesday, a wandering minstrel sings to the children, creatures from outer space arrive and each year around 1 December, Father Christmas comes. Not surprisingly it is common to see people sitting in the warm mall looking totally bemused.

A total society, created by the environment, develops in the centre. The centre newspaper – who decides editorial policy? – circulates; marriage partners are found; parties for centre employees occur. As multipurpose centres develop, it is possible to live, work, shop, obtain entertainment and totally exist within the centre. The sociologists have yet to study, in any detail, shopping centre culture although there have been a few studies of user participation (Downs, 1970). Keyes (1973) states: 'Malls are a classic case of something that fills millions of people's needs but is of no interest to sociologists'. In an interview reported by Kowinski (1978) a newspaper editor comments: 'If you had to pick one thing that would typify civilization in the United States in the twentieth century, a front-running candidate would be the suburban shopping mall' (p. 34). Kowinski's study describes graphically how a centre culture has arrived in North America and how conflict will occur between the controlled centre society and the outside real-world society. This alternative society is present to a lesser degree in Australian cities and is appearing, but only sporadically so far, in Europe (Northen and Haskoll, 1977; *Deutsche Bauzeitung*, 1975). The megacultural attributes of the shopping centre, though, mean that its subculture will spread as rapidly as has the building of the centres. Perhaps in Europe it will be possible to prepare for, and defuse in advance, likely social conflict. Large centres 'are so powerful that they overwhelm everything else – there is nothing strong enough to balance them . . . towns disappear' (Kowinski, 1978, p. 47). But, Keyes (1973) argues that already in America, 'Malls aren't *part* of the community. They *are* the community' (p. 118).

References

ALEXANDER, I. and J.A. DAWSON (1978) *Survey Method and Codebook of a Census of Retail Employment in Shopping Centres in South Canberra* (Urban Research Unit, Australian National University).

APPLEBAUM, W. (1970) *Shopping Center Strategy: a Case Study of the Planning, Location and Development of the Del Monte Center, Monterey, California* (International Council of Shopping Centers, New York).

APPLEBAUM, W. and S.O. KAYLIN (1974) *Case Studies in Shopping Center Development and Operation* (International Council of Shopping Centers, New York).

ARKITEKTUR D.K. (1975) 'Lyngby Storcenter', *Arkitekur D.K.*, 19,(2), pp. 62-73.

BARTON ASCHMAN ASSOC. INC. (1977) 'Parking Demand at the Regionals', *Urban Land*, 36(5), pp. 3-11.

BEAUJEAU-GARNIER, J. and A. DELOBEZ (1970) 'Evolution de l'activité commerciale de la région parisienné', *Cooperation*, June, pp. 10-16.

BENETT, D.W. (1971) 'Land Costs Push Regional Centers Up and Out', *Appraisal*

Journal, 39, pp. 606-9.
BENNISON, D. and R.L. DAVIES (1977) 'Retail Change in North East England', in B. Fullerton (ed.), *North Eastern Studies, 1977* (University of Newcastle, Department of Geography), pp. 9-18.
BERRY, B.J.L., S.J. PARSONS and R.H. PLATT (1968) *The Impact of Urban Renewal on Small Business* (Center for Urban Studies, University of Chicago).
BOHALL, R.A. and A.Z. MACOMBER (1962) 'The Organization of the Wholesale Fruit and Vegetable Market in Washington D.C.', *U.S. Department of Agriculture, Marketing Economics Division, Market Research Report*, 324.
BROWN, L.E. (1976) 'Speciality Shopping Centres: the New Trend in Retailing', *Appraisal Journal*, 44, pp. 226-34.
BURNS, W. (1959) *British Shopping Centres* (Leonard Hill, London).
BUSINESS WEEK (1971) 'Shopping Centres Generate Shopping Cities', *Business Week*, 5(4), pp. 34-8.
CAMERON, B. (1977) 'U.S. Shopping Centre Development is only for Professionals', *Estates Gazette*, 29 October, 244, pp. 271-3.
CAMPBELL, R.W. (1974) 'Stages of Shopping Center Development in Major Latin American Metropolitan Markets', *Land Economics*, 50, pp. 66-70.
CENTRE FOR ADVANCED LAND USE STUDIES (1975) *Rent Assessment and Tenant Mix in Planned Shopping Centres* (Centre for Advanced Land Use Studies, Reading).
CHAIN STORE AGE (1978) 'Sharpening Sunbelt Strategy', *Chain Store Age (Executive)*, 54(3), pp. 55-8.
CHAPIN, F.S. (1965) *Urban Land Use Planning* (University of Illinois Press, Urbana).
COHEN, Y.S. (1972) *Diffusion of an Innovation in an Urban System* (University of Chicago, Department of Geography, Research Paper, 140).
COMITE BELGE DE LA DISTRIBUTION (1964) *Shopping Centres in Europe* (Comité Belge de la Distribution, Brussels).
COX, E.P. and L.G. ERICKSON (1967) *Retail Decentralization* (Michigan State University, East Lansing).
CTIFL (1976) 'L'approvisionnements en fruits et légumes du commerce intégré, associé et des grandes surfaces en Région Parisienne en 1975', *Centre Technique Interprofessionnel des Fruits et Légumes, Documents*, 51, pp. 41-52.
DARLOW, C. (1972) *Enclosed Shopping Centres* (Architectural Press, London).
DAVIDSON, T.L., S.C. McMILLAN and C.J. GLADFELTER (1960) *Some Effects of the Growth of Planned and Controlled Shopping Centres on Small Retailers* (School of Business Administration, University of Connecticut).
DAVIES, R.L. (1976) *Marketing Geography with Special Reference to Retailing* (Retail and Planning Associates, Corbridge).
DAVIES, R.L. and D.J. BENNISON (1977) 'Preliminary Effects of the Eldon Square Shopping Centre', *Estates Gazette*, 2 November, 244, pp. 709-13.
——— (1978) 'The Planning Repercussions of in-town Shopping Schemes', *Estates Gazette*, 8 April, 246, pp. 117-21.
DAWSON, J.A. (1974) 'The Suburbanization of Retail Activity' in J.H. Johnson (ed.), *Suburban Growth: Geographical Processes at the Edge of the Western City* (Wiley, London), pp. 155-75.
DEUTSCHE BAUZEITUNG (1975) 'Paradise on the Outskirts of the Town', *Deutsche Bauzeitung*, 109, pp. 37-48.
DISTRIBUTIVE TRADES EDC (1971) *The Future Pattern of Shopping* (HMSO, London).
DOUGLASS, L. (1958) 'Shopping Centre Design', *Traffic Quarterly*, 12, pp. 409-24.
DOWNS, R.M. (1970) 'The Cognitive Structure of an Urban Shopping Center', *Environment and Behavior*, 2, pp. 13-38.

DUERDEN, B. (1977) 'Community Facilities and District Centres' in URPI, *District Centres* (Unit for Retail Planning Information, Reading), pp. 23-33.

FANTUS COMPANY (1963A) *Study for the Re-location of Covent Garden Market* (Fantus Company, London, March report).

—— (1963B) *Study for the Relocation of Covent Garden Market, London* (Fantus Company, London, April report).

FIRST NATIONAL BANK OF ARIZONA (1972) *Shopping Center Survey Tucson Metro Area* (First National Bank of Arizona, Phoenix).

—— (1973) *Metro Phoenix Shopping Center Survey* (First National Bank of Arizona, Phoenix).

FORMAN, F. (1959) 'The Downtown Shopping Center', *Traffic Quarterly*, pp. 495-503.

FOSTER, J.R. (1967) 'The Effect of Shopping Centre Financing on the Opportunity for Occupancy by Independent Retailers', *Southern Journal of Business*, 2, pp. 25-37.

GANTVOORT, J.T. (1971) 'Shopping Centre versus Town Centre', *Town Planning Review*, 42(1), pp. 61-70.

GERN, R.C. (1970) 'The Middle-age Spread of Regional Shopping Centres – the 1970's', *Traffic Engineering*, 40(11), pp. 20-7.

GILAIN, P. and YVANOFF (1976) 'City 2: nouveau shopping center de centre-ville rue Neuve à Bruxelles', *Distribution D'Aujourd'hui*, 17,(10), pp. 26-30.

GRUEN, V. (1959) 'Retailing and the Automobile' in J.S. Hornbeck (ed.), *Stores and Shopping Centers* (McGraw-Hill, New York), pp. 96-114.

HARDING, C.V.H. (1968) 'Traffic Characteristics at Major Shopping Centres', *Australian Road Research Board Proceedings*, 4(1), pp. 208-232.

HENLEY, D.S. *et al.* (1970) *Market Processes in La Paz, Bolivia* (Michigan State University, East Lansing).

HIGHWAY RESEARCH BOARD (1966) 'Shopping Centers and Parking', *Highway Research Record*, 130.

HORTICULTURAL MARKETING COUNCIL (1962) 'Wholesale Fruit, Vegetable and Flower Markets in France, Italy and West Germany: Capital Assistance Available and Reconstruction Undertaken and Planned', *Horticultural Marketing Council, Technical and Economic Report*, no. 4.

HUBSCHMANN, E.W. (1968) 'Shopping Centers in Germany and the Old Central Shopping-Areas' in C. Christians (ed.), *Colloque International de Géographie Appliqué* (Report of Third meeting of IGU Commission on Applied Geography).

INSTITUTE FOR CENTRE PLANNING (1966) *Urban Centres and Changes in the Centre Structures* (Institute for Centre Planning, Lyngby).

ITE PROJECT COMMITTEE (1972) 'Transportation Considerations of Regional Shopping Centers', *Traffic Engineering*, 42, pp. 14-21, 63.

JOHNSTON, M.R. AND ASSOC. (1974) *Perth Metropolitan Region Retail Shopping Survey* (M.R. Johnston & Assoc., Perth).

JOHNSTON, R.J. and P.J. RIMMER (1967) 'The Competitive Position of a Planned Shopping Centre', *Australian Geographer*, 10(3), pp. 160-8.

JONES, C.S. (1969) *Regional Shopping Centres* (Business Books, London).

KEYES, R. (1973) *We, the Lonely People* (Harper & Row, New York).

KOWINSKI, W.S. (1978) 'The Malling of America', *New Times*, 10(9), pp. 30-55.

LIEPMANN, C. (1973) *L'integration des indépendants dans les centres commerciaux* (Institut Français du Libre Service, Paris).

LIM, W. (1974) 'Shopping Centers, Singapore', *Ekistics*, 219, pp. 114-15.

LION, E. (1976) *Shopping Centers: Planning, Development and Administration* (Wiley, New York).

LIPP, M.N. (1961) 'Lincoln Road Mall, Miami Beach', *Traffic Quarterly*, 15, pp. 441-7.

LSA (1978) 'Rungis fruits et légumes restructuration du marché', *Libre Service Actualité*, 21(661), pp. 22-3.

McKEEVER, R. (1953) 'Shopping Centres: Principles and Policies', *Urban Land Institute, Technical Bulletin*, 20.

McKEEVER, J.R. (1968) (ed.), *The Community Builder's Handbook* (Urban Land Institute, Washington).

MERENNE-SCHOUMAKER, B. (1974) 'Les grands centres commercaux en Belgique', *Bull. Societé Géog. de Liège*, 10, pp. 13-38.

—— (1976) 'Evolution récente des grands centres commerciaux en Belgique 1974-5', *Bulletin Societé Géog. de Liège*, 12, pp. 51-63.

MILLER, F.D. (1969) 'Trip Generation at Shopping Centers', *Traffic Engineering*, 39(12), pp. 32-5.

MITTENDORF, H.J. (1976) *Planning of Urban Wholesale Markets for Perishable Food* (FAO, Rome).

MOYER, M.A. (1973) 'Shopping Centers in Canada: Their Impact, Anatomy and Evolution', *Business Quarterly*, 38(2), pp. 23-31.

MOYER, M.S. and G. SNYDER (1967) *Trends in Canadian Marketing* (Dominion Bureau of Statistics, Ottawa).

MULTIPLE SHOPS FEDERATION (1967) *Shopping Centres in North West Europe* (Multiple Shops Federation, London).

NEVILS, R.C. (1977) 'A Study of Retail Shopping Center Atmospherics as a Buying Influence' (Ph.D. thesis, University of Arkansas).

NORTHEN, I. and M. HASKOLL (1977) *Shopping Centres* (College of Estate Management, Reading).

REDSTONE, L.G. (1973) *New Dimensions in Shopping Centers and Stores* (McGraw-Hill, New York).

—— (1976) *The New Downtowns: Rebuilding Business Districts* (McGraw-Hill, New York).

REGIONAL PLANNING COUNCIL (1969) *Detailhandelen i Egnsplanomradet* (Regional Planning Council, Copenhagen).

RILEY, H. *et al.* (1970) *Market Coordination in the Development of the Cauca Valley Region – Colombia* (Michigan State University, East Lansing).

ROBERTS, D.D. (1973) 'Management of Shopping Centres in the United States of America', *The Valuer*, October, pp. 624-32.

ROLPH, I.K. (1933) 'Location Structure of Retail Trade', *US Department of Commerce, Domestic Commerce Series*, 80.

ROUSE, J.W. (1962) 'Must Shopping Centres Be Inhuman?', *Architectural Forum*, 116, pp. 105-118.

—— (1963) 'The Regional Shopping Center: Its Role in the Community It Serves', *Ekistics*, 16, pp. 96-100.

SANSOM, R.L. (1975) 'Modern Issues Confronting Shopping Centers' in *Shopping Centers: the Next 15 Years* (International Council of Shopping Centers, New York), pp. 47-66.

SCHILLER, R. and S. LAMBERT (1977) 'The Quantity of Major Shopping Development in Britain since 1965', *Estates Gazette*, 242, pp. 359-63.

SHERBINI, A.A. (1966) *Planning Fruit and Vegetable Wholesale Market Facilities in Developing Countries* (FAO, Rome).

SHINEHOUSE, A.F. (1962) 'Financing Shopping Centers', *Banking*, 55, pp. 52-3.

SHOPPING CENTER WORLD (1978A) 'The Viability of Downtown Shopping Centers', *Shopping Center World*, 7(2), pp. 33-4.

—— (1978B) 'New Techniques in Lighting', *Shopping Center World*, 7(2), pp. 24-31.

SMITH, B.S. (1977) 'Central Area Development: the German Style', *Town and Country Planning*, 45, pp. 362-5.

SMITH, L. (1952) 'Department Store Trends in the Development of Shopping Centers', *Urban Land News*, 11.
—— (1954) 'Maintaining the Health of Our Central Business Districts', *Traffic Quarterly*, 8, pp. 111-22.
—— (1959) 'Analysis of the Earning Capacity of a Shopping Centre', *Appraisal Journal*, 24, pp. 305-20.
SMITH, P.E. and E.J. KELLY (1960) 'Competing Retail Systems: the Shopping Center and the C.B.D.', *Journal of Retailing*, 36(1), pp. 11-18.
SNAITH, W.T. (1959) 'How Retailing Principles Affect Design' in J.S. Hornbeck (ed.), *Stores and Shopping Centres* (McGraw-Hill, New York), pp. 2-29.
SPORCK, J.A. (1972) 'Les nouvelles implantations commerciales dans la métropole liegeoise, à la lumière de réalisations récentes: américaines, europeénnes, japonaises', *Revue de la société d'étude et d'expansion*, 250, pp. 193-203.
STERNLIEB, G. (1963) 'Future of Retailing in the Downtown Core', *Journal of American Institute of Planners*, 29, pp. 102-12.
STURTEVANT, P.S. (1959) 'Restrictive Lease Covenants in Shopping Center Leases', *New York University Law Review*, 34, pp. 940-55.
TAYLOR, E.G. and F.J. MILLER (1967) 'Baltimore Regional Wholesale Food Distribution Facilities', *US Department of Agriculture, Marketing Research Report*, 783.
J. WALTER THOMPSON CO. (1954) *The Shopping Center in the United States* (J. Walter Thompson, New York).
TUPPEN, J. (1977) 'Redevelopment of the City Centre: the Case of Lyon: La Part Dieu', *Scottish Geographical Magazine*, 93(3), pp. 151-8.
UEDA, N. (1975) *Designing Wholesale Markets for Asian Countries* (FAO, Rome).
UNITED STATES SENATE (1960) *The Impact of Suburban Shopping Centres on Independent Retailers*, Report of Select Committee on Small Businesses, 86th Congress, 1st session, Report 1016.
UNIT FOR RETAIL PLANNING INFORMATION LTD (1977) *District Shopping Centres* (Unit for Retail Planning Information Ltd., Reading).
URBAN LAND INSTITUTE (1965) 'Parking Requirements for Shopping Centers', *Urban Land Institute, Technical Bulletin*, 53.
—— (1966) *The Dollars and Cents of Shopping Centers, 1966* (Urban Land Institute, Washington, DC).
—— (1976) *Shopping Centre Development Handbook* (Urban Land Institute, Washington, DC).
WALKER, M. (1957) 'The Impact of Outlying Shopping Centres on CBD's', *Public Management*, 38, pp. 170-4.
WELCH, C.T. (1969) 'A Guide to Shopping Centre Planning', *National Building Research Institute, Pretoria, Bulletin*, 56.
WELCH, K.C. (1961) 'Parking for Large and Small Cars', *Traffic Quarterly*, 15, pp. 86-97.

8 GOVERNMENT INFLUENCES IN MARKETING

Many of the conflicts in the marketing system arise through an imbalance between the efficient use of marketing resources and institutions and the effective fulfilment of the varied demands of consumers. As the previous chapters have shown, this is not the only reason for conflict within marketing but at a broad scale many conflicts have this root cause. Within capitalist societies there is often pressure placed on government to control and stabilise the equilibrium between the conflicting actors in the marketing system. Specific policies then become a response to a particular conflict as the following examples illustrate. The control of hypermarkets in Belgium has developed as a response to the problems these channels have produced for other retailers and for the less mobile sectors of society. The imposition by colonial bureaucracies of a system of market centres in East Africa was a response to the perceived lack of marketing opportunities available to the rural population. Price regulation policies in Britain are a response to possible abuses of near monopoly situations by producers or retailers. Policies in France to provide independent retailers with a pension and to allow them to close their business is a response to a particular problem facing this minority group. The establishment of government controlled Agricultural Marketing Boards in Australia can be a policy which ensures a reliable marketing procedure for agricultural producers. These few examples show the very wide range of public policies which may be used to influence marketing systems. In these examples the ultimate purpose of the policy is either to protect some group, often a minority, from potential exploitation or to make marketing a more efficient sector of the economy.

Although the detailed policies are very different within communist countries the broad policy aims are surprisingly similar to those in capitalist societies. The rationalisation of wholesale warehousing in the USSR is an attempt to improve marketing efficiency, as is the planned introduction of supermarkets into some of the larger cities in Eastern Europe. Policies to ensure adequate retail provision in the small settlements in the Hungarian Plain aim to ensure access to retail facilities for the minority rural population. The relocation and redesign of market patterns in China aims at improving the efficiency of the retail sector. The overall philosophy underlying government control of the marketing system is quite different in communist and capitalist economies but effectively many of the policies are tackling common problems arising from a basic conflict between efficient marketing institutions and the effective satisfaction of segmented consumer demand. There is a fundamental equity paradox in marketing in the developed countries and it is beginning to appear elsewhere, with the most efficient channel system being aimed toward satisfying only one consumer segment. Usually, but not always, this is the middle class, mobile, 'full-nest', family group. The rôle of government, therefore, is to ensure that minority groups have access to marketing systems even though such systems may be far from optimal from an economic or financial standpoint. Conversely, there is in most marketing systems an in-built conservatism which discourages innovation and change and in which relatively inefficient (from an economic viewpoint) institutions have attained powerful positions simply through their larger numbers or by political activity. Consequently in many marketing systems there are areas where activities with low levels of economic efficiency dominate the system. The rôle of government in these cases is to ensure a more efficient allocation of economic resources for the ultimate benefit of the total society.

Policies to Create More Efficient Distributive Institutions

There are several concepts of efficiency and contrasting political philosophies utilise different concepts. In a free enterprise economy efficiency may be related to the degree of competition within marketing. So it is argued that increased competition and increased efficiency go hand in hand; whereas in command economies, efficiency may be measured as the cost of distribution and the more efficient marketing practices reduce the overall costs in the marketing system. Mattsson (1969) in considering the different levels of efficiency resulting from corporate, rather than public, policy stresses the concept of efficiency as a balance between goal fulfilment and the ratio between output and input. From a corporate viewpoint a high output to input ratio reflects a high level of efficiency but a government with a political philosophy of controlling prices in an oligopolistic industry group would seek a low level of efficiency measured in this way. An efficient market channel might therefore be one in which a balance exists between corporate or institutional goals of a high output/input ratio and the goal of society is defined as an overall low output/input ratio through the total marketing system. These goals need not be incompatible if government policy stimulates and controls different types of marketing activity. By encouraging, for example, vertically integrated channels a high output/input ratio may be achieved by the company but in total the marketing costs to society may be lower than in a fragmented channel. But in stimulating the development of vertically co-ordinated institutions government may also need to control the market power of such institutions to ensure a low overall output/input ratio.

Mattsson stresses the need to qualify definitions of efficiency in terms of the groups involved:

> The efficiency of a marketing system can be judged from various standpoints. For example, the view may be that of the individual component in the system, or of the whole system, or of external components (suppliers, consumers), or of society as a whole. And obviously the chosen standpoint must be declared. Halbert (1965, p. 145) maintains that 'an inability to decide whose values should be the controlling ones in terms of which productivity is to be measured' has been holding up progress as regards efficiency measurements in the marketing sector. (Mattsson, 1969, p. 33).

None the less, governments have initiated policies which have aimed to improve the productivity of the distributive trades but few have been monitored as to their effect, nor have the wider implications for the efficiency of the overall system been considered. It would be wrong to view efficiency as synonymous with productivity (Takeuchi, 1977). Policies frequently arise as a response to an immediate conflict within marketing and efficiency considerations relate to the particular parties in conflict. It is perhaps not surprising therefore that the mix of policies relating to marketing in a country often contains policies whose goals are themselves in opposition.

One area where a number of policies have been effective is in the control of 'restrictive marketing agreements'. Within the USA particularly, these policies have been crucial in conflict resolution within market channels and have had a major effect on spatial patterns of the provision of marketing services (Hollander, 1965; Grether, 1966). The overall goal of these policies is to preserve and increase competition in line with a political philosophy that 'increased marketing efficiency comes with increased competition'. But as Palamountain shows, much of the procompetitive marketing legislation in the USA is the result both of a conflict between wholesalers and chain store groups and also the purchasing advantages chain stores were able to extract from manufacturers. By using their market power chain stores and other large corporations were able to increase their market power at the expense of wholesalers and more directly small independent traders. Although their economic power was in question wholesalers had a strong political voice and 'the Robinson-

Patman Act, one of the two federal acts resulting from intertype conflict in the 1930s, offers further illustration of the political repercussions of economic conflict' (Palamountain, 1968, p. 188). Palamountain shows, in some detail, that the Robinson-Patman Act although in conception a response to governmental (Fair Trade Commission) recommendations about limiting chain store activities in abusing their market power turned, in effect, into a much broader policy to protect small traders and in turn wholesalers:

> Although the original bill was written by wholesalers and designed primarily to improve their position, it was almost invariably presented as a bill to protect the small *retailer . . .* wholesalers were also able to disguise the bill's particularism by stating their goals in terms of some of the dominant political themes of the day. (pp. 200-1).

So price discriminations which had the effect of lessening competition or tending to create a monopoly in any line of commerce were made illegal. Furthermore, purchasing discounts had to be made on 'proportionately equal terms' to all purchasers. The Robinson-Patman Act has served to protect wholesalers and small retailers from the full rigours of competition. While, artificially, there are more distributors in the market than there would be without such legislation and so it is procompetitive, the same legislation limits competition in making illegal certain competitive activities. As Preston (1973) states, 'it is not obvious that the range of competitive alternatives has been increased simply because a greater number of firms is involved' (p. 328). Governments can respond to marketing conflict in a draconian fashion such that the relative position of the parties in conflict is simply reversed. The control of restrictive marketing arrangements with policies such as the Robinson-Patman Act with an avowed goal of increasing efficiency with procompetitive legislation can result in, effectively, activities which are 'Anticompetitive and inconsistent with the objectives of a competitive economy' (Gwinner *et al.*, 1977, p. 359).

The Robinson-Patman Act is only one of several policies, in the USA, with avowed procompetitive goals. Table 8.1 summarises the major legislation along these lines since the Sherman Act of 1890. The Sherman and Clayton acts underlie many of the recent attempts in the USA to control the expansion of dual distribution. In its simplest form this is marketing through both owned and independent outlets. Thus, in selling the same product a vertically integrated firm is in direct competition with a small independent operator. It is very easy for market power to be used

Table 8.1: Major US Federal Laws Affecting Marketing Decisions

Act	Purposes
Sherman Act (1890)	Prohibits contracts, combinations, or conspiracies to restrain trade, establishes as a misdemeanor monopolising or attempts to monopolise.
Clayton Act (1914)	Prohibits specific practices such as price discrimination and exclusive dealer arrangements in which the effect may substantially lessen competition or tend to create a monopoly.
Federal Trade Commission Act (1914)	Created the Federal Trade Commission, gives the Federal Trade Commission investigatory powers to be used in preventing unfair methods of competition.
Robinson-Patman Act (1936)	Prohibits price discrimination that lessens competition among wholesalers or retailers, prohibits producers from giving disproportionate services or facilities to large buyers.
Wheeler-Lea Act (1938)	Prohibits unfair and deceptive acts and practices regardless of whether competition is injured. Places advertising of foods and drugs under the jurisdiction of the Federal Trade Commission.
Celler-Kefauver Act (1950)	Prohibits any corporation engaged in commerce from acquiring the whole or any part of the stock or other share of the capital or assets of another corporation when the effect substantially lessens competition or tends to create a monopoly.
Consumer Goods Pricing Act (1975)	Prohibits the use of price maintenance agreements among manufacturers and retailers in interstate commerce.

to create difficulties in the independent channel:

> A firm which is vertically integrated has several levels at which it may make a profit and if such a firm is engaged in dual distribution then there would be less necessity or compulsion for it to make a profit at a given level than for an independent competitor who operated only at that level. (House of Representatives, 1964, p. 10).

Dual distribution is not in itself unlawful but a number of marketing

arrangements which can result from dual distribution are counter to
both the Sherman and Clayton Acts (Grether, 1966; Preston and Schramm,
1965).

Resale Price Maintenance has been the direct subject of several acts
culminating in the Consumer Goods Pricing Act, of 1975; RPM allows
manufacturers to set resale prices with the aim of stopping large retailers
from selling products at such low prices that smaller and financially
weaker retailers could not compete. Various states in the USA passed laws
to allow RPM and interstate trade was covered by Federal Law. The growing strength of larger marketing companies pressing for the abolition of
RPM and an increased awareness that distributive efficiency was possible
without a plethora of small independent traders together have led to
acts prohibiting RPM. This pattern of policies towards RPM is repeated
in many countries (Yamey, 1966A). The abolition of RPM has caused a
reduction in the number of small independent traders but it is impossible
to estimate its precise quantitative impact. 'A widespread use of r.p.m. is
said to preserve too many small retail shops operating at a low rate of
efficiency' (p. 176). Such is the view of Kjølby (1966) reporting the situation in Denmark. In Sweden the major structural changes in retailing
in the mid 1950s followed the abolition of RPM in 1955. Change has
been more gradual in Britain as RPM has been abolished in a piecemeal
fashion with freer pricing allowed at various times through the 1950s
and 1960s on different groups of goods. The abolition of RPM was seen
as a move to improve retail efficiency: 'there was evidence that many of
them [i.e. small-scale shopkeepers] were sufficiently efficient, or could
become so by means of co-operative activities with or without the
assistance of wholesale dealers, to continue in business' (Yamey, 1966B,
p. 287). Generally in Europe and North America RPM is viewed as a
restrictive marketing arrangement but it took largescale lobbying by
large marketing corporations before this view became widely held, with
the necessary change in the concept of efficiency.

A second group of policies with efficiency goals are those aimed at
restricting the entry of firms into the marketing system or alternatively
encouraging firms to leave the system. Unrestricted entry can mean the
operation of a large number of marginal enterprises many of which soon
die. This is particularly the case with small shops but also occurs in all
other parts of the marketing system: 'The ease with which the pensioner
or heir to a small legacy can set up in retail trade is only equal to the
rapidity with which he can (and does) go bankrupt or suffer a less dramatic extinction' (Smith, 1948, p. 90). These high birth and death rates
among small shops represent an 'inefficient' use of economic resources

and have provoked governments into attempts to restrict entry.

Many governments have enacted this type of legislation. In Italy, for example, there are stringent licensing regulations controlling entry but they not only control the birth rate of small shops but also control the entry of new large stores. The regulations have the additional effect of providing protection from large store competition and increasing the likelihood of growth of existing small shops. Laws relating to entry elsewhere in Europe are less stringent and usually relate, as in the Netherlands and Austria, to a training requirement for the potential entrant. Control of entry in the UK is through the development control and land use planning powers of local government authorities. By restricting shop sites the policy of selective control of shop birth is effective. Such a policy affects only shops at new locations (Dawson and Kirby, 1977), and Smith (1971) has argued strongly for an alternative policy approach which depends upon a training requirement for entry irrespective of whether new locations are concerned. Restrictive entry policies have been aimed at large stores as well as small and this will be returned to later when the policies aimed at controlling market power are considered in the second part of this chapter.

The Italian legislation, however, presents an interesting case, for while the legislation was designed to restrain excess competition between small retailers and to allow them to become more efficient through protected growth it has inhibited development of efficient largescale retailing. Even supermarkets and department stores have to obtain a trading licence and these have been granted in very small numbers. Approximately 250 supermarket licences were granted between 1965 and 1975 in the whole of Italy. Consequently there has been little stimulus from this legislation for reorganisation or rationalisation in either retailing or wholesaling (Dawson, 1976B). The large retail groups find this licensing policy particularly restrictive to their development and although the policy has served to reduce conflict between large and small traders it has inhibited trends towards a more efficient marketing system.

Exit promotion schemes have been introduced in the Netherlands and France. Under such schemes small shop operators, usually the owners, are provided with a state pension. In France,

over the years many thousand small scale entrepreneurs have invested their savings in small shops with a view to ultimately realising these assets on retirement. With a combination of inflation and the changed competitive position in retailing these shopkeepers now find that instead of having a sizeable retirement nest egg their shop is unsaleable

and of little value . . . Consequently they find themselves forced to
continue working, past the normal retirement age, without being able
to adapt themselves or their shop to the new conditions in retailing.
(Dawson, 1977B, p. 47).

The French Government, in 1972, passed legislation and set aside welfare
funds to allow this type of retailer to cease trading. This type of policy
not only allows distributive rationalisation but also may be viewed, more
broadly, as an antipoverty measure (Roy, 1971; Reynaud, 1972).

A third approach to improving marketing efficiency is through positive policies which encourage modernisation and investment in particular
parts of the marketing system. There are here a wide range of policy
options relating to all marketing functions and a few examples prove
this diversity.

One of the problems of retail provision in Hungary is the efficient distribution of basic retail services in rural areas. The state controlled retail
sector has never proved efficient in rural areas. Under the New Economic
Mechanism private traders have been encouraged in villages and on the
periphery of provincial towns where the supply of goods has been un-
satisfactory. 'It is primarily for this reason – better supplies to rural and
outlying areas – that the regime has taken a number of noteworthy steps
to increase the number of private traders' (Robinson, 1973, p. 141). These
policies include expanding the number of commodity groups that may be
handled in private trade, changing the method of licences for private
traders, securing state supply channels for private operators and various
tax and pension concessions to private traders in outlying districts. So a
mix of policies has been devised to improve the efficiency of retailing in
certain types of location.

The problems facing government in supplying rural areas with adequate
retail facilities are not uniquely Hungarian. Throughout the Eastern bloc
and Western Europe similar problems face rural traders. It is curious that
while the Hungarians have encouraged private enterprise to participate in
retailing to increase efficiency in these areas, throughout Western Europe
the response has been to increase governmental intervention in rural
retailing. In Norway a variety of subsidies has been provided to 'single
shop' communities (Kirby, 1976). A study of the Netherlands in 1975
showed that there were 1,100 rural communities without shops and proposed a state sponsored co-operative agency and state subsidised travelling shops; and a report in Britain advocates a greater degree of government action (National Council of Social Service, 1978). Concern in Britain and France about rural retailing has led to many calls for more state,

and particularly local authority intervention in an endeavour to make rural shop provision more efficient (Joseph, 1977; Commissariat Général du Plan, 1976).

Positive help for other types of retailing has come in a variety of forms. In the Soviet Union there are attempts to introduce supermarket and self-service retailing in urban areas. Samsonov (1971) quotes surveys of the USSR and Czechoslovakia showing how customer waiting time is reduced in selfservice stores and how employee productivity is raised. In the USSR there are plans for converting half the conventional shop network to selfservice with an expected, dramatic increase in efficiency: 'The introduction of self-service means an approximate 15% increase in the capacity of the trade network compared with conventional stores' (Samsonov, 1971, p. 74). Eastern Europe also is following this policy with similar anticipated results. Whether such changes occur remains to be seen. Again primarily with urban areas in mind, Japan has a series of government policies designed to encourage voluntary and co-operative chains (Yoshino, 1971). Through funding by the Japan Development Bank loans are made available to the wholesale and retail components of a prospective chain. An extensive government directed information campaign exhorts retailers to join and form chains and again financial inducements have been offered to participating retailers. Related to this whole programme are training schemes for both wholesale and retail management. There is a package of closely related government sponsored activities which together implement the policy of voluntary group growth.

A similar approach exists in respect to the development of wholesaling in Japan. Brief mention has been made in Chapter 5 of the establishment of new distribution centres in suburban Japan. In 1963 the Council on Urban Redevelopment under the auspices of the Ministry of Construction argued the need for suburban warehouse and truck terminals. The recommendations of the report were translated into policy in 1966 when 27 cities were officially designated as suitable for new distribution centres. These policies have been strengthened by additional reports on the advantages of multifunctional terminals (Nittsu Research Institute, 1972) but the implementation of the policies has not kept pace with the growth of the physical distribution industry. Loan availability and financial incentives for investment have been the major *carrots* in the implementation of the policy but the policy has lacked a *stick* which would have increased the spread of distribution centres. With the enactment of the Distributive Facilities Establishment Act, land acquisition became simpler and considerable progress was made on truck terminals but little on multifunction facilities. An example of development resulting from this governmental initiative is the Keihin Truck Terminal which serves as a collection and delivery terminal for the south of Tokyo and as a transport base for Tokyo to Osaka-Kobe traffic. Originally envisaged as a comprehensive distribution facility, the lack of centralised management has hindered multifunctional development. Around 40 major line-haul companies and 300 transport companies use the terminal, with many individual companies having exclusive use of particular berths and platforms. Around 7,000 vehicles per day use the facility and many of these are involved in relaying freight rather than in primary delivery/collection activities. The government initiative had resulted by 1977 in a total of three major truck terminals serving metropolitan Tokyo. The truck terminal element is only one aspect of the wholesale development strategy operated by the Japanese Government. Various joint distribution and delivery services have been developed with government backing. Many started relatively small but have subsequently grown. The East Nihonbashi centre in Eastern Tokyo for example started as a joint effort of six wholesalers in 1968 to pool and unify their transport fleets. By March 1976, 300 wholesalers were participating in the venture. One consequence of such centres is that the number of freight vehicles in operation is reduced, in the case of East Nihonbashi by 10 per cent (Toyota Transport Environment Committee, 1977). As with the social policies related to small shop operations, government policies aimed at establishing distribution centres have wider implications than improving marketing efficiency. Such policies also relate to urban traffic management problems and to more general urban environmental and energy conservation issues.

The wider ramifications of marketing policy are perhaps more clearly seen in agricultural activities where governmental intervention in marketing practices is often part of a total rural development programme. Marketing policies in these situations have to show a positive approach if they are to gain acceptance by smallscale producers operating close to the margin. Guaranteeing a price for grain, for example, is widely used as a government policy with only slight variations (FAO, 1976). In India minimum support prices and procurement prices are established by the government as an incentive to expand production but such a policy establishes a more stable market for grain. The guaranteed price system in Peru aims to stabilise producer prices for grain and so again stabilises marketing arrangements and in turn promotes a more efficient marketing system. Marketing boards, as shown in Chapter 6, are used widely by governments as a means of regulating and promoting marketing changes. Some recent studies have stressed not only the importance of direct interventionist policies but also the considerable rôle government has in providing the 'legal framework, weights and measures and the provision of adequate infrastructure, e.g. feeder roads and market places' (Mittendorf, Barker and Schneider, 1977, p. 44). In the same vein Mittendorf (1976) argues that when smallscale enterprises are involved, as is invariably the case in developing countries, then a major area of policy initiative must be in training and education so that participants in marketing actually understand what is going on. It has also been suggested that these education policies should be extended to government officials to increase their awareness of marketing problems and solutions (Spinks, 1970). The development, jointly by the Iranian Government and FAO, of the Iran Centre for Agricultural Marketing Development is typical of this type of policy geared towards the educational facet of marketing development.

There is great variety, as these few examples have shown, in the type of positive policy which government can pursue to promote greater efficiency in the marketing system. In all countries, even Eastern Europe, government can take a positive stand on marketing reform, being both a direct participant in marketing and a stimulant to private enterprise activity. The relationship between private traders and state agencies is described by Kriesberg and Steele (1972) who argue that, in developing countries at least,

> There appears to be a need for positive actions by public agencies to provide some of the basic services and to create an environment conducive to private marketing firm expansion. There is also a question whether spontaneous development of marketing firms, in the absence of facilitating policies and programs, will provide efficient and equitable linkages between producers and consumers. (p. 25).

Such a view is equally applicable to the developed countries of the world.

One of the reasons for governmental intervention in the marketing system is the resolution of conflict between marketing institutions. It is assumed that by resolving conflict marketing becomes more effective and efficient. The fourth group of policies with which the first part of this chapter is concerned deal directly with conflicts created by competition for land by marketing activities and comprise integrated policies for land use planning. The duty of the land use planner is usually the balancing of economic efficiency with social equity in the allocation of land uses and it is proposed to return to the equity issues and policies in the second part of the chapter. Although this task of 'reconciling conflicting objectives in order to achieve a balance under which the different groups in a community are provided with the greatest opportunities, choice and

satisfaction' (Mills, 1974, p. 61) is central to planning policy, the planner
still has a duty to develop regions, towns and functions such that their
economic efficiency is improved. In many planning policies it is difficult
to distinguish the efficiency and equity components but in some instances planners pursue particular land use policies which are stimulants
to economic efficiency. As marketing activities are fundamental to urban-
ism and urban growth so both regional and urban planners have become
involved in allocating marketing activity to particular places.

Of the major marketing activities it is retailing which has been the
focus of attention in land use policies. Wholesaling, agricultural marketing and even facilitating agencies such as banks and insurance have been
dealt with on an *ad hoc* basis within urban and regional development
plans. In very few instances in Britain, where land use planning is considered to be at an advanced stage, is wholesaling a topic at an interurban
or regional level, and even within towns policies are extremely hazy.
Retailing, perhaps because of the more obvious consumer link, is subject
to planning policies at several levels.

At both interurban and intraurban levels the cynosure of most policy
makers has been and continues to be central place theory and the notion
of a planned hierarchy of shopping areas. Central place theory has provided a rationale for directing new retail floor space to particular towns
and within towns the 'tidying' of retailing into a sequence of different
sized shopping areas is clearly a policy of economic efficiency. There is
extensive criticism of central place theory as a model of the way cities
function (Carter, 1972; NEDO, 1970) but the spatial efficiency of the
model and the possibilities it provides for improving retail efficiency
endears it to retail planners (Szumeluk, 1968). Grove and Huszar (1964)
utilised the central place model to evaluate service and retail provision
in the interurban network of Ghana. The study suggests a future pattern
of development which would direct capital investment and create a nested
hierarchy of towns in respect of their retail and service provision. The
planning of the settlement network to service the population of the re-
claimed land in the major projects in the Netherlands was based on the
principle of service centres (Thijsse, 1968). Mills (1974) and Thorpe
(1975), by considering British local authority planning proposals, show
the frequent use of the idea of a retail hierarchy as a model for retail
planning.

Within urban areas central place theory has been widely used as a policy
to create a more efficient network of shopping areas. Retailing in Sydney
is planned in this way as it is in London and many other smaller towns
and most notably in the British new towns. The development of plans

based on central place theory undoubtedly has helped the retail industry develop, in the 1950s and early 1960s, more efficiently but the industry has passed into another phase of development at least in urban Britain and central place theory is now of little relevance —yet it remains the basis of many plans.

Land use planning policies relevant to retailing efficiency are not concerned exclusively with the size and location of shopping areas. Decisions on the balance between the retail strength of town centre and suburbs have to be made both as national policy and for individual cities. Major policies exist on attitudes towards city centre redevelopment; again both national and local policies are designed. The redevelopment of a town centre, as for example in Newcastle-upon-Tyne (Davies and Bennison, 1978), is the result of planning policies and decisions and has improved the effectiveness and efficiency of retailing. The same is true of the redevelopment schemes in Chicago described by Berry, Parsons and Platt (1968) and of almost all the other downtown schemes in the USA (Redstone, 1976). Such policies represent positive contributions to improving market efficiency but they raise many questions of social equity from a consumer viewpoint (*Town and Country Planning*, 1974). Urban land use policies and zoning regulations (Bartelt, 1960; Nelson, 1958) can have far reaching effects on marketing activities even at a very broad level. Hollander (1973) argues that

> Postwar American policies that have encouraged highway construction and the development of suburban and family housing have probably done as much as any other phase of government action in shaping contemporary retailing. Conceivably town-planning and land-use control may turn out to be among the most powerful external variables that help shape our forthcoming retail structure. (p. 340).

It could be argued that in Britain this is already the case while environmental planning policies, already this side of the horizon, will also have considerable impact on marketing practices, particularly in respect of the transport function.

Very broadly, public policies aimed at improving retail efficiency fall into four classes. First are those seeking to *control restrictive marketing practices*, secondly are policies *restricting entry* or promoting the exit of inefficient firms, thirdly are positive attempts *to encourage more efficient marketing practices* and finally there are attempts *to improve the spatial efficiency of the location of marketing institutions*. Although efficiency in the marketing system is a somewhat nebulous concept it does not need to be equated with perfect competition which Newman (1965) argues is the criterion of market efficiency, for there is a considerable literature on market efficiency (Preston and Collins, 1966) most of which ignores the institutional and organisational basis of marketing. An efficient marketing system will have, when viewed from a seller viewpoint, a high output/input ratio but when viewed by the buyer will have a low output/input ratio. Almost all the policies discussed in this chapter have aimed to improve efficiency as viewed by the seller but there are also government policies aimed at creating an equitable marketing system from the buyer's point of view and it is to these policies that attention is now turned.

Policies Aimed at a More Equitable Marketing System

Although many government social policies have a marginal impact on marketing systems only two major policies will be discussed. These are first those dealing with the control of market power and secondly those relating to consumer protection.

Policies aimed at the control of market power often seek to curb the activities of large organisations to prevent monopolies developing and buyer choice being limited. Some of these policies are similar to those controlling restrictive market practices but while some policies result in increased marketing efficiency, as discussed in the first part of this chapter, others may limit moves to increased efficiency if these trends are likely to generate monopolies. The distinction between monopolies which are in the public interest and those which are not is a difficult one to make. Agricultural marketing in the USA is governed by umbrella antitrust laws making monopolies illegal but alongside these is more specific legislation such as the Agricultural Fair Practice Act of 1967 and the Agricultural Marketing and Bargaining Act of 1969 which allow agriculturalists to form co-operative bargaining associations. Agricultural co-operation is deemed to be in the public interest but potentially dangerous monopolies could be created easily.

Within developed Western style economies, policies to control monopolies in the marketing system are widespread. Reports on the competition policy in OECD member countries are issued each year and a considerable part of these reports comprises discussion on monopoly regulation. In the United Kingdom the Fair Trading Act of 1973 consolidated and strengthened regulations on mergers and in particular reduced the relevant market share criterion for defining a monopoly from a third to a quarter. The Trade Practices Bill in Australia, also of 1973, prohibits mergers if the effect may be to tend to result in a corporation substantially controlling the market. Antimonopoly legislation may also be enacted at a local level. In Denmark prior to 1966, for example, the Danish Trades Act prohibited retailers from having more than one shop in the same municipality. While this legislation effectively controlled any potential local monopoly it also limited the possibility of chain store development. A revised act, of 1966, with transitional arrangements terminating in 1970, lifted these restrictions but national antimonopoly laws still exist. Given the highly fragmented nature of retailing, however, considerable concentration and merger is possible before monopoly situations emerge. In Denmark, such concentration is occurring (Institute for Future Studies, 1976) but is not infringing antimonopoly legislation.

A second form of policy aimed at limiting market power particularly in retailing is that associated with control over the development of large establishments rather than large organisations. This policy is administered in a variety of ways but its rationale is common to many countries. In Britain and Australia, for example, control is within the land use planning legislation and permission for new developments such as hypermarkets or shopping centres can be refused if they are not integral to the accepted planning strategy for the area or if they are thought likely to be detrimental to providing all consumers with retail facilities. In Belgium, Italy and France, on the other hand, special commercial committees have been set up by government to judge the acceptability of proposals for new large stores (Coville, 1974). In all cases the reasons for limiting their growth stems from the effect such stores have on existing retail provision and the consequent possible reduction in shopping opportunities for minorities of consumers. With the development of large, more efficient stores so small, and sometimes less efficient, stores close and the density of retailing is decreased so that consumers have to travel further to visit shops. For consumer segments with low mobility such a change can cause deprivation. It can be in the interest of society, therefore, to control widespread development of such stores although this development would increase marketing efficiency. Most governments take the view that social equity considerations, in this case, take precedence over improved marketing efficiency and some limit on large store development is a widespread policy.

In France, after an initial period when hypermarkets were allowed to develop virtually unchecked, legislation was enacted in 1973 to limit future expansion. For four years prior to 1973 commercial development commissions existed but their remit was to comment and advise on new retail developments of 3,000 m^2 and over. The Loi d'Orientation du Commerce et de l'Artisanat of 1973 gave effective powers of control

to the commissions who were able to accept or reject development proposals. The potential developer has the right of appeal if the application
is rejected but the overall policy is one of controlling the widespread
development of large units:

> The need for some type of legal and administrative curbs on large
> scale development increasingly became apparent to the French govern-
> ment as studies were made of the impacts of hypermarkets and
> discount stores on small supermarkets and traditional retailing. During
> 1972 there were 62 new hypermarkets in France and in the following
> year a further 49. This rapid growth of giant stores together with an
> equally rapid increase in new supermarkets (more than 250 in excess
> of 400 sq. metres in both 1972 and 1973) provided a strong argument
> for the advocates of limiting the growth of large scale retailing. (Dawson,
> 1977A, p. 14).

The resulting law allowed each of the 95 Départements to set up a committee to adjudicate on all applications for major projects in the département. The committees have to consider applications in terms of three
broad criteria:

(1)   national levels of commercial activity;
(2)   the evolution of retailing in the département;
(3)   the balance among types of trade in the département.

There has been considerable debate on the justification of the policy
and on its results (Hermand, 1975). Undoubtedly the rate of opening of
new developments has slowed since 1973 but it is likely that this would
have happened in any case. Départements have interpreted the law in
different ways so there is some variation in the degree of control exer-
cised, but overall it seems likely that the policy has resulted in fewer
large developments than would otherwise have been the case. Unable to
consider new developments, corporations have looked towards both
new developments outside France (Fournier, 1978; Dawson, 1976A) and
expansion by merger and regrouping (Rousseau, 1977). One side effect
of the policy 'has been to accentuate the concentration of large commercial groupings and hence to reinforce their power' (Freis, 1978, p.
45).

Although the policy's effectiveness in controlling new development
has been evaluated there is no analysis of the success or failure of the
policy's real rationale. As a consequence of the policy, have shopping

facilities for older, poorer, less mobile, central city residents become more accessible, or at least have they not become less accessible? Small shops in urban France continue to close in large numbers and are encouraged to by other legislation, mentioned earlier — providing state pensions for private retailers.

Control of hypermarket type development in the United Kingdom has been much stronger. The main aim has been to reduce the disruptive effect on consumer behaviour caused by new large stores on the urban periphery and to control likely traffic congestion resulting from hypermarket development. The reports, some of which are summarised in Lee and Kent (1976, 1978), of planning appeal inspectors dealing with hypermarket application, invariably focus on the anticipated impact on existing town centres and an analysis of likely traffic generation and congestion given the existing road network. Both topics are central to the Department of the Environment (DoE) directives on plan preparation. Development Control Policy Note 13 of the DoE in 1977 in discussing town centre impact states that 'The economic base of such a centre is likely to be particularly vulnerable to the effects of large store development in edge of town or out of town locations'. And, under a section on Highway Considerations it states:

> A large new store will generate substantial traffic of shoppers and staff in cars and of commercial vehicles serving the store. This may effect substantially the volume and composition of traffic on the road network both near the new store and over a wider area related to the drawing power of the store.

With central government directives the freedom of action of local government is limited but Davies and Sumner (1978) have shown that local authorities perceive the likely impact of such stores very differently and consequently can have different attitudes to their development. In protecting town centre shops from outer suburban competition, it is argued that viable shopping facilities in the town centre are more convenient to a larger proportion of the population than would otherwise be the case.

Concern for the shopping facilities available to segments of the population with low levels of mobility is also evident in land use plans for the provision of local shops. Typical is the policy applied in Bexley, a suburban South London Borough. The strategy plan proposes 'to encourage the provision of local shopping facilities within a half-mile walking distance of all households in the Borough' (London Borough of Bexley, 1975, p. 31). Such an aim is typical of most British land use planning. Even when the proportion of non-car owners is small it is often still pursued as a desirable policy. Inevitably it means that encouragement is given to small independent shop operators and some measure of protection is afforded to them from serious competition in the form of large mass merchandising operations. So, for example, in Canberra, where the tradition of British planning principles remains strong and although car ownership is extremely high, a system of neighbourhood shopping centres and corner shops has been planned. The centres are linked, by pedestrian ways, to the housing developments in the neighbourhoods and the vast majority of households are within 800 metres of a neighbourhood centre. One result of this is that hypermarket style operations have been confined to locations in regional shopping centres where their costs are higher than would be the case if they were freestanding at peripheral sites (NCDC, 1970). Such a policy typifies the balance between efficiency and equity which underlies all land use plans concerned with retailing.

A quite different area of public policy intervention, but again one related to providing a fair marketing system, is that of consumer protection. Conflict between buyer and seller is a common feature of all marketing systems and in almost every country there is some legislation to protect the consumer from marketing malpractice. In periodic markets in Africa, for example, market officials have some control over selling practices. In Yorubaland, Hodder (1969) points out that market by-laws on sanitation are quite strict and that there are also intricate procedures for policing the market and dispute resolution. Smith (1962) similarly points to supervisors in Hausa markets making sure that gross trading injustices are not perpetrated. Consumer protection, although present, is very weak. In Europe and North America legislation protecting the consumer is, as might be expected, stronger and more formalised. Common weights and measures and various other standards are legally imposed and regularly policed and false description of goods or false advertising also are areas where protection policies have evolved. Borrie and Diamond (1968) provide an extensive account of consumer law in Britain and advocate its extension and ultimately the preparation of a 'consumer's charter'. Through consumer protection legislation inbalances in consumer-retailer relationships are corrected, with the operation, in consequence, of a more equitable marketing system.

Consumer protection legislation in the USA shows three phases and Ford (1978) argues that the 'enactment of consumerism legislation at the state level has preceded the institution of similar policies by the federal government' (p. 49). The earliest activity by government was in the late nineteenth century, culminating in a series of acts dealing with deception, branding and adulteration of foods and drugs. A second bout of activity in the 1930s extended the earlier acts to several non-food items and introduced clearer legislation on deceptive practices. A third phase began in the 1950s and continues to the present day and is typified by a much wider range of legislation. The increased activity in recent years, not just in the USA, stems from a number of changes in marketing and society.

First, consumers have become more sophisticated and with better communication, more knowledgeable about products. Consequently, consumers are more critical of product failures and demand ways of seeking legal redress from manufacturers and suppliers. Secondly, with mass merchandising methods it is easy for defective products to be distributed rapidly and a profit taken by unscrupulous operators. Thirdly, the number of products on the market has increased as technology has developed. Many of these products are untried and untested by consumers, so it is difficult for consumers to evaluate product safety. There is then need for government based safety testing. Finally, consumers are increasingly willing to assert their rights under the existing legislation. To this end there are ever increasing numbers of consumer organisations in operation which among other activities monitor consumer protection legislation.

In a consideration of governmental policy activity within marketing it is immediately apparent that policies within a society are piecemeal with no overall view of how marketing activities should develop. This is as true for countries with command economies as it is for those with market economies. The mix of policies existing in a country is a response to the perceived mix of marketing conflicts occurring in the particular marketing system. It is worth remembering that the perception of a conflict by a policy making agency may occur well after a conflict has begun. Political activity by one group of participants may serve to make government aware of a conflict. The lobbying of small retailers seeking protection in 1930s Belgium or 1960s France is an example of the lag between a conflict occurring and a government's perception and acknowledgement of its existence. Not every marketing channel conflict is resolved by government but increasingly they are drawn into marketing relationships. Government policies are piecemeal and they cover an ever wider range of marketing activity. Often policies, because of their fragmented nature, are counterproductive. For example, encouragement may be given to investment in retailing on one hand but planning permission refused for the stores resulting from the investment programmes.

The range of marketing activity subject to government policy is extremely wide and policies are implemented by different levels of government. National policy on competition and local policy on shop opening hours may exist alongside each other on the statute book. Even the same area of activity may be treated differently in different countries. For example, shop hours in Denmark are controlled by a national policy while in Australia it is the concern of state government, with some of the major cities having Saturday afternoon opening while shops in other cities close at noon. In the USA the absence of restrictions on evening selling hours 'and the almost total inefficiencies of Sunday closing laws provide further encouragement for suburban shopping' (Hollander, 1973, p. 346) and, as Hollander (1972) points out elsewhere, give a positive boost to the convenience store movement. When relatively minor matters such as shop opening hours are controlled by public policy it is not surprising that there are few aspects of marketing which are not influenced in some way by government activity and policy.

Often this influence is not a consequence of policies directly aimed at the marketing system but results from the indirect effect of policies aimed at other economic or social sectors. General labour laws and wage policy, for example, can have impact on marketing although they are of more general applicability. The adoption of policies of labour redistribution through selective taxation, as with the British Selective Employment Tax (Reddaway, 1970; Cuthbert, 1971) produces change throughout the whole marketing system. Similarly policies on energy conservation which seem likely in the USA in the late 1970s and 1980s will have significant effects on all parts of the marketing system, from refrigerated transport to shopping centre location.

Despite the plethora of government policies influencing the marketing system, there are few analyses of the effectiveness of particular policies. Clearly it is difficult to develop a cause-and-result type analysis for policy evaluation as the objects under study are themselves changing irrespective of any effects of government policy. There are many studies of the evolution of policies, including important comparative descriptions such as those included in Boddewyn and Hollander (1972) but in comparison there are both few full analyses of the effects of policy and few attempts to monitor changes created by policy directives. There are some studies of the success or otherwise of marketing boards but considering the many policies effective at any one time and the great variety of these, evaluations are few in number.

Carson's (1967) classic work on comparative marketing points to the different emphasis individual countries place on government intervention in business. While broad policy aims may be common among countries, often the ways to these goals are quite different. An OECD report of 1973 reviewed distributive development among member countries and allied this to a study of government policy. For OECD member countries it concluded:

> This conclusion has wider validity both beyond the OECD group and to all marketing activity.

> Governments increasingly recognise the importance of the distribution sector. The scope, variety and responsible nature of the distribution sector is such that there is no unique prescription for the formulation of government policy relating to the distribution area . . . Some governments are concerned in varying degrees by the problems posed by the distribution sector. Some governments are continuing to explore new and to adapt existing policies to deal with specific problem areas, including the social and economic position of small enterprises, inflation, productivity and resource needs, including manpower and financial requirements. (p. 40).

While not a universal panacea, government action can help considerably towards making marketing systems both more efficient and more equitable.

References

BARTELT, L.F. (1960) 'Shopping Centers and Land Controls', *Notre Dame Lawyer*, 35, pp. 184-209.

BERRY, B.T.L., S.J. PARSONS and R.H. PLATT (1968) *The Impact of Urban Renewal on Small Business: The Hyde Park-Kenwood Case* (Center for Urban Studies, University of Chicago, Chicago).

BODDEWYN, J.J. and S.C. HOLLANDER (1972) *Public Policy toward Retailing* (Lexington Books, Lexington, Mass.).

BORRIE, G. and A.L. DIAMOND (1968) *The Consumer, Society and the Law* (Penguin Books, Harmondsworth).

CARSON, D. (1967) *International Marketing* (Wiley, New York).

CARTER, H. (1972) *The Study of Urban Geography* (Arnold, London).

COMMISSARIAT GENERAL DU PLAN (1976) *Rapport de la commission: Commerce, services et artisanat* (La Documentation Française, Paris).

COVILLE, G. (1974) 'Le développement des grandes surfaces commerciales en Europe et les problèmes qu'il pose', *Problèmes Economiques*, 1396, pp. 26-30.

CUTHBERT, N. (1971) *The Effects of Selective Employment Tax in Retail Trade in Northern Ireland* (The Queen's University, Belfast).

DAVIES, R.L. and D.J. BENNISON (1978) *The Eldon Square Regional Shopping Centre: the First Eighteen Months* (Retail Planning Associates, Corbridge).

DAWSON, J.A. (1976A) 'Hypermarkets in France', *Geography*, 61, pp. 259-62.

——— (1976B) 'Public Policy and Distribution in the E.E.C.' in R. Lee and P.E.

Ogden (eds), *Economy and Society in the E.E.C.* (Saxon House, Farnborough), pp. 256-71.

—— (1977A) 'Control over Large Units in France: the Loi Royer and Its Effects', *Retail and Distribution Management*, 6(4), pp. 14-18.

—— (1977B) 'French Help for the Independent Trader', *Retail and Distribution Management*, 5 (4), pp. 47-8.

DAWSON, J.A. and D.A. KIRBY (1977) 'Problems and Policies Affecting the Small Shop', *International Journal of Physical Distribution*, 7(5), pp. 244-54.

FAO (1976) *National Grain Policies* (FAO, Rome).

FREIS, J. (1978) 'Government Intervention in France: How Has It Affected Development?', *Retail and Distribution Management*, 6(2), pp. 41-5.

FORD, G.T. (1978) 'Adoption of Consumer Policies by States: Some Empirical Perspectives', *Journal of Marketing Research*, 15, pp. 49-57.

FOURNIER, M. (1978) 'Carrefour: un adulte qui continue sa croissance', *Libre Service Actualité*, 668, pp. 35-7.

GRETHER, E.T. (1966) *Marketing and Public Policy* (Prentice-Hall, Englewood Cliffs).

GROVE, D. and L. HUSZAR (1964) *The Towns of Ghana: the Role of Service Centres in Regional Planning* (Ghana Universities Press, Accra).

GWINNER, R.F. *et al.* (1977) *Marketing: an Environmental Perspective* (West, St Paul).

HALBERT, M. (1965) *The Meaning and Sources of Marketing Theory* (McGraw-Hill, New York).

HERMAND, H. (1975) 'Loi d'orientation: anachronique, inadaptée', *Libre Service Actualité*, 548, pp. 103-7.

HODDER, B.W. (1969) 'Markets in Yorubaland' in B.W. Hodder and U.I. Ukwa (eds), *Markets in West Africa* (University of Ibadan Press, Ibadan), pp. 3-109.

HOLLANDER, S.C. (1965) *Restraints upon Retail Competition* (Michigan State University, East Lansing).

—— (1972) 'United States of America' in J.J. Boddewyn and S.C. Hollander (eds), *Public Policy toward Retailing* (Lexington Books, Lexington, Mass.), pp. 367-403.

—— (1973) 'Retailing and Public Policy: Retrospect and Prospect' in F.C. Allvine (ed.), *Public Policy and Marketing Practices* (American Marketing Association, Chicago), pp. 339-51.

HOUSE OF REPRESENTATIVES (1964) *The Impact upon Small Business of Dual Distribution and Related Vertical Integration: Report of Sub-committee on Distribution Problems to Select Committee on Small Business* (US Government Printer, Washington, DC).

INSTITUTE FOR FUTURES STUDIES (1976) *A Study of the Evolution of Concentration in the Danish Food Distribution Industry* (Commission of the European Communities, Brussels).

JOSEPH, M.E. (1977) *The Village Shop in Rural Mid-Wales* (Department of Geography, St David's University College, Lampeter).

KIRBY, D.A. (1976) 'Planning and the Small Shop – the Scandinavian Example', *Retail and Distribution Management*, 4(5), pp. 41-2.

KRIESBERG, M. and H. STEELE (1972) 'Improving Marketing Systems in Developing Countries', *US Department of Agriculture, Foreign Economic Development Service, Staff Paper*, 7.

KJØLBY, H. (1966) 'Denmark', in B.S. Yamey (ed.), *Resale Price Maintenance* (Weidenfeld & Nicolson, London), pp. 145-77.

KOBIK, V. (1968) 'Principles of Constructing a Retail Trade Network in Czechoslovakia', *Journal of Retailing*, 44(1), pp. 45-53.

LEE, M. and E. KENT (1976) 'Planning Inquiry Study', *Donaldsons Research*

Report, 3 (London).
―――― (1978) 'Planning Inquiry Study 2', *Donaldsons Research Report*, 5 (London).
LONDON BOROUGH OF BEXLEY (1975) *Shopping: an Interim Policy* (Bexley Council, Sidcup).
MATTSSON, L-G. (1969) *Integration and Efficiency in Marketing Systems* (Economic Research Institute, Stockholm).
MILLS, E. (1974) 'Recent Developments in Retailing and Urban Planning', *Planning Research Applications Group, Technical Paper*, 3.
MITTENDORF, H.J. (1976) 'Facilitating Services for Agricultural and Food Marketing Systems in Developing Countries' in D. Izraeli, D.N. Izraeli and F. Meissner (eds), *Agricultural Marketing for Developing Countries*, vol. 2. (Wiley, New York), pp. 3-20.
MITTENDORF, H.J., E.J. BARKER and H. SCHNEIDER (1977) *Critical Issues on Food Marketing Systems in Developing Countries* (OECD, Paris).
NATIONAL COUNCIL OF SOCIAL SERVICE (1978) *The Decline of Rural Services* (NCSS, London).
NCDC (1970) *Tomorrow's Canberra* (National Capital Development Corporation, Canberra).
NEDO (1970) *Urban Models in Shopping Studies* (Distributive Trades EDC, London).
NELSON, R.L. (1958) *The Selection of Retail Locations* (F.W. Dodge, New York).
NEWMAN, P. (1965) *The Theory of Exchange* (Prentice-Hall, Englewood Cliffs).
NITTSU RESEARCH INSTITUTE (1972) *Outlook and Plans for Physical Distribution in a Megalopolis – a Long Range Study* (Urban Distribution Research Section, Nittsu Research Institute, Tokyo).
OECD (1973) *The Distribution Sector: Evolution and Government Policies* (OECD, Paris).
PALAMOUNTAIN, J.C. (1955) *The Politics of Distribution* (Greenwood Press, New York, reprint).
PRESTON, L.E. (1973) 'Marketing Organization and Public Policy' in F.C. Allvine (ed.), *Public Policy and Marketing Practices* (American Marketing Association, Chicago), pp. 321-36.
PRESTON, L.E. and N.R. COLLINS (1966) 'The Analysis of Market Efficiency', *Journal of Marketing Research*, 3, pp. 154-62.
PRESTON, L.E. and A.E. SCHRAMM (1965) 'Dual Distribution and Its Impact on Marketing Organization', *California Management Review*, 8, pp. 61-9.
REDDAWAY, W.B. (1970) *Effects of the Selective Employment Tax* (HMSO, London).
REDSTONE, L.G. (1976) *The New Downtowns: Rebuilding Business Districts* (McGraw-Hill, New York).
REYNAUD, P. (1972) *Les petits commerçants face à la cessation d'activité* (Credoc, Paris).
ROBINSON, W.F. (1973) *The Pattern of Reform in Hungary* (Praeger, New York).
ROUSSEAU, H. (1977) 'L'hypermarché: mythe et réalité', *Chroniques d'actualité de la S.E.D.E.I.S*, 16(8), pp. 318-44.
ROY, M. (1971) *Les commerçants: entre la révolte et la modernisation* (Seuil, Paris).
SAMSONOV, L. (1971) 'Problems in the Development of Retail Trade', *Voprosy ekonomiki*, 12, pp. 61-79.
SMITH, A.D. (1971) 'Small Retailers: Prospects and Policies', *Committee of Inquiry on Small Firms, Research Report*, 15 (HMSO, London).
SMITH, H. (1948) *Retail Distribution*, 2nd edn (Oxford University Press, Oxford).
SMITH, M.G. (1962) 'Exchange and Marketing among the Hausa' in P. Bohannan and G. Dalton (eds), *Markets in Africa* (Northwestern University Press, Evanston), pp. 299-334.
SPINKS, G.R. (1970) 'Attitudes towards Agricultural Marketing in Asia and the Far

East', *Monthly Bulletin of Agricultural Economics and Statistics*, 19(1), pp. 1-9.

SUMNER, J. and K. DAVIES (1978) 'Hypermarkets and Superstores: What do the Planning Authorities Really Think?', *Retail and Distribution Management*, 6(4), pp. 8-15.

SZUMELUK, K. (1968) *Central Place Theory: Its Role in Planning with Particular Reference to Retailing*, Working Paper 9 (Centre for Environmental Studies, London).

TAKEUCHI, H. (1977) 'Productivity in Retailing: Retail Structure and Public Policy', *Journal of Retailing*, 53(1), pp. 35-46, 94.

THIJSSE, J.P. (1968) 'Second Thoughts about a Rural Pattern for the Future in the Netherlands', *Papers of Regional Science Association*, 20, pp. 69-75.

THORPE, D. (1975) 'Town Planning for Retailing', Seminar Papers, Research Report 20 (Manchester Business School, Retail Outlets Research Unit).

TOWN AND COUNTRY PLANNING (1974) 'Redevelopment in Two City Centres', *Town and Country Planning*, 42(2), pp. 119-28.

TOYOTA TRANSPORT ENVIRONMENT COMMITTEE (1977) 'Urban Physical Distribution in Japan: a Survey', *The Wheel Extended*, 6(4), pp. 6-43.

YAMEY, B.S. (1966A) *Resale Price Maintenance* (Weidenfeld & Nicolson, London).

—— (1966B) 'United Kingdom' in B.S. Yamey (ed.), *Resale Price Maintenance* (Weidenfeld & Nicolson, London), pp. 249-98.

YOSHINO, M.Y. (1971) *The Japanese Marketing System* (MIT Press, Cambridge, Mass.).

9 CONFLICT, RESPONSE AND MARKETING CHANGE

The institutional relationships which define a particular marketing system result from the operation of many types of marketing process. The processes vary spatially with the differences in the economic, social, political and legal frameworks within which marketing operates. Change in these processes and consequently change in the system is constantly occurring. A marketing system, and the processes which comprise it, has strongly developed spatial and temporal dimensions. Much of the discussion in the previous chapters has concentrated on patterns and processes within the spatial dimension. It is worthwhile asking, however, why does change occur in the temporal dimension?

A Crisis-Response Model

Many examples in earlier chapters have shown that change in the system occurs with an action—reaction—synthesis sequence. It has been argued that marketing systems evolve through this process but that a frequent implication of action and reaction is conflict among the actors. Synthesis occurs with the resolution of the conflict. Change takes place therefore both in the actors themselves and in the processes and relationships linking together these actors. It is in this way that the system changes. Many of the changes in retailing, wholesaling, producer marketing and consumer behaviour can be shown to be constructed in this way. Fink, Baek and Taddeo (1971) have isolated, in a general way and for undifferentiated organisations, four phases in the reaction-synthesis part of the change process. The applicability of this concept to marketing has been dealt with briefly and at a theoretical level by Stern and El-Ansary (1977), and it is certainly worthwhile considering the concept in more detail and adding an initial phase associated with the original action.

In the Fink, Baek and Taddeo model an action occurs and a *crisis* results which demands reaction on the part of some or all of the actors in the marketing system. The following four phases of reaction are identified:

(1)   the shock phase;
(2)   the defensive retreat phase;
(3)   the acknowledgement phase;
(4)   the adaptation phase.

The shock phase is the immediate result of the perception of a crisis by a participant in the marketing system. An action occurs and as a consequence relationships in the system change. When the group losing power perceives the change then it enters the shock phase. The changes may be seen as a threat to survival, a threat to the objectives or a loss of channel power. The concern of the group is to survive and to think of non-competitive ways to regain the former position. There tends to be a refusal to accept the new situation as anything but a very short-term set of relationships and a frequently held view is that the new activity group, selling technique or whatever has caused the crisis, itself will not survive. Much effort can be expended showing how unlikely survival of the new state is and how efficient and socially valuable the former state was. There is virtually no positive reaction in the shock phase.

The second phase begins as positive reaction occurs. The primary concern ceases to be personal survival and becomes both a co-operative effort to survive and the hindering of the success of the original active element. Short-term aims remain uppermost and the long-term strategies which were being pursued prior to the crisis remain in a state of limbo. Requests for co-operative effort may extend to appeals to similarly 'unfairly' treated or disenchanted actors in the system, to government to introduce legislation to control the changes taking place or even to society at large. Powerful lobbies can be created and major campaigns mounted to gain sympathy for the power-loss group. This type of activity can result in the power-gain group similarly lobbying for their own cause and becoming distracted from their own longer term goals. The defensive retreat stage comprises the aggressive phases of conflict resolution — battle lines are drawn and battles are fought.

The third phase extends gradually from defensive retreat. Some parties to the co-operative defensive tactics realise positive action is required and ultimately other parties reach similar conclusions. The acknowledgement phase consists of an internal re-evaluation of activities with a view to co-existence through structural change in the marketing institution and its relationships. It must be stressed that within a widely perceived crisis some participants may still be in the negative defensive retreat stage while others are looking positively for ways to come to terms with the change. During this phase alternative long-term goals are assessed in the light of the new relationships in the system. Tentative decisions might be made towards a preferred long-term policy and general activities cease to be totally governed by former functions and the former place of the institution in the system. Activities result from the current situation. As the acknowledgement phase proceeds, so seeds are sown for another initial action phase which itself will result in a new crisis response, perhaps by another group in the system. Change in the marketing system becomes selfperpetuating.

The final phase is the adaptation phase and consists of the effective resolution of the original conflict. During this phase new relationships become established and one cycle in the change process becomes complete. The institution has adapted to its new position in the system and can pursue long-term objectives of growth. The adaptation phase usually involves taking positive decisions which result in actions which themselves create a crisis for some other member of the system. Not only is change selfperpetuating but it is also selfsustaining to the marketing system with 'crisis' provoking actions integral to the continued existence of the system. Activity in the adaptation phase is the result of empirical and logical strategies which aim at maximising the selfinterest of the particular institution which perceives a crisis. An innovation in management methods may be adopted or some technological innovation in another function of the institution might occur. The essential point is that new activity, which creates the next crisis, is both a real and tangible change and results from logical *internal* processes in the system.

These empirical, logical and internally derived real activities constitute one group of actions which start the crisis-response cycle. Secondly, there are also activities which impinge on the system but which come from outside the marketing system. Thirdly there are actions motivated by theory and the pursuit of an abstract goal. This third type of action may be internal or external to the system. Before considering these three types of catalyst to the crisis-response model it is worthwhile to discuss briefly an application of the basic model.

If it is considered that an institutional action which creates a crisis diffuses through the operators in that institutional sector with some adopting the action sooner than others, then the perception of the crisis will also spread through the group as a diffusion process. Some operators will perceive the crisis sooner than others and begin their cycle of response. At any one time, therefore, there are likely to be participants at a variety of stages of the cycle. Even when some of the parties involved have adopted positive responses there are likely to be some, having only just perceived the crisis, still in the shock phase. When the model is considered in terms of individual actors it may be related to temporal diffusion models. We are also dealing with activities which vary through space and there is in operation both a simple spatial diffusion of the crisis-response cycle and a more complicated spatial diffusion of the various temporal lags involving individuals. A perceived crisis will spread spatially as the action provoking the crisis itself spreads. There will then be a simple spatial diffusion of a shock phase and subsequent phases through the affected population. There may be parts of the region or country where the perception of the crisis is retarded or the whole cycle process operates more slowly, because the marketing system has developed a particular spatially determined set of internal relationships. In earlier chapters it has been pointed out that marketing systems vary spatially and so their developmental process, as modelled by a crisis-response cycle, will also have a spatial component. It is possible therefore that the crisis-response model can be both disaggregated temporally to allow for the individual activity of operators in the marketing system and also disaggregated spatially to allow for the spatial variations in relationships in the marketing system.

Some changes among retail grocery institutions in Europe or North America serve as an example of the application of the model. The development of large retail chains may be considered as a primary action. When independent retailers perceived this potential competition the shock phase began. Independent retailers went to considerable efforts to show how chain stores could not survive, how their advertised lower prices were not really lower if all consumer costs were taken into account and how much better was the service provided by the traditional independent trader. Long-term development plans were shelved as short-term survival became the main goal.

The second phase was marked by co-operative efforts to obtain legislation to restrict chain store activity and to ensure 'fair trade' practices. The small business lobby can have a strong political voice and its activities typify the defensive retreat phase. Independent traders in this phase were less concerned with competing in retailing practices with the chain stores than they were with protecting their own interest. Wholesalers were also called on to co-operate in seeking restrictive legislation. Campaigns were mounted to try to enlist the shopping public as a whole and great play was made with notions of the friendly independent trader and the faceless chain store. The strength of the independent lobby caused the chain stores themselves to play the same game and seek government legislation which would further their goals. Resale price maintenance was attacked, as were the various successes of the small business lobby in restricting the spread of chain stores.

The third phase of the cycle began with the realisation by some of the more progressive elements in independent retailing that more positive policies were required. A number of structural adaptations were tried — some were successful, others failed. Selfservice techniques were evaluated, co-operative purchasing schemes were tried, contractual vertical integration through organisations such as voluntary groups was considered, the provision of a greater range of customer services and changing the merchandise mix were also considered by many operators. Within this phase preferred strategies, often involving several of these potential responses, were worked out. Voluntary group formation and the adoption of selfservice were a common combined response. The independent trader moved into a position where he could compete, in retail terms, with the chain stores. The beginnings of new potential conflicts and crises are apparent in these actions.

The fourth phase is the adoption of new growth strategies, the successful operation of various types of contractual integration of organisations and the successful adoption of new selling techniques. The improved market position of independent grocers subsequent to voluntary group formation itself creates a shock phase in the chain store sector.

The action of the development of supermarkets by the chain stores led the independents to respond by creating more integrated forms of voluntary association and themselves adopting supermarket methods. The chain stores, after shock and defensive retreat, have looked to greater vertical integration and to the adoption of discount store and hypermarket methods and have again caused a crisis and subsequent lobbying for legislative protection by the independent retailer and wholesaler. The grocery trades at a general level have passed through a number of crisis-response cycles.

Individual operators of independent grocery stores currently are at various stages in these cycles. For example while some are taking defensive positions over supermarket expansion, others are several stages ahead and are considering how they can adapt to discount store and hypermarket competition. The survey on the problems of small shop operators reported in Dawson and Kirby (1979) showed that some retailers were still advocating a return of RPM to protect them from supermarket competition and others were wanting government to take action to reduce property tax so that their competitive position would be improved. Both attitudes are typical of the retailers in the defensive retreat stage. Even in the same suburb, however, there were independent traders who had joined voluntary groups and passed through another crisis of superstore/discount store competition and were operating their own supermarket within a vertically integrated and successful voluntary chain.

On some occasions retailers out of phase by one cycle combine to generate defensive policies. In Britain, for example, in the last few years there has been considerable lobbying by independent traders, some of whom want legislation to protect them from supermarket development while others see the emergence of discount stores and hypermarkets as the crisis from which they require protection. Both groups of independent traders, together with some wholesalers, are lobbying for governmental intervention and are mounting public awareness campaigns in a unified attempt to control the market power of large integrated marketing corporations. Although individuals are in different cycles of change, their defensive positions are similar and they can effectively co-operate. Within the overall crisis-response pattern of independent and chain/conglomerate company the individual participants, at any one time, can span a range of phases in the cycle of change.

The spatial variation in the model stems from the spatial diffusion of chain store growth, supermarkets and other organisational and technological changes. In Britain effective chain store competition in the grocery trade developed in the larger towns during the 1930s and in medium sized towns in the 1950s (see Chapter 4). Only since the late 1960s have small country towns had a full representation of chain stores and by this stage chain stores were operating supermarkets. Only in the 1970s therefore are independent stores in villages feeling the main thrust of competition from the chains and so are in crisis and taking up the same sort of defensive positions urban independent retailers took in the 1950s and 1960s.

There is a temporal and spatial lag in the pattern of crisis perception and response and this leads to a slightly different set of responses. Those responding later are able to use the experience of earlier participants but they still appear to pass through all the crisis-response phases despite having precedents to study. Village grocery retailers have perceived crisis and undergone a defensive retreat and in many cases have entered an acknowledgement phase. The attitudes in defensive retreat differ from those of their urban counterparts both because of their different operating environment and also because they have learnt from the urban responses of the 1950s and 1960s. Attitudes in defensive retreat in the rural sector have concentrated much more on stressing the social services the traditional rural retailer provides and have used arguments of social equity in their requests to government for protective legislation. The spatial dimension shows itself both in the spread of innovation in the acknowledgement phase and in the way different environments create different response patterns.

Other examples could be taken to show the applicability of the model. The pattern of change in developing countries after the establishment of European or American based marketing groups follows the crisis-response model. The introduction of a marketing board into the agricultural marketing subsystem could be considered in the same way. Many of the changes under way in marketing result from the conflicting operations of two or more groups and these changes may be analysed in terms of crisis, defensive retreat, acknowledgement and adaptation phases.

Triggers to Provocative Action

The crisis-response model begins with an action that acts as a catalyst and provokes conflict. Some of these actions are logically intrinsic to the process of change as it has been modelled but there are the two other sources of (a) an external stimuli and (b) political or theoretically based power shifts. There would seem to be a tendency in the process of change in the marketing system for external stimuli to become increasingly important as the catalyst to change.

The first type of stimulus for change is that associated with innovation within the institution and is the result of a rational analysis of a situation by marketing policy makers. A series of alternative logical responses to a situation may be analysed and a preferred form of action involving change, and often involving innovation, will be developed, diffused and adopted within the overall organisation. Changes in management structure in a marketing company, many of the changes in consumer behaviour, the acceptance of new techniques in physical distribution and many of the locational changes, particularly the suburbanisation action involving marketing institutions, are all of this type. The action is a rational organisational response to a given situation. There is a copious literature, effectively summarised by Zaltman, Duncan and Holbek (1973) on organisational change and its relationship with innovation. It is apparent that it is this type of action which occurs in the acknowledgement phase of the crisis-response model.

The second source of action is that external to the institution and has origins in the attitudes and changes taking place in society generally. In marketing activities in recent years there has been a considerable growth in what has been termed *social* or *ecological* marketing. Traditionally marketing has been user or customer orientated, with the corporation serving the user and the general needs of society; the needs of the environment have not been considered. An alternative and more recently canvassed view of marketing is one in which user needs are subjugated to those of the environment and society generally, which together provide the pivot of the system: 'In the societal view of marketing, the needs of society and the environment have the highest priority, and the needs of the individual and the corporation are relegated to a lower position'

(Gwinner *et al.*, 1977, p. 562). The traditional attitude of marketing institutions having considerable power to effect social change but with a very limited social ethic has been questioned increasingly in North America since the late 1960s (Schneider, 1968; Clasen, 1967). The ecology movement posed basic questions to marketing philosophy, with authors such as Segal (1969) calling into question the morality of the marketing system. The responsibilities of institutions in the marketing system have changed as social pressures have increased. Lavidge (1970) provides five examples of areas of growing responsibility:

(1)   consumerism;
(2)   the provision of facilities for the underprivileged;
(3)   marketing of social and cultural services;
(4)   the day-to-day functioning of the economy;
(5)   the use and pollution of society's resources.

Many of these growing responsibilities revolve around the debate on efficiency and social justice mentioned in the last chapter, but all represent responses of society to marketing activities and all create action and change in the marketing system.

The increased social pressures on marketing institutions have spread from North America to Europe and many of the actions of marketing institutions now are stimulated by social attitudes. Once the crisis-response cycle is initiated by pressure from outside the marketing system, then the response process continues and the cycle may pass through several sequences. In the 1970s there would seem to have been an increased propensity for social activity to be the catalyst for marketing change (Kangun, 1972; Feldman, 1971). This may be symptomatic of a wider movement in all organisations. Terreberry (1968) for example states 'that contemporary changes in organizational environments are such as to increase the ratio of externally induced change to internally induced change' (p. 590). The growth of the system based philosophy in social science inevitably leads to a concern with relations between systems and the way a system develops owing to changes in the overall environment in which the system operates. While external social stimuli to marketing activity have increased in real terms, there has also been an increase in their importance as perceived by social scientists.

The third source of activity to initiate the crisis-response cycle is the application of power, both political and otherwise and both internal and external to the marketing system. It could be argued that the extending social influence over marketing is a result of a changed balance in power relationships such that society now has more power than marketing institutions. Social power is such a nebulous concept however that this argument becomes tenuous particularly when the diffuse social power is compared with the directed power wielded by government or some marketing institutions. Mallen (1978) has explored the potential for the abuse of power in marketing channels and pointed to the range of conflicts which can result when a market channel becomes controlled by centrally controlled policies. The conflicts created by the use of economic power within marketing channels have been pointed out in earlier chapters. A channel leader or channel *captain* can initiate actions not for any empirical logical reason but as an exhibition of status and to consolidate the power base already existing. Such actions can act as a trigger to the crisis-response cycle. Similarly government may take political actions and exert marketing power merely to prove it has political power and again such action may be the catalyst to a cycle of responses. In the case of the channel leader, the source of action is internal to the marketing system but with government it is external.

There are many types of power in this context. The power to influence prices is a common government ploy; the power to influence patterns of supply to consumers often resides with the channel leader; the power to influence location may rest with land use planners and even occasionally geographers. El Ansary and Stern (1972) consider power as the extent to which the marketing strategy of *j* is controlled by *i* and this relates to the interdependence of *i* and *j*. Interdependence may be considered as the extent of the contribution one firm makes to the profits of another or the difficulties faced by the firms if the interdependency links are severed. There are several studies of power relations in marketing channels and in many cases power plays result in actions which create crises for other marketing institutions.

Within the group of power motivated actions it appears that actions stimulated by non-marketing organisations are becoming more common in comparison with those triggered by organisations integral to the marketing system. The rôle of government at all levels is increasing (see Chapter 8). This pattern within the group corresponds to the generally increased importance of outside influences promoting change in marketing.

This increase in external influences produces a reverse effect whereby marketing itself, extends its influence beyond its traditional boundaries. As marketing matures and 'broadens its function and scope, marketing will become increasingly relevant during the 1970's to the fulfillment of man. And as the impact of marketing on society increases, so does the social responsibility of marketing people' (Lavidge, 1970, p. 28). The concepts of marketing and distribution have been applied to health care, education, population control programmes, insurance services and even the provision of tennis courts (Sheth and Wright, 1974). Most aspects of marketing involve the delivery of a way of life. The demands for different lifestyles and the ways they are delivered to the consuming public vary from place to place. While marketing is becoming concerned with these broader issues of changing life styles, its central emphasis remains in the provision of tangible goods and services in response to consumer demand. Many of the problems implied in this goal relate directly to the spatial variation in marketing processes. Marketing is, and will continue to be for some time, a vital activity of all societies whether communist or capitalist, subsistence or postindustrial.

References

CLASEN, E.A. (1967) 'Marketing Ethics and the Consumer', *Harvard Business Review*, 45, pp. 79-86.

DAWSON, J.A. and D.A. KIRBY (1979) *Small Scale Retailing in the United Kingdom* (Teakfield, Farnborough).

EL-ANSARY, A.I. and L.W. STERN (1972) 'Power Measurement in the Distribution Channel', *Journal of Marketing Research*, 9, pp. 47-52.

FELDMAN, L.P. (1971) 'Societal Adaptation: a New Challenge for Marketing', *Journal of Marketing*, 35, pp. 54-60.

FINK, S.L., J. BAEK and K. TADDEO (1971) 'Organizational Crisis and Change', *Applied Behavioral Science*, 7, pp. 15-37.

GWINNER, R.F. *et al.* (1977) *Marketing: an Environmental Perspective* (West, St Paul).

KANGUN, N. (1972) *Society and Marketing* (Harper & Row, New York).

LAVIDGE, R.J. (1970) 'The Growing Responsibilities of Marketing', *Journal of Marketing*, 34, pp. 25-8.

MALLEN, B. (1978) 'Channel Power: a Form of Economic Exploitation', *European Journal of Marketing*, 12(2), pp. 194-202.

SCHNEIDER, K.R. (1968) *Destiny of Change* (Holt Rinehart & Winston, New York).

SEGAL, R. (1969) *The Americans: a Conflict of Creed and Reality* (Viking, New York).

SHETH, J.N. and P.L. WRIGHT (1974) (eds) *Marketing Analysis for Societal Problems* (Bureau of Economics and Business Research, University of Illinois, Urbana).

STERN, L.W. and A.I. EL-ANSARY (1977) *Marketing Channels* (Prentice-Hall, Englewood Cliffs).

TERREBERRY, S. (1968) 'The Evolution of Organizational Environments', *Administrative Science Quarterly*, 12(4), pp. 590-613.

ZALTMAN, G., R. DUNCAN and J. HOLBEK (1973) *Innovations and Organizations* (Wiley, New York).

AUTHOR INDEX

PLACE INDEX

377